THINKING
THROUGH
DANCE

The Philosophy of
Performance and Practices

This book is dedicated to the memory of Chris Challis (1937-2012), who contributed greatly to the philosophy of dance and was an inspirational teacher, colleague and friend.

THINKING
THROUGH
DANCE

The Philosophy of

Dance Performance and Practices

Edited by Jenny Bunker, Anna Pakes

and Bonnie Rowell

DANCE BOOKS

Cover photograph:
Dancers, Marika Rizzi, Darrell Jones
Photograph, Simon Ellis

First published in 2013 by Dance Books Ltd.,
Southwold House, Isington Road, Binsted, Hampshire, GU34 4PH

ISBN: 978-1-85273-165-6
A CIP catalogue for this title is available from the British Library

Printed in Great Britain

Contents

Contributors

Henrietta Bannerman is Head of Research at London Contemporary Dance School. She is also a freelance lecturer specializing in dance history, aesthetics and critical studies. She has gained an international reputation for her papers on American and British contemporary dance which she has presented at conferences including those held by the Society of Dance History Scholars and the Congress on Dance Research. She has published papers in journals such as the British *Dance Research*, the American *Dance Research Journal*, *Research in Dance Education*, *Forum for Modern Languages* (Special Issue) and in 2011 an article on Graham and release-based techniques in *Journal of Dance and Somatic Practices*.

Julia Beauquel has a PhD from the University of Lorraine, in France, prior to which she practised contemporary dance for many years. Her PhD thesis, entitled *Aesthetics of Dance: Definitions, Choreographic Expression and Understanding*, is due to be published in French in early 2014 at Presses Universitaires de Rennes. She is co-editor of the collected papers from an international conference on Philosophy and Dance that she co-organized: *Philosophie de la danse* (Presses Universitaires de Rennes, 2010). Her main interests are in aesthetics, philosophy of art, philosophy of mind, philosophy of language, action theory, ontology and metaphysics.

Catherine Botha lectures in Philosophy at the University of Johannesburg, South Africa. Her areas of research specialization and interest are hermeneutics, the history of philosophy (especially the work of Heidegger and Nietzsche), and aesthetics (most particularly the philosophy of dance). She is also a registered ballet teacher of the Royal Academy of Dance, and is passionate about theatre, dance and the arts.

Kristin Boyce is an ACLS New Faculty Fellow in the Humanities Center and Department of Philosophy at Johns Hopkins University. She received a doctorate in Philosophy from The University of Chicago in 2010. She is the recipient of numerous awards including the ACLS New Faculty Fellowship, a Post-Doctoral Fellowship from Stanford University, and a Josephine De Karmán Dissertation Fellowship. Her work has been published in *The Journal for Philosophical Research*, *The Henry James Review*, and *Dance Research*. She is currently working on two book projects: *Why Wander Into Fiction? Analytic Philosophy, Literature and the Elucidation of Confusion* and *An Anscombian Approach to Philosophy of Art*.

Jenny Bunker is Lecturer in Philosophy at the University of Roehampton and has previously taught at the University of Oxford and the University of Southampton. Her research focuses on early modern philosophy, the history of aesthetics and contemporary issues in the philosophy of art, alongside a developing interest in legal and political philosophy. She was involved in organising the *Thinking Through Dance* conference which took place at Roehampton in early 2011. Her forthcoming monograph *Spinoza and Theology* (co-authored with Daniel Whistler) is due to be published by T and T Clark.

Jane Carr first worked as a dancer, gaining experience in ballet, contemporary dance and collaborative cross arts projects. Jane also worked for over fifteen years at Morley College, south east London, to provide opportunities for adults and young people to participate in dance. She has taught in a range of conservatoires/universities and currently leads the BA (Hons) Dance and Professional Practice at the University of Bedfordshire. Since completing her PhD at Roehampton University, she has continued to research the intercorporeal negotiation of significance in dance performance, resulting in publications related to both how dance is appreciated and to specific examples of practices ranging from British (underground) jazz to performance-installation.

Noël Carroll is Distinguished Professor in the Philosophy Program at the Graduate Center of the City University of New York. His most recent three books are *On Criticism, Art in Three Dimensions* and *Living in an Artworld*. He is a past president of the American Society of Aesthetics and a former Guggenheim Fellow. He has worked as a journalist, including as a dance critic, and he has written five documentaries including *Dancing with the Camera* and *The Last Conversation: Eisenstein's Carmen Ballet*.

Jonathan Owen Clark is currently Head of Research at Trinity Laban Conservatoire of Music and Dance, London UK. His research interests include aesthetics, phenomenology, and historiography. He is also an active composer and sound artist.

Renee Conroy is an Assistant Professor of Philosophy at Purdue University Calumet. Publications on dance include essays in *The Continuum Companion to Aesthetics, Feminist Aesthetics and the Philosophy of Art, The Journal of Aesthetics and Art Criticism*, and the *American Society for Aesthetics* newsletter. Conroy has presented papers on philosophical issues in dance at regional and national conferences of the American Philosophical Association and the American Society for Aesthetics. She has also served the ASA as a two-time member of the Selma Jeanne Cohen Prize selection committee and co-organizer of the ASA Pacific Division conference.

Raf Geenens obtained degrees in philosophy and in dance studies from the Universities of Brussels, Leuven and Paris VIII Vincennes. He has held visiting positions at Columbia University, New York City, and at the Centre Raymond Aron (Ecole des Hautes Etudes en Sciences Sociales), Paris. He is currently Assistant Professor at the Institute of Philosophy, University of Leuven, Belgium. His primary research interests are in the field of political and legal theory, yet Geenens also has a vivid interest in the history and the philosophy of dance.

Graham McFee is a Professor of Philosophy at California State University, Fullerton (USA) and formerly Professor of Philosophy in the University of Brighton (UK). His main research interests lie in the philosophy of Wittgenstein and in philosophical aesthetics (especially the aesthetics of dance); and he has lectured and presented on these topics both nationally and internationally. Until 2004, he was Vice President of the British Society of Aesthetics. His principal publications include *Understanding Dance* (Routledge, 1992), *The Concept of Dance Education* (Revised Edition: Pageantry Press, 2004), *Artistic Judgement* (Springer, 2011), and *The Philosophical Aesthetics of Dance* (Dance Books, 2011).

Geraldine Morris danced with the Royal Ballet during the 1960s and subsequently took various degrees, ending in a PhD on the dance movement style of Frederick Ashton. Morris is a Reader in the Dance Department of the University of Roehampton where she teaches on both BA and MA courses, as well as supervising PhD students. Her monograph, *Frederick Ashton's Ballets: Style, Performance, Choreography* was published in 2012 by Dance Books.

Larraine Nicholas is a dance historian and a senior lecturer at the University of Roehampton. She is the author of *Dancing in Utopia: Dartington Hall and its Dancers* (2007). Published papers include 'Leslie Burrowes: A Young Dancer in Dresden and London, 1930–34' (2010) *Dance Research*, 28:2. A new book, *Walking and Dancing: Three Years of Dance in London, 1951-1953*, is due for publication in 2013.

Anna Pakes is Reader in Dance at the University of Roehampton. She has been teaching philosophical aesthetics to dance students (first at Laban, then at Roehampton) since 1997, and has published a number of articles on diverse philosophical themes related to dance, such as the mind-body problem, the epistemology of dance practice as research and Husserlian phenomenology. Her main research interest currently is the ontology of dance, on which she has presented work at the American Society for Aesthetics Pacific Division meetings in 2011, 2012 and 2013, as well as the London Aesthetics Forum (2013). She is completing a monograph, to be published by Oxford University Press, on the ontology of dance.

Efrosini Protopapa is a London-based choreographer, teacher and writer. She works as a Senior Lecturer in Dance at the University of Roehampton, and is the artistic director of the performance group *Lapsus Corpi*, who have presented work in festivals throughout the UK, Germany, Holland and Greece. She has also performed in works by Ivana Müller, Tino Sehgal and Yvonne Rainer, and has published on experimental dance practices and contemporary European choreography. She is a Director on the Board of Performance Studies International and General Editor of the *PSi Manifesto Lexicon*.

Bonnie Rowell was formerly Principal Lecturer in Dance Studies and Head of Subject for Dance and Music at the University of Roehampton, London, now retired. Her monograph *Dance Umbrella: The First Twenty One Years* was published by Dance Books in 2000. Chapters in dance collections include *Fifty Contemporary Choreographers*, edited by Martha Bremser and Lorna Sanders; *Contemporary Choreography: a Critical Reader*, edited by Jo Butterworth and Liesbeth Wildschut; *Dance, Education and Philosophy*, edited by Graham McFee, and, co-written with Rachel Duerden, *Bodies of Sound*, edited by Sherril Dodds and Susan C. Cook.

Acknowledgements

The idea for this book emerged during and following a conference held at the University of Roehampton on 27th February 2011, entitled *Thinking Through Dance: the Philosophy of Dance Performance and Practices*. We are grateful to all those who presented at and attended the conference for their stimulating arguments, enthusiasm and encouragement. Similarly the University of Roehampton's Department of Dance, which hosted the conference, has supported the development of this volume from its very early stages, as has the Philosophy programme in the Department of Humanities at the same institution. Thanks also to the British Society of Aesthetics, the Society for Dance Research and American Airlines who sponsored the February 2011 event; to Raj Seghal, Sara Houston, Geraldine Morris and Graham McFee for agreeing to serve on the conference committee; and to Julia Noyce and her team for their exceptionally efficient and good-humoured administration. There is a range of other individuals without whom this book might never have seen the light of day. Stephanie Jordan, Andrée Grau, Toby Bennett and Norman Hirschy all assisted greatly in steering the volume toward publication. John Rowell was a generous host enabling a crucial writing retreat. Special thanks also go to David Leonard of Dance Books for his receptivity and encouragement. And we are very grateful too to Elizabeth Morrell for her expert editing and patience as the manuscript was prepared for publication.

Introduction

Jenny Bunker, Anna Pakes and Bonnie Rowell

Dance as an art form poses unique philosophical questions. It foregrounds the human body in movement and stasis, and human action as the manifest substance of the dancework. Dance challenges us to understand the dynamics of agency, and to probe the connection between the dancer's somatic experience and the viewer's understanding. Dance works are typically devised through collaborative activity in the studio and not routinely notated; their re-instancing depends, at least partly, on the physical capacities and bodily training of future generations. So, as a performing art which generates repeatable works as well as performance events, dance also inflects ontological and identity questions in interesting ways. Furthermore the embodied character of dance works poses questions about the kinds of meanings they generate, and indeed the kinds of thinking developed in different sorts of dance activity. These questions become particularly acute as dance forges a space for itself within the academy and begins to test traditional assumptions about knowledge and associated institutional conventions.

This book seeks to take up some of these philosophical challenges, in an effort to think clearly about what is at stake in dance as an art form. It draws on strategies of argument and existing literature in philosophical aesthetics, but develops both in new directions: through the focus on dance as distinct from other artforms; through the confrontation with insights from a range of philosophical traditions; and through the presentation of a variety of viewpoints, from those of professional philosophers of art to those of dance practitioners, as well as some who have claims to both camps.

The book explores a range of themes in the philosophy of dance, including key questions concerning embodiment, personhood, meaning, ontology, identity and the nature and relevance of philosophical enquiry to dance as an art form, thus reflecting some of the topics being considered in dance and philosophy internationally today. It is aimed primarily at dance scholars and practitioners who are inquisitive about what philosophy can bring to our understanding of dance, and at philosophers curious about dance and its potential to illuminate problems of art, mind, language and metaphysics. We hope it will also appeal to undergraduate and masters students who want to discover the application of philosophy in dance studies, or explore the significance of the performing arts within aesthetics. The volume also serves as a resource for university teachers of courses in dance studies and philosophy of art, pinpointing themes and issues of current concern.

The book is made up of a series of essays, selected and developed from much shorter papers given at the *Thinking through Dance* conference held at the University of Roehampton in February 2010.[1] Organized by a group of academics drawn from the dance and philosophy departments at Roehampton, the conference was partly designed to respond to student interest, and partly motivated by recent evidence of the inclusion of dance in mainstream philosophical consideration of the arts.[2] A call for papers was sent to interested parties around the world from both dance and philosophy, with an intentionally wide brief: to submit papers on any theme relevant to philosophy and dance. Response to the call was surprisingly enthusiastic, with seventy-eight proposals, received from five different continents, for papers covering an array of topics. Twenty of these papers were selected for inclusion in an intense one-day event, which attracted 108 delegates, including participants from the US, Norway, France, Belgium, Germany, Luxembourg, Italy, Turkey, Ireland, South Africa, New Zealand, as well as the UK. Contributors were academics from both dance studies and philosophy (some of whom are, or were, also dance practitioners), and included some new and some well established scholars (most notably Noël Carroll and Graham McFee).

In this volume, our aim is to demonstrate something of the breadth of research that was in evidence at that *Thinking through Dance* conference, whilst also developing in-depth arguments around the themes considered in the fourteen essays selected for inclusion. The essays draw on different philosophical traditions, including analytic, phenomenological and poststructuralist, and the primary focus is on theatre dance in the Western tradition, although the issues discussed have a much broader sweep. That the focus of most of the authors here is Western theatre dance is not intended to deny the philosophical interest of non-Western or non-theatre dance forms, nor to impose a way of thinking on dances and movement practices developed under alternative conceptual and cultural frameworks. We envisage that broadening the cultural remit of the discussion might challenge or reaffirm the various conclusions drawn here with respect to Western theatre dance. Such a project would no doubt contribute fascinating insights to the reflection begun here on what we consider basic questions in the philosophy of dance: about what it means to be or witness a dancer moving, about the nature of choreography, dance works and performances, and about the interest and value of a dialogue between philosophy and dance. In asking these kinds of questions, the volume speaks to a renewed pre-occupation with the philosophical significance of dance, which is

---

1 The conference received funding and support in kind from the following organizations: British Society of Aesthetics; Royal Institute of Philosophy; Society for Dance Research; University of Roehampton, London, and American Airlines.

2 See below p.11.

evident in the contemporary academy as well as dance practice. The nature of and context for this renewed interest, as well as the ways in which it is addressed by this volume, are the focus for the rest of this introduction.

Dance and philosophical aesthetics

Dance is traditionally considered under-represented within philosophical aesthetics. The reasons are complex and include the disputed status of dance as one of the fine arts, the neglect of the body (and by extension dance as an art of the body) in philosophical enquiry generally, and the still relatively marginal position of dance within the cultural institution, at least within the US and the UK (see Sparshott 1988, pp.3-82). That said, recent overviews of analytic philosophy of art and aesthetics have included sections on dance.[3] Similarly, there have been panels on dance programmed at recent aesthetics conferences, for example, the American Society for Aesthetics Pacific Division meetings in 2007 and 2011, the American Society for Aesthetics annual meeting in 2012.[4] Moreover, the Spring 2013 issue (Volume 71:2) of the *Journal of Aesthetics and Art Criticism* included a collection of articles on dance in its symposium devoted to Dance Art and Science. So, although dance has not received much attention from analytic philosophers of art, neither is it entirely neglected.

If a recent surge of interest in dance is evident in analytic aesthetics, this development builds on the groundwork laid by the few philosophers who, in the second half of the twentieth century, have devoted significant attention to the art form. Susanne K. Langer (1953 and 1957), David Best (1974), Julie Van Camp (1981), Selma Jeanne Cohen (1986 [1982]) and Betty Redfern (1983) all made important contributions to showing the philosophical interest of dance and to working through some of the philosophical problems posed by danceworld practice and discourse. Francis Sparshott's two extensive studies (1988 and 1995) engage with an impressive array of philosophical themes and provide important analysis of core issues such as definition, ontology and identity. Similarly Graham McFee's work (1992, 2004 and 2011) develops a sustained reflection from a different perspective on the same issues, alongside considering questions of meaning, understanding and appreciation. And David Davies (2004 and 2011), although not exclusively concerned with dance, considers it

---

3 See, for example, Noël Carroll in Levinson (ed.) 2003, pp. 583-593; Francis Sparshott in Kivy (ed.) 2004, pp. 276-290; Julie Van Camp in Davies, S. et al. (eds.) 2009; Graham McFee in Gaut and McIver Lopez (eds.)2005, pp. 683-694; Renee Conroy in Ribeiro (ed.) 2012, pp.156-170.

4 Further evidence is the successful establishment by Aili Bresnahan of a dance and philosophy Google discussion group, which at the time of writing numbers 29 members. See https://groups.google.com/forum/?fromgroups#!forum/dancephilosophers.

at key points in the development of his arguments. Noël Carroll similarly has given detailed attention to dance and dance examples in the context of publications which consider a range of artforms and philosophical themes (for example, 1999 and 2012) and has recently published a collection of philosophically informed critical writings on dance (2011).

In addition, there has been debate on central issues in the philosophy of dance within the pages of relevant journals. For example, Monroe C. Beardsley, Noël Carroll and Sally Banes explored contrasting perspectives on what defines dance in *Dance Research Journal*, (see Beardsley 1982; Carroll and Banes 1982), with Gregory Scott (1997 and 1999) and David Davies (2004 and 2011) picking up the thread of the debate. Nelson Goodman's comments on dance (1974) sparked debate in the *Journal of Aesthetics and Art Criticism* between Adina Armelagos, Mary Sirridge and Joseph Margolis (see Sirridge and Armelagos 1977, 1983; Armelagos and Sirridge 1978, 1984; Margolis 1981) on issues of identity, notation and authenticity (a debate which is re-examined in Julia Beauquel's essay in this volume). In the *British Journal of Aesthetics*, Julie Van Camp (1996) and Trevor Whittock (1997) discussed metaphor and meaning in dance, whilst articles by David Carr (1987, 1997) have explored dance as meaningful action, the same author developing an account of dance as an exercise of practical reason or wisdom over a number of decades (1978, 1984, 1999). Recent work in contemporary neuroscience on mirror neurons has also inspired and informed philosophical reflection (Montero 2006), although the findings of such research, and the extent to which neuroscience can explain or justify claims about kinaesthetic empathy in dance, are still contentious (see, for example, McFee 2011, pp.185-206; Foster 2010; Reason and Reynolds 2011; Conroy and Van Camp [eds.] 2013).

However, the extent of the analytic philosophical literature on dance – and of focused debate – is much smaller than that relating to other artforms such as music or literature. This has inevitably affected the depth and range of philosophical research in the domain. Indeed, despite the important articles identified above, there remains a paucity of sustained discussion on dance within the pages of major journals in philosophical aesthetics, and a correspondingly small number of collections of essays specifically devoted to the philosophy of dance, few of which are still in print. Some of these volumes are essentially conference proceedings (Fancher and Myers, [eds.], 1981), whilst some (like the present volume) are collections of essays developed out of conferences or symposia (McFee [ed.] 1999; Beauquel and Pouivet, [eds.], 2010)[5]. Some bring together writings all or a portion of which have been previously published in diverse contexts elsewhere (Copeland and Cohen,

---

5 Alvarez, Pérez and Pérez-Carreño (eds.)(2010), although it has a broader performing arts focus, includes three important contributions on dance, including one by Graham McFee.

[eds.] 1983; Sheets-Johnstone, [ed.] 1984). It is notable that there have been no philosophy of dance anthologies published in English in nearly fifteen years. This stands in stark contrast to the proliferation of publications on analytic philosophy of music, for example, and indicates the gap into which this collection steps.

The influences and context of this anthology extend beyond analytic philosophy, however. As a number of the essays in this volume suggest (those by Jane Carr and Jonathan Owen Clark particularly) dance practitioners and writers have often been drawn to the phenomenological tradition initiated by Edmund Husserl, and developed in the work of, for example, Maurice Merleau-Ponty, whose reflections on embodied existence have received much attention in dance. Maxine Sheets-Johnstone's seminal publication *The Phenomenology of Dance*, first published in 1966, laid groundwork for future writings by dance scholars such as Sondra Horton Fraleigh (1987), Jaana Parviainen (1998) and Susan Kozel (1994, 2007). A recent edition of *Dance Research Journal* (Franko [ed.] 2011) bears witness to the continuing interest and development of phenomenological thinking about dance, and includes articles by two of the authors also represented in this volume (Jonathan Owen Clark and Anna Pakes).

The development of dance studies and dance theory

Another factor profoundly affecting the evolution of the philosophical literature on dance has been the significant development of dance studies – as a field or discipline – within the academy. A range of factors has contributed to this shift within the last few decades. There has, for example, been an increase in the amount of dance research conducted, creating sufficient momentum to propel scholars into common interest groups. Alexandra Carter's introduction to the first edition of *The Routledge Dance Studies Reader* (1998) notes the fragmentary history of the study of dance and how her volume signals a shift towards more coherence and greater recognition: though dance has long been a topic of research within different domains, attention to it has been sporadic and not unified in 'a solid body of serious literature'; only now (in 1998), she suggests, is dance able to 'fully claim its status as a culturally significant and intellectually viable field for study' (p.1). This expansion of dance research may also be linked to developments within dance practice, perhaps particularly the development of contemporary or modern dance, although dance scholarship has not been solely concerned with this genre. Modern and contemporary dance tend towards self-reflexivity and have a self-conscious relationship to their own history, arguably embedding a research – even a philosophical – imperative within the dance practice itself (see Carroll 2003, and the essays by Kristin Boyce and Efrosini Protopapa in this volume). The development of modern dance also helped to give dance a broader presence in the cultural life of the US and the UK, which in turn has helped legitimize the practice as an object of study. Opportunities for scholars to publish (in specialist journals and with reputable publishers) have increased and been enabling for the growth of dance research.[6]

There has also been a proliferation in the US and the UK in the number of university dance departments, or performing arts faculties with a significant dance presence. This has both enabled, and been made possible by, the development of academic degree programmes (at BA, MA, MFA and PhD level) focused on dance study, both practical and theoretical. New generations of dance scholars as well as practitioners graduating from these courses, have a fresh awareness of the intellectual issues raised by dance. What is more, the institution of degree programmes required articulating a rationale for the value of dance study, a rationale which could also be relevant beyond the realm of formal dance education. The work of the analytic philosophers mentioned earlier was instrumental in articulating the conceptual foundations for dance in higher education, at least in the UK: arguments developed by Betty Redfern, David Best, David Carr, Gordon Curl and Graham McFee were incorporated in the rationales for new dance degree programmes.

These institutional shifts have coincided with broader developments within the humanities, in which structuralist and poststructuralist theories (developed in linguistics, philosophy and literary criticism) have challenged the premises and commitments of study in many domains. This 'Theoretical revolution' has questioned the nature of knowledge, challenging enlightenment values of reason, objectivity and progress, deeply embedded in earlier humanities research. Poststructuralist theory (inspired by the seminal work of Jacques Derrida, Roland Barthes and Michel Foucault) argues that learning is always bound up with the operations of power, the supposedly neutral approach of academic research excluding and suppressing certain domains as not worthy of attention. By questioning the legitimacy and procedures of established disciplines, this theoretical critique arguably carved out a space for dance as a previously marginalized or excluded domain of practice and enquiry.

The 'Theoretical revolution' has also shaped the way in which the emerging discipline of dance studies (or what Janet O'Shea in the introduction to Carter and O'Shea's second edition, 2010, of the *Routledge Dance Studies Reader* calls the 'new dance scholarship') engages with its object. Although the influence of (predominantly French) poststructuralist and postmodernist theory was felt relatively late in dance studies (during the

---

6 On the development of dance scholarship in the late twentieth century, see also Malnig (ed.)(2000), Franko (2009) and Giersdorf (2009).

1980s and 1990s), it is still pervasive today. A new interest in the cultural history and politics of the body meant both a new interest in dance, and the opening up of a space for the study of dance as an embodied practice. Similarly, the poststructuralists' critique of the ways in which knowledge is formed and bound up with operations of power, and of the binary oppositions dominating 'traditional' philosophy (mind over body, speech over writing, language over embodiment), enabled a critique also of the existing disciplinary arrangements within the academy, again opening a critical space in which new areas like dance studies could take a foothold.

Interpretative practice in dance in the 1980s and 1990s also bears the mark of poststructuralism's influence, in the methodologies that treat the dance work as a kind of text (the premises of these methodologies are examined and critiqued in Graham McFee's essay in this volume). Drawing on the work of Derrida and Barthes, writers like Susan Leigh Foster (1986), Mark Franko (1993) and Janet Adshead (1999) used the textual analogy to open dance works up to a new kind of scrutiny – not in terms of their aesthetic appeal or the ways in which they expressed their creators' ideas and emotions, but in terms of the meanings that transcended the artist's horizon and in terms of their political connotations and implications. Thus, the textual analysis of dance links with the critique of how the viewer is positioned and with a critique of dance representation. A concern with how dance represents gender, race and class is very prevalent still within dance studies.

The influence of poststructuralist and postmodernist thinking on dance studies constitutes an alternative lineage for philosophy of dance. The distinctiveness of this tradition is vividly illustrated by two recent special issues or series devoted to the subject: a (2005) edition of *Topoi* (volume 24:1) entitled 'Philosophy and Dance', and edited by Susan Leigh Foster, Philipa Rothfield and Colleen Dunagan; and *The Drama Review*'s special series of articles on choreography and philosophy, (Lepecki [ed.] 2006 and 2007). Interestingly, neither the articles nor the editorial introductions of these special issues make much (if any) reference to the analytic tradition in philosophy of dance, revealing how the field has become bifurcated, with little dialogue between perspectives though there is undoubtedly some common thematic ground. It is part of the purpose of this volume to reveal the interests shared between different philosophical perspectives, whilst recognizing the distinctiveness and divergences of the various traditions. At least by bringing diverse perspectives into the same volume in relation to a common focus (dance), critical dialogue between views is made possible.

Philosophical approaches of this volume

So, although all the following essays consider some aspect of the nature of dance and dance experience, they do so employing a variety of different theoretical perspectives, and from the standpoint of very different sorts of expertise. Their organization is predicated upon broad themes, which take into account views developed by the dance profession alongside views from professional philosophers. Some take as their primary focus the dancer, the choreographer or the spectator, or the relationship between them; some look to the work of philosophers for guidance on issues raised in dance scholarship, some turn to dance as a means by which to elucidate or foreground philosophical problems in the wider arena of art.

In selecting the essays, we have taken into account currently contested topics in dance scholarship, such as the nature and status of practice in practice-led research; the relevance (or otherwise) of traditional theoretical frameworks to current dance practices; the rise in popularity of phenomenological accounts within the profession and in dance scholarship, not least because they bring to the fore the dancer's agency; the resurgence of interest in notions of kinaesthetic empathy, now twinned with research in cognitive science.

We have also taken into account the seeming marginalization of analytic aesthetics within dance scholarship in recent years by including a number of essays built on an analytic approach: the essays by Graham McFee, Raf Geenens, Julia Beauquel, Anna Pakes, Renée Conroy, Geraldine Morris, Noël Carroll and Kristin Boyce, for example, could all be said to adopt essentially analytic strategies of argument and to respond to debates current in analytic philosophy of art. Of course, the umbrella term 'analytic philosophy' already covers a range of diverse approaches and influences, represented here to some extent, from McFee's Wittgensteinianism to the concern with philosophy of action evident in Beauquel and Boyce; from Pakes's platonist metaphysics to the references in the work by Carroll and Morris to contemporary debates in philosophy of mind and art. Some of the essays (for example, those by Jane Carr, Henrietta Bannerman, and Catherine Botha) choose to argue from a theoretical base that seeks to reconcile analytic and continental traditions. Others, by Jonathan Owen Clark and Efrosini Protopapa, are rooted more squarely in phenomenological and postmodernist traditions, though they speak more broadly because of their thematic concerns. Two of the essays, by Bannerman and Larraine Nicholas, draw on philosophical writings (by C.S. Peirce and R.G. Collingwood respectively), which are difficult to categorize but which help elucidate particular features and problems of dance and dance scholarship.

The themes explored

Our themes map a trajectory from the specifics of dance performance to the place of dance art in philosophy: beginning with an interrogation of the performer, moving through dance works in performance; tackling the nature of dance expression and finally the relationship between dance and philosophy.

In Part I, 'Dancers and people dancing', the dancer is considered in terms of her expert craft; her humanity; and her perceived connection with the spectator. Graham McFee's '"Admirable legs", or the dancer's importance for the dance' explores the embodiment of danceworks and the dancer's instantiating role. He targets for critique two sets of claims often made about danceworks and their performers: first, the (poststructuralist) idea that dance works are reducible to open 'texts' whose authors are now 'dead'; and secondly, the notion that dancers are performing artists, in the sense of co-authors of the work they instantiate. Against the first set of claims, McFee urges an account of danceworks as intentional. Against the idea that dancers are artists, McFee draws a distinction between the roles and responsibilities of the dancer and the choreographer, roles which are analytically distinguishable, though they may be performed by the same person(s) in some cases. McFee is concerned to stress that to deny an authorial role for (typical) dancers is not to neglect or ignore dancers' contributions or achievements. Indeed, his concern is precisely to value correctly that contribution. McFee's discussion draws on and develops arguments about identity, notationality and persistence put forward in his other published work, through this critique of tenets of danceworld discourse which often pass unchallenged.

Raf Geenens' emphasis is on the dancer's humanity. Geenens' essay 'Bodies and movements or persons and actions?' reexamines David Michael Levin's celebrated 1973 article 'Balanchine's Formalism'. In that article, Levin argues that Balanchine reveals the defining conditions of dance in a manner that fits the modernist project in the Greenbergian sense. Geenens questions the nature of the expressiveness of the human body on which Levin's argument rests and secondly asks whether it is ever indeed possible for dance to refer to nothing outside of itself.

Drawing on the work of Rosalind Krauss and Stanley Cavell, Geenens argues that Levin fails crucially to distinguish between artistic materials and artistic medium. In contrast to materials, medium is always convention-dependent: artworks refer to their historical context for their meaning, so that expression is inevitably more than mere formal relations. Moreover, he challenges the reductionism of Levin's account, arguing that the specificity of dance is dependent upon seeing persons dancing. So, if a choreographer, such as Balanchine or Sasha Waltz, wants to play down, or eliminate the human element, then s/he can do so only by using a considerable amount of artifice. Geenens concludes that it is above all the humanity of the dancer that is the defining quality of dance works, even those dance works that are apparently formalist in nature.

Jane Carr's 'Embodiment and dance: puzzles of consciousness and agency' also focuses on the humanity of the dancer, this time to reflect upon the dancer's felt experience, her connection with the audience and how this may shed light on the philosophical problem of dance expression. Carr draws on her experience as dancer, choreographer, and academic to consider dance expression, in particular, the dancer-audience connection. In their consideration of dance expression David Best (and later, Graham McFee) emphasize the relationships between the observable features of a dance and their context. But, swayed by her case studies of dancers' experiences of dancing, Carr urges a more interdisciplinary approach that draws on insights from phenomenology and the social sciences to interrogate the relationships between consciousness, intention, feeling and action and to develop her account of how dance expresses. Prompted by some dancers' insistence on the perceived energy that passes between dancer and audience in performance, Carr considers the concept of kinaesthetic empathy as a way to explain this exchange. While accepting the argument that direct kinaesthetic connection between dancer and audience is problematic in explaining a dance's significance, this does not mean that a kinaesthetic sense does not have a bearing on how dance is experienced as an artform.

In Part II, 'Dance works and their performances', we focus on the dance work and its instantiation. This trio of essays poses questions concerning dance ontology, dance work identity and authentic performance. The essays explore the nature of the dance work, the conditions that must be satisfied in order for two distinct dance performances to be instances of the same work, and the question of appropriate performance interpretation to instantiate choreography.

The section begins with Anna Pakes' essay 'The plausibility of a platonist ontology of dance'. Platonism (with a small 'p', note) offers one way of characterizing the ontological status of dance works: for the platonist, dance works exist as abstract objects which can be instantiated in multiple individual performances. Pakes notes the paucity of the literature on dance ontology and that the discussion concerning musical works is much further advanced. She borrows from this tradition (particularly the work of Peter Kivy and Julian Dodd) to develop a sophisticated version of the platonist ontology of dance capable of plausibly negotiating such difficulties as the tension between the eternal existence of dance works and the historically situated nature of their performances. Nonetheless, Pakes ultimately concludes that platonism fits the ontology of dance less comfortably than it does that of music. If a musical work can be identified as a sound-structure, the parallel for dance is harder to identify. Again, context and intention seem to play a role in constituting the meaning of dance works – this fact is difficult to square with the platonist's model of dance works as abstract, relatively mind-independent objects. In drawing this conclusion, however, Pakes points to the possibility of a much richer debate about dance ontology, and indeed to lessons that ontologists as such could learn from the problems of accounting for art works such as dances.

In her essay, 'The *Beat* goes on: reconsidering dancework identity', Renee Conroy addresses the question of what it is that fixes the identity of a dancework as the particular piece of art that it is. She illustrates this problem, with the intriguing example of two very different performances of Mark Dendy's *Beat*.

Conroy outlines three *desiderata* for a theory of dance work identity: that it be non-revisionist in relation to actual dance practice; that it be metaphysically substantive – simply offering a formula for re-identifying works is not enough; and that it be accessible in the sense of making acts of identification achievable in practice. With these criteria in place, Conroy turns to a careful critical examination of three candidate theories of dancework identity. She first considers notationalism as presented by Graham McFee, followed by Julie Van Camp's legal model and last explores what she labels the canonical performance view. While the three approaches are found to be fruitful and illuminating in their own ways, Conroy nonetheless identifies a number of limitations with each theory. One issue that comes sharply into focus is the difficulty of finding a model that can satisfy the second *desideratum*. The best theories we have currently available, Conroy concludes, may offer a procedure for re-identification, but a truly metaphysical account of identity remains elusive.

Geraldine Morris's essay 'What should dancers think about when performing? Issues of interpretation and identity in ballet' identifies and explores a problem in contemporary ballet practice, arguing that dancers often tend to misperceive and misrepresent choreographic works as sequences of classroom steps. She diagnoses the problem as a mismatch between, on the one hand, the values of ballet training regimes, which emphasize positions, individual steps and perfect execution; and, on the other hand, choreographer expectations and artistic choices, which may stress opposing qualities such as speed and flow. Morris seeks to develop an account of performance interpretation which might help overcome the problem. Drawing on philosophical literature about performance interpretation in (classical) music, she explores the importance of stylistic and historical knowledge, alongside attention to the score, for appropriate performance. Only when choreographic choices and stylistic features are correctly perceived and valued, she argues, will ballet choreography – as distinct from academic dance movement – be made visible, and the significance of these ballets as artworks become apparent.

Part III, 'Dance, expression and representation', revisits issues pertaining to dance expression touched upon in the essays of Part 1, this time by turning to theories of artistic expression and representation across the arts and considering their adequacy in relation to a range of dance works, including contemporary dance theatre works that, it may be argued, challenge traditional theoretical frameworks.

Noël Carroll's 'Expression, music and dance' examines how music and dance work together to project expressive properties, that is the kinds of properties designated by attributions like 'the music is *angry*' or 'this dance is sad'. These appear to be the kinds of properties that only sentient beings can bear, so a philosophical problem arises in explaining how such characterizations can apply to music and, indeed, other non-sentient objects. Carroll proposes in this regard an 'imitation theory of musical expression': in other words, it is in virtue of resemblance(s) between the music and the behaviour of, say, a sad person that the music expresses sadness. The expressive properties that music projects, however, are often diffuse: they are more mood-like than emotion-like in that they lack the object directedness, or referential apparatus, of emotion. When music and dance conspire, dance (whether narrative or not) supplies the reference, particularizing and rendering explicit the general feeling tone suggested by the music. Carroll also proposes an account of how we are able to perceive emotional properties in dance with music, suggesting that this capacity depends on a more general 'mind-reading' ability, by which we imitate others 'in order to get a fix on their emotive states'. Finally, Carroll considers cases where music and dance seem to work in opposition rather than concert: the function of the dance here, he argues, is still to concretize the emotional quality of the whole, but in this case by recalibrating the mood of the music.

In 'Physical and aesthetic properties in dance' Julia Beauquel takes as her starting point a debate between two contrasting views of how dance is understood. One view claims that, because it involves the human body as its medium, dance is naturally expressive. The second, opposing view sees style as the key element: style mediates choreographic intention and dances are comprehensible to the extent that we understand the conventions of the style and of the technique associated with it. Beauquel disputes both views and borrows from action theory to consider how dance movements' expressive properties are related both to the choreographer/performer's active intentions and to the body's subjection to factors outside of intentional control (such as the force of gravity). Arguing that the expressive properties of dances supervene upon their physical properties, Beauquel proposes a continuity rather than dichotomy between the natural and the stylistic. She thus explains the importance of both perceptual and cognitive faculties, expression and style, patiency and agency, to the appreciation of dance.

Henrietta Bannerman, in her essay 'Visible symbols: dance and its modes of representation' seeks to reconcile traditional accounts of artistic representation as imitation with the claim that contemporary dance theatre stages (rather than copies) the real: in the words of Norbert Servos, 'it does not pretend, it *is*'. Bannerman argues that a more sophisticated account of dance representation is required to move beyond these opposing views and recognize that dance theatre possesses *both* symbolic richness *and* a physical immediacy, combined in what she terms, following Susan Kozel, a 'physical symbolic'. She explores Susan Foster's (1986) account of dance representation as a potential advance on mimetic theories, and then further develops her own account of dance signification through a discussion of Charles Sanders Peirce's semiotics. In particular, Peirce's triadic typology of signs as symbols, icons and indices is examined as a means of elucidating the complex way in which dances represent. The fruitfulness of this typology is demonstrated through detailed and illuminating analyses of moments from two works of contemporary dance: Jérôme Bel's (1997) work *Shirtology* and Hofesh Shechter's (2010) *Political Mother*.

In his essay 'The Intrinsic significance of dance: a phenomenological approach', Jonathan Owen Clark seeks to justify a phenomenological methodology as that best suited to an appreciation of the art form. Other approaches, such as those derived from poststructuralism, critical theory, semiotics or historicist hermeneutics tend to over-emphasize dance works' socio-cultural and historical contexts, thereby neglecting the 'foundational nature of dance as movement, the distinctive way in which it reveals and epitomizes our *animate* nature'. To support his argument, Clark investigates the controversial topic of kinaesthesia, approached through Adorno's notion of 'Mimesis' which Clark likens to Husserl's concept of 'pairing', arguing firstly the case for kinaesthesia as a sensory modality in its own right (following Maxine Sheets-Johnstone) and secondly, its profound relevance to dance appreciation. Husserl argues that kinaesthesia is important to perception of all objects irrespective of whether we are looking at movement or not, and this, Clark notes, has the effect of uniquely situating dance. These insights lead Clark to propose six theses on dance's intrinsic significance, which relate to: path-dependency and spatial trajectory; the 'three-foldedness' of dance; imaginative and projective aspects of kinaesthesis; the virtualization of expression; intermedial interpenetration; intercorporeality and intersubjectivity.

In Part IV, 'Dance and philosophy, dance as philosophy', four essays consider the inter-relationship of dance and philosophy, drawing on diverse strands of philosophical thinking which illuminate reflection on dance.

Catherine Botha's project in her essay 'Dance and/as art: considering Nietzsche and Badiou' is spurred by Alain Badiou's characterization of dance as non-art. In denying art-status to dance, Badiou draws on Nietzsche's use of dance as a metaphor for thought. In Badiou's hands, as Botha shows, it becomes a metaphor for the infinite thinking subject's shedding of its bodily limitations. For Botha, this picture relies on a narrow understanding of the nature of dance and a similarly narrow reading of Nietzsche's account of it. She devotes the next section of her essay to uncovering a richer reading of Nietzsche which avoids both the problem of relegating the body to a secondary position and the inference that dance cannot be art. In the final part of her essay, Botha turns to the question of how best to define art. Rejecting various versions of the institutional theory, Botha proposes an alternative in which both artistic intentions and audience expectations – two themes dear to Nietzsche himself – play a pivotal role.

Larraine Nicholas's essay 'Dance and the historical imagination' examines the role and character of the imagination in the work of the dance historian. She begins from phenomenological observations about the spontaneous occurrence of mental images during the research process, and recognizes (following Antonio Damasio) that such images can include the aural and the kinaesthetic as well as the visual. Nicholas probes the relationship between this mental imaging and imagination generally, and seeks to discover how the two are connected in historical thought. She explores R.G. Collingwood's account of historical thought as 'imaginary', but argues that Collingwood's constructive and rational characterization of the historical imagination, though undoubtedly important, leaves little space for what springs to mind when thinking about the past. To elucidate this, Edward Casey's notion of 'imagining how' – as distinct from 'imagining that' – proves helpful: imagining *how* is focused on how it would *feel* if this were the case, rather than whether a given state of affairs could conceivably exist. Such imagining how is important to the breadth and humanity of historical study, since it enables sympathy (if not empathy) with the dance historian's subjects.

In 'The thinking body: dance, philosophy and modernism' Kristin Boyce points out that the phrase 'philosophy of dance' can be understood to refer to two different things, either philosophy which takes dance as its object, or philosophical reflection that is carried out by dance works themselves. Her project is to develop a modernist account of dance that can clarify the second possibility. She identifies and outlines a standard approach, common to the work of three theorists (Sally Banes, Noël Carroll and Roger Copeland) influenced by Clement Greenberg's modernism. This approach is found to be able to demonstrate that philosophical reflection is present in the pieces of some choreographers, but not to draw a necessary connection between a dance's philosophical contribution and its achievement *as art*. Boyce argues that this mutual dependence can be illuminated on the basis of her own, alternative account, which draws on the conception of modernism offered by Stanley Cavell and Michael Fried.

Efrosini Protopapa continues this theme in her essay 'Choreography as philosophy, or exercising thought in performance'. Focusing on the specific case of Jérôme Bel, Protopapa considers in detail a lecture performance which the choreographer delivered in 2008 instead of, but apparently focused on, a previous performance work *The Last Performance* (1998). In his lecture performance Bel claims that the ideas he explored within *The Last Performance* are more effectively dealt with in words. Protopapa disputes this claim, arguing that the later lecture performance is instead a clever exposition of the impossibility of exactly reproducing a live performance. In this respect, what Bel is actually doing in the lecture, Protopapa contends, is choreographing a new work: a notion of choreography that fits with Deleuze and Guattari's formulation of philosophy as 'the art of forming, inventing and fabricating concepts'. Protopapa develops these ideas, taking into account Hélène Cixous's thoughts on the difference between a writer, albeit one who like herself writes philosophically, and a philosopher: the writer is focused on exploring dimensions of the other; the philosopher owns what s/he says. In this sense, Bel is a philosopher as well as a writer/artist.

We hope that this volume helps consolidate the development of philosophy of dance over the last few years. For the field to grow further, sustained discussion around key issues seems crucial. Although we are aware that it offers only a sample of work in the field, the volume will have served its purpose if it sparks debate and draws in to the on-going discussion a wider range of scholars interested in dance and philosophy. At the very least, we hope to show how dance remains fertile ground for philosophical investigation.

References

Adshead, Janet (ed.). *Dancing Texts: Intertextuality in Interpretation*, London: Routledge, 1999.

Alvarez, Inma, Hector J. Pérez and Francisca Pérez-Carreño (eds.). *Expression in the Performing Arts*, Cambridge: Cambridge Scholars Publishing, 2010.

Armelagos, Adina and Mary Sirridge. 'The Identity Crisis in Dance.' *Journal of Aesthetics and Art Criticism*, 37:2, 1978, pp.129-140.

Armelagos, Adina and Mary Sirridge. 'The Personal Style and Performance Prerogatives', in Sheets-Johnstone, Maxine, (ed.), *Illuminating Dance: Philosophical Explorations*, Cranbury: Associated University Presses, 1984.

Beardsley, Monroe C. 'What is Going on in a Dance?', *Dance Research Journal*, 15:1, 1982, pp.31-36.

Beauquel, Julia and Roger Pouivet (eds.). *Philosophie de la danse*, Rennes: Presses Universitaires de Rennes, 2010.

Best, David. *Expression and Movement in the Arts: A Philosophical Enquiry*, London: Lepus Books, 1974.

Carr, David. 'Practical Reasoning and Knowing How', *Journal of Human Movement Studies*, 4, 1978, pp.3-20.

Carr, David. 'Dance Education, Skill and Behavioural Objectives', *Journal of Aesthetic Education*, 18, 1984, pp.67-76.

Carr, David. 'Thought and Action in the Art of Dance', *British Journal of Aesthetics*, 27:4, 1987, pp.345-357.

Carr, David. 'Meaning in Dance,' in *British Journal of Aesthetics*, 37:4, 1997, pp.349-366.

Carr, David. 'Further Reflections on Practical Knowledge and Dance a Decade On', in McFee, Graham (ed.), *Dance, Education and Philosophy*, Oxford: Meyer and Meyer Sport, 1999.

Carroll, Noël. *Philosophy of Art: A Contemporary Introduction*, London: Routledge, 1999.

Carroll, Noël. 'The Philosophy of Art History, Dance and the 1960s', in Banes, Sally (ed.), *Reinventing Dance in the 1960s: Everything was Possible*, Madison: University of Wisconsin Press, 2003, pp.81-97.

Carroll, Noël. *Living in an Artworld: Reviews and Essays on Dance, Performance, Theatre and the Fine Arts in the 1970s and 1980s*, Louisville: Evanston, 2011.

Carroll, Noël. *Art in Three Dimensions*. Oxford: Oxford University Press, 2012.

Carroll, Noël and Sally Banes. 'Working and Dancing: A Response to Monroe Beardsley's "What is Going on in a Dance?",' *Dance Research Journal*, 15:1, 1982, pp.37-41.

Carter, Alexandra (ed.). *The Routledge Dance Studies Reader*, London:

Routledge, 1998.

Carter, Alexandra and Janet O'Shea (eds.). *The Routledge Dance Studies Reader*, 2nd edition, London: Routledge, 2010.

Cohen, Selma Jeanne. *Next week, Swan Lake: Reflections on Dance and Dancers*, Middletown: Wesleyan University Press, 1986 [1982].

Conroy, Renee and Julie Van Camp (eds.). 'Symposium: Dance Art and Science', *Journal of Aesthetics and Art Criticism*, 71:2, 2013, pp.167-210.

Copeland, Roger and Marshall Cohen (eds.). *What is Dance? Readings in Theory and Criticism*, Oxford: Oxford University Press, 1983.

Davies, David. *Art as Performance*, Malden, MA, Blackwell Publishing, 2004.

Davies, David. *Philosophy of the Performing Arts*. Malden: Wiley-Blackwell, 2011.

Davies, Stephen, Kathleen Higgins, Robert Hopkins, Robert Stecker and David Cooper (eds.). *A Companion to Aesthetics*, Oxford: Blackwell, 2009.

Fancher, Gordon and Gerald Myers (eds.). *Philosophical Essays on Dance: with Responses from Choreographers, Critics and Dancers*, New York: Dance Horizons.

Foster, Susan Leigh. *Reading Dancing: Bodies and Subjects in Contemporary American Dance*, Berkeley: University of California Press, 1986.

Foster, Susan Leigh. *Choreographing Empathy: Kinaesthesia in Performance*, London: Routledge, 2011.

Foster, Susan Leigh, Philipa Rothfield and Colleen Dunagan (eds.). 'Philosophy and Dance', *Topoi*, 24:1, 2005.

Fraleigh, Sondra Horton. *Dance and the Lived Body: A Descriptive Aesthetics*, Pittsburgh: University of Pittsburgh Press, 1987.

Franko, Mark. *Dance as Text: Ideologies of the Baroque Body*, Cambridge: Cambridge University Press, 1993.

Franko, Mark. 'Un-disciplined Questioning', *Dance Research Journal*, 41:1, 2009, pp.v-vii.

Franko, Mark (ed.). 'Dance and Phenomenology: Critical Reappraisals', *Dance Research Journal*, 43:2, 2011.

Gaut, Berys and Dominic McIver Lopes (eds.). *The Routledge Companion to Aesthetics*, London: Routledge, 2005.

Giersdorf, Jens Richard. 'Dance Studies in the International Academy: Genealogy of a Disciplinary Formation', *Dance Research Journal*, 41:1, 2009, pp.23-44.

Kivy, Peter (ed.). *The Blackwell Guide to Aesthetics*, Oxford: Blackwell, 2004.

Kozel, Susan. *As Vision Becomes Gesture*, PhD thesis, Colchester: University of Essex, 1994.

Kozel, Susan. *Closer: Performance, Technologies, Phenomenology*, Cambridge: MIT Press, 2007.

Langer, Susanne K. *Feeling and Form: A Theory of Art developed from Philosophy* in a New Key, New York: Charles Scribner's Sons, 1953.

Langer, Susanne K. *Philosophy in a New Key: A Study in the Symbolism of Reason, Rite, and Art*, Cambridge: Harvard University Press, 1957, 3rd edition [1942].

Lepecki, André (ed.). 'Dance Composes Philosophy Composes Dance: Series on new Choreography', *The Drama Review*, 50:4 (Part I), 2006, and 51:2 (Part II), 2007.

Levinson, Jerrold (ed.). *The Oxford Handbook of Aesthetics*, Oxford: Oxford University Press, 2003.

McFee, Graham. *Understanding Dance*, London: Routledge, 1992.

McFee, Graham. *The Concept of Dance Education*, expanded edition, Eastbourne: Pageantry Press, 2004 [1994].

McFee, Graham. *The Philosophical Aesthetics of Dance*, Alton: Dance Books, 2011.

McFee, Graham (ed.). *Dance, Education and Philosophy*, Oxford: Meyer & Meyer Sport, 1999.

Malnig, Julie (ed.). 'Trends in Dance Scholarship' and 'Dance Research: Perspectives on the Past, Outlook Towards the Future', *Dance Research Journal*, 32:1, 2000, pp.39-77 and pp.110-137.

Margolis, Joseph. 'The Autographic Nature of the Dance', *Journal of Aesthetics and Art Criticism*, 39:4, 1981, pp.419-427.

Montero, Barbara. 'Proprioception as an Aesthetic Sense', *Journal of Aesthetics and Art Criticism*, 64:2, 2006, pp.231-242.

Parviainen, Jaana. *Bodies Moving and Moved: A Phenomenological Analysis of the Dancing Subject and the Cognitive and Ethical Values of Dance Art*, Tampere: Tampere University Press, 1998.

Reason, Matthew and Dee Reynolds. *Kinaesthetic Empathy in Creative and Cultural Contexts*, Bristol: Intellect Books, 2012.

Redfern, Betty. *Dance, Art and Aesthetics*, London: Dance Books, 1983.

Ribeiro, Anna Cristina. *The Continuum Companion to Aesthetics*, London: Continuum, 2012.

Scott, Gregory. 'Banes and Carroll on Defining Dance', *Dance Research Journal*, 29:1, 1997, pp.7-22.

Scott, Gregory. 'Transcending the Beardsleyans: A Reply to Carroll and Banes, in *Dance Research Journal*, 31:1, 1999, pp.12-19.

Sheets-Johnstone, Maxine. *The Phenomenology of Dance*, London: Dance Books, 1979 [1966].

Sheets-Johnstone, Maxine (ed.). *Illuminating Dance: Philosophical Explorations*, Lewisburg: Bucknell University Press, 1984.

Sirridge, Mary and Adina Armelagos. 'The In's and Out's of Dance: Expression as an Aspect of Style', *The Journal of Aesthetics and Art Criticism*, 36:1, 1977, pp.15-24.

Sirridge, Mary and Adina Armelagos. 'The Role of "Natural Expressiveness" in Explaining Dance', *The Journal of Aesthetics and Art Criticism*, 41:3, 1983, pp.301-307.

Sparshott, Francis. *Off the Ground: First Steps to a Philosophical Consideration of the Dance*, Princeton: Princeton University Press, 1988.

Sparshott, Francis. *A Measured Pace: Toward a Philosophical Understanding of the Arts of Dance*, Toronto: University of Toronto Press, 1995.

Van Camp, Julie. *Philosophical Problems of Dance Criticism*, PhD thesis, Philadelphia: Temple University, 1981.

Van Camp, Julie. 'Non-Verbal Metaphor: A Non-Explanation of Meaning in Dance', *British Journal of Aesthetics*, 36:2, 1996, pp.177-187.

Whittock, Trevor. 'Dance Metaphors: A Reply to Julie Van Camp', *British Journal of Aesthetics*, 37:3, 1997, pp.274-282.

Part I

Dancers and People Dancing

1. 'Admirable legs';
or, the dancer's importance for the dance

Graham McFee

Introduction

My chief concern in this essay will be to defend, somewhat indirectly, the importance of the embodiment of dances against some of its critics.[1] The readings of those critics (perhaps called 'postmodernist readings') attack the idea of *danceworks* – as performables – by denying 'the dance' that unity required for fit objects for understanding. And by the term 'performable' is meant a suitable object for performance, one that can be performed on one occasion, and the very same object re-performed at another time or place. We see *this* dance or *that* play on the particular occasion when we see the performance, even though we accept that there are typically differences between tonight's performance and another night's; and that many such differences will be irrelevant to our identification of the artwork. This idea is central to a commonsense view of what is involved in being a performing art.[2]

By contrast, for some writers a dance is an open text (often, *just* a text) with features subject to a continuous, and typically unconstrained, process of interpretation.[3] Here, there can be no *one* enduring thing to call *the dance*,

---

1 This essay thereby further develops ideas explored in my recent monograph (McFee 2011b), winner of the Selma Jeanne Cohen Prize for Dance Aesthetics 2010-12.

2 Thus, happenings (as 'one-off' art-events) are not *performables* in this sense: hence *happening* is not a performing art.

3 For 'open text', see Rubidge 2000. As examples of theory, Stephanie Jordan (2000, p.63) explicitly adapts a passage from literary theorist Stanley Fish to the effect that it is:
> ... our framework for seeing that give dances their shape, making them, rather than, as is usually assumed, arising from them. Thus the facts of the dance, rather than being the objects of interpretation, are its products. [her modification of his text]

And, for Fish (1980, p.vii), there can be no entity which remains the same from one moment to the next: and hence, applied to dance, no *dancework* as such. For there is, in effect, no object for interpretation here, but only what is composed *from* interpretation. Similarly, this view typically identifies its alternative as a form of *absolutism* which:
> ... supposes that cultural artefacts contain a pure, intrinsic worth that is timeless and universal. Thus it privileges the 'object of value' rather than the process of evaluating ... (Dodds 2011, p.15)

The contrasting view, then, finds no such object, as above. Instead, as Briginshaw (2001, p.18) might put it, the dancework is '... always in the process of constructing and being constructed'. [Note: there are of course many differences amongst the views thus loosely characterized.]

since each of the structures of interpretation has equal claim. Moreover, as interpretations, they are not uniquely identified with any particular embodiment, especially once little weight is given to the idea of authorship of texts (see What is wrong with postmodernist readings? below).

Although, as we will see, my defence rejects such a view and emphasizes the necessary embodiment of dances, meeting this task does not need a specific theory of embodiment, once we better understand the part played by *dancers*. But my discussion of dancers also comments, in passing, on Théophile Gautier's passion for ballerinas' legs – the 'admirable legs' of Eugénie Fiocre in *Néméa* (July, 1864: Gautier 1986, p.305) or for Fanny Elssler whose 'beautiful legs [resembled] ... an antique statue worthy of being cast and lovingly inspected' (Gautier 1986, p.23). For this does not sound like *my* concern with dancers.

Art and embodiment

Before turning to discussion of the contribution of the dancer to the dancework, I begin by briefly elaborating the place of that *dancework* (as work of art), sketching the picture of *art*, and hence of some danceworks as artworks, as it might apply here. That is, I begin from the sense in which, as I would put it, artworks are made to be meaning-bearing: that, as a whole, they embody (roughly) the intelligence of their creators. Thus:

> If we wanted to say something about art that we could be quite certain was true, we might settle for the assertion that art is intentional. And by this we would mean that art is something we do, that works of art are something we make. (Wollheim 1973, p.112)

In this sense, the features or characteristics of any artwork derive from its author or authors – sometimes seen easily and directly, sometimes in a much more indirect fashion. For, as in typical artworks, (artistic) meaning here is embodied in this or that particular way (movement, sound, and so on). Thus, Karole Armitage's *The Watteau Duets* (1985) is rightly thought '... a concentrated exploration of two important ballet conventions: the pas de deux (or duet form) and pointework' (Banes 2007, p.314) with '... a frank carnality that most earlier ballets [...] only gestured toward' (Banes 2007, p.315); and in which Armitage '... seems [...] to move on pointe precariously, like a tightrope walker – not through lack of technique but as a result of the daring, extreme positions of her legs and torso' (Banes 2007, p.316). But, even when these seem remarks about artists' thoughts or achievements, these are descriptions of the intention-as-embodied: in that sense, then, descriptions *of the dancework*. Hence 'what is meant' cannot ultimately be divorced from this embodiment – in contrast to, say, the report of a traffic accident, where the same meaning might occur expressed differently.

Further, this explains why similar or related artworks differ: their meaning, in being differently embodied, is a different meaning.[4] Stressing in this way the *embodied* nature of artistic meaning (and artistic value) re-affirms its intentional character. And one aspect of my critique is directed at views seeking to deny or minimize that fact: say, by characterizing dances as (just) *texts*.

What is wrong with postmodernist readings?

Some theorists – often calling themselves post-structuralists or postmodernists[5] – have endorsed a radical view here. Beginning under the heading 'the death of the author', since their primary concern was initially with literature[6] (or perhaps even with writing more generally), they stress, not the author's *death* at all, but the disappearance from discussion of novels (and the like) of the concept *author*, with its implications of *intention*. On this view, literary works are merely instances of writing, with the author an abstraction, and meaning determined by the reader. Relatedly, a contrast (sanctioned by literary theory) is drawn between text and work, where the *text* is just 'a concatenation of signs subject to multiple interpretations' (Lamarque 2000, p.457), but where the *work* is (or may be) constrained by purpose, context, genre: this *work*-concept, which seems to imply authorship, is also disparaged. And more than just *avowed* post-structuralists take this line. For instance, there are scholars who feel that the concept *literature* '... artificially separates the study of 'literary' texts from adjacent areas of cultural practice' (Bennett 1979, p.11); and is unhelpful for that reason – 'literature is just text'. But, as Peter Lamarque (2000, p.457) puts it, 'By assigning priority to texts over works, poststructuralists in effect sideline altogether the category of literature ...'. This denies literary value (and, *mutatis mutandis*, artistic value).

Further, there is an additional issue: for, in the case of literature, a theory designed for language is being applied to the linguistic – literary works have *words* as their components, at least in some sense. The application to dance requires an additional step, to explain how a theory constructed for application to words can be augmented to apply to movement. Moreover,

---

4 See McFee 2011a, pp.47-54.

5 See, for example, Goellner and Murphy (1995, p.ix) on the aim:
  ... to read dance as literary critics read texts – especially given dance's unstable meanings, its dense net of reference to other movements ...
And, as below, literary critics are here theorized as rejecting the *work*-concept, and the concept of *literature* as such.

6 NB As quoted above (footnote 3), Jordan (2000, p.63) explicitly draws on Stanley Fish; likewise, many authors in Goellner and Murphy (1995) are explicit in their starting point in literary theory.

it cannot appeal here to *artistic meaning* for movement, since precisely this distinctive sense of 'artistic' is being denied. And notice that this is not a critique of a *kind* of dance (call it 'postmodern dance'),[7] but a perfectly general critique of features which – were its advocates right – are common to much dance, even if this regularly escapes notice.

But what postmodernists deny is not what I have asserted.[8] The dispute does not concern the place (for understanding the artwork) of the planning of this or that person: postmodernists rightly recognize that, in itself, *intending does not make it so*. Hence, they want to address the object produced, not the thoughts or plans that produced it: they rightly refuse to begin from the actual thoughts of this or that person. I too reject the confused view of intention such a picture adopts. So (as Beardsley [1970, p.33] urged) I will be '... a poem reader, not a mind-reader', in looking to the meaning *embodied* in the poem. And similarly for dance.

Two problems for typical postmodernist accounts arise here. First, in denying the role of the author, the imported theory about linguistic meaning seems to imply (a) that (say, for a poem) the *words alone* ('the text') could carry any weight; and then concludes (b) that these words are somehow ambiguous, or in need of interpretation.[9] This result follows, even for words, *only* when the context of the production of those words (their 'utterance') is set aside. (The words, 'Mary had a little lamb', may be equivocal between a concern with animal husbandry and a concern with dinner. But, in context, their utterance is typically not misleading.[10]) So this is a poor account of language. Then, second, artworks (here, our poem) carry with them the specific and crucial contexts of *art*; they must be appreciated *as art*, or they will be misunderstood – since this *is* a poem. And the requirement that one understand them as *poetry* returns us to what has been called their 'history of production' – to the time and place of their production and/or reception.

In ignoring both the facts about language and those about art, our postmodernists miss much that is important in granting intelligibility to

---

7 Compare McFee 2004, pp.204-207.

8 Compare McFee 2011a, pp.85-95.

9 As Wittgenstein (PI §201) points out, there must be 'a way of grasping a rule which is *not an interpretation*'; and, for these purposes, expressions resemble rules. For the speaker's own understanding of what he said is not an interpretation.
Standard abbreviations are used for the works of Wittgenstein:
Wittgenstein, 1953/2001 – PI
Wittgenstein, 1969 – OC
Wittgenstein, 1980 – CV
Wittgenstein, 1993 – PO

10 In his unpublished inaugural lecture at Kings College, London, Charles Travis offers – as a third possibility – that 'Mary had a little lamb' might speak 'of medical novelties'. Again, we can imagine this being obvious in context.

artworks. Further, their view runs counter to at least three connections between intention and (genuine) meaning. First, meaning is intentional. Contrast the yawn, at some dull meeting, which just *occurs* with the one where I catch your eye and yawn extravagantly. From both, the observer (my boss!) might learn something. But my deliberately yawning is an attempt to *mean* something; to communicate to you how dull I find the meeting. From the 'natural' yawn, by contrast, my boss finds out just how bored I am – the very last thing I wanted her to know! So, in one case, there is no genuine *communication*, and no message: for it was not intended communication, meant communication. At most, my (genuine) yawn might be a symptom of something. Second, causality alone cannot yield meaning. The cracks in the wall *appear* to spell-out a loved-one's name: they not only *do not* do so, they *could* not (insofar as they really are just cracks).[11] Since these cracks just occur naturally, there is nothing that they *mean* (although they too might be symptomatic of something: PI §354). The third point, more specific to artworks, is that one cannot just make of them whatever one wants – although the key thought here (that artworks can be *misperceived*) only implies *some* constraint, as contrasted with the unconstrained 'anything goes'. Neither are the features of artworks *accidental* (unless someone decides they shall be). So (roughly) an artist's intelligence must be seen behind the artwork. The objections of many who disagree rest simply on assuming a 'one right answer' version of constraint.

And, of course, the case of danceworks offers another significant difference here: for danceworks typically incorporate bodies in motion. And it remains unclear how these points *could* have a bearing there.

Further[12], it is easy to render problematic the commitments of those who see the choreographer as producing an endlessly open *text*, to function as a catalyst for the dancer's performance, the reaction of the audience, or some combination of them. For this view denies that there is a distinguishable, and relatively persistent, *dancework*. Yet being a *performable* involves precisely such distinguishability and persistence. And even such theorists treat danceworks as performables in practice: they compare this performance *of the work* with another performance (or one by another company); they regard rehearsals as *for* performances, and those performances as *of the work* at issue; and, again, that is what the notators are notating. All this reiterates the traditional ontology of *the performable*.

Moreover, those who urge publicly that one's 'reading' of artworks lacks *any* constraint do not typically mean what they say: they *do* regard, say, the words in the poem as constraining *to some degree* and *in some way* what can

---

11 Thus, artworks are not 'naturally occurring', not accidental (except where someone decides to go with the accidental).

12 As pointed out by Renee Conroy (2012, p.158)

be made of that poem.[13] First, they do not really think that each of us has a different 'reading' (although that claim is often heard) – such that, say, 200 million Americans might have 200 million different readings. At best, they are just recognizing some diversity. Second, they do not really believe that, say, *King Lear* could be 'read' as a farce, nor that Goya's *Saturn Eating His Children* could be seen as jolly: some cases *offered* just seem too implausible. And that reflects the *features* of those artworks.[14] Moreover, they grant some basis to, say, the organization of books in a book store – mysteries here, science fiction there, and romances over there. Perhaps some such decisions are arbitrary. But the majority are not.[15]

These ideas, taken together, show how artworks are best understood via such concepts as 'meaning', 'intention', 'artist': for the first two ideas suggest *meant* or *intentional*; the third suggests a *constrained meaning*.[16] Once such meaning is recognized as not dependent on some artist's psychology, we are well on the way to locating the meaning-as-embodied in the dance or poem by acknowledging a set of personal properties here: that is why the sculpture could be expressive, witty, and so on, while such concepts could not apply to the meteorite (see Ground 1989, pp.25-26) – even when one could be mistaken for the other, as a pair of Danto-esque 'confusable counter-parts' (Danto 1981, p.138). And these properties of danceworks

---

13 Derrida's 'reading' of Searle, in *Limited Inc.* (Derrida 1988), might seem to suggest that I am wrong: for here he seems to read elements of Searle's text without regard to its context or the constraints the words provide. At best, though, this seems a joke – when the misreading does not seem gratuitous.

14 The impact of titles seems revealing here. For example, consider Hockney's *Rubber Ring Floating in a Swimming Pool* [1971], where '... the arrangement on the canvas reads two ways, as the depiction of the scene in the title, and as a comment on the work of [...] contemporary painters' (Hockney 1976, p.20). As Hockney (1976, p.241) said, '... it's almost copied ... [from a photograph] ... I was so struck by the photograph's looking like a Max Ernst abstract painting that I thought, it's marvellous, I could just paint it.' Without the title, it might be mistaken for an abstract work. A similar impact of the title sustains Alphonse Allais's joke all-white painting, *Anaemic Young Girls Go to Their First Communion in a Snowstorm*.

There are also works where – although the work might be 'read' a certain way – the title gives reasons to prefer another reading. For instance, a Joseph Epstein sculpture in the chapel of New College, Oxford, might be taken as a woman being martyred by stifling with tight wrappings. Faced with the title, *The Raising of Lazarus*, one sees the figure as male and takes the expression quite differently. (I owe this example to Terry Diffey, from his PhD thesis: *Aesthetic Judgements and Works of Art*, University of Bristol, 1966.)

15 The alternative view, that *all* interpretations are arbitrary, somehow reflecting their origins in language, is (as Bernard Williams [2002, p.6] said) ' ... a tissue of mistakes.' As he continues, 'If [the word] *dog* is an arbitrary sign for a dog, it is at any rate a sign for a dog, and that must mean it can refer to a dog: and a dog is a dog, not a word'.

16 NB these points actually go for, say, all writing – only the one below stresses directly the connection to art.

should not be taken to indicate the thoughts or feelings of dancers. And hence to our concern with embodiment for dances.

Dancers instantiate the dance

Here, I want to address the dancers specifically. For dance has a distinctive place among the performing arts. Not merely are typical danceworks *performables*, in the sense that the *very same dance* can be re-performed on another occasion (despite the differences between such performances), but danceworks depend on the specific physicality of the dancers. Thus musicians fit exactly Urmson's account of performing arts: they bring about '... those things [...] of which the witnessable work consists' (Urmson 1976, p.243) – that is, they *make* or *cause* the sounds that instantiate the musical work. But dancers do not *cause* the dance; rather, they *are* the dance – their movements instantiate it.

To expand this thought, recall here Merce Cunningham (1984, p.27) saying:

> you can't describe a dance without talking about the dancer. You can't describe a dance that hasn't been seen, and the way of seeing it has everything to do with the dancers ...

Cunningham's first point is just that one only really encounters the dance itself *in performance*. Then Cunningham is right that, in a sense, '... you can't describe a dance that hasn't been seen': that is, one uninstantiated. Further, only in performance is a particular dancework fully determinate – since the features or details of performances make concrete all the places where the dancework itself under-determines those performances.

So the dance as we encounter it is principally composed of the bodies of dancers in motion – although there is a role for music, costume, and so on. Thus the embodiment of the dance depends on the dancers: that gives us a purchase on the necessity of embodiment. It also allows recognition of another feature of the dancer's contribution to the dance performance. For the dancer's activities (along with others) bring the concrete dance-performance into being. Thus, for example, Collingwood (1938, pp.320-321) writes that:

> the author [...] demands of his performers a spirit of constructive and intelligent co-operation [...] where performers [...] are not only permitted but required to fill in the details.

This seems exactly right if one were trying to capture the role of dancers in making concrete what is under-determined in *the work itself*. So one aspect of that contribution will be through the dancer's mastery of the 'craft' of instantiating the dance – from the score, or from the choreographer's instructions, or whatever. And this 'craft-mastery' aspect is easily missed.

Further, on some occasions, this 'craft-mastery' aspect is sufficiently distinctive in respect of a particular dancer to give a new nuance to the role or part being danced: to generate what might be called a distinctive *performers' interpretation*. But even this is typically within the manner of a particular dance company of delivering, say, *Swan Lake*. Although one might pick out the more distinctive of these performer's interpretations, perhaps as virtuoso performance, in typical cases they really amount to doing what each dancer *must* do – to making the dance itself concrete, given the powers and capacities of his or her body.

Dancers as building blocks

But does this exhaust the dancers' typical contribution? Some writers have thought that *therefore* the dancework itself involves a contribution from the dancer. Here, Collingwood's own conclusion is puzzling – he writes: 'Every performer is co-author of the work he performs' (Collingwood 1938, p. 321). At best, this seems hyperbole for effect! For what could it mean, taken literally, to assign the dancer a role as 'co-author'?

The problem here, as we shall see, is that the role of author of the work has already been used up – typically correctly assigned to the choreographer, although there are a number of cases to consider. Certainly dances that depend, wholly or in part, on improvisation by dancers: such cases can be set aside as *special*; but even here the choreographer *decides*. And that point seems even stronger if the dancer's role, in practice, involved offering some movement suggestion which the choreographer accepted (or did not). Should dancers be rightly seen as 'co-authors' (in Collingwood's expression) of danceworks they perform?

Since in this context the term 'art' means (fine) art, *artists* are makers of it. But the emphasis here on the importance of the dancer does not identify a role for that dancer as artist in the sense of *author* of that work. Of course, the term 'artist' is used in other ways – and dancers might be artists in those craft-mastering ways ('This surgeon is an artist!'); but we are not considering them here. Nor is this claim merely about words: with Wittgenstein, I urge, 'say what you choose' (see PI §79), but worry about what *contrasts* you are drawing.

Then the fact that most dances can be performed with different casts highlights an absurdity in assigning authorial responsibility to dancers in such cases: for then, having a different cast would make each performance a different artwork. But that is just to reject the idea of a performing art, as multiple, or re-performable, on which *the very same work* can, in principle, be performed on other occasions, at other times and in other places, with other casts.

It may help to consider the expression 'performing *artist*' here, since it is widely used. My point throughout is just that authorial responsibility identifies one sense of the term 'artist'; one commonly used in respect of all the arts. And that sense clearly applies to the performing arts. But, there, it is taken up by a role *other than* that of performer. Of course, as above, we can use the term 'artist' to mean other things too. Yet, first, doing so is likely to mislead and, second, an account of this other sense of 'artist' is then needed.

Let us consider in more detail the authorial role for dance. Since works in performing arts are indeed *multiples*, the abstract object that is the *dance* can be made either by making a recipe (such as a score) or by creating a ('first') performance. Perhaps only a few dances are composed by writing a score, with most composed by working in the studio with dancers – making the abstract object that is the artwork by making a performance. In either case, the artist will make the final decisions. Thus the artist, as author, has a clear role, even for performing arts like dance.

In our typical dance performances, recognizing only one artwork acknowledges at most one *authorship*. Moreover, that artwork is not *just* its performances: like a play, it can persist unperformed, at least for a time. In both cases, the role of author is logically separable from that of performer. Hence *this* is the context in which the dancer (or dancers) *cannot* be artists in the relevant sense, since authorship of the work already exhausts that role. Such an author is not necessarily one *person*, of course; but that point need not detain us long, since it is familiar from, say, cinema. For what is important here is precisely *authorial* responsibility, in the sense in which a Beethoven symphony is *Beethoven's*. And it cannot matter if this responsibility resides in one person or (typically in films) in many. Hence, if Lloyd Newson '... wanted to create a situation in which dancers and choreographers collaborated on work' (Mackrell 1992, p.50; see also Mackrell 1997, p.114), when *DV8: Physical Theatre* performed *My Sex Our Dance* (1986), described as '... a collaboration between Newson and Nigel Charnock' (Mackrell 1992, p.123), the responsibility rested with Newson *and* Charnock. And that was just traditional authorial responsibility, as makers.[17] So, although they *did* perform the piece, that was a separate role: indeed, we can imagine just that piece performed by other dancers – especially when its recording on film or by notation gives these others relatively easy access. In any case where that work is performed, it will be *their* work – the work of Newson *and* Charnock:

---

17 This is part of the logic of the performing arts. As Paul Thom (1993 p.181) puts it:
    ... the performers are present in the same way the audience is, and in a way that the author need not be.
In fact, it would be better to write 'cannot be', since the author's role is completed prior to performance, a point Nelson Goodman (1966 p.114) recognized in characterizing autographic arts as ones where (for music) '... the composer's work is done when he has written the score' (see McFee 2011b, pp.42-52).

that is what it means to call dance a 'performing art', or to see danceworks as performables.

Moreover, some companies might ascribe the authorial responsibility to the *whole* company (as Alvin Ailey sometimes did), sometimes at least meaning to include the composers of the music, the lighting, costume, and set designers. Again, if this is where the authorial responsibility rests, so be it. On other occasions, these roles might be thought ancillary to the construction of the dance (which would involve taking a view of what constituted the dance), such that the responsibility rested with the choreographer. Both positions are applied to films on some occasions, as when the director gets his/her own prize, and the producer accepts the prize for the film itself. And, as above, a choreographer who invites improvisation in the preparation of his/her dances retains that authorial responsibility: he/she typically decides which pieces of improvisation from the rehearsal room make it into the final work, and when the piece is finished. Again, if this responsibility is distributed to all members of the company, then they jointly form 'the choreographer'. But that role – and that responsibility – necessarily differs (in a *performing* art, like dance) from the roles and responsibilities of the performers of the finished work, or even (viewed as roles) of the work in the process of completion (say, at 'try-outs').

It would be of interest to know why the term 'artist' is so attractive here, such that dancers have applied it to themselves, even when many accept that they are the performers of the work; and do not (indeed, logically, cannot) be its authors, that being a separate role. But most discussions of this point seem either to focus on the dancers' contribution to the authorial process, as just discussed and set aside, or to the use of the term 'performing artist', viewed as a way to improve the status of the dancer.[18] Yet that can only be done by elaborating a role for the dancer: and my strategy is to do that, as a way to recognizing its important difference from the authorial role. For it is a characteristic of performing arts to have these two roles, performer and author, even when the same person fulfils both.

In this context, then, the term 'performing artist' is ultimately unhelpful: it could pick-out those who instantiate works in the performing arts, such as dance, to recognize their artistry (their craft-mastery); or it could refer to those involved in works of one-off performance art, *happenings*. But these are very different: we probably mislead ourselves if we confuse one with the other. Of course, some of the 'practitioners' involved in a happening may just be performers – as typical dancers are: but there might be some who

---

18 The most promising alternative would stress the role of the dancer in instantiating the dance (and especially of what I call 'performer's interpretation'); but, since this must be contrasted with the authorial role, it will be very confusing to use the term 'artist' for both.

are the artists in such a case. Moreover, only those in the happenings might plausibly be thought *artists* (in some cases, not all) in the sense, previously identified, that picks out the *authors of artworks*. By contrast, that is not the right way to see the activities of (typical) dancers – dancers being *artists* would, at best, turn dances into 'happenings'. Hence dancers are not artists precisely *because* dance is a performing art, one with a role for *performers*. And that is the role the dancers fill!

So, of course, dancers sometimes *seem* like artists in the sense of *authors*: for instance, when dancers offer movement ideas for some composition; but then the choreographer decides – the responsibility remains with the choreographer. Similarly, improvisation by dancers can itself be put aside: the *order* to improvise operative here is a choreographer's order. Further, one must recognize the number of 'hats' (roles) in play: dancers may have at best a role in the process *other than as dancers* – thus a choreographer may make solos for himself or herself. *But* even the solo a choreographer makes for himself is a *performable* (part of a performing art); hence it can in principle be re-performed on another occasion, including (typically) by someone else.

Authenticity in performance

Clearly, dancers – like musicians – achieve something praiseworthy (at least in typical cases); so, in denying that dancers are artists, I am *not* denying that their contributions (and especially their achievements) are laudable. But one must understand both what dancers (and other performers) *do* achieve – hence what *is* laudable (when it is). And what they *do not* – indeed, strictly speaking, *cannot* – achieve.

As noted already, what dancers achieve is (a) instantiating the danceworks – without them, there would be no work to be confronted. Then, sometimes, (b) doing that by offering a version or interpretation of the work – what I have called 'performer's interpretation' (McFee 1992, p.103), as we speak of Pollini's interpretation of Schoenberg's opus 19, contrasting that with Glen Gould's version; or, again, of Glen Tetley's interpretation of his *Pierrot Lunaire* (1962), contrasting it with that of Christopher Bruce. Both of these areas of attainment by dancers are laudable; and especially the second. Without the first, there would be no dances to view; while the second often explains part of our interest in particular dance performances. Thus one might attend a particular performance *in order* to see so-and-so's interpretation of such-and-such a role – as one might also for a play or an opera. So that some times one wonders how such-and-such a dancer would carry so-and-so role: for my generation, the male dancers for whom this question was raised were Nureyev and, later, Baryshnikov. Not all performances need be taken as seriously – and hence as distinctively – as this: one need not insist on a performer's interpretation in *all* cases. (Or, sometimes, another dancer might perform Nureyev's performer's interpretation – say, as a stand-in for Nureyev's staging of a ballet.)

Our musical example reminds us that, since both Pollini and Gould offer 'versions' of the same artwork, a trip to the concert-hall to hear *either* interpretation counts as an encounter with Schoenberg's opus 19 – the artwork itself. Just the same is true of our typical dances. Thus the performer's contribution, although praiseworthy, stands against another contribution: namely, that of the *author* of the artwork, the *artist*. For typical dancers – like pianists and opera-singers – do not *initiate* the artwork: they are not ultimately responsible for that work (despite bearing a heavy weight in terms of the work's performance). So the artist's role as *author* is crucial, not least because the two roles just ascribed to the performers in a performing art only make sense against this background. For (in that context) one can only *perform* a dance when there *is* a dance – when it has been choreographed. Further, the author typically has a role when the audience considers in which category of art the work is appropriately understood.

This conclusion points to a *difference* only: in particular, the activities of artists are *not* being rated more highly (nor less highly) than those of dancers, but merely some differences here recognized. We are valuing each, but differently. Thus, this is not an attempt to downplay the importance of dancers – say, to dis-value the dancer. Rather the plan is to *rightly* value the dancer. In fact, that is the main thrust of this essay! That means seeing differences between dancer's value and artist's value, without ranking either more highly. Recognizing important differences was not meant in any way to the detriment of the dancers.

The stress on *authorship* as explaining what is central to being an artist allows us to put aside a plausible-sounding counter-example in which an inferior dance becomes recognized as an artwork because of the contribution of an outstanding performer in 'delivering' it. In effect, this will be one of two or three possible cases, reflecting the prior status of the 'inferior' dance. Thus, is that dance an artwork? As a first case, suppose we grant that it is, and recognize the dance we are seeing – although revitalized – as the very same dancework as previous performances. Then it is still ascribed to its previous choreographer (or whomever): it is still his/her dance, and any plaudits *for the dance* (or any brickbats) belong to that original author. Here, the revitalized version allows us to see the dance for what it was; or to see what is in it. But, insofar as the *responsibility* for the dance continues to rest with its original author, there is no temptation to think here of the performer as author.

But suppose that the 'new' dance is a transfiguration of its previous incarnation, either wholly or in part. The simplest case here might be the transfiguration of a folk dance: so let that be our second case. Here, the 'original' dance was not an artwork; and it is the performer's contribution that now makes it one. So it is a bit like finding inspiration in a tree – the tree is not an artwork, but one's painting is. Or perhaps more like a kind of Readymade: one writes a name ('R. Mutt, 1917') on a urinal, and then it becomes one's own artwork. But now the 'performer' does count as the *author* of the artwork: it has become his or her work. So there is no confusion.

Then, as our third case, imagine a minor artwork brought to life in performance. Since this is not merely a repeat of our first case, the performer must have contributed *more* than in that example. As this might be expressed, it is not merely his *dancing* – his performance – that is being admired. But then what is? The temptation must be to say that it is *his dance*: but now the performer counts as, at least, a co-author – it is his/her dance that is being praised: as we might say, his/her *dance*, and not just his/her *dancing*. Of course, in this case, the dancer would be an artist in the sense under discussion – that is, to the degree that is indeed his/her dance. So, to the degree that the dancework is recognized as the dancer's, to that degree the dancer is seen as *author* – and hence as artist. But, to that degree, we no longer regard that person (or persons) simply as the *dancer*. (Thus, for analytic purposes, the performance-role of the dancer is separated from the authorial role.)

Why is any of this important? In part, the answer lies in trying to get an accurate assessment of the areas of possible attainment of dancers – not to offer them a comparison (with the achievements of artists) which claims too much for their legitimate activities. Rather, we should celebrate *these*; and not bewail a failure to attain what was actually unattainable in principle. So one implies neither too much nor too little about them. Perhaps fewer self-proclaimed artists in the world of performing art may mean a happier regime, because fewer *prima donnas*. But due weighing is also crucial to an appropriate valuing of the craft-related attainments of dancers.[19] So that someone might say, with justice and with pride, 'No, I'm not an artist – that is because I've spent my time, energy, and creativity on being one *hell* of a dancer!'

What are the contingencies of instantiating dances?

Then, when we *do* see dances, we see the *dancers* (as Cunningham recognized). So every performance reflects, in some way or other, features of the dancer(s) involved – not only of the dancers, of course; but centrally of

---

19 Here, I would reiterate in particular the complexity of turning abstract choreography into a concrete dance performance, the creativity of the *dancer's* role, and the sense in which (like members of other professions: McFee 2010, pp.128-129) dancers may be called on to resolve new or unfamiliar situations.

them. Even attempts to evade this point ultimately reinforce it. Thus, Alwin Nikolais (1998, p.116) writes:

> I used masks and props – the masks, to have the dancer become something else; and the props, to extend his physical size in space.

But these then *become* the features of the dancer *as we experience them*! Here, we recognize (first) that, in this way, features such as these become properties of the dance – and hence of the dancers; and (second) that the features of the dance *on any occasion* are set by the properties of that particular performance. Thus, many factors may have an impact on what movements, and such like, get performed to instantiate (say) Christopher Bruce's *Ghost Dances* (1981) – the impact of different casts, of different performance spaces, of different companies (with differing technical prowess); and even just of a different *night* will be among explanations of differences between performances of the very same dancework.

Yet, now, which features of the performance one *sees* – danced by this company on that occasion – are (*crucial*) features of the dance, such that one might criticise a performance which failed to include them, and which are the contingencies of *this* performance? In illustration, consider some cases where compliance with a notated score generates the dancework. Then imagine a performance uncontentiously *of that work*, but failing to comply with our score – clearly the score includes some constraints not *crucial* for the work. So, here, dance-performances based on this score will reflect some features crucial to the dance (perhaps) but also some other constraints. And this case is not merely a philosopher's fantasy: the Stepanov score for *Swan Lake*[20] presents precisely this situation. In my language, this score is not *adequate* for *Swan Lake* just because it does not identify *solely* the constraints from the dancework itself, but only for some performances of that work.

So far, we have recognized the key role of the dancer in bringing the dance into a form with which the rest of us can interact: as Cunningham reminded us, 'you can't describe a dance that hasn't been seen'. But we have also recognized that some of the features of this performance may reflect facts about the dancers not themselves crucial features of *the dance*.

A further complication is that much dance today, in being made on the bodies of particular dancers, reflects closely the powers and capacities of those dancers. Then what might – for other works – be mere contingencies of performance seem here to be crucial features of these works. Yet we must go carefully, for we do not want to say that, as a matter of logic, *only* dancer X can perform this work – even if that were the contingent truth at a certain time. Thus, to repeat the familiar example, it is widely claimed that Petipa

---

20 As commonly, this score was not made by the dancework's choreographers, Ivanov and Petipa, but composed 'after the fact': it is usually ascribed to Nicholai Sergeyev.

put the thirty-two *fouettés* in Act III of *Swan Lake* (1895) because at the time
he had a dancer, Pierina Legnani, who could perform this, when few could
(compare Mackrell 1997, p.7). So suppose that, at that time, *only* Legnani
could perform this segment of the dance.[21] Still, the requirement is just for
a dancer *able* to do so. If there *were* only one, that would just be a practical
matter. And that is how any other requirements here should be regarded.
Thus, almost exactly this problem was faced by Martha Graham's company,
in wishing to continue to perform dances which Graham herself could no
longer manage – it was not enough to find someone who knew the steps,
say. Instead, what was required was a *quality* of dance that was (fairly) easy
to recognize in performers – and especially in those lacking it – but much
harder to describe.

The point can be illustrated by contrasting a merely *technical* performance
of, say, Schoenberg's pianowork opus 19 with an *expressive* one. For that
difference *is* reflected in differences in what the performer *did* (say, in
differential pressure on the piano keys), rather than just what he/she felt. So
the differences were *in the performances*, even when those differences cannot
here be *described* more fully. The mistaken description of the differences
here being *imperceptible* highlights the problem: while the differences were
perceived well enough, there seemed no way to *describe* those differences
more exactly.

The moral here – perhaps unsurprisingly – is that we may not always be
able to *say* how we do these things; but that need not preclude our doing
them successfully. For becoming skilled observers will allow us to give due
weight to the contributions of individual performers.

The problem concerning the place of the *dancer* amounts to giving due
weight to the importance of the dancer as *instantiating* the dancework; so
that, when one sees that work, one *always* sees it by seeing this or that dancer.
The features of the dancework *as we confront them* are always composed out
of the bodies of this or that collection of dancers. Then clearly the dancers
make some contribution here: recording that contribution is (for me) giving
a place to their *distinctiveness*.

Of course, one must only give *due* weight here: it is as easy to over-rate
the dancer as to under-rate him or her. Recognizing the dancer's *physicality*
must grant that the physicality here is *of a dancer* – stressing only the
biology (the anatomy and physiology; or even the neuro-physiology) must
be confusing oneself, since those alone do not identify a *dancer*. Here, we
might profitably return to Théophile Gautier's fascination with the legs of
ballerinas: say, with the 'admirable legs' of Eugénie Fiocre, the 'intelligent

---

21 Notice that I am careful to treat this 'feat' as a part of the choreography, treating it
as an open question whether others might perform it (so, not as inserted just to show off
the talents of this dancer).

legs' of Thérèse Elssler (Gautier 1986, p.35), or the 'slender legs of Mlle Taglioni' (Gautier 1986, p.39). This fascination might be mistaken for a concern with the person. And Gautier sometimes wrote as though his concern was just with the dancers (as persons) and not with dance at all: that *all* that dance amounts to is '... nothing more than the art of displaying elegant and correctly proportioned bodies in various positions favorable to the development of line' (Gautier 1986, p.29).[22]

Yet, in reality, Gautier's interest in the legs was as the legs of *dancers*: he was not, for example, someone at the stagedoor who inspects these legs in their 'real life' location. So this is not just a concern with the person whose legs they are – with Eugénie Fiocre or Thérèse Elssler – but rather with these people *as dancers*. That is, with the impact of those legs on the experience of *this* dance – so that (even if he sometimes expresses the point differently[23]) Gautier is responding to the dance. For saying that these are always typically the legs of dancers is a way to relate their (observed) properties to those of the artworks they help to instantiate. And that *is* the topic concerning embodiment which has been our primary interest.

So stressing that these must be *dancers* involves the recognition, first, that (at the peripheries at least) what is and what is not dance, and hence a dancer (as performer of it), is a matter for debate within a culture – better, within that proper part I call 'The Republic of Dance'; and, second, that what is involved in being a dancer for these purposes (and especially the kind of dancer suitable to perform fine art-type dances) is a contextual matter.

Identity and danceworks

Thus far, I have elaborated places which, with justice, stress the importance of the performers in performing arts. Yet giving the dancers *an* importance does nothing to dispute the idea of a *dancework* (although some of our 'postmodernists' deny this). For, in typical cases, our dancers display their 'craft-mastery' as dancers by instantiating a particular dancework. Recognizing the sense in which dancers are *not* artists is one way to grant this point about both the importance of that dancework and the dancers' importance in permitting it an audience.

Here, there is typically only one *dancework*. Like the piece of music one listens to on Tuesday evening, the particular dance one sees counts as one (and only one) artwork. That fact is acknowledged in granting that, in the

---

22 Or, again: '[D]ancing has no purpose but to display beautiful bodies in graceful poses and develop lines that are pleasing to the eye. [...] Dancing is ill-suited for expressing metaphysical ideas' (Gautier 1986, p.16).

23 Perhaps *some* of Gautier's comments should be seen as about the dancer viewed as a *person*. But, to that degree, his interest was in the 'real thing', not the artwork.

same venue on Wednesday, that same artwork can be encountered *again*. This is typically independent of differences between the performances: both can be, say, *Swan Lake* despite a wide variety of differences. For being *the very same work* is not a matter of *similarity* here – as numerical identity judgments generally are not. Thus, the short, hairy boy who bullied me at school is the very same person as the tall, bald man getting the Nobel Peace Prize – we grant that in letting him inherit the estate of his (or the boy's) grandfather. Here there is numerical identity despite radical dissimilarity. Similarly, *one* artwork is recognized here, despite its diversities.

In practice, 'same-work' continuity for, say, *Swan Lake* tolerates a pretty wide range of diversity: diversity of company, staging, costume, and even movement. But all of this counts as *the very same* (numerically identical) artwork.[24]

Further – to repeat – this idea of *difference among performances* is central to the conception of a performing art as composed of *performables*; works that can be re-performed on another occasion: at best, we can argue about the *degree* of difference permissible, given that the outcome is a performance of *the very same* dancework.

Moreover, the performers or company rehearsing on Monday was (in principle) a rehearsal for *all* of the performances they would make of the work that week, rather than for only one of them (McFee 1992, p.93). This in turn speaks clearly for our sense of only one artwork here. For many works would seem to require many distinct rehearsals.

Of course, talking in this way about *performables* may not be the most important thing to say about the performing arts – perhaps I *stress* the essential repeatability of danceworks only because I grew up at a time when 'happenings' (that is, one-off performance events) were an issue. But one inevitably returns to repeatability as *among* the features of performing arts. That, in turn, localizes an aspect of the dancer's role: however unlikely (for reasons mentioned already), different dancers could *always* perform the roles in typical danceworks.

---

24 In fact, the discussion of 'same-work' continuity here effectively recognizes a framework (see McFee 2004, pp.229-231; McFee 2011b, pp.33-69) built around three kinds of cases:

(i) the standard token (say, for *Swan Lake*, the Ivanov and Petipa choreography);

(ii) the extreme token – properties very different from standard tokens, but still a token of that same type (say, Matthew Bourne's *Swan Lake*);

(iii) the new, but similar artwork – a token of a different type (say, the Mats Ek *Swan Lake*).

Of course, the examples are not crucial; the thought here is to illustrate sorting candidate *Swan Lakes* into categories, where only the first two preserve work-identity.

Dances as potentially worth preserving

The argument so far has spoken in favour of a posterity for danceworks. But perhaps danceworks *should* exist 'at a perpetual vanishing point' (Siegel 1972, p.1), such that they actually do vanish 'when they have had their day'. Of course, this must mean more than just that a particular work has failed the test of time (we would expect that in all artforms). Rather, the perspective of (some?) choreographers is that dances *should not* be preserved. But why, exactly?

As Renee Conroy (2007, p.2) makes plain, Mark Franko has urged the rejection of a posterity for dance, seeing a place only for 'radical re-invention', which '... involves actively rethinking dance history's uses as well as its meanings now' (Franko 1989, p.58). For Franko (1989, p.73) stresses that we clearly cannot realistically hope to bring to the stage a performance visually indistinguishable from, say, that encountered by the original audience at a Ruth St. Denis concert. That is surely correct. But, insofar as our interest is the artistic one, why should we want to, anyway? That is not typically a goal when staging a dance that our own company performed last season: why should it become one in this case? Talk of the 'old myth of repeatability' here hides a profound confusion: if one can re-perform *any* dancework (and that *must* be possible, if danceworks count as *performables*), then a particular work can be *repeated*. Commonsense tells us that the 'repeat' is quite likely *not* to be qualitatively indistinguishable from the previous performance – but serious thinking about performing arts *begins* from the fact that performances with significantly different properties can nevertheless be performances of the very same artwork.

Some theorists (perhaps Franko 1989 again, at least in this early work[25]) might be committed to an ontology whereby the dance exists *only* at the moment of performance, drawing on parallels in literary theory, such that '[t]here is no original work to which subsequent instantiations [...] must necessarily conform' (as Sarah Rubridge [2000, p.207] remarks). Now, this view of *existence* is odd. As Drid Williams (2004, p.72) points out:

> It is as though we are being asked, '*where* is, e.g. *Swan Lake*, when no one is performing it?' Otherwise sensible, rational people who would hoot at the question, 'where is spoken language when it is not being spoken?' [...] do not hesitate to ask this question about dancing.

As though there were a good answer! And, as noted earlier, even such theorists treat danceworks in line with the traditional ontology of *the performable*; comparing this performance *of the work* with another performance (or one

---

25 Some later works of Franko may embody, or seem to embody, a different conception. But a view resembling this one is also found in Franko 1996, pp.25-52.

by another company); regarding rehearsals as *for* performances, and those performances as *of the work* at issue.

Moreover, a work which *remains* in the repertoire is not a set of indistinguishable performances. So too much is being asked of our historical case if one insists that repeating the work requires indistinguishability from some past performance. (Which?) Now imagine that one goal in preserving a work for posterity is simply to keep that work in the repertoire. Then (a) doing so draws on the under-determination of performance by dancework; the continuity of that very dancework allows for difference. And (b) recording that dance itself (and especially what, if anything, is crucial to that dance) in a notated score will be a very suitable way forward. For, first, notationality is not just about preservation (especially preservation 'in the long run'); rather, it offers a basis for clearer judgments about the *present* of a dancework, in ways that bear on its future; second, preservation of some kind is required for 're-performables'; that is, for performing arts. Since that applies as much to the performances on Tuesday and Wednesday of this week as to those in some future, the need to make identity-judgments cannot simply be put aside here; third, reliance on memory (and especially memory alone) is clearly problematic; and, fourth, reliance on recording by, say, video or DVD is also problematic (since it preserves the *whole* of one performance, with no method of sorting the crucial from the contingencies).

Should choreographers be happy to let their works die with (say) a particular cast, as Franko (1989, p.73) seems to assume, even though that was not necessary – and given that the dancework's place in posterity was not the sterile one sometimes associated with reconstruction, or preservation, or dance history more generally? The notated score, for instance, precisely offers a freedom here; exactly as much freedom as one wants and certainly freedom in line with the standard treatment of 'classics' from the past, which can be kept vivid in performance. And, of course, dancers – and their craft-mastery – will be key for such vividness.

A theory of embodiment?

If, as urged initially, the role of embodiment encompasses the place of the dancer in typical dances, perhaps we can see why an abstract or theoretical account of embodiment has no place here. In effect, there are two related considerations. The first concerns the specificity of the embodiment of dances: that this embodiment involves these particular dancers on these particular occasions – to speak more generally is just to have abstracted from the particular occasions. The same is not true for, say, visual artworks such as typical paintings or sculptures: they are relatively unchanging. So the need to stress embodiment in those cases is primarily to show that the specific *meaning* (or some such) of paintings or sculptures cannot be detached from the artworks themselves – that they are not just means to an otherwise specifiable end! Of course, that point must be urged for dances too. Yet it does not require *special* explanation in the dance case.

But that leads to the second issue. For the embodiment itself amounts to locating artistic meaning here in the transitory movement of dancers (among other sources). As we saw initially, dancers have a role in performing arts different from that of, say, typical musicians: and that role resides precisely in embodying the dance. So am I suggesting that a theory of embodiment suitable for dances is needed, to replace (say) one from painting? No, because, in effect, the centrality of human agency here leaves nothing unsaid: as Wittgenstein[26] liked to put it, 'In the beginning was the deed'. That is, we are *agents* who can, therefore, perform certain actions. And, while able to do certain things, we cannot always say *how* we do them. Further, those actions have normative possibilities: they can be good or bad (like, say, chess moves), and they can embody meanings. The typical case here is genuine meaning, which is intentional: it occurs in 'hand language', such as American Sign Language or Padgett, as well as in speech and writing. And recognizing its connection to humans as *agents* contrasts it with behaviour that permits insight into agents but without that intentionality (what David Best [1978, pp.138-162] calls 'percomm') – typified by the involuntary yawn mentioned earlier; a possibility shared with, for instance, some non-human animals.

No doubt the craft-mastery involved in training in dance has a bearing here. But it simply offers a more sophisticated range of *actions*: that just stresses again the role of *action* in the embodiment of artistic meaning for danceworks.

On another occasion, we can attempt to clarify precisely the kinds of resources that may be appropriately deployed in understanding dance. There, we should begin by contrasting the *conceptual* with the *empirical*; or, if this is different, recognizing Frege's point – that '[e]rror and superstition have causes just as much as correct cognition' (Frege [1918] 1984, p.351). Lest this seem too gnomic, think how it might apply to a chess game: the causal story (in terms of changing states of my brain, say) behind my chess move can never explain why this is, or is not, a *good* move in chess since a poor move too will have a causal story of the same kind. To apply: since there is always *some* causal story describing the causal basis – or physical substrate – of one's judgment, that story can never be explanatory of the normativity of that judgment. And it is normativity, within dance identification and appreciation, that concerns us here.

As with human action more generally, precisely what action has been

---

26 On Certainty §402; Culture and Value §161 p.31 Philosophical Occasions p.395; Quoting Goethe, *Faust I*, opening scene in the *Studierzimmer.*

performed to constitute a dance depends on the 'description under which' that action was performed: correctly identifying the action requires capturing that description – I *really did* score the goal in football; but it is much less clear that I damaged the goal-netting, although that was a consequence of the goal I scored. And similarly for actions in dances, which might be described in terms of changes to the musculature or (where appropriate) by a technical term from classical ballet: say, as an *arabesque de face*; or even by reference to its place in the dancework under consideration, which might even involve denying that the technical term fitted it. But such 'descriptions under which' can play no role in causal explanations, since how an event is characterized does not guarantee whether it will *cause* another, strictly speaking – the causal powers of a moving billiard ball are not changed by calling it 'the white' or 'the cue ball', nor those of (what is in fact) a bullet by describing it differently: say, by giving its chemical composition. Once this point is granted, we shall regard fewer and fewer events in the human world as explicable causally, especially those where humans are agents.

Thus, even if parrots have greater visual acuity than typical humans, or if macaque monkeys display kinds of 'mirror reflex' (McFee 2011b, pp.189-193) arguably important in understanding other movements, we will not give seats in our performance spaces to either such parrots or monkeys. Whatever the extent of their causal powers, they can never genuinely *see* nor appreciate dances. So what we share with them can never be crucial, for understanding dance requires conceptual powers, involving cultural concepts, which both lack.

At the least, the central interpretative categories required here are either those of the *artform* of dance or (occasionally) those of human action, with its implicit appeal to the cultural. A theory of embodiment would have no place under the second heading – that was Wittgenstein's point about the priority of action – while, if urged seriously under the first heading, it would simply become a theory of the meaning of *danceworks*; and here their status as performables would have its place.

So the project of this essay has urged the centrality of the place of the dancer for our understanding of the dancework: the dancer's contribution permits us to confront the dancework embodied; and hence to see the intentions embodied in the dance work (McFee 2011b, pp.130-135). Although recognizing the importance of authorship, this conception of danceworks, built on the commonsense view of dances as *performables*, stresses the centrality of a role for dancers *other than* as authors of danceworks. And now we have argued that the embodiment here should *not* be treated via an independent theory of artistic embodiment, but integrated into an account of human action, seen in its cultural context.

Conclusion: Do danceworks last for ever?

But what should one conclude about the durability of danceworks? Faced with the question, 'Do dance works last for ever?', I have no good reply; but three thoughts seemed to sketch a conclusion here:

First, unlike Julian Dodd (2007,[27] a 'yes' answer from me would not make danceworks *eternal* – each certainly has a beginning in time; and each could (in principle) have an end in time when it can no longer be performed.[28]

Second, a dancework 'can no longer be performed' when the traditions of performance[29] it requires have been lost – that is, when there are no longer dancers able to realize it. It might also be lost by being forgotten; but this seems merely a contingent loss (as though all copies of a particular play were thought lost, and then one found in a remote library): if there is material for reconstruction, then the dance is never lost completely. But the other condition limits the possibility of reconstruction.

Third, it is obvious that a full notated score, and a selection of other materials, would make a good 'time capsule' for a particular dance – it would probably allow that dance to return to the repertoire of the time; but only if the work could still be danced (if the requisite traditions of performance were not lost).

Notice that these comments concern an extant dance: so the moment of *authorship* – of being an *artist* in respect of this dance – has passed, and with it any residual questions about who the artist was. But there remain a number of key issues concerning that work's posterity; and, for them, the role of the dancers is crucial; in particular, their craft-mastery in the context of traditions of performance. If this is correct, it highlights (some of) what is wonderful about dancers!

---

27 For some discussion, see McFee 2011b, pp.289-306.

28 Compare Arlene Croce (1982, pp.28-29):

I watched Martha Graham's *Primitive Mysteries* (1931) die this season in what seemed, for the most part, scrupulous performances. The twelve girls looked carefully rehearsed. Sophie Maslow, who had supervised the previous revival, in the season of 1964-65, was again in charge. Everybody danced with devotion. Yet a piece that I would have ranked as a landmark in American dance was reduced to a tendentious outline, the power I had remembered was no longer there [...] Perhaps there's a statute of limitations on how long a work can be depended upon to force itself through the bodies who dance it.

For discussion, see McFee (2011b, pp.263-266).

29 Here, I am running together both what I called 'performance traditions' and 'traditions of performance' (McFee 2003, pp.121-143).

References

Banes, Sally. 'A New Kind of Beauty', in *Before, Between, and Beyond: Three Decades of Dance Writing*, Madison: University of Wisconsin Press, 2007, pp.311-319.

Beardsley, Monroe C. *The Possibility of Criticism*, Detroit: Wayne State University Press, 1970.

Bennett, Tony. *Formalism and Marxism*, London: Methuen, 1979.

Best, David. *Philosophy and Human Movement*, London: Allen & Unwin, 1978.

Briginshaw, Valerie A. *Dance, Space and Subjectivity*, Basingstoke: Palgrave Macmillan, 2001.

Collingwood, R. G. *The Principles of Art*, Oxford: Clarendon, 1938.

Conroy, Renee. 'Dance Reconstruction: Kinesthetic Preservation or Danceworld Kitsch?', *ASA Newsletter*, 27:1, 2007, pp.1-3.

Conroy, Renee. 'Dance' in Ribeiro, Anna C. (ed.), *Continuum Companion to Aesthetics*, London: Continuum, 2012, pp.156-170.

Croce, Arlene. *Going to the Dance*, New York: Alfred A. Knopf, 1982.

Cunningham, Merce. *The Dancer and the Dance: Merce Cunningham in conversation with Jacqueline Lesschaeve*, New York: Scribners, 1984.

Danto, Arthur. *The Transfiguration of the Commonplace*, Cambridge, MA: Harvard University Press, 1981.

Derrida, Jacques. *Limited Inc*, Evanston: Northwestern University Press, 1988.

Dodd, Julian. *Works of Music: An Essay in Ontology*, Oxford: Clarendon, 2007.

Dodds, Sherril. *Dancing on the Canon*, Basingstoke: Palgrave Macmillan, 2011.

Fish, Stanley. *Is There a Text in this Class?*, Cambridge, MA: Harvard University Press, 1980.

Franko, Mark. 'Repeatability, Reconstruction and Beyond', *Theatre Journal*, 41:1, 1989, pp.56-74.

Franko, Mark. 'History/theory – criticism/practice' in Foster, Susan L. (ed.), *Corporealities*, London: Routledge, 1996, pp.25-52.

Frege, Gottlob. 'Thoughts' in *Collected Papers on Mathematics, Logic and Philosophy*, Oxford: Blackwell, 1984 [1918].

Gautier, Théophile. *Gautier on Dance*, Guest Ivor (ed.), London: Dance Books, 1986.

Goellner, Ellen W. and Jacqueline Shea Murphy, (eds.). *Bodies of the Text: Dance as Theory, Literature as Dance*, New Brunswick: Rutgers University Press, 1995.

Ground, Ian. *Art or Bunk?* Bristol: Bristol Classical Press, 1989.

Hockney, David. *David Hockney: My Early Years*, London: Thames & Hudson, 1976.

Jordan, Stephanie. *Moving Music: Dialogues with Music in Twentieth Century Ballet*, London: Dance Books, 2000.

Lamarque, Peter. 'Literature' in Gaut, Berys and Dominic McIver Lopes (eds.), *Routledge Companion to Aesthetics*, London: Routledge, 2000, pp.449-461.

McFee, Graham. *Understanding Dance*, London: Routledge, 1992.

McFee, Graham. 'Cognitivism and the Experience of Dance' in Sukla, A. C. (ed.), *Art and Experience*, Westport: Praeger, 2003, pp.121-143.

McFee, Graham. *The Concept of Dance Education*, enlarged edition, Eastbourne: Pageantry Press, 2004.

McFee, Graham. *Ethics, Knowledge and Truth in Sports Research*, London: Routledge, 2010.

McFee, Graham. *Artistic Judgement*, Dordrecht: Springer, 2011a.

McFee, Graham. *The Philosophical Aesthetics of Dance*, Alton: Dance Books, 2011b.

Mackrell, Judith. *Out of Line: The Story of British New Dance*, London: Dance Books, 1992.

Mackrell, Judith. *Reading Dancing*, London: Michael Joseph, 1997.

Rubidge, Sarah. 'Identity and the Open Work', in Jordan, Stephanie (ed.), *Preservation Politics: Dance Revived Reconstructed Remade*, London: Dance Books, 2000, pp.205-211.

Siegel, Marcia. *At The Vanishing Point*, New York: Saturday Review Press, 1972.

Thom, Paul. *For an Audience: A Philosophy of the Performing Arts*, Philadelphia: Temple University Press, 1993.

Urmson, J. O. 'The Performing Arts' in Lewis, H. D. (ed.), *Contemporary British Philosophy (Fourth Series)*, London: George Allen & Unwin, 1976, pp.239-252.

Williams, Bernard. *Truth and Truthfulness*, Princeton: Princeton University Press, 2002.

Williams, Drid. *Anthropology and the Dance: Ten Lectures*, 2nd edition, Urbana: University of Illinois Press, 2004.

Wittgenstein, Ludwig *Philosophical Investigations*, Oxford: Blackwell, 2001 [1953].

Wittgenstein, Ludwig. *On Certainty*, Oxford: Blackwell, 1969.

Wittgenstein, Ludwig. *Culture and Value*, Oxford: Blackwell, 1980.

Wittgenstein, Ludwig. *Philosophical Occasions 1912-1951*, Indianapolis: Hackett, 1993.

Wollheim, Richard. *On Art and the Mind*, Harmondsworth: Allen Lane, 1973.

2. Bodies and movements or persons and actions?[1]

Raf Geenens

There are many ways to set about the question of what constitutes the 'modernism' of modern dance. Here, I will approach the question by focusing on David Michael Levin's influential essay, 'Balanchine's Formalism' (Levin 1983), first published in *Dance Perspectives* in 1973.[2] Levin's text makes familiar reading for most dance scholars and has helped to cement Balanchine's reputation as a paragon of modern ballet. Yet it has attracted surprisingly little critical attention.[3] By and large, it seems, Levin's argument has stuck.[4] My intention here is to put into question, not so much Levin's interpretation of Balanchine's work, but rather the peculiar account of modernism he derives from it.

Below, I start by summarizing Levin's argument (section I). After that, I will draw attention to two weaknesses in his argument that, if they do not invalidate his conclusions, at least significantly complicate the picture of modernism he puts forward (sections II, III). At the end of the text, I will lay out a number of modest and rather sketchy suggestions for a possible alternative account of modernism in dance (section IV).

That account is meant to be broader and more inclusive than the one proposed by Levin. Levin tends to equate, in a rather rigid manner, 'modernism' with 'formalism' and 'formalism' with 'Balanchine'. This has contributed to dance theorists trying to distance themselves – and their choreographers of choice – from the label 'modernism'. Sally Banes and Noël Carroll, for instance, explicitly accept Levin's account of modernism

---

1 In preparing this text for publication I have greatly benefited from suggestions made by the editors of this book and by Filip Mattens.

2 When citing Levin's text, my page numbers always refer to the text's republication in the seminal volume *What is Dance?* (edited by Roger Copeland and Marshall Cohen in 1983), which is the most widely available version of the text. (It was also reprinted in *Salmagundi* in 1976.)

3 The only serious critical take on Levin's text I am aware of, is by Marshall Cohen. In his essay on 'Primitivism, Modernism, and Dance Theory', Cohen extensively and convincingly questions Levin's interpretation of Balanchine's work, but pays disappointingly little attention to the philosophical details of Levin's argument about modern dance (Cohen 1983, pp.173 ff.).

4 Tim Scholl, for instance, incorporates Levin's view rather uncritically into his own account of the modernization of ballet (Scholl 1994, pp.109 ff.). Similarly, Noël Carroll and Sally Banes unquestioningly accept Levin's interpretation of Balanchine's work and the way Levin translates the Greenbergian programme into the discipline of dance (Carroll 2003; Banes and Carroll 2006), cf. infra.

and, in consequence, claim that the work of Yvonne Rainer, Trisha Brown and others belongs to a completely separate avant-garde lineage, which they call 'integrationism'. This 'integrationist' school (which also includes dada, surrealism, pop art and other movements) tried to blur the boundaries between life and art and was thus diametrically opposed to modernism and its purported 'purism' and 'formalism'.[5] It seems to me that such a strong dichotomy is not particularly plausible, if only because it obscures the extent to which the artistic concerns of supposedly 'integrationist' choreographers are related and indebted to the modernist project. Indeed, many of them were consciously contributing to that project.[6]

A complete recategorization of twentieth century dance falls outside the confines of this chapter. Yet I do believe that my account of what the modernist programme implies in the field of dance, is potentially more comprehensive than Levin's. That is, it might be able to make room for the concerns and endeavours of many twentieth century choreographers – both before and after Balanchine – who would fall outside modernism as defined in Levin's 1973 essay.

Section I

The central claim of Levin's text is very straightforward. Starting from Clement Greenberg's well-known teleological conception of modern visual arts, Levin wishes to demonstrate that a similar progressive movement can be perceived in the history of dance, a progression that would find its culmination in the later work of Balanchine. According to Levin, Balanchine's abstract ballets can be regarded as the choreographic equivalent of, say, the paintings of Frank Stella or the sculptures of David Smith. Just as these quintessential modern artists did in their art form, Balanchine brings to light the concealed essence of dance as a *sui generis* artistic medium.

The key term in Levin's analysis is 'formalism' (a term he borrows from

---

5 According to Banes and Carroll, these two avant-garde movements ('modernism' and 'integrationism') have run parallel to each other throughout the century in all artistic disciplines (Banes and Carroll 2006).

6 Regardless of the fact that one might want to label some of these 'integrationist' choreographers as 'postmodern' so as to chronologically distinguish them from earlier generations. For classificatory discussions on the modern(ist)/postmodern(ist) divide, see Banes (1987) (although Banes modified her position in 2006, cf. Banes and Carroll 2006, p.66) and see Levin's piece on postmodern dance (Levin 1990). In this latter text, Levin broadens his own definition of modernism (and surprisingly classifies Trisha Brown and Yvonne Rainer as both 'modernist' *and* 'postmodernist'). It is not clear how Levin's new definition rhymes with the one he gave in 1973. A rather critical take on Levin's new classification is provided by Judith Mackrell (1991).

Greenberg). Balanchine's choreographic language, Levin tells us, consists predominantly of abstract, geometric forms and departs from the academic tradition in that it is no longer narrative or theatrical. In Balanchine's work there are no more 'semantic elements', no more elements 'that must be taken as mimetic or in some other way representational'; Balanchine has done away even with 'distinctly allusive movements' (Levin 1983, pp. 124, 130).[7] Thus, dance has finally reached the point where movement, just like modernist painting or sculpture, 'refers to nothing outside of itself' (p.127). In Levin's view, Balanchine is the first to eliminate so radically everything that is figurative.[8] Balanchine reduces movement to 'purely literal movement', that is, to 'an objective modification in Euclidean space of the dancer's 'real' body' (p.132).

But that is not all. According to Levin, these pure, Euclidean movements still express something, even if they do so 'without the various resources of mimetic and symbolic convention' (p.123) and without referring to anything outside of the movements. What movements 'express' (in this slightly peculiar sense of expressing) is *the human body*. There is what Levin calls an 'intrinsic expressiveness' of the body (p.130), and Balanchine's genius lies in that he capitalizes on this expressiveness. The choreography allows the human body to express itself in its sheer physicality or 'corporeality'. Ultimately, Levin says, 'it is the body itself [...] that is revealed' (p.133).

If Balanchine manages to draw attention to his dancers' physicality, it is – according to Levin – primarily because his choreographic vocabulary emphasizes the *weight* of their bodies; Balanchine-dancing brings to the fore 'the tangible weight, the massive balances of the body' (p.132). For Levin, some of the most striking passages in Balanchine's ballets are these 'moments when we perceive the weight-presence of the dancers' (p.136). Balanchine's signature *pliés*, for instance, are 'an incontestable acknowledgment, or demonstration of the dancer's objective weight' (p.135). At such moments, we become aware of the force of gravity and

7 This claim can be disputed. As Cohen demonstrates, even in many of Balanchine's key 'modernist' ballets, storytelling is an essential part of the work (Cohen 1983, p.174).

8 As Stanley Cavell has argued, it is not obvious that modern art is modern because it *leaves behind* certain qualities or techniques, qualities or techniques that are purportedly inessential to the medium yet which artists in previous periods had – almost by mistake – kept on board: 'To say that the modern "lays bare" may suggest that there was something concealed in traditional art which hadn't, for some reason, been noticed, or that what the modern throws over – tonality, perspective, narration, the absent fourth wall, etc. – was something inessential to music, painting, poetry, and theater in earlier periods. These would be false suggestions. For it is not that now we finally know the true condition of art; it is only that someone who does not question that condition has nothing, or not the essential thing, to go on in addressing the art of our period.' (Cavell 1976, pp.219-220)

of the dancers' 'corporeal mass and weight' (p.137); we are reminded of their materiality, that is, their 'objecthood' (p.132).

This, then, is what seems to make Balanchine's work 'modern' in the specific, Greenbergian sense. Balanchine uses the medium of dance to reveal the essence of that medium, namely, pure movements and, underneath these movements real, weighty, material bodies. In most ballets, this essence – movements and bodies – remained hidden. Balanchine, however, pushes it into the limelight and leaves behind all theatrical and other superfluous stylistic elements. He thus responds to the call of 'the modernist aesthetic', which 'challenges the work of art to reveal, to make present [...] its defining condition as art' (p.127). And in the case of dance, it seems, that defining condition can be summarized as follows: bodies in motion.

Yet Levin adds one further element that defines the medium of dance and that is revealed by Balanchine, namely: dance's inbuilt potential to *overcome* the body's objecthood. If the dancer initially appeared as a weighty, three-dimensional mass, the choreographer eventually transforms the dancer into a 'weightless, optically intangible presence' (p.132). This 'suspension of weight' comes about by visually equating the dancer's body parts to purely geometric elements. Reduced to pictorial, seemingly weightless lines, limbs and torsos float around in a 'merely optical space' (p.137) – a space that is perfectly flat, the dimension of depth (and of mass) having been abolished. Thus, all bodily movement is reduced to a two-dimensional spectacle of abstract forms and lines.

The language of classical ballet already alluded to the possibility of such a reduction. Levin mentions several academic positions that are particularly apt at creating the illusion of a body that has become pure line. For instance, in an *arabesque allongée*:

> the torso – visually weightless – certainly touches the vertical leg, but touches without 'really' resting upon it. Somewhat as a balloon is connected to its string, the torso seems to float, meeting the leg only to contrive – for a breathtaking interval – an optical, or flat, pictorial symmetry. It is as if the leg/torso juncture were the intersection of two mathematical lines. (p.138)

In other academic positions as well, the torso and the head are visually reduced to weightless extensions of the leg, that is to say: they are not so much 'a distinct quantity supported by the legs, as they are a qualitative and linear continuation of the legs' (p.138).

This 'optical reduction of corporeal mass and weight' (p.137) has been perfected by Balanchine in the twentieth century. His formalist style deliberately and successfully – much more so than classical ballet – reduces legs, torso and head to equivalent, pictorial lines and thereby completely eliminates their materiality ('it is as if their substance has magically evaporated!' (p.137)). This total reduction of all body parts to mere geometric elements in a two-dimensional space, a possibility that was foreshadowed in the history of Western dance, is purportedly the key merit of Balanchine's formalism.[9]

This concludes Levin's story as to why Balanchine can be said to reveal the defining conditions of dance. Balanchine's vocabulary draws attention to the dancer *qua* material body, yet, at the same time, suspends the body's materiality by producing the illusion of a perfectly abstract, geometric spectacle. Thus, the essence of dance – an essence to which its history was more or less unconsciously progressing – is double: it is the body's material presence *and* the simultaneous disappearance of that physicality in optical space. It is this twofold quality that allows dance to create an aesthetic experience all of its own, and the growing awareness of this specificity is what propelled the historical development of dance towards its twentieth century apex, namely: Balanchine's formalism. This is why Levin claims that Balanchine articulates the 'truth' about the medium of dance, something 'which seems logically imperative at this given point in its history' (p.127). Note that Balanchine's work is now seamlessly integrated into Greenberg's account of modernism. If Greenberg's preferred abstract painters push their discipline towards its historical moment of self-disclosure, it is because they emphasize the materiality of the canvas – its flatness and its shape – while at the same time overcoming that materiality by immersing the spectator into a purely visual experience, what Greenberg calls 'opticality'. Balanchine's formalism, according to Levin, shows us that these same terms can be imported – almost literally – to describe the dynamics of modernism in the field of dance.

Section II

Despite the elegance of Levin's argument, I believe that his account of modernism in dance runs into severe difficulties. First, I would like to take issue with the claim that Balanchine, because he reduces ballet to a mere play of forms, does away with all 'symbolic conventions' or unleashes the body's 'intrinsic expressiveness'. My criticism here is largely inspired by the American art historian, Rosalind Krauss.[10] Although an admitted Greenbergian herself, Krauss introduces certain alterations and

---

9   Cohen extensively challenges Levin's assertion that Balanchine's ballets somehow swap mass and three-dimensional space for a purely 'optical', two-dimensional presence (Cohen 1983, pp.174-176).

10   At one point in his article, when describing David Smith's work, Levin himself refers to Rosalind Krauss (Levin 1983, p.144, n. 20).

complications into Greenberg's conceptual scheme and clears up some of the possible sources of confusion within that scheme.

Most importantly, she states that an artistic medium, properly understood, cannot be reduced to its material preconditions. Echoing a view already expressed by Stanley Cavell[11], Krauss argues that it would be ill-advised to treat the notion of 'medium' as a mere synonym of the *material supports of that medium*.[12] If an artistic medium can generate meaning, that is, if it can provoke specific, *sui generis* experiences that are felt to be meaningful, it is because it comes with a 'matrix' or a set of conventions that provide a specific way of apprehending reality or certain objects within that reality. In her discussions of such diverse artists as Richard Serra and Michael Snow, Krauss demonstrates that if these modernist artists explore their own artistic medium, they are not just laying bare its material preconditions. They are, rather more subtly, bringing to light that medium's internal syntax and its ingrained way of capturing reality (Krauss 1999a, p.25 ff.; 1999b, p.171 ff.).[13]

Elsewhere, Krauss expands on Greenberg's idea of formalism to dispel the notion that the paintings of, for instance, Frank Stella or Kenneth Noland derive their expressive quality from mere 'formal' relations, that is, from the arrangement of lines, forms and colours on the two-dimensional surface of the picture (Krauss 2010, pp.117 ff.). According to Krauss, we misunderstand our own aesthetic experience if we believe it to be derived from such empirical, visual design qualities. In fact, even our appreciation of purely abstract works of art depends on their participation in a web of referrals that reaches far outside and beyond the physical object. For instance, if we look at a painting by Frank Stella (I am following Krauss's example here), we also see – behind it, as it were – the paintings of Manet. And behind Manet we see Velazquez, and so on. In fact, looking through the surface of Stella's painting an endless, Louvresque gallery opens up that connects Stella to the history of Western painting. It is because Stella brings to mind this very long gallery and consciously dialogues with it, that his work can appear as meaningful to us at all. In other words, the flatness of Stella's works is treacherous. A painting might appear to be abstract and deprived of all figurative or 'narrative' elements. Yet what the viewer actually does, says

---

11 Cavell writes that '[the] idea of a medium is not simply that of a physical material, but of a material-in-certain-characteristic-applications' (Cavell 1976, p.221).

12 Krauss makes this claim on various occasions (see for instance Krauss 1999a, pp.26-27; 1999b, pp.164-165). For further discussion on the notion of 'medium' in art, see David Davies (2003).

13 Again, this dovetails with Cavell, who claims that 'the way [modern painting] changes – what will count as a relevant change – is determined by the commitment to painting as an art, in struggle with the history which makes it an art, continuing and countering the *conventions* and *intentions* and *responses* which comprise that history.' (Cavell 1976, p.222) (emphasis altered).

Krauss, is project onto the painting's flat surface another kind of narrative, one about the history of painting. And this narrative hinges not on the sheer physicality of the object, nor is it immediately given in our sense perception of the work. It rather depends on a number of conventions that allow the painting to point to a history that is not physically present but that is nonetheless there. That history is, literally, *re-presented* in the work because the work evokes it and simultaneously offers a specific interpretation of it. Thus, the work's flatness is hardly expressive 'in itself', but indisputably refers to things outside itself.

It is in this sense, I believe, that Levin can be said to operate with too simplistic a reading of Balanchine. Levin claims that the dancer becomes pure body, or movement, or line, and he emphasizes that this material, objective presence is somehow expressive in and by itself. According to Levin, Balanchine-dancing reveals the 'intrinsic', 'sensuous' expressiveness of the body, a body that thenceforth refers to nothing outside of itself: it has somehow escaped the symbolic realm to become pure presence.

Such a description, though, is highly inaccurate. It might be the case that spectators with a modernist sensibility spontaneously feel that Balanchine's choreography 'points' towards the movements themselves or towards the weight of the body. Yet it does not necessarily follow that one has left the narrative domain to reach a purely 'material' or 'formal' level. Even if one kind of narrative is being rejected – that of swans and princes – it is not hard to see that, once again, the dancing has been turned into a screen onto which one projects a narrative, be it now a narrative about the history of ballet. Balanchine, on this analysis, does not quite do away with conventions and representations.

At some moments, Balanchine even resorts to very unsophisticated mimetic conventions to convey that story. In *Serenade*, for instance, there is a noteworthy passage where the male protagonist and three female dancers hold hands and turn in a circle.[14] As the circle speeds up, they let go of their hands and softly run backwards as if they were falling, their weight pulled away by centrifugal forces. In actual fact, though, they are hardly falling and they are not quite giving in to gravity. They are rather *miming* the 'pull of gravity', in a way that is not significantly different from the way the movements of, say, swans are mimed in certain other ballets. Even when Balanchine does not use such crudely mimetic means (and usually he does not), it should be noted that perceiving a dancer as a set of floating, two-dimensional geometric lines, is not less fanciful than seeing in a waving arm the movements of a swan's wing, or seeing in the undulations of Doris

---

14 *Serenade* had its official première in 1935. I am basing my analysis on *Serenade* as performed by New York City Ballet in 2010.

Humphrey's dancers the waves of the sea.[15]

That is not to say that the desire for pure abstraction is not a part of the history of ballet, as Levin rightly contends. But that debt should be properly recognized. If, in Balanchine's ballets, we sometimes don't perceive torsos or legs but pure, geometric lines, it is because academic ballet has habituated us to see certain poses in that particular way. And if, in this respect, Balanchine's vocabulary strikes us as more radical (or more 'abstract') than academic ballet, it is precisely because it refuses us the closure that ballet usually gives: the reassurance that these abstract movements do, eventually, have meaning and fit into an overarching plot line. Thus, even this lack of closure only confirms to what extent Balanchine relies on prior experiences and expectations that are carried over from the history of academic ballet and without which his work could not appear to us as meaningful at all.

It is at least misleading, then, to state – as Levin does – that the 'body' or the physical properties of the work have suddenly become intrinsically expressive, without referring to anything outside themselves and without relying on any 'symbolic conventions'. Balanchine's work might not fit into a narrow balletic reading, but it is clear that any proper understanding of his work depends on acknowledging the set of conventions on which it depends – that is, on acknowledging a past that remains insistently present.

Section III

There is a second element in Levin's account of modern dance that I would like to take issue with. One can certainly grant it to Levin (and to Greenberg) that the story of modernism in art is that of a growing preoccupation of the artistic medium with itself, a gradual 'revelation' (Levin's preferred term) of the specificity of an artistic medium within that medium itself. What I do reject, however, is Levin's assumption that the specificity of dance can be summarized in such formal or crudely materialist terms as he proposes: pure bodies, pure movements, pure lines. If one strips away from dancing everything that is superfluous, is this what remains? Would the most 'frank' kind of dance, one that really reveals the truth about its own medium, be a dance in which the spectator is compelled to see nothing but an aggregate of bodies, movements, and lines?

I believe the specificity of dance can be defined in a richer way, one that does not fall into the positivist trap of reducing dance to its material preconditions, be it physical bodies or 'Euclidean' movements. My main objection to such

---

15 See for instance the phrase by Levin already quoted above: 'It is as if the leg/torso juncture were the intersection of two mathematical lines.' Note the usage of the words 'as if'. Levin seems to accept here that it does require a theatrical suspension of disbelief to see in the 'leg/torso juncture' nothing but the intersection of mathematical lines.

a reduction lies in that it is phenomenologically implausible. In watching dance, even dance of the modern, abstract kind, we do not just perceive bodies and movements. What we perceive first of all, I contend, is 'persons and actions', as Graham McFee once put it in a slightly different discussion (McFee 1992, p.55ff).

Let me illustrate this by briefly analyzing a fragment of German choreographer Sasha Waltz's celebrated piece, *Körper* (literally: bodies), first performed in 2000. Although not exactly choreographed in the vocabulary of Balanchine, the artistic intentions behind *Körper* can easily be made to fit into the scheme set up by Levin. What Sasha Waltz wants, quite literally, is to do away with everything in the medium of dance that tends to conceal or constrain its material basis, that is, the body. Waltz intends to show this material basis in a direct, unmediated manner; she wants to show the body as it 'really' is.[16] If one looks at Waltz's choreography in detail, however, it turns out that such a strategy of 'baring all' actually requires quite a bit of concealment.

Much of the choreography of *Körper* consists in a very slow, amorphous crawling on the floor. Waltz thus enrols two recognizable conventions (eliminating man's vertical posture, breaking with the usual rhythm of human movement) that are often used – at least within the contemporary continental vocabulary – to evoke the idea of the body as materiality, as pure 'flesh'. Part of that 'flesh'-logic is the idea that all body parts are equivalent: they are all sheer 'matter'. At certain moments in the choreography, though, it becomes clear that this is perhaps not the case. Dancers are not just material bodies, and in order to make them appear that way, Waltz has to hide quite a bit.

At one moment in the choreography, a dancer lying on the floor – in the original 2000 production this was Joakim Olsson – is invited by another dancer, Grayson Millwood, to roll sideways. Millwood gently puts his foot against Olsson's face in order to make him slowly roll to the side. What happened when I saw the piece, is that Olsson first had a small, spontaneous reaction of repulsion when that footsole was planted against his cheek. Olsson of course immediately corrected himself, readjusted to the choreography's slow-motion tempo and went into that sideward roll. Yet this brief, nearly imperceptible interruption in the smoothness of the choreography was very telling, because it showed just how deeply artificial

---

16 For Waltz, this artistic programme serves a broader, political purpose. According to Waltz, our bodies all too often 'lie' (be it on stage or in social life) because people only care about the outside and about the image they project. In an attempt to counter this 'alienation', her dancers (and people in general) should truly reconnect with their own body (cf. Waltz 2001). It is not certain, though, whether Waltz's choreographic strategies are consistent with this purpose.

it is to ignore, for instance, the distinction between a face and a foot.

Needless to say that such distinctions are very prominent in our perception of our own body, as well as in our perception of others. When encountering someone else, we do not first perceive a material, flesh-like entity, sections of which we subsequently identify as human body parts: we *immediately* see a familiar face, a wrinkled hand, or an endearing curve. That is to say, we never perceive human bodies as mere material things: we spontaneously see them as the embodiment of 'persons'. The different meaning we attach to different parts of the human body, far from reflecting a merely spatial or functional logic, is closely related to our perception of the other as an individual person who, among other moral features, is worthy of respect (think for instance of Emmanuel Levinas's emphasis on the face and the eyes of the other[17]) and capable of shame (think of our desire to conceal certain bodily functions).

In the same way, human movements are never mere mechanical movements. We are inclined to see them, even against our better knowledge, as meaningful and driven by intentions. Indeed, this inclination is so strong that it sometimes even extends to non-human movements. Imagine for instance a robot manipulating objects. If its 'hand' suddenly slows down to pick up a fragile item, we tend to perceive this movement as careful. Although we know there to be no intention behind the movement (let alone a genuine attitude of 'carefulness' or a 'caring' personality), it is difficult not to project such an intention onto the hand's movement.[18] Similarly, the very rapid approach of a fragile item will come across as careless or even brutish – regardless of the mover's actual intentions (or lack thereof).

I believe this 'moral' perspective on human bodies and movements cannot be suspended so easily. Even when looking at dance, we never simply perceive material bodies (even if the choreography is persistently pointing at these bodies), nor do we perceive the motions of these bodies as mere modifications in Euclidean space. Instead, we inevitably see *persons who are doing things*, that is, self-conscious beings who are deliberately executing certain actions. For instance, we see one person planting a foot in someone else's face.[19] If choreographers nonetheless want to create the illusion that

---

17 See Levinas 1969, and elsewhere.

18 I owe this example to Filip Mattens.

19 Compare the unfortunate passage from *Körper* described above with a passage in Mats Ek's choreography *Appartement* (first produced for the Paris Opera Ballet in 2000; I am basing my description on a performance by that same company in 2003). At a certain point in the choreography, Céline Talon sits on the floor while Nicolas Le Riche stands in front of her. Suddenly, Le Riche places the sole of his foot on Talon's face and leaves it there for a short moment. This surprising and slightly bizarre incident is introduced here by Ek, deliberately, as an interruption of the smooth, virtuoso dance sequence that preceded and that will take up again immediately thereafter. In Ek's piece, this sudden 'reality

persons are nothing but material bodies or want to present these persons'
deeds as pure, 'Euclidean' movements, they have to actively suppress our
perception of dancers as subjects. Of course, choreographers might try to
create such an illusion for legitimate artistic reasons. My sole claim is that
successfully doing so would require the complete negation of something
that is always already there: our perception of dancers as persons doing
certain actions.

A typical element in such attempts at negation is the illusion of equivalence
between all body parts. It is not a coincidence that Levin, in his discussion
of Balanchine's formalism, strongly insists on this point. Balanchine's style,
according to Levin, creates a visual equivalence between legs, head, arms
and torso, which no longer appear as distinct entities but all become 'pure
line'. For Levin, this geometric reduction of the human body represents the
summum of disclosure; dance's defining conditions are laid bare for anyone
to see.

But Levin's observations can just as well lead to the opposite conclusion.
Rather than an instance of revelation, Balanchine's vocabulary can be said
to conceal something, to wit the way we spontaneously perceive the head
or the torso as distinct from, say, legs or feet. If Balanchine indeed wants to
show pure bodies or pure movements, as Levin claims, he would actually be
attempting to suppress our perception of movements as intentional actions
executed by self-conscious individuals.[20] Thus, rather than pure disclosure,
another – profoundly theatrical – illusion is being created.

This, then, is the basic misunderstanding that I believe to be at work in
Levin's story about dance modernism. Levin claims that at the very bottom
of the medium of dance, when scraping away all superfluous theatrical
elements, one finds pure movement. And through these movements the
body expresses itself, not as a recognizably human body – since the distinct,
meaningful parts of the body are supposed to lose their distinctness – but
as 'mass' or 'line'. In other words, the dancer, who naturally appears on
stage as a person doing certain actions, is supposed to completely disappear

---

check' serves a very precise function: it interrupts the whirling spectacle of movements
and poignantly reminds us that these are the movements of real, recognizable, and very
fragile individuals. Thus, rather than trying to deny the subjectivity of his dancers, Ek
brusquely reminds us of it – and to great effect, for the image sticks in the mind even as
the dancing takes up again.

20 To my best knowledge Balanchine never reacted to Levin's text, but it is not obvious
that he would agree with Levin's interpretation of his work. On the contrary, Balanchine
himself seemed keenly aware of the impossibility of creating truly 'abstract' or 'formal'
dance in the way that Levin suggests. Consider for instance the following quote by
Balanchine: 'no dance can in itself be abstract [...] [Y]ou see moving before you, dancers
of flesh and blood, in a living relation to each other. What you hear and see is completely
real.' (Balanchine 1975, p.79)

behind her or his own movements.

My claim would be that this is not quite the end of theatricality. A reduction to 'objecthood', as Levin proposes, would not constitute a moment of (direct, unmediated) revelation. It would rather be a continuation of the logic of representation: the dancer is to give the illusion of being pure body, or pure movement. Even though the choreographer wishing to create such an illusion has a variety of well-known conventions at his disposal, it is an undertaking that is ultimately bound to fail – not least because the logic of modern art consists precisely in the unremitting unmasking of such illusions.

Section IV

What I have suggested above, is that the defining condition of dance as an artistic medium includes the fact that dance consists of 'actions' that are executed by 'persons'. The spectator may be seduced to see swans or geometric shapes, yet she also (and inevitably so) sees subjects who are deliberately doing things. In a way, dance movements are just that: deliberate actions by human beings. As this perspective is constantly available to the spectator (we cannot not see the dancer), choreographers have no choice but to somehow relate to and take into account this 'basic fact'.

At the same time, it is true that the history of dance provides a wealth of conventions and strategies that lead our attention away from the dancers qua persons. Dance movements typically 'break' with the way people naturally move in daily life: because the movements have a different and more elaborate shape, because the rhythm is distinct, or through some other mechanism (for instance, repetition). As a result, we might overlook that these movements are, in fact, actions executed by self-conscious subjects. Instead, we think of princes and swans or we revel in the abstract spectacle of whirling lines and shapes.

Thus, dancing is saddled with a fundamental duality. On the one hand, dance movements are actions performed by persons and can always be recognized as such. On the other hand, the dancing tends to obscure this basic fact or lead us away from it. Accepting Greenberg's account of modernism as a process of investigation and gradual revelation of a medium's specificity within that medium, the modernization of dance would then imply a progressive disclosure of this constellation. Modern choreographers would face the task of acknowledging that dance movements, although they evoke all sorts of things, can never fully conceal their all too human substratum. It seems to me that some of the most interesting moments in twentieth century dance are indeed those where choreographers have consciously played on this duality. Let me just give one example of a modern choreographer whom I believe to be unusually sensitive to this tension that sits at the very heart of the medium of dance: Bronislava Nijinska.

In her best known piece, *Les Noces* (made in 1923), Nijinska has appropriated the language of classical ballet in a very sophisticated manner.[21] For starters, she has done away with the perspectivism of classical ballet, both in spatial formations and in the posture of individual dancers who – instead of adopting *croisé*, *effacé*, or *écarté* positions – always find themselves in very stark, 'flat', front-facing positions.[22] Nijinska has also chosen to emphasize the geometric shapes inherent in the academic vocabulary. For instance, in the lateral *pas de bourrée* that dominate much of the choreography of *Les Noces*, the upper body is counter-leaning sideways in a very rigid manner, giving the movement a linear, metronome-like quality. Elsewhere, arms are extra rounded so as to form clearly visible circles. Several other features similarly contribute to the striking 'geometric' quality of Nijinska's vocabulary. Combined with the gruelling, repetitive rhythms of Stravinsky's music, *Les Noces* tends to come across as a very severe construction that pushes classical ballet's mechanical logic to its ultimate conclusion.[23] Indeed, *Les Noces* is often cited precisely because of its hard, constructivist aesthetic that reduces dancers to purely formal elements and seemingly strips away their individuality.

This would be to deny, though, that something totally different is going on in *Les Noces* as well. Despite its constructivist looks, the choreography simultaneously draws attention to what can only be described as the 'humanity' of the individual dancers. It does so, most prominently, by emphasizing the gaze and the faces of the dancers. For instance, the dancers' mostly front-facing orientation, without any sort of *épaulement*, never invites our eyes to glide through and beyond them towards the backdrop (in the way classical, 'perspectival' postures do) but instead forces us – quite literally – to face them, as persons. The same goes for other aspects of the

---

21 In what follows, I summarize an analysis of the choreography of *Les Noces* that I developed in more detail elsewhere (Geenens 2010).

22 In this same vein, Cohen argues that it makes no sense to catalogue Balanchine among the modernists favoured by Greenberg on account of the purported flatness or 'opticality' of his choreographies (Cohen 1983, pp.174-176). Balanchine deliberately articulates the physical stage space in three dimensions (not unlike Petipa), Balanchine's dancers are decidedly three-dimensional (they are 'turners' rather than 'jumpers'), and Balanchine's vocabulary massively partakes in the sculptural principle of *contrapposto*: human figures are shown in a-symmetrical poses with pelvis or shoulders slightly rotated around the vertical axis so as to introduce a spiral in the body and to create an illusion of depth and dynamism.

23 Nancy Van Norman Baer, for instance, describes *Les Noces* as 'anti-realist', and attributes this anti-realism to Nijinska's attempt to reinforce the abstraction inherent in classical ballet. Van Norman Baer emphasizes in particular Nijinska's bold usage of point shoes in *Les Noces*, which 'stripped naturalism from the movement' (Van Norman Baer 1986, p.34).

choreography. In the third scene the members of the corps de ballet form one long line with their forearms, and let their heads rest on it while calmly yet insistently looking at the audience – obliging us as it were to acknowledge their presence. And then there are of course the famous human pyramids at the end of the first and the fourth scene. These pyramids (often reproduced in photos of *Les Noces*) feature eight female dancers who are piled up, their heads forming a perfect, vertical line. As the lights slowly fade, the dancers' eyes linger unusually long on the audience. The strict geometry (a triangle made of bodies and a perpendicular made of eight pairs of eyes) does not prevent this tableau from exuding a touching vulnerability.

These and other strategies allow Nijinska to intensify the contrast between austere, 'dehumanizing' choreographic structures and, on the other hand, the presence of her dancers within these structures as recognizable individuals.[24] In *Les Noces*, this contrast ultimately serves a narrative purpose, since it symbolizes the contrast between the crushing weight of ritual and tradition on the one hand, and the hapless Russian peasants (and, in particular, their young daughters) who are subject to it, on the other. Yet this hardly diminishes the novelty and ingenuity of Nijinska's approach. Rather than relying on theatrical means, as so many of her contemporaries would have done, Nijinska chose to emphasize the specificity of her medium – namely: the tension between ballet's abstract vocabulary and the humanity of the dancing subject – and made it the privileged vector of expression. Thus, Nijinska focuses on an experience that is wholly specific to her own artistic medium; a medium she never reduces to its material support, instead bringing to light its internal differentiatedness. As we know from Nijinska's writings, it is her drive to 'modernize' the medium of ballet that brought her there; the pastoral theme of *Les Noces* (by and large forced upon her by Diaghilev) was at best a pretext to explore that modernist path.

Nijinska is not an isolated case. There are numerous other instances in the history of twentieth century dance where choreographers have shown proof of this same sensitivity. Indeed, I believe the works of many key choreographers can and should be understood as attempts to bring to light what they saw to be the particularity of their medium: the fact that dance lives off the tension between on the one hand stylized movements and, on the other, the presence of recognizably human subjects performing these movements. This tension is built into the medium of dance and thus differentiates it from other artistic mediums.

---

24 Stravinsky's music has been interpreted along similar lines. According to Richard Taruskin, Stravinsky's *Les Noces* plays on the contrast between familiar, recognizably human voices ('voices with which normal, cultivated Western listeners can identify') and, on the other hand, a musical score that is severe, mechanical, 'Russian', and deliberately 'antihumanistic' (Taruskin 1997, p.463).

This, ironically enough, is precisely what Levin overlooks. Levin claims, quite plausibly, that the progression of dance history is spurred by a growing awareness of dance's specificity as an artistic medium. However, in his eagerness to assimilate the history of dance to the history of painting and sculpture, he fails to take proper notice of what distinguishes dance from the visual arts described by Greenberg. The main difference, as I hope to have shown, lies in that dance can never be 'abstract' or 'formal' in the same manner as painting or sculpture can be, since the practice of dancing is inevitably interwoven with the figure of the dancer, who cannot possibly be erased or removed.[25] No matter how abstract or rigid the choreographic architecture, dance movements are always and at the same time recognizable as actions executed by persons. The choreographer's freedom in this regard is limited to dealing with this basic condition in a less or more lucid way.

Thus, dancing can be described as a medium that allows (or even obliges) the spectator to simultaneously adopt two perspectives: the spectator can be captivated by the movement spectacle and everything it evokes, yet, at the same time, she can see self-conscious persons deliberately doing certain actions. One advantage of this description, I believe, is that it can link up with the artistic concerns of many twentieth century choreographers, even of the so-called 'integrationist' creed (think of Rainer or Brown, but also some of their older colleagues), who – in one way or another – explored the tension between these two perspectives and thus investigated the specificity of their own medium. Of course, this claim requires further fleshing out. Yet if the scheme I am outlining here is defensible, it would allow the artistic efforts of many pioneering choreographers who do not fit into Levin's unduly narrow and materialist account of dance modernism, to be understood as part and parcel of the modernist project – which is only logical given that these choreographers often worked shoulder to shoulder with modernist artists from other disciplines. It is rather unfortunate that Levin, because of his attempt to fit Balanchine literally into Greenberg's story, cannot make conceptual room for their achievements. Possibly, it even prevents him from fully taking into account the merits of Balanchine himself.

---

25 It could be argued that even abstract painting and sculpture are not as 'abstract' or 'formal' as is sometimes assumed (cf. Schapiro 1995).

References

Balanchine, George. 'The Dance Element in Stravinsky's Music', in Lederman, Minna (ed.), *Stravinsky in the Theatre*, New York: Da Capo Press, 1975 [1949], pp.75-84.

Banes, Sally. 'Introduction to the Wesleyan Paperback Edition', in *Terpsichore in Sneakers. Post-Modern Dance*, Middletown: Wesleyan University Press, 1987, pp.xiii-xxxix.

Banes, Sally and Noël Carroll. 'Cunningham, Balanchine, and Postmodern Dance', *Dance Chronicle*, 29:1, 2006, pp.49-68.

Carroll, Noël. 'The Philosophy of Art History, Dance, and the 1960s', in Banes, Sally (ed.), *Reinventing Dance in the 1960s. Everything Was Possible*. Madison: University of Wisconsin Press, 2003, pp.81-97.

Cavell, Stanley. *Must we mean what we say?* Cambridge: Cambridge University Press, 1976.

Cohen, Marshall. 'Primitivism, Modernism, and Dance Theory', in Copeland, Roger and Marshall Cohen (eds.), *What is Dance?* Oxford: Oxford University Press, 1983, pp.161-178.

Davies, David. 'Medium in Art', in Levinson, Jerrold (ed.), *The Oxford Handbook of Aesthetics*, Oxford: Oxford University Press, 2003, pp.181-191.

Geenens, Raf. 'Une politique de l'abstraction ou les ruses chorégraphiques des *Noces* de Bronislava Nijinska', in Launay, Isabelle and Sylviane Pages (eds.), *Mémoires et histoires en danse*, Paris: L'Harmattan, 2010, pp.177-190.

Krauss, Rosalind. *A Voyage on the North Sea. Art in the Age of the Post-Medium Condition*, London: Thames and Hudson, 1999a.

Krauss, Rosalind. 'The Crisis of the Easel Picture', in Varnedoe, Kirk and Pepe Karmel (eds.), *Jackson Pollock. New Approaches*, New York: The Museum of Modern Art, 1999b, pp.155-179.

Krauss, Rosalind. 'A View of Modernism', in *Perpetual Inventory*, Cambridge: MIT Press, 2010 [1972], pp.115-128.

Levin, David Michael. 'Balanchine's Formalism', in Copeland, Roger and Marshall Cohen (eds.), *What is Dance?* Oxford: Oxford University Press, 1983 [1973], pp.123-145.

Levin, David Michael. 'Postmodernism in Dance: Dance, Discourse, Democracy', in Silverman, Hugh J. (ed.), *Postmodernism. Philosophy and the Arts*, New York: Routledge, 1990, pp.207-233.

Levinas, Emmanuel. *Totality and Infinity: An Essay on Exteriority*, Pittsburgh: Duquesne University Press, 1969.

Mackrell, Judith. 'Post-Modern Dance in Britain: An Historical Essay', *Dance Research*, 9:1, 1991, pp.40-57.

McFee, Graham. *Understanding Dance*, London: Routledge, 1992.

Schapiro, Meyer. 'On the Humanity of Abstract Painting', in *Mondrian: On the Humanity of Abstract Painting*, New York: Braziller, 1995 [1960], pp.9-17.

Scholl, Tim. *From Petipa to Balanchine. Classical Revival and the Modernization of Ballet*, London: Routledge, 1994.

Taruskin, Richard. *Defining Russia Musically. Historical and Hermeneutical Essays*, Princeton: Princeton University Press, 1997.

Van Norman Baer, Nancy. *Bronislava Nijinska: A Dancer's Legacy*, San Francisco: Fine Arts Museum of San Francisco, 1986.

Waltz, Sasha. 'Der Kanzler tanzt eher verklemmt' (interview with Sasha Waltz), in *Der Tagesspiegel*, 21 July 2001.

3. Embodiment and dance: puzzles of consciousness and agency

Jane Carr

During the last few decades the term 'embodiment' has become increasingly popular in the discourses of dance and particularly in those that draw on the traditions of modern dance developed in America and Europe in the early Twentieth Century. Certainly by the time I began teaching at Laban, in the early years of the new millennium, embodying the dance material was a taken for granted aim of many students and their teachers.[1] The term's popularity amongst many dancers is often closely related to a desire to foster a more holistic attitude to the person dancing as opposed to overly instrumentalist attitudes to the body as a tool to be brought under mental control. Yet a warning that the use of the term 'embodied' might serve to gloss over an implied dualism, that it is more often thought of as renouncing, was posited within philosophical aesthetics over thirty five years ago by David Best (1974, p.188). The term is also problematic in that its use in relation to dance may be informed by seemingly contradictory theoretical frameworks. For example Sondra Horton-Fraleigh, writing about dance from the perspective of existential phenomenology, describes embodiment as an articulate act (Horton-Fraleigh 1987, p.13). In contrast, Janet Adshead draws on the poststructuralist concept of intertextuality to account for the embodiment of ideas in dance in a manner which suggests the dancing body is rather the recipient of meaning (Adshead 1999, p.5). Such differences not only relate to their authors' founding their understanding of dance on contrasting philosophical traditions, but also to the emphasis placed on the dancer's experience in relation to what is understood as the dance work.

The following discussion of the concept of embodiment arises from my experiences as a dancer, choreographer and dance teacher and, further, draws on findings from five case studies informing my research amongst London based dance artists who perform their own work (Carr 2008). I start by recognizing the philosophical problems Best raises with regard to some common assumptions made in relation to dance practices. However, I then explore the difficulties in accounting for what dancers often value in performance within the framework provided by Best's post-Wittgensteinian

---

1 Laban, in London, is a conservatoire for the 'contemporary' dance that draws on traditions in European and American Modern dance. I taught there from 2006-2010.

analytic philosophical approach to meaning in dance.[2] Here I also refer to the more recent work of Graham McFee (1992, 2011) who takes up some of Best's arguments in relation to dance and whose philosophical approach similarly draws strongly on the work of Ludwig Wittgenstein. Consideration of the relationships between consciousness, intention, feeling and action leads me to develop an interdisciplinary approach towards embodiment in relation to dance that considers the significance of intercorporeal exchanges between choreographer, dancers and audience. Drawing on insights from both phenomenology and the social sciences, I explore the cultural dimensions of corporeal experience and agency that are important to an understanding of the interrelationships, not just between mind-body, but between consciousness-world and self-other. Here I suggest that the existential phenomenology developed in the posthumously published writing of Maurice Merleau-Ponty, is a valuable resource. His analysis of the 'double nature of the body as a thing among things' (Merleau-Ponty 1968, p.143) that is also the source of what is seen and touched, offers a useful perspective from which to conceptualize dance as an art form centred around human actions performed to an audience.

In the past divisions between analytic and continental philosophy made it difficult for those attempting to reconcile these two distinct viewpoints. However there is currently a more sympathetic attitude towards 'the rich confluence and cross fertilisation' between different philosophical approaches (Solomon 2003, p.338). Further, the more traditional philosophical aesthetics of Paul Crowther (1993), developed in relation to dance by Bonnie Rowell (2009), reveals how concepts from existential phenomenology may be brought into play with philosophical aesthetics. Drawing upon Rowell's account of embodiment in relation to dance, I conclude this exploration of embodiment by considering how Crowther's 'ecological' aesthetics may be developed to provide a basis for understanding the concept of embodiment in relation to current dance practices.

The problem of expression

Best's (1974) critique of expressionist aesthetics is useful as a starting point to consider how the philosophical problem of the relationship between mind and body has implications for how intentions and feelings are understood to

---

2 Analytic philosophy refers to related approaches to philosophy that developed in English speaking countries in the Twentieth Century. While there are variations in these approaches, the work of Ludwig Wittgenstein, and in particular Wittgenstein's analysis of meaning has been particularly influential to many philosophers in this tradition including David Best and Graham McFee: 'We are not analyzing a phenomenon (e.g. thought) but a concept (e.g. that of thinking), and therefore the use of a word' (Wittgenstein 1968, p.118).

be embodied in dance. His concern regarding the concept of embodiment is raised in relation to criticism of what, in the 1970s, was a common assumption: that a dance could express the 'inner' feelings of the dancer. Best shows how a dualist understanding of the mind-body relationship informed the still-influential modern dance practices that emerged in Europe and America in the early Twentieth Century. His post-Wittgensteinian philosophical method is used to dismantle the implicit dualism that, often emanating from an assumed universalism, underpinned the beliefs of the foundational figures of modern dance in the potential of individuals to communicate directly with their audiences. The ideals inspiring much modern dance are captured in the words of the influential dance artist Isadora Duncan: 'There will always be movements which are the perfect expression of that individual body and that individual soul...' (Duncan 1902, p.127).

Citing the movement theories of François Delsarte and Rudolf Laban, Best reveals how in order to account for the correlation between outward form and inner feeling, the early pioneers of modern dance often resorted to metaphysical or mystical beliefs or some inexplicable 'intuition' (Best, 1974, pp.79-85). For him such solutions are untenable since, he argues, the result is that a publicly shared understanding of art becomes impossible. Best points out that often underlying such resorts to metaphysics are assumptions regarding the existence of some hidden inner entity such as 'mind,' or a specific emotion that are the result of thinking in terms of 'meaning as naming' (Best 1974, p.18). Such concepts, he argues, are not things that can be pointed to and he warns against any attempt to capture their 'essence' (Best 1974, pp.15-21).

It is in the context of his determination to avoid dualism that Best raises his objections to Louis Arnaud Reid's account of embodied significance. Where Reid suggests a psycho-physical unity through which aspects of character and feeling are embodied, Best argues Reid's theory is still ultimately dependent on a dualist distinction between the physical and the mental.[3] Influenced by Wittgenstein's notion of 'seeing as,'[4] Best prefers to focus on

---

3 Best (1974, p.188), specifically cites Louis Arnaud Reid's (1974) statement that: 'To "see" character in a person's face, in his posture and gesture, is neither to perceive his body only nor to apprehend his character through his body, but to apprehend one single embodied person with distinguishable aspects [...] To feel happy, or anger, or at ease or in anxiety, is neither mental only nor physical only, but psycho physical. The aspects are indivisible and convey the idea of meaningful embodied experience.'

4 This concept is discussed by Wittgenstein in *Philosophical Investigations* (part II, xi, 1968, pp.193-229). He exemplifies the difference between the continuous seeing of an aspect and the 'dawning of an aspect' using the ambiguous duck/rabbit figure. The image does not change but what is seen – duck or rabbit – does, and this is related to discussion of the recognition of 'seeing as' in which it is understood that 'seeing as' consists of more than receiving sense data.

the act of perception as interpretation: 'The point is that to see character in a person's face is not to see the mental embodied in the physical, it is to interpret his physical expression' (Best 1974, p.188).

Best is careful to avoid a behaviourist approach to mind-body, which would disregard the relevance of a dancer's feelings (Best 1974, pp.66-73). However, working from his specific philosophical position, his focus is on the logical basis of what can be stated about the expressive capacity of dance rather than on the interrogation of the experience itself. He solves the logical problem of the relationship between feeling and action by suggesting that, rather than trying to infer inner feeling from outer behaviour (which for him is not logically possible), physical behaviour can be seen as a criterion of feeling. A dancer's actions are interpreted in relation to their context that, for Best, includes both the features of the performance and knowledge of the traditions relevant to its production. His approach allows for a variety of interpretations which, however, are not unlimited by virtue of their being dependent on the observable features of a dance.

The dancer's perspective

Paradoxically, many dancers themselves are also often critical of dualism, albeit for different reasons to those argued by David Best. As Anna Pakes (2006) reveals, dancers often regard dualism as fostering a separation of the mental and physical that runs contrary to their aims of working towards 'integration of mind and body' (Pakes 2006, p.88). However, as the discussion of Best's argument against Reid reveals, such aims may still be dependent upon an implicit dualism. Moreover, in spite of Best's protestations, the expressionist assumption that a dancer's actions provide some direct insight into her/his inner state or soul seems to have persisted: in the 1990s the British dance academic Jacqueline Smith-Autard found it necessary to argue against what she saw as a tendency towards dance as subjective self-expression (Smith-Autard 1994, p.5)[5]. More recently, the very title of a widely available text book,[6] *Choreographing From Within* (Green 2010), signals the author's proposition that choreography as an art 'involves the process of discovering movement that provides a window into your soul' (Green 2010, p.4). It may be argued that making and performing dance works and accounting for them philosophically are very different activities and thus dancers' ideas about dance are not required to be philosophically

---

5 In contrast to Best, Smith-Autard (2004, p.4) is happy to cite Reid's account of embodiment as psycho-physical unity in support of her views regarding meaning in dance.

6 That I came across this book via my undergraduate students' essays suggests it has been well promoted and distributed successfully.

accurate in order to be useful to their practice. Moreover, as Best rightly points out, 'not everything can be said about a dance' (Best, 1974, 178), but his approach leads him to set aside what dancers often want to talk about.[7] While the dancers' perspective should not be overemphasized in relation to that of the audience, I will argue that what dancers experience is often an important part of the complex of embodied negotiations through which the significance of dance is produced.

How dancers feel whilst dancing is often related to what that dancing means to them. In current practice, frequently adopted 'somatic' training methods focus dancers on their felt experience of motion and this may result in the dancer's increased sensitivity to the bodily sensations of emotion since, it can be argued, there is a dynamic congruency between emotion and motion (Sheets-Johnstone 2009, p.209). In contrast to the expressionist aesthetics of much early modern dance, today's dancers are aware their actions may be interpreted in different ways. Even so, there often remains a sense that their felt experience is an important part of a communicative interaction that takes place in performance. For example, the artists I interviewed emphasize some sort of relationship between dancer and audience when asked to describe what they experience, both as performer and audience, when a piece 'works'(Carr 2008, p.1). The 'independent' dance artist Gaby Agis describes: 'a dialogue or an exchange [...] of sensations, of memories, of energies, of resonances with something the artist has communicated' (Agis, cited in Carr 2008, p.155). In discussing a performance by Deborah Hay, another independent artist describes how: 'Within her performance she was able to embody something that altered space [...] and its effect was felt' ('Artist D,' cited in Carr 2008, p.155). While Nina Anderson, whose own work draws on Egyptian dance traditions, commented about the dancers in the performances she most enjoyed: 'You feel that emotionally they've kind of got you somewhere' (Anderson 2003 cited in Carr 2008, p.158). For these dancers, a sense of embodying the dance not only seems to be important to how they perform movements but contributes to what one artist described as the 'energy' between performer and audience and another as a sense that performer and audience 'journey together.'('Artist B' and Sushma Mehta cited in Carr 2008, pp.156-157).

Dancers and dance theorists often make use of theories of kinaesthetic empathy to explain the sense of connection between performer and

---

7 I included discussion of Best (1974) in seminars with students at Laban over a period of four years from 2006-2010. My own interests may well have shaped the undergraduates' responses and some students inevitably struggled with a philosophical text. However those who found the problems with Expressionism he raises interesting and relevant to their experience expressed dissatisfaction with his solution.

audience.[8] The most famous early example is by the dance critic John Martin. Writing about the modern dance that developed during the 1930s, Martin describes 'the inherent contagion of bodily movement, which makes the onlooker feel sympathetically in his own musculature, the exertions he sees in someone else's musculature...' (Martin 1983, p.22). For Martin this empathetic capacity facilitates what he terms 'metakinesis' in which the movement is 'a medium for the transference of an aesthetic and emotional concept from the consciousness of one individual to that of another' (Martin 1983, p.23). Best, however refutes the significance of kinaesthesia, arguing that a kinaesthetic empathetic response somehow caused by watching dance should not be confused with its meaning (Best 1974, pp.144-147).

More recently, a renewed interest in kinaesthetic empathy draws on research in neuroscience into the neural basis for mirror responses to another's movement. Susan Foster, for example, refers to the research of the neuroscientist Vittorio Gallese to claim that 'the same neurons fire when [movement] is performed and when it is witnessed' (Gallese 2001, Foster 2011, p.165). Yet while many dancers have welcomed scientific research that seems to validate their experience, the philosopher Graham McFee questions the validity of the neuroscience upon which such claims are based (2011, pp.193-199). Further, following many of Best's arguments, he finds no place for reference to the kinaesthetic sense as part of any explanation of a dance (McFee1992, p.2011). He challenges assumptions that mirroring someone's movement gives direct access to their (inner) feelings and thoughts since this again raises the problematic assumption that psychological 'inner' states can be inferred from outer behaviour (2011, pp.190-191).[9] For McFee, dance is actively understood as an intentional act within culture. Responding to current theories of kinaesthetic empathy that refer to the function of mirror neurons, he thus argues against the relevance of locating the biological cause of a seemingly automatic mirror response to the understanding and appreciation of dance as art (McFee 2011, pp.192-200).

Whether or not McFee's analysis of the validity of the findings of neuroscientists is correct, this latter point in his argument is certainly convincing: even if neuroscientists could locate a specific neuron that,

8 Although there is some confusion over its precise definition, dancers tend to use the term kinaesthetic to refer to all the felt sensations relevant to the body in dance. More specifically kinaesthesia may refer to 'a sense of movement through muscular effort' (Sheets-Johnstone 2009, p.164) but is also sometimes understood to include proprioceptive awareness of the body's position in relation to space and gravity.

9 For McFee (as with Best before him) the problem of other minds cannot be resolved by 'the argument from analogy' which seeks to draw general conclusions about the relationship between conscious experience and behaviour from the limited case of an individual's own experience.

without exception, fires in all humans in response to seeing the same motor action it would, as McFee states, only explain how that action is recognized and not its significance within a dance work. There would also be the further problem that there may be no guarantee people would experience the motor neuron firing in the same way.[10] McFee is thus right to argue that neither mirror reflex nor mirror neurons can provide for the significance of a dance since this is the product of a culturally informed understanding of dance as an art form. However, that the assertion of direct kinaesthetic empathy between dancer and audience is problematic does not mean that the kinaesthetic sense has no bearing on how dance is experienced as art. Yet McFee doubts the need to postulate a separate kinaesthetic sensory modality (McFee 2011, p.186). For him the audience's experience is understood as visual and he sees attempts to explore how awareness of bodily sensations might inform the understanding of dance as prioritizing what the dancer experiences at the expense of the audience (McFee 2011, p.188). I will argue that whatever its biological basis, a kinaesthetic modality is important to the understanding of much current dance practice. Moreover, as part of an embodied understanding of dance, it is relevant to the experience of both dancer and audience. However, before I continue to argue for the importance of a kinaesthetic modality I will first explore how dancers experience intention as embodied.

Intention and action

In consideration of intention as embodied, a distinction is made between the intention of the dancer and the choreographer, notwithstanding that in practice they can be closely interrelated.[11] Not sharing Best's suspicion of the term 'embodiment,' McFee (2011) allows for a dance work to embody choreographic intention. However, he avoids the dualism Best warns against since he is careful to avoid explaining choreographic intention as 'what is in the artist's head' (McFee 2011, p.131). It is evident from McFee's account of the intentionalist debate[12] that he considers intention in a

---

10 This raises the philosophical 'knowledge argument' concerning whether a physical description of a brain state associated with a particular sensation (or quale) is all there is to know. A brief summary of this debate and the related issues surrounding subjective consciousness can be found in Anthony Freeman (2003).

11 For example, the artists who were the case studies for my research (Carr 2008) all performed their own work. Their positions as both choreographer and dancer revealed a particularly close interrelationship between dance and dancer. But even when the roles are taken by different people they overlap. (Editor's note: see McFee's essay in this volume for further discussion of the respective roles of choreographer and dancer.)

12 The debate regarding the relevance of the author's intention to understanding a work of art was raised by William K. Wimsatt Jr. and Monroe C. Beardsley. They objected to

'hypothetical' sense in which there is no need for a psychological or causal explanation of the relationship between intention and action (McFee,2011, pp.136-137). According to McFee, understanding of the choreographic intention embodied in the work is based on publicly observable actions that can be interpreted in relation to the known context within which the work was made. Hence intention is 'ascribed' (McFee 2011, p.131) to the choreographic act.

In relation to the dancer's intention, McFee recognizes the dancer's role in embodying the dance as an act through which the dance is 'instantiated' (McFee 2011, pp.175-180). However, he argues this act of embodiment needs no further theorizing. For him it is enough to recognize that, 'dancers are agents capable of performing certain actions' (McFee 2011, p.181). Yet it may be worthwhile exploring just how the dancer is understood to instantiate the dance. For many dancers, bodily awareness is intrinsic to how they understand intention as embodied in their artform and the sense of self and agency they can enjoy through dance. The Australian dance artist Sandra Parker, for example, guides dancers to focus on bodily feeling as the source of new movements.[13] Similarly, a kinaesthetic sensibility may also inform the recreation of rehearsed actions in performance so that they are 'embodied' by the dancer: a process one artist describes as 'weaving his being through the structure' (Artist D 2003, cited in Carr 2008). In order to explore how kinaesthesia is important to the dancer's sense of agency in embodying dance, I will examine the relationships between conscious intention, awareness of action, and the action itself within a social context.

Culture, consciousness and agency

Understanding of the relationship between intention and action can be informed by drawing on the findings of other disciplines. In particular, the social sciences offer analyses of the relationship of individual agency (or the capacity to bring about what is intended) to social structures. This is a topic of extensive debate that cannot be adequately covered here.[14] However, it

---

what they saw as 'the intentional fallacy' in literature stating: '...the design or intention of the author is neither available nor desirable as a standard for judging the success of a work of literary art' (Wimsatt and Beardsley 1978, pp.294-295).

13 This approach was explored by the Australian dance artisit Sandra Parker in a workshop at the University of Lincoln, October 26, 2011.

14 In sociology both functionalism and structuralism emphasize systems and structures which tend to constrain individuals who are viewed as fitting into proscribed roles. In contrast, humanist and hermeneutic approaches to the social world emphasize the significance of individual actions unfettered by the constraints of structure. Attempts to provide theoretically for an understanding of human agency as dialectically related to society include the structuration theory of Anthony Giddens (1991) and Pierre

is important to recognize that, in contrast to the dancer's understanding of embodiment through which they experience a sense of agency through instantiating the dance, within the social sciences cultural embodiment is often perceived as occurring tacitly, at a level of consciousness that may not be readily available to self-awareness and may even be viewed as limiting agency. Hence, for those interested in the creative acts of artists, the question arises: 'How does human agency exert itself despite the enormous pressures of social conditioning?' (Noland 2009, p.1)

By belonging to a culture, people share ways of moving. Some aspects of a shared movement culture may resemble what are understood as signs – usually common gestures that people are able to identify as meaningful according to culturally shared codes. However, the sociologist Pierre Bourdieu describes tacitly understood 'differences in gesture, posture and behavior which express a whole relationship to the social world' (Bourdieu, 1979, p.192). These differences are both structured and structuring of behaviour and are part of what he terms the 'habitus.' This is described by him as a 'disposition that generates meaningful practices and meaning giving perceptions' (Bourdieu 1979, p.170) that is shared by members of the same cultural group and that is part of the 'hidden conditions' through which culture is absorbed at a level beneath everyday conscious awareness (Bourdieu 1979, p.28). That the cultural anthropologist Ted Polhemus considers dance to be a 'crystallization' (Polhemus 1998, p.180) of the more general bodily culture that informs it, suggests dance carries tacitly understood significance that is important to how it is understood and appreciated.

For the dancer, the habitus informs the underlying bodily organization of daily life and hence influences her/his dancing. However, dance styles may also be considered as requiring a specific habitus that may or may not be closely related to the dancer's own cultural background. Getting a 'feel' for a particular dance style enables dancers to perform, or even improvise, in the appropriate manner without necessarily focusing attention on movement choices. The distinction between conscious choice and more habitual response is complicated by the permeability of the boundary between actions that can be performed seemingly unconsciously and those that require conscious monitoring.[15] While people's movements may embody a

Bourdieu's (1979) theory of habitus and field. Chris Shilling (1996) and Thomas Csordas (1994) specifically explore embodiment from the perspective of the social sciences.

15 The role of conscious awareness in relation to action is a topic of debate in the field of consciousness studies that draws on findings in neuroscience, psychology and philosophy. Of the many and complex models put forward, those that argue for embodied consciousness are the more consistent with both how dancers experience the relationship between awareness and action and Merleau-Ponty's analysis of the interrelationships between self-other-world that is discussed below. See, for example, the dynamic

common culture or a dance style without their conscious awareness being directed to do so, dancers often focus conscious attention on details of their movement. In learning new dance styles or unusual sequences there may be awkwardness when dancers are faced with an unaccustomed bodily organization, but at a later stage this becomes part of a residual, or habitual feel for the movement so that conscious attention can be focused elsewhere.[16]

What adds still further complexity is that dancers may choose to change what is brought into focal awareness and this includes consciously interacting with the body's habitual systems. In the dance class dancers may shift their focus between consciously creating new movement habits (the required habitus of a particular style) and focusing on 'undoing' what has become habitual. Indeed it is the sense of conscious interplay with habitual systems that Carrie Noland (2009) argues is important to experiencing a sense of agency in embodying movement: 'If there is an enduring quality to the material body, then [...] it promises to disclose an aspect of human kinetic potential that has not previously been integrated into normative gestural routines' (Noland 2009, pp.213-214). By attending to the body in its most seemingly organic state, as in catching the moment when a reflex happens, dancers continually engage in a process of self-awareness.[17] Such a process however draws on a kinaesthetic sensibility that, as the dance anthropologist Deidre Sklar (2007) describes, is part of the habitus and as such needs to be considered as a part of culture.

Revisiting kinaesthesia

Kinaesthesia is important to many current practices in which dancers develop a high level of sensitivity to the bodily sensations produced by their movements. Today's skilled dancers not only draw on their bodily awareness to ensure their body is accurately placed in space and time but to shift their focus to the details of body actions. For example they might focus on the back of the rib cage to emphasize an in breath that initiates a move backwards. Further, in the terms of Laban effort analysis (Laban and Lawrence 1974) they are aware of the differences between movement qualities such as sudden and sustained, free and bound and so on. This enables them to have control over the compounds of effort qualities through time that structure the dynamic content perceived by the audience. Novice dancers may find this

---

sensormotor view of perceptual consciousness in O'Regan and Noë, 2001.

16 In this, I recognize the influence of Michael Polanyi's (1997) distinction between tacit and focal awareness.

17 That this also results in the increasing potential for control of the self has further implications for the experience of both agency and the limits on agency. See Carr (2010) for further discussion.

awareness difficult: they feel their leg is straight when their teacher can see it is still bent; they lack awareness of when and how they breathe and may not have control of the dynamic phrasing of their actions. However, the skilled dance artist not only has the physical awareness necessary to control her/his movements but a heightened kinaesthetic sense that allows her/him to be conscious of how that movement is structured in relation to a particular cultural framework. This then allows the dancer not only to monitor what her/his movements may look like to others but also to gauge how they may be understood within a particular cultural context.

One of the surprises in my previous research amongst experienced dance artists was how one of them seemed to utilize her skill in monitoring her actions even when she was not conscious of doing so. This was an artist who had been working with an emotional stimulus as a source for improvisation. Watching a video of herself improvising, she began to realize that she already had a much better idea of her dancing than she had envisaged. 'Lost' as she had been in a realm of emotional memories, she recognized she had retained a good sense of her actions and what they would look like (Artist A cited in Carr 2008, pp.151-152). Such experience raises questions as to whether in between the unconscious systems, such as reflex actions, and a fully conscious monitoring of movement, there is a form of inbuilt self-awareness that is perhaps enhanced through dance training.[18] Further, the experience of this dancer leads to consideration that this self-monitoring crosses between modes of consciousness so that kinaesthetic experience informs a visual sense of movement.[19]

The importance of kinaesthesia to dancers does not mean it is necessary to the audience's appreciation of dance. However, much current dance practice can be understood as orientated towards a kinaesthetic modality rather than having a more visually orientated focus on spatial forms and visual images. For example, one artist I interviewed was adamant that he created a particular dance as a flurry of movement because he 'didn't want anyone to grab onto an image' (Artist D cited in Carr 2008, p.149). The dynamic patterns that are created may be experienced kinaesthetically as meaningful without it necessarily being easy for people to articulate just what that meaning is.

---

18 As a skill this may be related to the everyday awareness of the self the sociologist Erving Goffman (1969) explores.

19 Shaun Gallagher and Jonathan Cole, (1995) explore the relationship between body image (which they define as the product of visual, conceptual, social and emotional knowledge of the body) and body schema (defined as the generally more habitual motor responses including reflexes that maintain balance). They suggest there is 'intermodal communication' between visual and 'proprioceptive' awareness that allows visual perception to inform and coordinate movement. The anthropologist, Deidre Sklar (2008) also explores the implications for dancers of research findings that haptic schema and visual schema are not developed separately and thus are innately interrelated.

The shift in dance practice towards a focus on kinaesthetic structural patterning in addition to, or instead of, an emphasis on more visually orientated geometric forms, is itself part of the changing history of bodily experience that Susan Foster (2011) describes. This changing focus in dance practice is paralleled by renewed interest in the importance of kinaesthesia to the experience of watching dance (Montero, 2006; Carroll and Moore, 2008; Reason and Reynolds, 2010). For example, Matthew Reason and Dee Reynolds, in their study of audiences' responses, argue for the importance of the kinaesthetic experience to the audience's enjoyment of dance (Reason, and Reynolds, 2010). For Reason and Reynolds it is important that the kinaesthetic empathy felt by the audience is their own experience projected back onto the dance in response to the action they see, rather than a direct intuition of what the dancer feels. In this way they avoid the essentialism of expressionism and allow for the impact of culture on kinaesthetic responses.

The audience's own kinaesthetic experience thus informs their understanding of the plays on dynamic structures that are important to much current dance practice. Such felt responses to dance are shaped by the habitus and thus understood in relation to culture. Viewed in this way, the kinaesthetic sense informs the interpretation of dance. Yet the question remains as to how a kinaesthetic sense accounts for the experience of 'communion' between audience and dancer that seems important to some dancers. It is possible that this experience of some connection between dancer and audience is imagined in response to the intensity of sensory experience watching dance. However in order to account for the intersubjectively felt experience that is important to them, many dancers have turned towards phenomenology.[20] Here the writings of Maurice Merleau-Ponty have been particularly influential and it is to an aspect of his existential phenomenology that I will now turn.[21]

---

20 An important initial text was Maxine Sheets-Johnstone's *The Phenomenology of Dance* first published in 1966. Sheets-Johnstone has continued to develop an influential phenomenological approach to dance focusing particularly on the evolutionary dimensions that shape human experience as founded in 'animate form' (Sheets-Johnstone 2009, pp.136-148). The work of Sondra Horton-Fraleigh (1987 and 2004) has also been very influential. There is not space here to do justice to their considerable contributions to the field.

21 Note that while kinaesthesia is a focus of phenomenological accounts of dance, it is not adequately accounted for by Merleau-Ponty himself (Sheets-Johnstone 2011, p.209, Shusterman 2008). Richard Shusterman (2008) situates Merleau-Ponty's resistance to recognizing the importance of kinaesthesia within his larger philosophical project to oppose representational explanations of human perception and action.

Merleau-Ponty and the re-conceptualization of self-other-world

So far I have explored some of the philosophical problems in accounting for the experience of a sense of communion between dancer and audience that dancers value. Bound up with how dance is understood in this manner are questions regarding how dance can embody conscious intention or agency and the relevance of kinaesthetic experience to understanding dance. In contrast to the analytic philosophy of Best and McFee, the existential phenomenology of Merleau-Ponty offers a means of accounting for the reciprocity of the experience between self and other. This provides for a sense of mutual interaction between dancer and audience without relying on an underlying dualism. In his final, posthumously published writing, Merleau-Ponty seeks to avoid the 'bifurcation' of the objective body (in itself) and the phenomenal body (for itself)(Merleau-Ponty 1968, pp.136-137).[22] Rather, the 'double nature' (Merleau-Ponty 1968, p.143) of embodied experience that he analyses accords well with understanding an artform in which the dancer is both the source of what the audience sees and of her/his own actions.

By exploring the phenomenological experiences of seeing, being seen and touching both one's own and another's hands, Merleau-Ponty reconsiders the complexities of reciprocal interrelationships between self-other across the different senses. This leads him to challenge the very basic foundations upon which the notion of individual, bounded consciousness is derived. Instead, he describes intercorporeality as 'a presumptive domain of the visible and the tangible, which extends further than the things I touch and see at present' (Merleau-Ponty 1968, p.143). It is important to recognize that in his analysis of intercorporeal experience Merleau-Ponty is not describing a simple direct connection between people based on an essential nature; rather he explores the complexities of interrelationships upon which any sense of a shared world is based. The relationship between self-other, as with that between the sensing-sensed self is never fully transparent, but rather brought to life through a dynamic of 'incessant escaping' (Merleau-Ponty 1968, p.148).

Merleau-Ponty explores the facticity of the world-as-lived in terms of an elemental but non material 'flesh' that he describes as: 'the coiling over of the visible upon the seeing body, of the tangible upon the touching body'(Merleau-Ponty 1968, p.146). The reciprocal experiences of vision and touch become interwoven not only with each other but also with

---

22 In doing so Merleau-Ponty makes an important distinction between his work and that of Jean-Paul Sartre whose distinction between the body for itself and body for others may be argued to continue a Cartesian dualism (Dillon,1998).

speech.[23] In his philosophy, the reversibility of, and interrelations between, sensory experience are manifested in the relationship between thinking and feeling: 'one must see or feel in some way in order to think' (Merleau-Ponty 1968, p.146). Hence, choreographic and performative acts that structure the world as lived may have ramifications for how we understand, even speak about the world. Following Merleau-Ponty's concept of 'flesh', ideas may be understood not as abstract entities put into a dance but as part of it.

In performance, the dancer and audience become part of a shared world of meaning. Merleau-Ponty's analysis of intercorporeal experience accords with how dancers sense the 'energy' of a performance that is dependent on all those present. Relevant to the experience of the audience is that Merleau-Ponty observes a qualitative difference in perceiving the world if we share that experience with another person, arguing that: 'It is not *I* who sees, not *he* who sees, because an anonymous visibility inhabits both of us' (Merleau-Ponty 1968, p.142). These words suggest how dancing for an empty auditorium is qualitatively different to dancing for someone, which is again different to dancing for a group of people.

Embodiment in an ecological aesthetics

The complexities of the relationships between self-other-world, that Merleau-Ponty articulates, lie at the heart of the 'ecological' aesthetics proposed by the philosopher Paul Crowther (1993) that has been developed in relation to dance by Bonnie Rowell (2009). Crowther's approach to philosophical aesthetics is rooted in the tradition of modern philosophical aesthetics that dates back to Immanuel Kant. Yet Crowther also draws on the more recent phenomenology of Martin Heidegger and Merleau-Ponty to develop an aesthetic theory that foregrounds human embodiment. Drawing particularly on the work of Merleau-Ponty he argues that 'ontological reciprocity' (Crowther 1993, p.2) is the fundamental basis of human experience. On Crowther's terms, that artists are caught up in a web of reciprocal relationships ensures that their work reflect modes of 'embodied inherence in the world' (Crowther 1993, p.7) and thus extend further than their individual understanding. Further, to appreciate art is itself an embodied act. Crowther's analysis of the reciprocity of the subject-object relationship may be developed to consider the embodied acts of both performers and audience as dependent on an intercorporeal realm that is culturally enmeshed. Such understandings will never completely converge: as the discussion of Merleau-Ponty above emphasizes, embodied

---

23 See in particular the discussion in Merleau-Ponty (1968, pp.152-155) where he makes references to the linguist's 'ideal' system of language. It is likely Merleau-Ponty is here alluding to Saussure, whose work he lectured upon.

significance is not to be understood as ever fully transparent. However, by exploring how, in responding to an art work we become part of a shared ecology, Crowther emphasizes the importance of trying to understand what others value (Crowther 1993, pp.199-200).

While Crowther focuses primarily on the visual arts, Bonnie Rowell draws upon his aesthetics in relation to dance to suggest: 'We have a twofold embodiment in dance, in that the object that is the dancer embodies the choreographer's intentions, but the dancer is also an intentional subject' (Rowell 2009, p.147). The twofold embodiment Rowell identifies is complex, not least because of variations in the terms of the relationship between choreographic intention and the dancer's intention: one dancer may perform work in a choreographic style that demands they match the very specific requirements of a particular company; another may make work on themselves, or collectively explore individual movement habits; still another may work for a choreographer who draws on each dancer's particular traits as material that may still come to embody the choreographer's own ideas. Further, as Rowell points out, choreographers may also foreground questions as to how the dancers' embodiment is to be read (Rowell 2009, p.140).

Additional complexities arise in consideration of the reciprocal interrelationships during a performance. For works which are the product of a separate choreographic act, intertwined with the relationships between dancer and audience are traces of those between dancer and choreographer which the dancer brings to performance and which are further informed by his/her interactions with other dancers, both in rehearsal and performance. During performance, the audience interacts with the dancer(s), their understanding of the choreographer's intention and other members of the audience. The interplay of these varied reciprocal interrelationships is vital to those times when a piece 'works.' The dancers and audience are actively engaged in the event of the performance as brought into being by the choreographer. They contribute to a shared world as lived to bring forth interpretations that emanate from embodied experience.

Conclusion

The Wittgensteinian analytic philosophies of David Best and Graham McFee are valuable in highlighting the philosophical problems underlying some common assumptions regarding how dance embodies intention and meaning. However, in arguing against the relevance of kinaesthesia to the appreciation of dance, they set aside consideration of how the structuring of bodily experience, through both dancing and watching dance, is experienced as significant. Following McFee's adherence to Wittgenstein's maxim that 'meaning is what explanation of meaning explains' (Wittgenstein cited in

McFee 1992, p.114), an explanation of the meaning of much current dance practice might direct the audience's attention to such aspects as changes in the flow of energy through the body, the various plays between tension and release and subtle changes in bodily organization. While these provide for visible movement qualities, to make sense of them the audience may also draw on their own awareness of bodily experiences, understanding of which is informed by the habitus. In the terms of Best's philosophical approach, what he and McFee might address is the manner in which dance foregrounds how corporeal experience informs 'seeing as.'

I have suggested that Merleau-Ponty's later existential phenomenology offers an alternative means of accounting for a sense of connection between dancer and audience without lapsing into dualism. His philosophy seems worlds apart from that of Best and McFee, yet he is concerned with a similar problem: how can what are thought of as the 'inner' and 'outer' dimensions of human existence be related? Best and McFee's responses to this dilemma are to reveal the philosophical problems in the assumption that inner feeling can be inferred from outer behaviour. In relation to dance they then explore how it is interpreted or understood as an object of perception. In contrast, Merleau-Ponty seeks to challenge the notions that detach sense experience from the world. Following Merleau-Ponty's rethinking of the relationship between body as object to others and body as sensing others, audience and dancer may be conceived as implicated in a shared realm of meaning. This, I have argued is in accordance with what some dancers value in performance. Instead of a void between singularities, Merleau-Ponty suggests potential sites of 'intertwining' that form the fabric of shared cultural lives. He does not offer a recipe for direct experience of the other but rather articulates the complexities of intercorporeal experience in which there is interplay between conscious modalities.

Merleau-Ponty's analysis of the interrelationships between self-other-world, is developed upon in the ecological aesthetics of Paul Crowther. Applied to dance, this aesthetic theory provides for the centrality of embodiment to understanding dance as art. Through exploration of how dancers experience embodiment I have suggested how a continual play between the dancers' kinaesthetic awareness and their motor habits provides for a sense of embodied agency. That currently this sense of embodiment is important to many dancers, results in works which often foreground kinaesthetic experience. To appreciate works with such a focus does not require knowledge that is *only* available to the dancer. However, understanding of them, as with much other dance, may be enriched by sensitivity to embodied experience and recognition of the intercorporeal exchanges that inform live performance.

References

Adshead-Lansdale, Janet (ed.). *Dancing Texts: Intertextuality in Interpretation*, London: Dance Books, 1999.

Best, David. *Expression in Movement and the Arts*, London: Lepus Books, 1974.

Bourdieu, Pierre. *Distinction. A Social Critique of the Judgement of Taste*, trans, Richard Nice, London: Routledge, 1984.

Carr, D. Jane. *Embodiment, Appreciation and Dance: Issues in relation to an exploration of the experiences of London based, 'non-aligned' artists*, unpublished PhD thesis, London: University of Roehampton, 2008, available at: http://roehampton.openrepository.com/roehampton/bit stream/10142/ 47593/13/openning.pdf.

Carr, Jane. 'Issues of Control and Agency in Contemplating Cunningham's Legacy,' conference paper presented at The Society for Dance Research: Dance History: Politics, Practices and Perspectives, University of Roehampton, 13th March 2010, available at http://www.sdr-uk.org/ temp/docs/2010 _SDR_dance_history_ symposium_proceedings.pdf.

Carroll, Noël and Margaret Moore. 'Feeling Movement: Music and Dance,' *Revue internationale de Philosophie*, 2008, pp.413-435.

Crowther, Paul. *Art and Embodiment*, Oxford: Clarendon Press, 1993.

Csordas, Thomas (ed.). *Embodiment and Experience*, Cambridge: Cambridge University Press, 1994.

Dillon, Martin C. 'Sartre's Phenomenal Body and Merleau- Ponty's Critique,' in Stewart, Jon (ed.), *The Debate Between Sartre and Merleau-Ponty*, Evanston: Northwestern University Press, 1998.

Duncan, Isadora. (1902 or 1903) 'The Dance of the Future,' in Copeland, Roger and Marshall Cohen (eds.), *What is Dance? Readings in Theory and Criticism*, Oxford: Oxford University Press, 1983, pp.262-264.

Foster, Susan (ed.). *Corporealities: Dancing Knowledge, Culture and Power*, London: Routledge, 1996.

Foster, Susan. *Choreographing Empathy: Kinesthesia in Performance*, London: Routledge, 2011.

Freeman, Anthony. 'What is it Like to be Conscious?' in *Consciousness: A Guide to the Debates*, Santa Barbara: ABC-CLIO, 2003, pp.219-238.

Gallagher, Shaun and Jonathan Cole. 'Body Image and Body Schema in a Deafferented Subject', in Welton, Donn (ed.), *Body and Flesh: A Philosophical Reader*, Oxford: Blackwell, 1998, pp.131-148.

Gallese, Vittorio. 'The "Shared Manifold" Hypothesis. From Mirror Neurons to Empathy', *Journal of Consciousness Studies* 8: 5-7, 2001, pp.33-50.

Giddens, Anthony. 'Structuration Theory: Past, Present and Future' in Bryant, Christopher G.A. and David Jary (eds.), *Giddens' Theory of Structuration: A Critical Appreciation*, New York: Routledge, 1991, pp.201-221.

Goffman, Erving. *The Presentation of Self in Everyday Life*, London: Penguin, 1969 [1956].

Green, Diana. *Choreographing From Within: Developing the Habit of Inquiry as An Artist*, Champaign: Human Kinetics, 2010.

Horton-Fraleigh, Sondra. *Dance and the Lived Body*, Pittsburgh: University of Pittsburgh Press, 1987.

Horton-Fraleigh, Sondra. *Dancing Identity: Metaphysics in Motion*, Pittsburgh: University of Pittsburgh Press, 2004.

Laban, Rudolf and F. C. Lawrence. *Effort*. London: Macdonald and Evans, 1974 [1947].

Martin, John. 'Metakinesis' in Copeland, Roger and Marshall Cohen (eds.), *What is Dance? Readings in Theory and Criticism*, Oxford: Oxford University Press. 1983 [1933], pp.23-25.

Martin John. 'Dance as a Means of Communication,' in Copeland, Roger and Marshall Cohen (eds.), *What is Dance? Readings in Theory and Criticism*, Oxford: Oxford University Press. 1983 [1946], pp.2-23.

McFee, Graham. *Understanding Dance*, London: Routledge, 1992.

McFee, Graham. *The Philosophical Aesthetics of Dance: Identity, Performance and Understanding*, Alton: Dance Books, 2011.

Merleau-Ponty, Maurice. *The Visible and The Invisible*, Evanston: Northwestern University Press, 1968.

Montero, Barbara. 'Proprioception as an Aesthetic Sense,' *The Journal of Aesthetics and Art Criticism*, 2006, 64:2, pp.231-242.

Noland, Carrie. *Agency and Embodiment. Performing Gestures/Producing Culture*, London: Harvard University Press, 2009.

O' Regan, J. Kevin and Alva Noë. 'A Sensorimotor Account of Vision and Visual Consciousness', *Journal of Behavioral and Brain Sciences*, 2001, 24:5, pp.939-1031.

Pakes, Anna. 'Dance's Body-Mind Problem', *Dance Research*, 2006, 14:2, pp.87-104.

Polanyi, Michael. *Personal Knowledge: Towards a Post-Critical Philosophy*, London: Routledge, 1997 [1962].

Polhemus, Ted. 'Dance, Gender and Culture,' in Carter, Alexandra (ed.), *The Routledge Dance Studies Reader*, New York: Routledge, 1998, pp.171-179.

Reason, Matthew and Dee Reynolds. 'Kinesthesia, Empathy, and Related Pleasures: An Inquiry into Audience Experiences of Watching Dance', *Dance Research Journal*, 2010, 42:2, pp.49-75.

Rowell, Bonnie. 'Dance Analysis in a Postmodern Age: Integrating Theory and Practice', in Butterworth, Jo and Liesbeth Wildschut (eds.), *Contemporary Choreography: A Critical Reader*, London: Routledge, 2009, pp.136-151.

Sheets-Johnstone, Maxine. *The Phenomenology of Dance*, London: Dance Books, 1979 [1966].

Sheets-Johnstone, Maxine. *The Corporeal Turn: An Interdisciplinary Reader*, Exeter: Imprint Academic, 2009.

Sheets-Johnstone, Maxine. *The Primacy of Movement*, expanded 2nd edition, Philadelphia: John Benjamins, 2011.

Shilling, Chris and Philip A. Mellor. 'Embodiment, Structuration Theory and Modernity: Mind/Body Dualism and the Repression of Sensuality', *Body and Society*, 1996, 2:4, pp.1-16.

Shusterman, Richard. 'The Silent Limping Body of Philosophy: Somatic Attention Deficit in Merleau-Ponty', in *Body Consciousness: A Philosophy of Mindfulness and Somaesthetics*, Cambridge: Cambridge University Press, 2008.

Sklar, Deidre. 'Remembering Kinaesthesia' in Noland, Carrie and Sally Ann Ness (eds.), *Migrations of Gesture*, Minneapolis: University of Minnesota Press, 2008, pp.85-112.

Smith-Autard, Jacqueline M. 'Expression and Form in the Art of Dance,' Keynote paper, Dance and The Child International, Sixth Triennial International Conference, Macquarie University, 1994.

Smith-Autard, Jacqueline M. *Dance Composition*, 5th edition, London: A&C Black, 2004.

Solomon, Robert C. 'Conclusion: What Now for Continental Philosophy?' in Solomon, Robert C. and David Sherman (eds.), *The Blackwell Guide to Continental Philosophy*, Oxford: Blackwell, 2003, pp.338-340.

Wimsatt, William K. Jr., and Monroe C. Beardsley. 'The intentional Fallacy,' in Margolis, Joseph (ed.), *Philosophy Looks at the Arts: Contemporary Readings in Aesthetics*, revised edition, Philadelphia: Temple University Press, 1978 [1954], pp.293-306.

Wittgenstein, Ludwig. *Philosophical Investigations*, 2nd edition, trans. G. E. M. Anscombe, Oxford: Blackwell, 1968 [1953].

Part II

Dance Works and their Performances

4. The plausibility of a platonist ontology of dance

Anna Pakes

Introduction

The ontology of dance addresses, amongst other issues, the puzzle of what a dance work is. That puzzle arises because, on the one hand, dances materialize in the actuality of the body moving on stage: they seem to depend on the body and to be made up of its movements. On the other hand, dance performances are (often) not simply isolated events: if I go to watch the Royal Ballet in Bronislava Nijinska's *Les Noces*[1] on three nights in the same week, I don't (typically) think that I have seen three different dances, but rather three performances of the same work.[2] So, dances are *embodied* in physical events, and are (or seem to be) also capable of *multiple* instantiation: they can be performed again and again, by different bodies, in different spaces, or performed simultaneously by different people in various locations. The ontology of dance works tries to explain what dance works must be to make this possible, examining what it is that performances are performances *of*.

Platonism offers one possible solution to the puzzle of the dance work.[3] A model for how that solution might be developed is presented by recent philosophy of music defending a platonist ontology of musical works (see, particularly, Kivy 1997 and Dodd 2007).[4] Such defence engages

---

1 First performed in Paris in 1923, with music by Igor Stravinsky and scenography by Natalia Goncharova, and revived by the Royal Ballet in 1966, 2001 and 2004 (Oberzaucher-Schüller 2013; see also http://www.rohcollections.org.uk).

2 The problem of identity in dance concerns *both* how three consecutive performances by the same company can be performances of the same work, *and* (the more complex issue of) what criteria might identify performances at different historical moments, by different companies, as being *of* the same work. Although these issues impinge on the ontology of dance works, I cannot consider them in detail here. Graham McFee (1992, 1994, and 2011) and Aaron Meskin (1999) consider them at greater length, as does Renée Conroy's essay in this volume.

3 Nelson Goodman's nominalism offers an alternative view (Goodman 1976), as does McFee's defence of a non-platonistic theory of dance works as types (McFee 1999, 2004 and 2011).

4 Although it derives from Plato's theory of forms, contemporary platonism in metaphysics neither defends Plato's views nor makes explicit reference to its historical origins. The orthographic convention of not capitalizing the term 'platonism' marks the contrast with

with what are, or appear to be, the deeply counter-intuitive consequences of the platonist view. In particular, from the categorization of musical works as eternally existing types, it follows that they are discovered rather than created by their composers, and that works are causally inert and unchanging. These implications seem to rub hard against the grain of musical practice and discourse. Typically, musical composition is treated as a process which brings new works into existence, thus creating things which did not exist before and with which we can interact in various ways. Works are typically considered capable of being heard in performance, for example, re-orchestrated or revised; they are said to influence other compositions, cause changes in musical taste or even in some cases provoke uproar and riot. None of these kinds of interaction seems logically possible if musical works are causally inert.

Platonism appears attractive, however, to the extent that it avoids the metaphysical commitments of certain other ontological positions, obeying the principle of ontological parsimony.[5] By contrast, for example, the contextualist ontology of Jerrold Levinson, makes historical facts about a work's genesis essential to what it is, and in the process formulates what appears to be a new ontological category (the 'indicated type') to accommodate this peculiarity. For its defenders, platonist ontology has the advantage, over views like Levinson's, of assigning musical works to an already familiar (albeit still controversial) ontological category into which other objects – words and natural kinds, for example – also fall. Thus, if we can accept types as '*bona fide* citizens of our ontology' (Dodd 2007, p.42), we can plausibly argue that musical works are types, provided the apparently counter-intuitive consequences can be explained away.

This essay explores whether and how one might argue the case for a platonist ontology of dance works. Although there has been some philosophical discussion of what dance works are, the literature is by no means as extensive, nor the debate as developed, as in philosophy of music.[6] Yet recent writing on the ontology of musical works is suggestive

---

the use of the term to refer to Plato's views or those of his followers. See Balaguer (2009)

5 The notion that entities should not be multiplied beyond necessity, commonly known as Occam's Razor, is deeply embedded in analytic philosophical thinking: it implies that, faced with a choice between two competing theories which are in other respects equally plausible, it is rational to prefer the one which implies the smallest ontology, or which minimizes ontological commitment. Accordingly, if an ontology of dance works is to be consistent with the principle of ontological parsimony, the fewer things or sorts of things it claims exist, the better. For further discussion of the principle of parsimony, see Thomasson (1999), pp.137-145.

6 On the nature of dances, see, for example, Sparshott (1995, pp.397-419) and McFee (1992 and 2011). The literature on music is too extensive to survey comprehensively within the scope of this essay, let alone a footnote, but includes seminal publications such

of how a platonist account of dance works might proceed, and it is part of the purpose of this essay to develop the characterization of dance works as eternal types. I will also address some key objections to the platonist view similarly suggested by the literature on musical works. Problems posed for platonism by the nature of dance as an art form distinct from music will also be considered. Ultimately, I will argue that platonism is less plausible in the context of dance ontology than that of music, and identify why. My broader agenda, though, includes a sketch of the value of detailed consideration of dance work ontology – the kind of analysis enabled by contemplating platonist ontologies of music – even though their dance parallel proves problematic in a variety of ways.

Platonism and the puzzle of the dance work

In order to assess the plausibility of platonism in the dance context, we first need to get clearer about what claims a platonist ontology of dance would make. In general terms, metaphysical platonism can be characterized as upholding the existence of abstract objects (Balaguer 2009); so, in our context, platonism is the view that dances are abstract objects (in some sense) and that they exist. To claim that dances are abstract is to recognize that they are in themselves neither physical nor mental entities. Performances happen in space and time, and consist of physical beings – dancers – doing physical things – movement or action. But however they may be related to performances, dances as such don't have concrete, spatio-temporal existence. It makes no sense to ask where *Swan Lake* is, unless we are talking about a particular performance thereof. [7] And thieves cannot make off with Nijinska's *Les Noces* in the way they might steal Leonardo Da Vinci's *Mona Lisa* (catastrophic lapses in museum security permitting).[8]

One might, of course, steal the notated score of one of these dances: but the disappearance of a copy of the score, even if it is the only one extant, does not entail the disappearance of the work, as it does in the case of the painting; if there is still the possibility of the work being performed (perhaps because it can be remembered, step-by-step, by one or more dancers), then the dance would not be lost. Similarly, making off with a video record of a

---

as Goehr (2007 [1992]), Levinson (2011 [1991]), Kivy (1993), Davies, S. (2004), Dodd (2007) and Davies D. (2011), as well as numerous journal articles by diverse authors. For an overview, see Kania (2012, section 2).

7 The first ballet of this title, choreographed to Pyotr Ilych Tchaikovsky's score by Julius Reisinger, premièred in 1877. Many contemporary productions claim to derive from the 1895 version choreographed by Marius Petipa and Lev Ivanov. See Cohen (1982, pp. 3-15) and Demidov and Fanger (2013).

8 This hypothetical example derives from a thought experiment developed in Kivy (2002, p.202).

dance is not the same as making off with the work as such. Like the notation, this is one representation of the dance, not the dance itself. Dance works do not exist in spatio-temporal actuality, and so cannot be the objects of actions like theft.[9] But nor are they simply ideas in the minds of individuals, for if they were, they would not exist as publicly accessible, shareable things. We do, after all, debate the features and significance of a ballet like *Swan Lake*. It is difficult to see how this could be possible if that dance existed only within an individual's thought process: any 'debate' would just be a clash of subjective perspectives, with nothing objective or independent to appeal to in reconciling differences. Such an object is provided in a platonist ontology, which posits dances as abstract existents, that existence considered (at least relatively) independent of human thought processes – or at least such would be the claim of a platonist ontology of dance.

Platonism in the ontology of the performing arts has an intuitive plausibility when it is characterized in this very general way. Indeed, the account of the puzzle of the dance work with which this essay began (and which seems, to me at least, eminently plausible) already makes some platonist assumptions: notably, that there exists some thing (a dance), which is not in itself material, but which can be instanced in performance. It is hard to see how we could do without some conception of dance or choreographic works in everyday and scholarly discourse and practice. There are often 'runs' of performances of the same dance over a number of nights, or tours of a work to different locations. People debate the authenticity of various performances or productions of *Swan Lake*, say. And when discussing the development of a choreographer like Jérôme Bel, it makes sense to explore his trajectory work-by-work rather than performance-by-performance.[10] Platonism thus offers a way to mark the distinction between performances and works, recognizing that there is some sort of object at stake in the production and reception of dance, music and theatre, beyond the immediacy and physical presence of performances.

Although it is not the only option, then, platonism is one way to explain what performances are performances *of*, one way to identify what we mean

9 That is, dance works cannot be the object of physical actions like theft, as distinct from forgery or plagiarism. There are plenty of examples of choreographic material being 'stolen' in the sense of being used and not attributed to the choreographer. Witness, for example, the recent allegations against Beyoncé who used choreography by Anne Teresa de Keersmaeker in the video for the song *Countdown* (Trueman 2011). However one judges the ethics of Beyoncé's action, the action itself is not of the same order as putting a painting under one's arm and walking out of the Louvre.

10 See, for example, Ramsay Burt's entry on Bel in Bremser and Sanders (2011), which (like the other chapters) charts the evolution of the selected choreographer's dances, providing a list of works as well as a bibliography at the end.

when we call different performances instances of, say, *Swan Lake*, *Les Noces*, or *The Show Must Go On*.[11] Performances instance works, which are abstract objects that exist independently of any particular instantiation. In this general sense, then, platonism seems hardly contentious, although some might initially balk at the idea that dances are not physical, given the ubiquity of the notion that dance is an art of the body, and *the* physical art form *par excellence*. But this very general characterization of platonist ontology is only a beginning and we need to make it more specific if we are to grasp its implications. If dances are abstract objects, what kinds of abstract objects are they? After all, there are many different sorts of things which could qualify as abstract objects: numbers, mathematical theorems, properties, relations, meanings of sentences, fictional characters and musical works, for example. Although these are all (arguably) abstract entities, there seem to be significant differences between them, suggesting that the term 'abstract objects' generalizes over a range of distinct ontological categories.

Eternal existence and creatability

Insofar as the ontology of dance has been discussed at all in the philosophical literature, the dance work is most commonly conceived as a type, of which there can be many possible performance tokens (see, for example, Margolis 1959; McFee 1992, 1994, 1999, 2004 and 2011; Meskin 1999). But the idea of a 'type' might be cashed out in a number of ways. The platonist conception maintains that types are abstract objects which do not belong to the spatio-temporal world, and so must be causally inert, unchanging and either timeless or *eternally* existent things. Julian Dodd, for example, sees musical works as pure types, that is, as entities which are 'abstract, unstructured, and both modally and temporally inflexible (i.e. incapable of having properties other than those they actually have, and incapable of change in their intrinsic properties over time)' (2007, p.4). It is worth emphasizing here the nature of types is contested, and Dodd certainly does not articulate a consensus view. As already suggested, different conceptions of types are developed in, for example, Jerrold Levinson's account of musical works as indicated types (Levinson 1980), and Graham McFee's discussions of dance identity (McFee 1992, pp.88-111; 1994; 1999; 2004; 2011, to which an appendix, pp.289-306, explicitly takes issue with Dodd's characterization of types). Even Peter Kivy (who also defends a platonist ontology of music) accepts that types are not necessarily viewed platonistically (Kivy 1983, p.109). Nonetheless, when they are, it seems

---

11   Choreographed by Jérôme Bel, and first performed in Paris in 2001. A filmed performance (dir. Aldo Lee and recorded at the Teatro Nacional San Joao in Porto, Portugal) was published by the Association R.B. Jérôme Bel also in 2001.

they must have the characteristics Dodd identifies. And musical works, according to a platonist type ontology, exist eternally.

A consequence, then, is that musical works cannot therefore be created by their composers – because they pre-exist acts of composition, they can only be discovered. This might immediately make us question the plausibility of a platonist ontology, given the apparent centrality within art practice of the idea that artists *make something*. According to Levinson, this is 'one of the most firmly entrenched of our beliefs concerning art [that] art is creative in the strict sense, that it is a godlike activity in which the artist brings into being what did not exist beforehand' (Levinson 2011, p.66). But this belief is not shared by all, indeed Levinson's particular articulation of it seems bound up with Romantic conceptions of the artist as genius, not universally accepted nor historically generalizable. For Kivy, the idea of composers discovering or inventing their works is not nearly as counter-intuitive as it may initially appear, indeed it better fits some forms of musical practice than Levinson's 'godlike activity'. Nor does thinking of composers' work in this way necessarily imply that their works or activities are therefore less valuable. No one doubts the value of work by Isaac Newton or Albert Einstein though they discovered, rather than creating, respectively gravity and the theory of relativity. Musical 'creation' is similar to scientific discovery, involving comparable creative intelligence and imagination, without implying that the product emerges *ex nihilo*. The activity of composition is still (or can still be) creative in the sense of 'revealing [...] what has always been there, but which no one has yet had the genius and the creative imagination to see' (Kivy 1993, p.43).

Perhaps also the idea that dances are discovered rather than created is not as implausible as it might intuitively appear, at least not radically at odds with the phenomenology of 'creative' choreographic processes. When making a dance, a choreographer typically gathers a group of dancers together in a studio and either asks the dancers to try out patterns of movement the choreographer has sketched in advance ('discovered' on her own body in advance of the rehearsal), or asks them to improvise around some premise or preconceived questions about a particular theme, movement practice or artistic problem. The movement generated is experienced, observed and evaluated, some elements selected for elaboration and refinement, others rejected or set aside. Either the choreographer, or the choreographer in collaboration with the dancers, edits the material. And with the gradual accumulation of phrases of movement – and effective transitions between distinct passages being developed – the work begins to take shape until it reaches a point where it appears complete and/or viable as a performable entity. In many ways, this feels more like a process of discovery than it does Levinson's 'godlike activity which the artist brings into being something which did not exist beforehand'. In a sense, the materials – and the potential to structure them in the way the work ultimately does – are all already there in the choreographer's and dancers' movement resources, which may include their physical training, actional predispositions and ingrained physical habits, as well as or instead of a pre-existing codified movement vocabulary. And we do not automatically view choreographic activity as less creative because it involves uncovering and exploiting some movement possibilities within a given range.

Two issues are raised here. One is whether, in making a work a choreographer fashions something that is more than the sum of its parts. A recent book by Peter Lamarque (2010) examines this issue (though without detailed consideration of dance), exploring whether the 'composition' of pre-existing materials, when it reaches a state of relative completion, makes any substantive change in or to those materials and/or the world (see particularly Chapter 2, pp.33-55). Because this issue impinges on a broader debate within philosophy about material constitution, and the distinction between constitution and identity, I have insufficient space to consider it here.[12] However, I will examine the second issue raised by the creatability debate, namely whether or not the model of choreographic creation as 'discovery' – which seems to fit the typical pattern of contemporary processes – is plausible through a range of dance practices. Certainly it seems plausible in the context of the deflationary account of choreographic 'creation' underpinning much postmodern dance experiment.[13] But what, for example, are we to make of cases where a dance artist (Martha Graham, say, or José Limón) have seemingly created not just a work or series of works but an idiosyncratic movement language or idiom, out of which their works are then constructed? In such cases, the choreographers do not appear (at least at the beginning of their careers) to be fashioning dances out of pre-existing materials – they are also creating the movement palette on which they draw in particular dances.

One response here would be to argue that the Graham or Limón movement idioms are themselves 'discoveries' of ways of moving from within a given

---

12 As Lamarque's (2010) discussion makes clear, this broader debate considers a range of questions relevant to the ontology of art: a statue is formed from a lump of clay, but is the clay identical with the statue, or is it non-identical but constitutive of it? What is the nature of constitution? For an overview of these issues and debates, see also Wasserman (2009).

13 See, for example, Banes (1987). Also relevant here is the response to Beardsley (1982) in Carroll and Banes (1982), which argues that 'task' dances like Yvonne Rainer's (1964) *Room Service* reveal the flaws in Beardsley's characterization of dance as a superfluity of expressiveness because they constitute dances composed of unembellished ordinary actions. This debate is examined in more detail by Davies (2004, p.17) and (2011, pp.10-17), and is discussed briefly in Henrietta Bannerman's essay in the present volume.

possible range. This range includes existing codified dance lexicons but also the resources of human movement from other non-dance contexts. Thus Graham's movement 'language' is developed in reaction to ballet and in relation to fundamental structures of human movement, like the pattern of breathing which grounds the signature Graham movement of contraction-and-release (Bannerman 2010). On this view, perhaps, Graham discovers rather than creates a choreographic idiom, because she works with existing movements and structures.

A model for how such an argument might go is presented by Dodd (2007), as he responds to criticism from Robert Howell (2002) that he misrepresents the nature of the musical work type. Howell contends that, alongside eternally existent, platonistically conceived types, there are types that are brought into existence by human practices: musical works offer one example, words another. Word-types only come to exist 'when some community establishes a practice of producing (and recognizing) concrete sound and visual items (noises, marks on rocks, and so on) that instantiate the relevant pattern and so have the property that underlies it' (Howell 2002, p.118). These types are created – or brought into existence – by the practices concerned. Dodd disagrees, arguing that one can recognize the contribution of the linguistic community and its practice without compromising the eternal existence of types: '[f]or the Platonist [sic], human practices *are* crucial to understanding language-use, but their function is not that of bringing word-types into existence; it is that of bringing word-types into languages' (Dodd 2007, p.78). One might similarly argue that Martha Graham's innovation is to bring movement types into a dance technique or vocabulary. She does not create the pelvic contraction or the dart pose (for example), but codifies their use.[14] In a way this seems more plausible even than the verbal language case that Howell and Dodd explore, given that the range of possible elements of a dance technique is grounded in the physical capacities of the human body. Some movements are physically possible, others not; choreographers cannot create previously impossible movement, they can only manipulate within certain biologically and physiologically given parameters. There remains, of course, the difficulty of arguing for the eternal existence of dance works as types if they are dependent on the existence of the human body. Since the body is an entity with a history as well as a biology, it can hardly be said to exist eternally (either ontogenetically or phylogenetically). I begin to address this problem below.

---

14 For a description and analysis of Martha Graham's movement resources, see Bannerman (1998). Editor's note: Bannerman's essay in this volume also includes brief comment on the 'dart' pose.

The temporality of instancing

There is, then, another difficulty for platonism which becomes apparent if we elaborate a little further the implication that works as types exist eternally. If they are eternal existents, doesn't this imply that they can always have had instances or tokens? It seems to suggest that even if Graham's *Lamentation*[15] happened not to be tokened until 1930, say, there was nonetheless the possibility that it might have been because the work has always existed, even prior to Graham's 'discovery' of it. The implication is that, even before Graham developed her new movement idiom, indeed her vision of the nature of dance and what it could express, *Lamentation* might have been instanced. But the work seems to depend on that idiom and that vision. Like other movement idioms and codified lexicons, the Graham style is an historical artefact. How can dance works that depend on historical artefacts be eternal? It does not appear plausible to suggest that the movement structure of *Swan Lake* – to give another example – could have been instanced in the paleolithic era, since the vocabulary of classical ballet (more specifically of late-nineteenth century Russian ballet) had not yet been developed, and Marius Petipa's and Lev Ivanov's work is premised upon that vocabulary. Even where the movement resources are not specialized dance vocabularies, there is a problem here. It is difficult to see how the movement structure which is (or is associated with) Steve Paxton's *Satisfyin' Lover*,[16] composed of so-called 'ordinary' walking, could have been instanced several centuries before, when 'ordinary' human comportment (let alone its significance in the theatrical context) must have been very different to that of 1960s America.[17]

But it may be that this gets the platonist view wrong, and that a type's eternal existence does not imply that it can always have had instances. Indeed Dodd claims that Levinson (1980) makes this mistake with regard to the platonist account of musical works. For Dodd, the identity of musical works as types is not fixed by the possibility of having instances, but by the conditions a token must meet in order to be a token of that type. Why claim that a type which cannot be instantiated at a particular moment does not

---

15 First performed in 1930 in New York City by Graham herself. See Jowitt (2012), the BBC documentary *Dancemakers, Martha Graham* (London: BBC, 1992) and the commercially distributed VHS, *Martha Graham Dance Company* (New York: Nonesuch, 1998).

16 First performed in 1967 at the University of Utah. See Banes (1987, pp.60-61), in which the score of the work is also reprinted (pp.71-74).

17 This problem also extends forwards to the possibility of present-day and future instantiations of dances whose movement idioms and styles have been lost. There is insufficient space to develop the discussion of this phenomenon here, though it is tackled in my (forthcoming) monograph. Geraldine Morris's essay in this volume addresses related questions.

itself exist at that moment? The type *child born in 2050* cannot have tokens in 2013, but according to Dodd it still exists – it's just impossible for it to be instanced until 37 years later. Consider the difference between the putative type *round square* and the type *child born in 2050*. One can argue for the existence of the latter in a way one cannot for the former. Even if the type *child born in 2050* has no tokens, and cannot have had any tokens to date, the condition that an object would have to meet to be a token of that type is clear. It is not evident, meanwhile, that there are – or, indeed, that there could ever be – conditions capable of being fulfilled for something to qualify as a round square (Dodd 2007, p.65). And the *Swan Lake* case is more like the future child than the round square. Thus, on the platonist view there is a condition a performance would have to meet to be a token of the *Swan Lake* type in the paleolithic era (just as there is in 1895 and 2013), before the vocabulary of Russian ballet classicism was even a twinkle in some unsuspecting caveman's eye.

These remain contentious arguments, and their residual counter-intuitive flavour has pushed many philosophers of music towards preferring a contextualist alternative to musical platonism.[18] Levinson (1980) argues that musical works are types, tokened in performance, but not pure sound-structures because they have historical, intentional and aesthetic properties that mere sound structures do not. The flaws in the platonist view are for him amply demonstrated via thought experiments in which the same sound structure is instanced in work by different composers at different historical moments. Whereas the platonist would be forced to argue that the different composers in these cases 'discover' the same work – the sound structures being identical – Levinson maintains that contextual facts about the compositions' genesis are essential to their being. Thus, two composers working in different contexts to produce identical sounds structures have nonetheless composed two different musical works, with different aesthetic and artistic properties:

A work identical in sound structure with Schoenberg's *Pierrot Lunaire* (1912), but composed by Richard Strauss in 1897 would be aesthetically different from Schoenberg's work. Call it 'Pierrot Lunaire*'. As a Straussian work, *Pierrot Lunaire** would follow hard upon Brahms's *German Requiem*, would be contemporaneous with Debussy's *Nocturnes*, and would be taken as the next step in Strauss's development after *Also Sprach Zarathustra*. As such, it would be more *bizarre*, more *upsetting*, more *anguished*, more *eerie* even than Schoenberg's work, since perceived against a musical tradition, a field of current styles, and an *oeuvre* with respect to which the musical

18 As well as Levinson's seminal article (1980), see, for example, Howell (2002) and Davies (2001).

characteristics of the sound structure involved in *Pierrot Lunaire* appear doubly extreme. (Levinson 1980, p.11.)

That the works have different properties indicates – via Leibniz's Law – that they are not the same, despite the identity of sound structure.

Analogous thought experiments can be developed in the dance context. A work identical in movement structure (or maybe costumed movement-structure) to Graham's *Lamentation* but composed in 1895 would be more strikingly unusual in its graphic simplicity, more shocking in its manipulation of the body, and particularly its groundedness and motivation of the movement from the pelvis. Indeed, in the late nineteenth century, this dance might have been capable of being read only as a grotesque, the soloist taking on the veneer of an anguished Carabosse,[19] power curbed by her imprisonment in a fabric tube. More plausibly, perhaps, a university dance student might, in unhappy but complete ignorance of post-modern dance history, hit upon the same movement structure as evident in Paxton's *Satisfyin' Lover*: a series of walks by groups of dancers from stage right to stage left, interrupted by pauses in which the dancers stand or sit at given intervals (Banes 1987, pp.60, 71-74). In the student's case, his dance lacks the originality of Paxton's and looks like a rather tired attempt to revalidate the pedestrian, rather than a fresh look at movement possibility and a celebration of the unifying force of the everyday. The properties of the student's hypothetical work seem to change again if he makes this dance self-consciously, in *homage* to Paxton and the postmoderns, exploring how the meaning of the act of walking has changed in the light of post-Judson dance history. The platonist, meanwhile, seems committed to arguing that the same work is produced in all three cases because the movement structure is identical. And yet these dances have quite different meanings, linked to their various derivations.

Levinson's charges are by no means unanswerable, and two lines of response are suggested by Kivy. One is that there is no distinction in Levinson's analysis of his thought experiments between properties which are essential and those which are accidental. This same problem has bedevilled 'so magisterial a metaphysical principle' as Leibniz's law, against which Levinson seems to assume that there is no appeal (Kivy 1993, p.60). Yet, Kivy claims, our ordinary language and intuitions do make such a distinction: and if the properties which distinguish the two superficially indiscernible works are merely accidental, then the platonist view has not been dismissed. The crux then becomes whether the semantic content or

---

19 The evil fairy in Marius Petipa's (1890) *The Sleeping Beauty*, 1890: see Wiley (1985) and Scholl (2004).

'aboutness' of dances, as historically and artistically specific interventions, is essential to what they are. Kivy's second objection is methodological, pointing out the wild impossibility of Levinson's examples which 'stretch our intuitions to the breaking point', formed as those intuitions are 'by the perfectly ordinary, eminently possible' (Kivy 1993, p.62). To expect to be able to draw sound conclusions from our intuitive responses to such cases is unreasonable, Kivy claims. Interestingly, perhaps, though the example of the 1895 *Lamentation* seems as implausible as Levinson's hypothetical cases, the student (unwittingly or wittingly) aping Paxton does not. But what is clear is that intuitions about such thought experiments can pull both ways, and this might make us question whether they provide a sound basis for developing either the platonist or anti-platonist view.[20]

Moreover, one of the things at issue in the above discussion is whether there is an equivalent in dance to the pure sound-structures which appear pivotal in platonist ontology of music. In attempting to develop a platonist ontology of dance, we might be tempted to identify dances with movement structures, discovered in the choreographic process and instanced in performance. So if musical works are individuated according to how they sound, are dances then individuated by how they look? That doesn't seem quite right, since the relation between music or sound-score is arguably also essential to what dance works are: without Tchaikovsky's music, the movement structure typical of *Swan Lake* does not appear in the same way; if we watched Petipa and Ivanov's choreography against the acoustic backdrop of a Radiohead album, for example, I doubt that we would be inclined to call this the same dance work.[21] The problem, then, is that the multi-dimensionality – and multi-sensory appeal – of dance as an art form seems crucial to the nature and meaning of dance works, yet denied as soon as one privileges the visual over the aural. And yet characterizing dances as movement-with-sound structures seems somewhat arbitrary: why not movement-with-sound-with-lighting or movement-with-sound-with-lighting-with costume structures? And so on. There may not be sufficient consensus around the centrality of particular elements across dance genres to be able to say what kinds of intrinsic properties dance works generally have. The lighting might change for some works (Petipa's *Sleeping Beauty*) without loss of meaning or work

---

20 On the role of intuitions in philosophy, see Pust (2000). The reliance of some types of philosophical argument on appeals to intuition has increasingly come under scrutiny with the development of experimental philosophy: see Knobe and Nicholas (eds.)(2008).

21 Of course, there is also the issue of how far it is possible to see the Petipa and Ivanov choreography in performance, given the lack of visual records of the original production and the problem of determining just how much survives in the contemporary performance of the ballet. Again, this pertains to the philosophical problem of dance identity, which there is insufficient space to consider properly here, though it is examined in Renée Conroy's essay in this volume and in my (forthcoming) monograph.

identity, yet be essential to others (Russell Maliphant's *Two*[22]). This is an issue explored some time ago by Adina Armelagos and Mary Sirridge (1978), and perhaps accounts for the still contested status of notation as a way of articulating the essentials of a dance.[23] Although there is also debate about musical notation – and the idea of works as sound-structures suits some musical practices better than others – that idea at least makes more general sense than the notion that dances are simply movement structures, the latter not being capable of isolation from their contexts in quite the same way.[24]

The platonist might, at this point, adjust her view to a claim that dances are *action*-structures rather than movement-structures. But, as I shall argue below, however we construe the idea of 'action-structure', it does not sit comfortably with a platonist metaphysics. Action, as opposed to mere movement, is partly constituted by its intentional and enabling contexts, and yet platonism typically construes abstract objects as 'independent of intelligent agents and their language, thought and practices' (Linnebo 2011). They would have to be in order to be eternal existents. Thus if dance is appropriately conceived as action, it is difficult to see how its works could be categorized as eternal types.

Movement, action and independence

The importance of conceiving of dance as action rather than as 'pure' movement has been well rehearsed by McFee (1992) and David Carr (1987). Briefly, it is not the presence of particular movements or types of movements in a dance work which make it dance, but rather intentional and contextual factors concerning the description under which the action is performed and the frame within which it is placed. Just because Daniel Larrieu's dance *Waterproof* looks (at least in some sections) like synchronized swimming, does not make it such rather than dance; performed in a swimming pool, it is nonetheless created as contemporary choreography, by a dance artist and company, within the context of a commission from a dance institution.[25]

---

22 First performed in London in 1999, by Dana Fouras, and restaged with Sylvie Guillem in Dance Umbrella, 2005. This latter production also exists in film version, broadcast as part of 4Dance: Rise and Fall on the UK's Channel 4 in December 2010.

23 McFee (2011) considers in detail the question of whether, and under what conditions, notation can be held to articulate the essential properties of a dance.

24 Meskin (1999) argues that dance works and productions are 'indicated action-sound-lighting-costume-setting type sequences' (p.47), but because he follows Levinson in treating works as indicated types, rejecting the platonist view, his claims about the importance of these various contextual elements do not contradict his metaphysical commitments as they do the platonist's.

25 This example is not used by either McFee or Carr, but it vividly illustrates their point.

But it is not simply the institutional context which counts here, rather it is the way in which certain actions, performed in relation to particular sets of conventions, are meaningful in a manner that mere movement, being simply physical behaviour, is not. Artworks seem to have their meanings essentially because they are products of artistic action.[26] What the work is about – and, if works are essentially meaningful, what it is – depends on how it relates to the surrounding context of art practice and artistic problems, of which artists themselves may be either explicitly or implicitly aware. The context is embedded in what they make, whether they are conscious of it or not.[27]

This, then, is one sense – generalizable to the other arts – in which dance works are constituted by action. But there is also another sense in which a dance work is action, brought out perhaps by the characterization just mentioned of the dance as an *action-structure*: that is, dances are not (just) movement structures, but rather patterns of activity, which can be re-instanced at different moments and (typically) in varying contexts (though the extent of possible variation remains to be specified). The same characterization might be applied to theatre (conceived as a performance rather than literary art) but not to painting or even music. Although, of course, making music involves action on the part of the performers, it is the sound(s) generated rather than the action itself that constitutes or instantiates the work. Thus, 'the creative powers of a composer or musician are causally linked to the organization of materials which have existence and identity apart from the artist's agency' (Carr 1997, p.351). This is not the case in dance, where the dance work is instanced in – not by means or virtue of – the performer's action.

This is not to say that choreographed movement, and indeed choreographic works, depend on *particular* dancers: those dance practices which produce performables that can be multiply instanced in different contexts may change their casting without loss of work identity. But choreographic works remain *generally* dependent on dancers and their action. Drawing on Amie Thomasson (1999), we might further specify that dependence as generic

---

Waterproof was created in 1986 and performed live at the Piscine Jean Bouin in Angers, then made into a film directed by Jean-Louis Letacon. See the *Tights, Camera, Action!* series (1992) on the UK's Channel 4.

26 Editor's note: Graham McFee argues for this view in his account of dance embodiment in this volume.

27 Indeed, there are ontologies of art developed from this insight which claim that the work is not the artefact (or performable type) created by the artist, but rather 'the action-type that [the artist] performs in discovering the structure of the work' (Currie 1989, p.75). An ontology of artworks along similar lines, which claims that they are the 'performances' of the artists who make them, has been defended by David Davies (2004) and recently extended by him to the performing arts, including dance (Davies 2011).

and historical. It is generic because works typically depend not on specific dancers, but on there being or having been some dancers or other who *could* embody the movement. And it is historical because, arguably, although the process of making (or, indeed, discovering) dance works involves dancers, once the work is made it persists even in their absence, though people are necessary to its re-instancing. We might conceive – in the kind of implausible thought experiment dreamt up by ontologists of art – of some miraculous instancing of J.S. Bach's *Air on a G String* by the wind rustling through trees and over apertures in, say, a pile of dead wood to produce the right notes of the right timbre in the right order and configurations. But even with a miraculous conjunction of natural circumstances, a dance work seemingly cannot appear independently of human action. Thus, if platonism is the view that there are such things as dance works, that they are abstract objects, and that they are 'independent of intelligent agents and their language, thought and practices' (Linnebo 2011), then it is this latter claim that proves most problematic. It is the failure of dance works to meet the independence condition for abstract objects that throws serious doubt upon the plausibility of a platonist ontology of dance.

Some concluding thoughts

I have by no means examined all of the ways in which a platonist ontology of dance might be construed, nor considered all the issues raised by such an ontology. Whether other solutions to the puzzle of the dance work are more plausible than platonism is also a topic for other occasions. I hope it is also clear that I have not tried here to set platonism up as a straw man, easily knocked down when we grasp its counter-intuitive implications. Platonist philosophers of music like Kivy and Dodd are well aware of the work that must be done to offset the counter-intuitive implications of their positions, positions they defend in spite of these implications, and – at least in Kivy's case – in spite of the fact that he is 'a down-to-earth, sensibly empirical fellow, and the [platonist] view about musical works and performances [...] has the reputation of being starry-eyed metaphysics' (Kivy 1993, p.59). What is more, platonist ontologies of art do recognize the challenge of doing ontology of art within a broader context in which metaphysical naturalism is in the ascendency, a view which would tend to reduce dance works to their physical dimension, or eliminate them from ontology altogether.[28] Assimilating dances to platonistically conceived types involves commitment to entities which some consider metaphysically suspect, but it does make

---

28 It is not just artworks that risk elimination on this spectrum of views, but ordinary objects: for a discussion of the challenge and a defence of the existence of everyday things, see Thomasson (2007).

for neat theory which avoids adding *still further* categories of things to an arguably already overpopulated universe.

Equally, understanding the problems of a platonist ontology of dance might push us towards reconsidering the philosophical goals and methodological principles of general metaphysics, within whose context it has proven so difficult to develop plausible and generally accepted ontologies of art works. The thorniness and interest of the problems is evidenced by the wealth of contemporary philosophical work on this theme.[29] Within these debates, dance has so far received scant attention. At the very least, taking platonism seriously can help us to be clearer about what is at stake in this scarcely explored territory.

References

Armelagos, Adina and Mary Sirridge. 'The Identity Crisis in Dance,' *Journal of Aesthetics and Art Criticism*, 37:2, 1978, pp.129-140.

Balaguer, Mark. 'Platonism in Metaphysics', in *Stanford Encyclopedia of Philosophy*, online, Zalta, Edward N. (ed.), Stanford, 2009.

Bannerman, Henrietta. *The work (1935-1948) of Martha Graham (1894-1991) with Particular Reference to an Analysis of her Movement System: Vocabulary and Syntax*, PhD thesis, Roehampton Institute, University of Surrey, 1998.

Bannerman, Henrietta. 'A question of somatics the search for a common framework for twenty-first-century contemporary dance pedagogy: Graham and Release-based techniques', in *Journal of Dance and Somatic Practices*, 2:1, 2010, pp.5-20.

Beardsley, Monroe C. 'What is Going on in a Dance?', *Dance Research Journal*, 15:1, 1982, pp.31-36.

Bremser, Martha and Lorna Sanders. *Fifty Contemporary Choreographers*, 2nd edition, London: Routledge, 2011 [1992].

Carr, David. 'Thought and Action in the Art of Dance,' *British Journal of Aesthetics*, 27:4, 1987, pp.345-357.

Carr, David. 'Meaning in Dance,' in *British Journal of Aesthetics*, 37:4, 1997, pp.349-366.

Carroll, Noël and Sally Banes. 'Working and Dancing: A Response to Monroe Beardsley's "What is Going on in a Dance?",' *Dance Research Journal*, 15:1, 1982, pp.37-41.

---

29 For an historical survey of work on the ontology of art, which includes discussion of contemporary philosophy, see Livingston (2011). Kania (2012), Davies (2009) and Thomasson (2005) explore methodological issues pertinent to the ontology of art.

Cohen, Selma Jeanne. *Next week, Swan Lake: Reflections on Dance and Dancers*, Middletown: Wesleyan University Press, 1982.

Currie, Gregory. *The Ontology of Art*, New York: St. Martin's Press, 1989.

Davies, David. *Art as Performance*, Malden: Blackwell Publishing, 2004.

Davies, David. 'The Primary of Practice in the Ontology of Art', *Journal of Aesthetics and Art Criticism*, 67:2, 2009, pp.159-171.

Davies, David. *Philosophy of the Performing Arts*, Malden: Wiley-Blackwell, 2011.

Davies, Stephen. *Musical Works and Performances*, New York: Oxford University Press, 2001.

Demidov, Alexander P. and Iris M. Fanger. 'Swan Lake', *The International Encyclopedia of Dance*, online version, Cohen, Selma Jeanne (ed.), Oxford: Oxford University Press, 2013.

Dodd, Julian. *Works of Music: an Essay in Ontology*, Oxford: Clarendon Press, 2007.

Goehr, Lydia. *The Imaginary Museum of Musical Works*, 2nd edition, New York: Oxford University Press, 2007 [1992].

Goodman, Nelson. *Languages of Art*, Indianapolis, Hackett Publishing, 1976.

Howell, Robert. 'Types, Indicated and Initiated', *British Journal of Aesthetics*, 42:2, 2002, pp.105-127.

Jowitt, Deborah. 'Martha Graham', in Cohen, Selma Jeanne (ed.), *The International Encyclopedia of Dance*, online version, Oxford: Oxford University Press.

Kania, Andrew. 'The Methodology of Musical Ontology: Descriptivism and its Implications', *British Journal of Aesthetics*, 48:4, 2008, pp.426-444.

Kania, Andrew. 'The Philosophy of Music', in *Stanford Encyclopedia of Philosophy*, online, Zalta, Edward N. (ed.), Stanford, 2012.

Kivy, Peter. 'Platonism in Music: A Kind of Defense', *Grazer Philosophische Studien*, 19, 1983, pp.109-129.

Kivy, Peter. *The Fine Art of Repetition: Essays in the Philosophy of Music*, Cambridge: Cambridge University Press, 1993.

Kivy, Peter. *Introduction to a Philosophy of Music*, Oxford: Clarendon, 2002.

Knobe, Joshua and Shaun Nichols (eds.). *Experimental Philosophy*, New York: Oxford University Press, 2008.

Lamarque, Peter. *Work and object: explorations in the metaphysics of art*, Oxford: Oxford University Press, 2010.

Levinson, Jerrold. 'What a Musical Work Is', in *Journal of Philosophy*, 77:1, 1980, pp.5-28.

Levinson, Jerrold. *Music, art, and metaphysics: essays in philosophical aesthetics*, revised edition, Oxford, Oxford University Press, 2011 [1991].

Linnebo, Øystein. 'Platonism in the Philosophy of Mathematics', in *Stanford Encyclopedia of Philosophy*, online, Zalta, Edward N. (ed.), Stanford, 2011.

Livingston, Paisley. 'History of the Ontology of Art', in *Stanford Encyclopedia of Philosophy*, online, Zalta, Edward N. (ed.), Stanford, 2012.

McFee, Graham. *Understanding Dance*, London: Routledge, 1992.

McFee, Graham. '"Was that *Swan Lake* I saw you at last night?": Dance Identity and Understanding,' *Dance Research*, 12:1, 1994, pp.21-40.

McFee, Graham. 'Technicality, Philosophy and Dance Study', in McFee, Graham (ed.), *Dance, Education and Philosophy*, Oxford: Meyer & Meyer Sport, 1999, pp.155-188.

McFee, Graham. *The Concept of Dance Education*, Eastbourne: Pageantry Press, 2004.

McFee, Graham. *The Philosophical Aesthetics of Dance*, Alton: Dance Books, 2011.

Margolis, Joseph. 'The Identity of a Work of Art', *Mind*, 68:269, 1959, pp.34-50.

Meskin, Aaron. 'Productions, Performances and their Evaluation', in McFee, Graham (ed.), *Dance, Education and Philosophy*, Oxford: Meyer and Meyer Sport, 1999, pp.45-61.

Oberzaucher-Schüller Gunhild. 'Les Noces', Cohen, Selma Jeanne (ed.), *International Encyclopedia of Dance*, online edition, Oxford: Oxford University Press, 2012.

Pakes, Anna. *Choreography Invisible: The Disappearing Work of Dance*, New York: Oxford University Press, forthcoming in 2014.

Pust, Joel. *Intuitions as Evidence*, London: Routledge, 2000.

Scholl, Tim. *Sleeping Beauty: A Legend in Progress*, New Haven: Yale University Press, 2004.

Sparshott, Francis. *A Measured Pace: Toward a Philosophical Understanding of the Arts of Dance*, Toronto: University of Toronto Press, 1995.

Thomasson, Amie. *Fiction and Metaphysics*, Cambridge: Cambridge University Press, 1999.

Thomasson, Amie. 'The Ontology of Art and Knowledge in Aesthetics', *Journal of Aesthetics and Art Criticism*, 63: 3, 2005, pp.221-229.

Thomasson, Amie. *Ordinary Objects*, New York: Oxford University Press, 2005.

Trueman, Matt. 'Beyoncé accused of 'stealing' dance moves in new video', in *The Guardian*, 10th October 2011, retrieved from http://www.guardian.co.uk/stage/2011/oct/10/beyonce-dance-moves-new-video?intcmp=239, accessed 23/1/2013.

Wasserman, Ryan. 'Materian Constitution', in *The Stanford Encyclopedia of Philosophy*, online, Zalta, Edward N. (ed.), Stanford, 2009.

Wiley, Roland John. *Tchaikovsky's Ballets: Swan Lake, Sleeping Beauty, Nutcracker*, Oxford: Clarendon Press, 1985.

5. The *Beat* goes on: reconsidering dancework identity

Renee Conroy

In 1985 Mark Dendy and Company (now Dendy Dancetheater) surprised New York dance enthusiasts with *Beat*. Intriguingly, inaugural audiences showed only modest interest in two of the work's most prominent features: Dendy's rhythmic use of movement-cum-vocalization and his tongue-in-cheek choreography. Original viewers seem to have been captivated by the fact that every member of *Beat*'s gender-mixed cast performed the athletic quartet topless because Dendy's unisex treatment of choreography and costuming embodied a timely commentary on gender roles.[1]

A decade later, the University of Washington Chamber Dance Company (CDC) opened its annual program with a performance of *Beat*. What these dancers offered Pacific Northwest audiences, however, did not appear to be an artwork designed to invite serious reflection on social issues. This time, under the direction of Mark Dendy and CDC founder and artistic director Hannah Wiley, the dancers – whose previously meager garments were entirely black and white – were fully clad in shiny blue tank tops, baggy red shorts, and cherry-coloured Converse. They bore greater resemblance to comic book superheroes than to the pale, androgynous, half-naked athletes of the New York premiere. As a result, many Seattleites read what was previously taken to be a politically provocative piece of dance art as a light-hearted mockery of sports or the 'Jane Fonda' exercise craze. Reviews of CDC's performances suggest that, because the change in costumes attenuated the original socio-political character of the work, Northwest audiences attended to *Beat*'s choreographic strengths and weaknesses more fully than had their earlier New York counterparts.[2]

This otherwise minor anecdote is significant because it reflects a ubiquitous danceworld phenomenon. Although dance insiders acknowledged the disparities between the mid-80s offerings by Dendy and Company and the later CDC performances, all were accepted unequivocally as presentations of the same work of dance art. The ease with which members of the

---

1 See Anderson (1986), Kisselgoff (1990) and Carbonneau (2000). This assessment is also based on anecdotal evidence, including personal conversations with Dendy and Wiley.

2 See Speer (2005), Kurtz (2000) and Conklin (1995). Although small choreographic amendments were made to accommodate the talents of the CDC dancers, *Beat*'s basic choreographic elements remained consistent across the performances discussed here.

danceworld embraced Dendy's substantive artistic changes raises a familiar philosophical question: given their many obvious differences, in virtue of what was each of these dance events an instance of Dendy's artwork *Beat*?

The more general question, 'What conditions must be satisfied for two qualitatively distinct dance performances to be presentations of the same artwork?' is widely regarded as worthy of philosophical attention.[3] The need for a comprehensive account of dancework identity is *normatively pressing* because having a clear conception of what is necessary for a work of dance art to 'remain the same despite change' is a prerequisite for ensuring that responsibility for its creation and value-laden consequences is attributed correctly, justice is meted out when conflicts of interest arise (as in cases of copyright dispute), and full appreciation of any particular dance art performance is possible. Answering this question is also *practically important* because some theory of dancework identity is required to make good sense of standard danceworld practices that reflect the typically 'flexible' character of danceworks. These include: the choreographic commonplace of on-going experimentation and revision with respect to a single work as it is performed multiple times; the activity of preparing a dancework for the stage by means of a rehearsal process that involves dancers' constant development and improvement; and the critic's recognition that there may be poor or mistake-filled instances of any given work. In addition, the question of what is required for two dance events to be performances of the same artwork is *philosophically compelling* because it is a challenge to formulate an adequate metaphysical theory responsive to the ductility of dance art creations.[4]

In light of these considerations, it is remarkable that the sizable philosophical literature dedicated to dancework identity is relatively bereft of argumentative topography. When the dust settles and one surveys this intellectual battlefield, one finds several clear camps but almost no evidence

---

3 See Anderson (1983), Armelagos and Sirridge (1978), Sirridge and Armelagos (1983), Carr (1997), Cohen (1982), Goodman (1976), Margolis (1981), McFee (1992, 2004, 2011), Rubidge (2000), Sparshott (1995); and Van Camp (1981, 1994, 1998, 2006).

4 This subject is also of interest in light of recent public discussion about artistic plagiarism following the release of Beyonce's 2011 music video *Countdown*. In the original version, several works by noted modern choreographer Anne Theresa De Keersmaeker (*Rosas danst Rosas* (1980) and *Achterland* (1990)) were borrowed from liberally without credit. As a result of the public controversy that ensued, Knowles released a second version of the video without reference to De Keersmaeker's works. While this case was important for bringing the subject of dancework *copyright* to public attention, it was never claimed that Knowles' original video performance was *numerically identical* to either of the De Keersmaeker creations that were inappropriately 'quoted'. Hence, it is beyond the scope of the present discussion. However, as danceworks become increasingly available in filmic and on-line formats, the question of which conditions must be satisfied to produce a performance of any given work of dance art will become increasingly pressing, as the controversy surrounding *Countdown* indicates.

of their encounters.[5] With respect to most substantial philosophical discussions one can both identify a range of competing views and plumb published debates that develop a 'standard set' of objections and responses relative to each. Given that dialectical exchanges are often the locus of the most profitable philosophical work, it is unfortunate that there has not been more interest in developing an interactive argumentative landscape with respect to dancework identity.

With this in mind, my aim is to revitalize conversation about this subject in service of both philosophical and practical goals. Several rich treatments of dancework identity have not had their theoretical feet put to the fire of sustained public critique, and there is at least one potential account implicit in dance practice that has not yet received philosophical attention.[6] Given that there are at least three underdeveloped approaches to dancework identity – to which I refer as notationalism, the legal model, and the canonical performance view – that appear to be improvements over other less sophisticated accounts, it is useful to ask whether any can deliver on the promise it holds forth.[7] My provisional claim is that none can, and my goal is to indicate why each is *prima facie* inadequate.

Although the arguments that follow are critical, my objective is constructive. Our collective thinking about dancework identity is impoverished by having competing accounts co-exist in philosophical texts independent of one another, related only as islands in an intellectual archipelago. The first step toward a cure for this academic ailment is to collect alternative models under one critical umbrella. If we reflect on the conceptual relationships between the views I discuss here – and weigh thoughtfully their relative strengths and weaknesses – we will have laid the foundation for improved conversations about when and why any dancemaker's *Beat* goes on.

5 Notable exceptions include several works by Van Camp (1981, 1998) in which suggestions offered by Goodman, Margolis, and Sirridge and Armelagos are treated and criticized directly. McFee (2011) also addresses Goodman's theory of dancework identity in detail.

6 The two main contemporary philosophical theories of dancework identity – to which I refer as notationalism and the legal model – have not been the subject of (much) published critique, though both have been discussed in conference settings. Carr's brief published discussion of the former (1997) is an exception.

7 Less sophisticated, but popular and intuitive, accounts include the thesis that two dance events are performances of the same dancework just in case both *express* the same affective or cognitive content and/or *exemplify* the same movement structure. See Anderson (1983) on idealism and materialism, and the critique in Sparshott (1995, pp.412-415). See also Carroll (2003, pp.587-592).

Preliminary desiderata

I begin by offering three minimal desiderata for an adequate philosophical account of dancework identity. First, I recommend that all viable dance-art-related theory be responsive to well-established institutional facts rather than revisionist with respect to core danceworld practices or values. Hence, any account that runs contrary to dance experts' all-things-considered identity claims will be, to that extent, undesirable.[8]

Second, because we seek an account of dancework *identity*, any satisfactory answer to the relevant 'same as' question must be genuinely metaphysical. Proposals that tell us only how to reliably re-identify a choreographer's artistic creation across diverse performances but fail to articulate *what makes* these performances instances of the same artwork will, therefore, be regarded as metaphysically inadequate. In addition, any account that on conceptual grounds forces us to conclude that a great number of danceworks and/or performances are indeterminate will be rejected. In line with more traditional subjects of metaphysical inquiry (such as persons, ships, statues, and lumps of clay), indeterminacy with respect to works of dance art should be the exception not the rule.

Third, on my view no reasonable account of dancework identity will make it practically impossible for well-informed members of the dance community to identify any given work correctly. Nor will it render 'same work' judgments unduly difficult for dance experts to furnish. On the assumption that the identity conditions of danceworks are deeply connected to what dance insiders *do* on the basis of their well-informed danceworld beliefs, the default position must be that such conditions are not only epistemically accessible in principle, but that the things relevant to their obtaining can be recognized in many actual cases by people who know what to look for.

With these desiderata in hand, we are prepared to explore three relatively neglected responses to the query, 'What makes it the case that the performances by Dendy and Company and the performances by CDC were equally instances of Mark Dendy's provocative *tour de force, Beat?*'

---

8 I do not attend to nominalism as defended by Goodman (1976) since its theoretical consequences flout a number of central dance art traditions. For clarification about the sense in which I take the metaphysics of art to be beholden to artworld practice, see Davies (2006, 2013). I also assume throughout that works of dance art are different in kind from (sets of) performances given that they persist after particular dance events have ended. Consistent with the views advocated by McFee (1994, 2004, 2011) and Pakes (http://roehampton.academia.edu/AnnaPakes, especially 'Talks' 2011, 2012), I maintain they are some kind of abstracta. I remain agnostic about whether they are best thought of as Platonic entities, types, norm-kinds, or abstract artefacts.

Notationalism

To begin, it is worth considering how a person unfamiliar with the history and conventions of theatre dance might approach this question. An intuitive first move would be to draw analogies to the other performing arts. For example, one might note that two putative performances of *King Lear* can differ greatly yet be instances of Shakespeare's play as long as both involve the dramatic recitation of (some critical number of) the lines Shakespeare penned. And one could acknowledge the same kind of phenomenon *mutatis mutandis* with respect to Beethoven's *Third Symphony* or Wagner's *Tristan und Isolde*. Hence, a natural thought would be that, just as in the other performing arts two appreciably different performances are instances of the same artwork only if both exhibit a high degree of fidelity to some authorial inscription that serves as a 'recipe' for producing public presentations of that work, so two appreciably different dance performances are instances of the same dancework just in case both satisfy instructions given in some kind of suitable movement notation. This is very close to the idea expressed by Graham McFee's 'Thesis of Notationality'. One might articulate his view as follows:

> A and B are instances of the same dancework X only if both are dance performances that satisfy (instantiate to some reasonably high degree) an 'adequate score' of X, where this is a text written in a form of notation deemed acceptable by those knowledgeable about dance art for preserving the kind of dancework in question.[9]

The upshot of the Thesis of Notationality is that, because dance is a *performing* art, a crucial part of the answer to the 'same as' question with respect to danceworks is 'fidelity to a(n adequate) score' in the same way a crucial part of the answer to the 'same as' question with respect to musical works or plays is fidelity to an authorized score or script.[10]

---

9 I have re-formulated McFee's first published expression of the Thesis of Notationality (McFee, 1992: 97-98) to capture the core of his notationalist theory as it applies to dance. McFee's original version is broader than my expression given that it is designed to show how dancework ontology and identity can be understood on a model that applies to all performing artforms. However, in his second book on dance, McFee presents the thesis as follows: '. . . The Thesis of Notationality . . . states that a work is a token of a particular type if it satisfies a notation agreed by the knowledgable in that field to be an adequate notation for that *dance*' (McFee, 2004: 21, emphasis mine). McFee returns to his original formulation in his 2011 monograph.

10 McFee emphasizes the continuity between dance and the other performing arts as follows: 'danceworks are typically performing artworks, physical artworks, and also multiple artworks . . . recognising dance as a performing art is recognising typical danceworks are *performables*, in the sense that the *very same dance* can be re-performed on another occasion (despite the differences between such performances . . .)' (McFee,

Before evaluating this proposal, it is important to note that McFee's Thesis of Notationality is designed to do several conceptually distinct, though interrelated, things: (1) capture the ontological character of dance art creations; (2) articulate a foundation for sound 'same as' judgments on the part of practitioners and dance audiences; and (3) highlight the normativity 'built in' to dance art performance (in virtue of which some things that happen on stage may appropriately be commended while others may be criticized). Although McFee's emphasis with respect to this thesis has varied, he makes clear in his most recent monograph *The Philosophical Aesthetics of Dance: Identity, Performance and Understanding* that part of his aim is to make conceptual progress with respect to our metaphysical grasp of dancework identity.[11]

The idea that the metaphysical 'same as' question with respect to danceworks can be answered by appeal to scores has intuitive plausibility and has been given robust philosophical defense. Hence, it is valuable to explore how it might fare under scrutiny. I refer to any account of this general kind as a notationalist account of dancework identity, taking McFee's Thesis of Notationality as only one expression of this view.

The first ostensible weakness of notationalism is the fact that many danceworks are never scored.[12] As a result, notationalist approaches appear to flout my second desideratum: the identity conditions for most dance art creations will be indeterminate given that most extant danceworks lack the requisite metaphysical foundation. The second putative Achilles' heel of any notationalist theory is the well-rehearsed fact that those choreographers who have their works scored rely on a multi-party interpretation system that invites the possibility of compounded misapprehensions, thereby attenuating the plausibility of the presumption that working from notation will ensure numerical identity across performances.[13] This practical reality

---

2011, p.33). Thus, his Thesis of Notationality is premised on the idea that there is some theoretical overlap between how one should approach identity questions about performables like musical works or plays and similar questions about danceworks, though he is careful to highlight important disanalogies (McFee, 2011, pp. 34, 55-56, 84-87).

11 McFee, 2011: 36-39, 62.

12 In recent years, there has been increased attention to the preservation of danceworks and to the value of using notation, but new works of dance art are more often preserved in film than notation. Note the importance attached by the Dance Heritage Coalition to archival 'footage' compared to its sparse comments about scores (http://www.danceheritage.org/, accessed 1/20/13). Statistics cited on the Labanotation Bureau (LBN) website confirm preservation by notation to be minimal relative to the use of other means: only 4-6 danceworks per year are notated and added to the Bureau's archives (http://www.dancenotation.org/, accessed 1/20/13).

13 The procedure involves interpretation of rehearsals and performances by the notator, the filtering imposed by the notation system itself, and interpretation (often by a further

suggests that any version of notationalism will likely violate the first of my proposed desiderata in addition to running afoul of the second.

While these objections are compelling from the perspective of life in the studio, the defender of notationalism has a succinct response: what secures identity across performances is not any actual score but only an *in principle possible* score, i.e., the potential 'recipe' for producing performances of the work in question that *would be* deemed acceptable by a set of dance experts. In light of this qualification, the fact that many works of dance art are not scored may be dismissed as philosophically irrelevant. Furthermore, the fact that it is challenging to ensure that identity is maintained across performances given current dance notation praxis gets no grip on the theoretical point that it is possible *in principle* to preserve all essential choreographic sequences in some kind of text. Unless it can be shown that, as a conceptual matter, some dance art movement cannot be captured in any kind of notation, the potential for mishaps inherent in the current system of notating and restaging danceworks is simply a misfortune.[14] Hence, even if current scoring practices are imperfect and available forms of notation remain underutilized, these facts pose no threat to notationalism as a theory of dancework identity.

But there *is* something philosophically amiss with views that attempt to answer the relevant metaphysical question by appeal to thoughtfully crafted symbolic texts. In the end, notationalism, regardless of how it is qualified, can provide a satisfactory response only to the epistemic question, 'On what grounds is a person justified in believing that two distinct performances are instances of the same work of dance art?' because scores merely *represent* essential features of danceworks: they do not *constitute* them. Notation is a way of capturing for future reference those aspects of danceworks that are already work-constitutive and are, therefore, essential for some reason other than (and conceptually prior to) the fact that they have been carefully recorded. Thus, any theory giving pride of place to notation can, at best, tell us how to reliably re-identify a particular dancework across performances; it cannot answer the metaphysical question at hand.

Here it is instructive to consider the importance of 'score adequacy' in McFee's Thesis of Notationality.[15] In short, his need to appeal to an

---

party) of the score in order to restage the dancework. For more information about the process of dancework notation and subsequent restaging from notated scores, see Hutchinson-Guest (1991), Whitley (2000) and Brennan (2002).

14 To date, no developed case for the claim that dance movement is in principle un-notatable has been offered. Some arguments in this direction are suggested by Armelagos and Sirridge (1978). For criticisms, see Van Camp (1981) and Margolis (1981). For rejoinders to Margolis, see Sirridge and Armelagos (1983).

15 McFee appeals to 'adequate scores' in all his monographs on dance, but gives the

'adequate score' to rule out deficient transcripts indicates that scores cannot be the metaphysical bedrock of dance art creations. This is evident when one reflects on discussions dance insiders – including choreographers, style coaches, and notation specialists – have about the degree to which some notated text is an apt documentation of a given dancework. Such debates typically include critiques of the impugned score by reference to the choreographer's expressed wishes, the performance history of the piece, the expressive point or 'aura' of the work, the style of the choreography, etc. The logic of this kind of conversation reveals that the answer to the question, 'Which elements of this dancework are necessary and which are variable?' cannot be given by reference to anything the score *actually* says since the point of the discussion is to determine what the notation *should* prescribe. And that question is always resolved by appeal to a variety of 'extra-textual' dance art-related matters, many of which go well beyond considerations about movement vocabulary into issues of style, historical context, and authorial intentions.

Thus, the fundamental philosophical problem with the notationalist approach to dancework identity is this: if we want to honor current danceworld practice by regarding some textual representations as too shoddy to be relied upon while countenancing others as trustworthy resources, then we must conclude that it is whatever *makes* a score adequate – rather than the score itself – that is metaphysically fundamental. Notation is a powerful epistemic tool for identifying works of dance art in and across performances, but scores do not *establish* identity conditions.

The notationalist has several obvious responses at his disposal. First, he can claim that once a condition of 'adequacy' has been specified, it is appropriate to appeal *directly* to scores to answer metaphysical questions about what is required for two performances to instantiate the same dancework given that any 'adequate' score will include all and only the artwork's essential features.[16] Second, the proponent of this view can deny that the distinction between dancework identity and dancework identification is as 'clean' as I have suggested, and argue that my attempt to prize apart these two kinds of 'same as' questions is theoretically artificial. I address both rejoinders briefly.

First, I concede that building 'score adequacy' into a notationalist theory of dancework identity makes it practically legitimate to appeal directly to

---

concept its most full-blooded explication in his 2011 book. For McFee's treatmemt of 'adequate score' see: McFee (2011, pp.56, 61, 74, and especially 80-84); McFee (2004, pp.226-229); and McFee (1992, pp.97-99 and 104-106). Although I do not address this aspect of McFee's proposal, part of what he means by 'adequacy' is context-sensitive. Hence, for McFee scores are 'adequate' to preserve works for particular purposes rather than 'adequate' *tout court*.

16 See McFee (2011, p.80).

notational records to answer identity questions, but reply that any proposed account of this kind will have the resources to address the metaphysician's concerns in only a thin way. For if we begin by declaring an 'adequate score' to be one containing all and only *essential* elements of a given piece of dance art, then *by definition* any dance performance that satisfies the prescriptions of an 'adequate score' will possess the properties required to be an instance of the notated work.

However, the key question for the philosopher interested in dancework identity is not whether complying with a stipulatively perfect set of instructions for *The Moor's Pavane* will successfully yield a performance of Jose Limon's masterpiece. Instead, the fundamental – and more challenging – question is: *why* are the particular elements specified by the 'adequate score' those that must be satisfied to produce a performance of this dancework? Notationalism has little help to offer here even if, like McFee, the notationalist insists that the answer rests with determinations made by those knowledgeable in the artform. For unless one can say something substantive about the kinds of reasoning in which experts engage – and about what count as *appropriate* reasons in this context – the fundamental philosophical question about dancework identity remains unanswered.

Second, the notationalist might defend himself against my charge that he has offered a theory of dancework identification rather than dancework identity by arguing that the practical need for danceworld experts to make *judgment calls* in many cases indicates there is no clean line between metaphysical and epistemological 'same as' questions with respect to dance art. As McFee writes:

> if it is impossible to determine for dance cases which identity-judgement is sound, then no identity-judgement can be sustained. As with most 'social objects' which admit of numerical identity, *their ontological questions are mingled with the epistemological ones* – that is part of what Quinton (1982 p.98) means in talking of 'fruits of human contrivance'. So that, for danceworks, we could not distinguish the purely ontological [from the purely epistemological issues] – as we could in the case of persons.[17]

Putting aside the reasons for which it might be argued that identity questions about persons demand a different kind of philosophical treatment than is appropriate for artworks, one might think the epistemic and metaphysical are 'intermingled' with respect to danceworks because as putative 'social objects' – roughly analogous to laws, money, rules of etiquette, and insurance policies – danceworks seem to exist and have normative import only in virtue of humans' shared commitments, theories, and practical-artistic endeavours. This is, in part, what McFee means when

---

17 McFee 2011, p.38, emphasis mine.

he refers to 'The Republic of Dance.'[18] Since the category 'work of dance art' is the 'fruit of human contrivance' rather than a natural kind like 'sodium chloride' or 'cumulus cloud', danceworks come into being only as a result of our collective agreement to treat selected acts or performances in special ways and survive only if people continue to recognize a certain set of malleable rules with respect to them. And as Morris Weitz famously argued, extending socially-constructed concepts – or applying them to novel or difficult cases – always calls for decision-making on the part of stake-holders in the relevant communities and never waits on the discovery of new, mind-independent facts.[19] As a result, one might contend it is incoherent to separate metaphysical and epistemic 'same as' questions with respect to dance artworks since marking a clear division between them suggests that, although danceworks qua 'social objects' depend on us for both their existence and persistence, facts about them (including those related to their identity conditions) may be beyond our epistemic grasp.

My brief response to this substantive line of argument is as follows: it is specious to think that because danceworks are 'social objects' questions about their metaphysical characteristics and questions about the conditions under which we are justified in believing (or asserting) certain things about them *must* be conceptually entwined. The social conventions that make possible things like dance art, laws, and driver's licenses need not be transparent to – let alone remedially understood by – individuals who engage them effectively, thereby ensuring their survival. People can make reliable and thoroughly justified judgments about when they are confronted with a particular 'social object', and about how to respond to it appropriately, without understanding anything about its metaphysical foundations. The checker at my local grocery counter is justified in believing (on various, complex grounds) that the twenty dollar bill I hand her is a putative piece of legal tender I am entitled to exchange for Kellogg's and Dinty Moore products, and is also justified in verifying that my particular offering is genuine by using a counterfeit-detection device. In our transaction, she reaffirms the metaphysical basis of money qua volatile marker of like-minded persons' willingness to accept a special bit of paper to settle debt. But she need not be aware that she is, in part, constituting the shared conventions that 'make money work' as she does her job. Hence, the conditions she must satisfy to know that any particular silken swath is a legitimate piece of legal tender are entirely separate from those she must fulfill to understand the metaphysics of monetary value and exchange. This suggests that, even with respect to

---

18 See McFee (1992, pp.71-72) for an 'institutional style of answer' (not a definition) to the question of what makes something art, drawing on Diffey (1992). McFee maintains this position and language in his 2004 and 2011 monographs.

19 See Weitz 1956, pp.27-35 (especially 30-32).

things widely acknowledged to be 'fruits of human contrivance', epistemic criteria are both practically and conceptually distinct from metaphysical criteria.

The legal model[20]

Suppose what is (or should be) written in some kind of notation is not that in virtue of which two dance events are performances of the same work of art. Nonetheless, given their putative powers of dancework preservation, scores might play an important role in answering our question about *Beat's* identity conditions. For example, while the constituent features of any particular dancework might not be secured by an 'in principle possible adequate score', they might depend on how people regard performances *in light of* scores or other available forms of 'fixation'. This possibility is suggested by Julie Van Camp's approach to dancework identity, which emphasizes procedures surrounding the legal protection of choreographers' creations. Although her treatment of American copyright law – and its potential application to the issue of dancework identity – has varied, one might construct the following proposal after first treatment of this subject:[21]

> A and B are instances of the same dancework if and only if they are dance performances determined by lay observers (acting as representatives of the dance art community) to exhibit 'substantial similarity' as defined by current legal practice.

In her early work, Van Camp recommends adopting a 'two-prong approach' analogous to the American legal procedure for settling cases of alleged

---

20 Julie Van Camp's work (1981, 1994, 1998, and 2006) is the inspiration for this suggestion although she describes her approach as 'pragmatist' in the spirit of John Dewey and C.S. Peirce (2006). And in attending to the ways in which consideration of legal practice can usefully amplify our understanding of artwork identity, she writes, '*I do not mean to suggest that the art legal community should be the leading paradigm for understanding all art,* but only that its long-established practices show the *theoretical effectiveness of pragmatism* in explaining an important set of practices to establish identity' (2006, p.47, emphasis mine). This reflects a shift from her earliest work in which her apparent suggestion was that a fruitful theory of dancework identity could be modeled closely after the legal procedure for settling dance art-related copyright disputes (1981, pp.149-150, 170). To indicate that my proposal is merely crafted after Van Camp's work, I refer to any theory that emphasizes the importance of art-relevant law as a 'legal model'.

21 Van Camp offers this synopsis of her early approach: 'The proposal here is that an identity theory must include two things: a standard for identity, through notation, and a test for application of that standard, namely substantial similarity . . . as determined finally by lay observers . . . Legal determinations of identity directly involve the issues of philosophical identity, and illustrate the viability of a two-pronged test of identity using both notation (or fixation) to set an ideal for absolute identity and a lay observer test to apply that ideal and specify actual identity of specific performances' (1981, p.171).

copyright infringement of choreographic works.[22] First, in the legal context, litigation can be pursued only if there is an absolute (or ideal) standard for the choreographic work that renders it protected under the relevant 1976 copyright law. This standard is constituted by a form of 'tangible fixation' of the choreography, which may be a choreographer-approved score of the work, a choreographer-approved film of a performance, and/or a choreographer-approved rehearsal video. Second, litigation is resolved only when there is a determination on the part of a jury of 'lay observers' – constituted by 'typical [dance] audience members' or 'ordinary spectators' rather than dance experts – that the performance claimed to violate copyright law bears 'substantial similarity' to the standard that establishes legal protection.[23] In her early work, Van Camp proposes that

---

22 I mark a distinction between *danceworks* and *choreographic works* that follows the legal language related to copyright protection. Although the category 'choreographic work' is vague, it might be best understood to refer to 'planned movement, set into a time frame, for the benefit and enjoyment of the passive observer' (Traylor, cited in Van Camp, 1994). Hence, as I treat the difference between works of dance art and choreographic works, the category 'choreographic work' is broader than that of 'dancework' insofar as it may include designed movement sequences featured in circus acts, parades, ice-skating and gymnastic routines, and plays (Van Camp, 1994, p.3). In contrast, the category 'dancework' refers only to works of art created within dance-related traditions. The category 'choreographic work' is also narrower than that of 'dancework' in this respect: while the former refers only to movement sequences or designs, the latter encompasses the complete artistic object the choreographer offers to audiences: including stage design, costuming, musical accompaniment, and anything relevant to the way in which the performed movements are *seen or experienced* by audience members. Thus, on my view, the set of conditions that must be satisfied for two performances to be of the same choreographic work can differ from those that must obtain for two performances to be of the same dancework because a dancework might not have 'planned movement, set into a time frame, for the benefit and enjoyment of the passive observer' as an essential component. This is arguably the case with task dances and improvised works that follow the traditions of the Judson Dance Theater.

23 On Van Camp's view there is *no formula* for determining what counts as 'substantial similarity'. One performance is 'substantially similar' to another just in case a jury of 'ordinary observers' declares it is on the basis of comparing those performances to the choreographer-approved standard and considering testimony by qualified members of the dance community (the choreographer, members of the original cast, notation specialists, and dance critics). Van Camp writes of the legal case that the relevant kind of similarity is 'determined finally by lay observers' and that the testimony of experts is 'relevant and admissible, but not conclusive on the jury of lay observers' (1981: 171). She also notes that while 'Infringement of all types of artworks is determined according to the ordinary observer test' (where this is also described legally as a test of substantial similarity according to 'ordinary spectators', 'average observers', or the 'average reasonable man', see FN 97) there is difficulty in applying the generic 'reasonable man standard' to the dance case (1981, pp.175-6). She proposes that in the context of theorizing about dancework identity we understand 'lay observers' as 'those who know how to look' insofar as they have 'experience as audience members of dance performances' (1981, p.175). Thus,

dancework identity be understood as involving these same elements: (1) a choreographer-supplied standard that sets an absolute criterion to which all identity-conferring judgments must appeal, and (2) a 'lay observer test', an identity-conferring verdict handed down by a group of average dance audience members pronouncing a particular performance to exhibit 'substantial similarity' to the choreographer's standard.

This version of the legal model raises a number of practical concerns. First, given its implicit reliance on status conferral, the theory is too formal to describe how identity-constitutive judgments are actually (or could reasonably be) made in the danceworld. On one reading of Van Camp's early suggestions, a dance performance is a public presentation of some particular work of dance art only if some practical equivalent of a jury of average dance art viewers decides it is an instance of this work, thereby *bestowing* the relevant artwork-status on the performance as a result of some (quasi-organized) deeming procedure. It has, however, been widely recognized that philosophical accounts of art-related matters modelled on structured decision-making procedures fail to capture the complex, and typically informal, path by which various kinds of status is granted in the context of art practice.[24]

Second, for most danceworks, there is no choreographer-approved form of 'fixation'. Since the existence of such a standard is a prerequisite for the kind of communal judgments that, on any version of the legal model, constitute the identity of particular dance art performances, many will be metaphysically indeterminate on this view. Third, even if we consider only those public presentations for which an appropriate standard exists, the choreographer-approved notations or films that constitute this standard are often inaccessible – or unintelligible – to the individuals upon whose judgments facts about the identity of any particular performance depend, viz., average dance art observers. And, fourth, when typical 'ordinary' audience members are confronted with two appreciably different performances presented as interpretations of the same dancework, they

---

on Van Camp's earliest suggestion the members of the jury whose decisions establish substantial similarity (hence, dancework identity) need no special dance training and are likely *not* to be dance art experts since they need be only 'typical audience members', that is, people with some experience viewing dance art (1981, p.176).

24 George Dickie famously changed his institutional theory of art from one that required 'status conferral' (Dickie, p.1974) to one that required only 'status achievement' (Dickie: 1984) in response to the objection that his earlier formulation implied an organized system of deeming too formal and artificially constrained to capture what goes on within the institution of art. Although Van Camp's focus is the achievement of 'status as the *same* artwork' rather than 'status as an artwork', the same objection applies to this version of the legal model. Van Camp's later suggestions in the pragmatist spirit, however, accommodate this potential problem (see Van Camp: 1994, 1998, and 2006).

often either disagree with one another about whether these exhibited the kind or degree of similarity required to support a 'same work' verdict or retreat to agnosticism. Hence, even if we consider only the limited set of dance art performances that are genuine candidates for identity-conferring judgments on the legal model, the consensus needed for them to be metaphysically effective is often not forthcoming.

The aforementioned are practical concerns about one version of the legal model, and the theory could be modified to accommodate some of them. For instance, in later work Van Camp addresses worries that might arise if the 'jury' whose decisions are constitutive of 'same work' status is closely analogous to the kind utilized in legal cases. She recommends that rather than appeal to a select panel of average dance art viewers to supply identity-establishing judgments we think of the group whose determinations count as constituted by the *whole* of the dance art community; including audience members who are dance professionals, 'ordinary observers', and those with an intimate relationship to the work under scrutiny.[25] This suggests a modified version of the legal model:

A and B are instances of the same dancework if and only if they are dance performances determined by members of the dance art community (including lay audience members, dance professionals, and specially qualified experts) to exhibit 'substantial similarity' as understood within the context of dance practice.

This modification, however, does little to dispel many of the practical concerns already articulated. First, for most cases, regardless of how the 'jury' is constituted or how informal the joint decision in favor of 'substantial similarity' might be, the relevant standard against which effective judgments might be made does not exist.[26] Hence, even if one expands the notion

---

25 Van Camp first offers this broader formulation in 1994: 'I would suggest a drastically different approach, both in the dance community and in the special context of copyright infringement. *The identity of a work (and whether it is 'substantially similar') should be considered a matter of agreement by the community.* In dance generally that community includes the choreographers, performers, audience, critics, historians, and so forth. The dialogue as to what counts as a work is carried on in conversations, formal and informal, oral and written. *The practices of this dance community define what counts as the 'same' work'* (1994, pp.74-75, emphasis mine). For similar recommendations see Van Camp 1998, p.401 and 2006, p.42.

26 In 1998 and 2006, Van Camp does not mention explicitly the 'two-prong test' that figured in her earlier writing. However, any theory of dancework identity modelled closely after legal procedures associated with the copyright of choreographic works must maintain this element of her earlier view to secure a reasonable analogy between legal practices directly related to identity and philosophical theory. Furthermore, if no standard is required, it is unclear to what community members' judgments about 'same work' status should appeal to count as reasonable.

of 'ordinary observer' to include all manner of dance experts and opts to describe 'same artwork status' in terms of status-achievement rather than status-conferral, most dance performances (and the works of which they might be performances) will be metaphysically indeterminate. Second, even if the 'typical dance audience' is populated largely with dance specialists and we consider only cases for which there is an appropriate 'standard' to guide decision-making, it will remain inaccessible to most and unintelligible to many. After all, even savvy dance professionals are not expected to be able to read notation as a matter of course. And if the relevant form of fixation is a choreographer-approved video of the work, the standard in light of which 'same work' judgments are to be made is not likely to be available even to audience members who are dance professionals. Third, if some kind of 'consensus' is *required* for an identity-constitutive judgment to be made on the part of the relevant observers, it seems even less plausible that this will be reachable when dance experts are added to the mix than when those whose judgments count are simply 'average audience members'. It is in the nature of dance insiders to debate about matters of detail in cases average audience members would not find difficult given that, as a result of their training, the dance practitioners often perceive fine-grained movement disparities that escape the watchful eyes of their non-professional counterparts.

Practical concerns aside, there are two reasons for which no philosophically adequate theory of dancework identity can be constructed by analogy to legal practices surrounding copyright litigation, both of which turn on the fact that any such account must include Van Camp's original 'two prongs': the absolute standard for identity and some kind of communal judgment made on the basis of this criterion.[27]

First, given that the relevant observers' judgments are made in light of an antecedent standard, what matters metaphysically is the process by which a score and/or film *becomes* a standard, not any viewing group's determination that a particular performance is (or is not) 'substantially similar' to it. Indeed, the need for an *absolute* standard implies that declarations made by the relevant community members are merely public recognitions of identity conditions that already obtain.[28] As a result, the legal model appears to be on all fours with notationalism insofar as it is better understood as a theory of dancework identification than dancework identity.

Second, since any account of dancework identity modeled after the relevant legal practice must claim that *both* the choreographer-approved

---

27 See note 28.

28 This is implied by the label 'lay observer test', even if 'lay observer' is extended to include those with extensive training in various dance art-related matters. Tests are epistemic devices, i.e., ways of *determining whether* something is the case, not ways of *making* something the case.

standard and the decision made by some audience in light of it are metaphysically necessary, all such theories require us to embrace – or vacillate between the acceptance of – two apparently contradictory claims: (1) the metaphysical constraints on any given work of dance art are constituted by the choreographer's judgment, and (2) the metaphysical constraints on any given work of dance art are constituted by (some kind of) communal ruling that may be in direct conflict with the choreographer's judgment. Given that the principle of non-contradiction is a limiting condition on every philosophical thesis, no version of the legal model can provide an adequate account of dancework identity.

The defender of Van Camp's general line might respond by pointing out that my first line of critique is but a thinly veiled version of the classic 'Euthyphro problem', which is given its most famous art-related expression by Richard Wollheim.[29] In presenting a variation on Plato's famous dilemma designed to challenge institutional definitions of art, Wollheim writes: 'The crucial question to ask of the definition is this: Is it to be presumed that those *who confer status upon some artifact do so for good reasons, or is there no such presumption?* Might they have no reason, or bad reasons, and yet their action [in claiming some object to be an artwork] be efficacious given that they themselves have the right status – that is, they represent the artworld?'[30] My first objection turns on the idea that the legal model confronts a similar dilemma: either the verdicts of the relevant jury members are metaphysically basic, in which case *no reasons* can be given to justify their judgments; or these audience members have good reasons for their verdicts, in which case it is *the content of these reasons* – rather than any proclamatory act – that constitutes facts about dancework identity.

To reply, the proponent of the legal model might point out that institutional theories of art are not necessarily undermined by Wollheim's dilemma because a path can be eked out between its horns. As Derek Matravers argues, 'Institutionalists need to deny, on pain of falling on the first horn of Wollheim's dilemma, that there is a reason such that, for everything that is a work of art, it is a work of art for *that* reason. However, they need not be impaled on the second: they can maintain that, for everything that is a work of art, there is *some reason or other* why it is a work of art.'[31] That is, while members of 'The Republic of Art' do not magically turn objects and performances into works of art by arbitrary fiat, there is also *no static set of reasons* to which those with a stake in art must appeal for their decree that something is art to be effective. Many different kinds of considerations may count as legitimate reasons to grant or deny art-status depending on the case.

---

29 Thanks to Anna Pakes for this suggestion.

30 Wollheim, 1980, p.60, emphasis mine.

31 Matravers, 2007, p.254, emphasis mine.

If Matravers is correct, then the theoretical heart of institutionalism can be maintained without forfeiting the idea that reasons play an important role in the process by which something becomes an artwork. Following his lead, one might defend the legal model by claiming that while members of the relevant dance-art jury must appeal to 'some reason(s) or other' supplied by the choreographer's standard, it is nonetheless *their decision in light of these reasons* that ultimately secures 'same dancework' status.

The apologist for the legal model might also argue that if the above line of defense is effective with respect to my first objection, a successful rejoinder to the second is not far behind. According to this critique, any version of the legal model might force us to accept a contradiction – namely, that some dance performance both is and is not a presentation of a particular work of dance art – because it is always possible for the choreographer's prescriptions to be at odds with the consensus reached by audience members. This conclusion is unavoidable only if taking the 'two prongs' of the legal model seriously requires us to treat them as *equally* metaphysically important (or as crucial in the same way), which anyone who follows Van Camp's lead should reject. Instead, the advocate of the legal model is best served by recommending that the choreographer contributes to the identity-status of dance art performances *only* by supplying the 'jury' with a set of contextually substantive reasons (encapsulated in the approved form of fixation) on the basis of which 'same dancework' verdicts must be reached. Given that the standard is a metaphysical prerequisite in this process, the dancemaker's contribution to the identity of his or her work is significant and to be taken seriously. But it is not the standard that renders the Joffrey Ballet's performance on Friday, May 11, 2012 an instance of Lar Lubovitch's *Othello*, nor is it what Lar Lubovitch might say about this performance in light of his proffered criteria. Instead, it is the *decision* on the part of audience members with access to the reasons supplied by Lubovitch's standard that is metaphysically effective: only *their* final assessment makes it the case that some dance event is, indeed, an instance of his ballet *Othello*. Hence, the second line of critique can be overcome by extending considerations relevant to the first.

I challenge both rejoinders by suggesting that they rely on a potentially suspect analogy between the legal model and the institutional theory of art. After all, as Matravers puts it, institutionalism escapes Wollheim's dilemma only if it is plausible that it is *not* the case that 'there is *a* reason such that, for everything that is a work of art, it is a work of art for *that* reason.'[32] However, the legal model cannot avoid the version of the Euthyphro Problem it confronts by following Matravers' lead because, on this view, every performance of a particular work of dance art is an instance of *that* work

---

32 *Ibid.*, emphasis mine.

(rather than any other) for only one reason, viz., the event is determined to bear substantial similarity to the choreographer's supplied standard. Of course, there is still a judgment call to be made on the part of those who confer 'same dancework' status on dance art performances; many different kinds of reasons could be brought to the table in defence of the claim that a particular occasion of dancing does (or does not) exhibit the *kind* of similarity to the choreographer's paradigm needed to be countenanced as a performance of his or her artwork. The problem for the defender of any version of the legal model is that the contextually relevant reasons come from a single, highly specific source: the dancemaker's approved form of tangible fixation. This is not the case when members of the artworld make determinative art-status judgments given that they have a panoply of resources upon which to draw to justify their claims, including all of art history, art theory, art criticism, philosophical aesthetics, *and* any explicit statements made by the generative artist. Although this disanalogy does not entail the legal model cannot meet the objections I have offered, considering these in conjunction with the practical difficulties that beset any view that takes its lead from current American copyright law should give one pause about the prospects of crafting a viable philosophical account of dancework identity after Van Camp's proposals.

The canonical performance view[33]

If we cannot create an adequate account of dancework identity by direct appeal to notational records or analogy to current legal practices, perhaps it would be fruitful to consider the possibility that the metaphysical constraints on any particular dancework are supplied by one of its performances. This idea has intuitive plausibility because choreographers do not (typically) create works of dance art by putting pen to paper and drafting a blueprint that specifies their essential features. Instead, the way danceworks are stereotypically made suggests that most become determinate only through rehearsal and, finally, in performance. As Gordon Fancher (1981, pp.3-4) writes,

> Since the choreographer's control over his work extends to the level of performance, what he creates will necessarily involve the elusiveness that we associate with performance. Such elusiveness, of course, emerges in the other performing arts but it does not play a central role *in fixing the identity of individual works*. Because the choreographer's work is so *intimately related to the final [first public] performance* he is less like the dramatist or composer and more like the sculptor or painter in enjoying a certain kind of control over his work. [my emphases]

---

33 Thanks to Laurence BonJour for suggesting this approach.

Fancher's remarks suggest a close connection between the identity conditions of danceworks and their public presentations. Along similar lines Angela Kane notes, 'This issue of identity [requires us to recognize that] . . . there is a *dialectical relationship between first and subsequent* performances of a dance work.'[34] Hence, although no one to date has developed an account according to which the identity conditions of dance art creations are constituted by facts about individual dance concerts, this theoretical avenue is worthy of exploration.

In defence of this approach to dancework identity, one might argue as follows: works of dance art, like almost all artistic offerings, start off as basic thematic ideas – coupled with an inchoate set of hopes and desires – in the minds of their creators. But, unlike many other artworks, they begin to acquire their identity-constitutive features only when the generative artist and her dancers collectively engage in the project of conducting movement experiments, an endeavor that constitutes a significant part of any rehearsal process. In many cases, the abstract object that is the *choreographic work* emerges quite late in the rehearsal game. And even when the choreography is finally set (for a particular run of performances), there is still the important matter of correlating it with light plots, deciding from which wings of the stage entrances will be made and where exits will be taken, determining whether the costumes are functionally suited to accommodate choreographic demands, and so forth. As a result, the abstract art object that is the *dancework* becomes determinate only after a series of exhaustive dress rehearsals, and is often fully realized for the first time only on opening night.

Thus, reflection on the standard process of dancework creation might suggest that many works of dance art do not acquire their identity conditions until some point in their performance history and that, therefore, the essential features of most danceworks are constituted by what occurs during some live performance. If so, then it is the features of some privileged performative event – including its movement structure, staging, lighting, costuming, and musical accompaniment – that constitute the metaphysical constraints on the abstract object that is the work. This theory is both consonant with facts about how danceworks are typically made and supported by the fact that audience members often take great interest in certain performances (e.g., the (in)famous opening night of Nijinksy's *The Rite of Spring* or Pavlova's execution of *The Dying Swan*), using them as benchmarks against which all other putative public presentations of a given dancework are both understood and evaluated.

These considerations suggest the following account, to which I refer as the 'canonical performance view':

---

34 Kane, 2000, p.73.

A and B are instances of some particular dancework if and only if both are dance performances that contain (to some reasonably high degree) the movement sequences and staging elements (e.g., music, lights, sets, costumes) that were a part of some canonical presentation of this work.

The idea that the essential features of works of dance art are 'fixed' in certain performances and that, therefore, acceptable 'same dancework' judgments must be made by appeal to performance history is an improvement over other views in at least two ways. First, the canonical performance view respects the first of my proposed desiderata insofar as it reflects the kinds of reasons dance insiders *typically* offer for claiming that some performance was (or was not) of a particular work of dance art. It is quite rare for 'same work' judgments to be made by appeal to scores, in part, because most danceworks are not scored and, in part, because most people – including dance art practitioners – cannot read dance notation. And it is almost never the case that dance insiders wait on the collective judgment of general audiences to draw conclusions in this domain. Hence, the canonical performance view appears more responsive to well-established facts about dance art practice than notationalism or the legal model.

Second, it is intuitively superior to its competitors because there is no possibility that recognized works of dance art will be metaphysically indeterminate on this view. If the essential features of every work of dance art are constituted by some performance(s), then the necessary metaphysical foundation will *always* be available with respect to works that make it out of the studio and onto the stage. If, however, the essential features of danceworks are constituted by actual notation or some kind of collective agreement in light of it, then any dance art creations that have not been preserved in some kind of fixation will lack the metaphysical prerequisites for numerical identity.

But while the canonical performance view seems an improvement over other accounts considered here, it cannot be developed easily into an adequate theory of dancework identity. First, on this proposal, there must be some *single* performance – the 'canonical' performance – whose properties constitute the constraints on the abstract object that is the dancework. The view cannot allow work-constitutive features to emerge from multiple performance events since, in practice, *any* element of one performance might not be present in another legitimately offered as a version of the same dancework. Since it is possible that for *any* particular thing that happens on stage one night something different might occur the next, the work's essential features cannot be appropriately limited unless there is only *one* performance that constitutes its identity conditions.

This creates a dilemma for the proponent of the canonical performance view: either the defender of this theory must make a *purely arbitrary* choice in favor of some single performance over all others or he must say that the identity conditions of danceworks are not *constituted* by what happens during any particular performance but by something else, e.g., the choreographer's intentions with respect to his/her creation or audiences' willingness to countenance multiple performance events as instances of the same work on the basis of visible similarities. In short, like the proponent of the legal model, the advocate of the canonical performance view faces a Euthyphro problem. If one performative event is metaphysically basic, then no reasons can be given for why *that* performance sets the relevant constraints on the abstract dance art object on pain of undermining the proposed view. If, however, reasons can be given in defence of the claim that one particular performance is authoritative with respect to the work's identity, then no performance *event* is metaphysically basic. Instead, it will be those things appealed to in the *reasons* for preferring one performance over others that capture what is at the metaphysical core of the work and that are, therefore, constitutive of its essential features.

In response, the defender of the canonical performance view might claim that the identity-constitutive performance is the *first* performance. While this response is intuitive, it is insufficient because it pushes the original problem back a level. We still confront the crucial question: which *features* of the inaugural performance are work-constitutive? This presents the defender of the canonical performance view with another dilemma.

The key problem is the unavoidable reality that any two live performances will differ from one another in some (if not many) ways. The defender of the canonical performance view cannot claim that *every* feature of the first public offering is identity-constitutive unless he is willing to accept that any dance event that does not possess this *exact set* of features is not a performance of the relevant work. Hence, the fact that no two performances are ever qualitatively identical will force the proponent of the canonical performance view to bite one of two equally unpalatable bullets. Either he must admit his theory entails that in practice every dancework is performed only once (which violates the first of our three desiderata), or he must find a philosophically adequate way to specify *which* features of the first performance are identity-constitutive. Unfortunately, there is no non-arbitrary way to specify which elements of the relevant performative event are essential to the work – and which are merely contingent – unless the work's essential features are constituted by something *other than* the performance itself. As a result, the advocate of the canonical performance view must either flout a fundamental norm of dance art practice or engage in blatant ad-hoccery.

Several other potential problems with the canonical performance view deserve brief mention. First, the defender of this approach must specify what makes some performative event 'inaugural' (or otherwise 'canonical') in a way that is both sufficiently determinate *and* does not beg the identity question.[35] Second, even if the defender of this view can provide an account of 'first/canonical performance' adequate to this task, he will have to face the theoretical consequence that danceworks that are only rehearsed, but never make it to the stage (or, perhaps, to dress rehearsal), are either metaphysically indeterminate or are all the same work of dance art. Third, the canonical performance view undermines the possibility of full-scale 're'choreography, as well as the leeway to allow lighting, costumes, and sets to be *significantly* altered over time (as in Dendy's *Beat*). Since it is a commonplace of dance art practice that danceworks grow and change over their performance history, the canonical performance view threatens to flout the first of my proposed desiderata. Finally, any approach of this kind is in danger of running afoul of my third desideratum because if the features of an 'inaugural' or 'canonical' performance of a dancework constitute its identity conditions, then even well-qualified dance insiders will lack access to the kinds of information required to make reliable identity claims about works from the distant past – such as those 'lost masterpieces' that are the objects of dance reconstruction – given that substantive data about their early performances is often inaccessible.

Reconsidering dancework identity

There are many possible variations on notationalism, the legal model and the canonical performance view, and some might have the resources to avoid the problems I have articulated here. That said, I hope this investigation has made two useful contributions to contemporary dance theory. First, it has laid the foundation for critical discussion about several accounts of dancework identity that have, unfortunately, remained relatively unexamined in recent years. Second, it has opened the door for dance theorists and philosophers to take renewed interest in this old issue and engage in richer interactive dialogue about what is at stake when dance insiders make identity judgments. Given that any critical responses to my arguments will improve the dialectic topography of this area of dance aesthetics, I welcome all with open arms. As Peter Kivy writes in the preface of *Authenticities*, 'What I hope there will be is the groundwork for future dialogue among [dancers] and philosophers together. I look forward to that, and to being, when it comes, in the thick of things.'[36]

---

35 That is, one cannot simply define the inaugural or canonical performance as the first to exemplify all of the work's essential features since the goal of this approach to dancework identity is to *specify what these features are* by reference to some special performative event.

36 Kivy, 1995, p.xiii. Thanks to Ann Baker, Laurence BonJour, Graham McFee, Ronald

References

Anderson, Jack. 'Idealists, Materialists, and the Thirty-Two Fouettes', in Copeland, Roger and Marshall Cohen (eds.), *What is Dance?*, New York: Oxford University Press, 1983, pp.410-19.

Anderson, Jack. 'Dance: Mark Dendy and Troupe at P.S. 122', *New York Times*, 14 October, 1986.

Armelagos, Adina and Mary Sirridge. 'The Identity Crisis in Dance', *The Journal of Aesthetics and Art Criticism* 37:2, 1978, pp.129-140.

Brennan, Mary Alice. 'Everything Little Movement has a Meaning all its Own: Movement Analysis in Dance Research', in Horton, Fraleigh, Sondra and Penelope Hanstein, *Researching Dance: Evolving Modes of Inquiry,*, PA: University of Pittsburgh Press, 1999, pp.283-308.

Carbonneau, Suzanne. 'Artist Notes: Mark Dendy', http://www.batesdance festival.org/ArtistNotes/dendy00.php, 2000, accessed 2/1/2013.

Carr, David, 'Meaning in Dance', *British Journal of Aesthetics* 37:4, 1997, pp.349-366.

Carroll, Noel. 'Dance' in Levinson, Jerrold (ed.), *The Oxford Handbook of Aesthetics*, New York: Oxford University Press, 2003, pp.583-593.

Conklin, J.L. 'Goucher, Towson students show promise in programs', http:// articles.baltimoresun.com/1995-05-02/features/1995122025_1_ goucher-towson-students-dance-students, 1995, accessed 2/1/2013.

Cohen, Selma Jeanne. *Next Week, Swan Lake: Reflections on Dance and Dances*, Middletown: Wesleyan University Press, 1982.

Davies, David. 'The Primacy of Practice in the Ontology of Art', *The Journal of Aesthetics and Art Criticism* 67:2, 2006, pp.159-171.

Davies, David. 'Dancing Around the Issues: Prospects for an Empirically Grounded Philosophy of Dance', *The Journal of Aesthetics and Art Criticism* 71:2, 2013, pp.195-202.

Dickie, George. *Art and the Aesthetic: an Institutional Analysis*, Ithaca: Cornell University Press, 1974.

Dickie, George. *The Art Circle*, New York: Haven Publications, 1984.

Diffey, Terry. *The Republic of Art*, New York: Peter Lang, 1992.

Fancher, Gordon. 'Introduction to the Essays', in Fancher, Gordon and Gerald Myers (eds.), *Philosophical Essays on Dance*, New York: Dance Horizons, 1981, pp.1-15.

Goodman, Nelson. *Languages of Art: An Approach to a Theory of Symbols* 2nd edition, Indianapolis: Hackett Publishing Company, Inc., 1976 [1969].

Guest, Ann Hutchinson. *Labanotation: A System of Analyzing and Recording Movement*, 3rd edition, New York: Routledge/Theatre Arts Books, 1991

Moore, Anna Pakes, Andrea Woody, several anonymous reviewers, and the editors of this volume for valuable comments on earlier versions of this essay.

[1954].

Kane, Angela. 'Issues of Authenticity and Identity in the Restaging of Paul Taylor's *Airs*', in Jordan, Stephanie (ed.), *Preservation Politics: Dance Revived Reconstructed Remade*, London: Dance Books, 2000, pp.72-8.

Kisselgoff, Anna. 'Review/Dance; Of Movement for Movement's Sake', http://www.nytimes.com/1990/01/13/arts/review-dance-of-movement-for-movement-s-sake.html, 1990, accessed 2/1/2013.

Kurtz, Sandra. 'Take two', http://www.seattleweekly.com/2000-07-12/arts/take-two/, 2000, accessed 2/1/2013.

Kivy, Peter. *Authenticities: Philosophical Reflections on Musical Performance*, Ithaca: Cornell University Press, 1995.

Margolis, Joseph. 'The Autographic Nature of the Dance', *The Journal of Aesthetics and Art Criticism* 39:4, 1981, pp.420-27.

Matravers, Derek. 'Institutional Definitions and Reasons', *British Journal of Aesthetics* 47:3, 2007, pp.251-57.

McFee, Graham. *Understanding Dance*, London: Routledge, 1992.

McFee, Graham. *The Concept of Dance Education*, expanded edition, Eastbourne: Pageantry Press, 2004.

McFee, Graham. *The Philosophical Aesthetics of Dance: Identity, Performance, and Understanding*, Hampshire: Dance Books, 2011.

Pakes, Anna. 'The Plausibility of a Platonist Ontology of Dance', conference presentation at the 'Thinking Through Dance' conference, Roehampton University, London, 2011.

Rubidge, Sarah. 'Identity and the Open Work', in Jordan, Stephanie (ed.), *Preservation Politics: Dance Revived Reconstructed Remade*, London: Dance Books, 2000, pp.205-215.

Sirridge, Mary and Adina Armelagos. 'The Role of 'Natural Expressiveness' in Explaining Dance', *The Journal of Aesthetics and Art Criticism* 41:3, 1983, pp.301-07.

Sparshott, Francis. *A Measured Pace: Toward a Philosophical Understanding of the Arts of Dance*, Toronto and London: University of Toronto Press, 1995.

Speer, Dean. 'University of Washington Chamber Dance Group: Martha's Mysteries', http://www.ballet-dance.com/200502/articles/UWCDG20050203.html, 2005, accessed 2/1/2013.

Van Camp, Julie. 'Philosophical Problems of Dance Criticism', PhD dissertation, Temple University, 1981.

Van Camp, Julie. 'Copyright of Choreographic Works', in Breimer, Stephen E., Robert Thorne and John David Viera (eds.), *1994-95 Entertainment, Publishing and the Arts Handbook*, New York: Clark, Boardman, and Callaghan, 1994, pp.59-92.

Van Camp, Julie. 'The Ontology of Dance' in Kelly, Michael (ed.), *The Encyclopedia of Aesthetics*, New York: Oxford University Press, 1998, pp.399-402.

Van Camp, Julie, 'A Pragmatic Approach to the Identity of Works of Art', *Journal of Speculative Philosophy* 20:1, 2006, pp.42-55.

Weitz, Morris. 'The Role of Theory in Aesthetics', *The Journal of Aesthetics and Art Criticism* 15 :1, 1956, pp.27-35.

Whitley, Ann, 'More than an Expert Scribe? The Human Dimension', in Jordan, Stephanie (ed.), *Preservation Politics: Dance Revived Reconstructed Remade*, London: Dance Books, 2000, pp.132-140.

Wollheim, Richard. *Art and Its Objects, Second Edition with Six Supplementary Essays*, Cambridge: Cambridge University Press, 1980.

6. What should dancers think about when performing? Issues of interpretation and identity in ballet

Geraldine Morris

This essay is about performance interpretation in ballet. My discussion centres on three philosophical issues. Firstly, I consider the extent to which performances of choreographed dances are artistic renderings of the choreography as distinct from merely aesthetic executions of the movement. In doing so I separate the artistic from the aesthetic, which allows me to distinguish between performances of choreography and renderings of academic dance; the two require different kinds of knowledge.[1] This leads to my second concern, the notion of choreographic intention. My point is that an artistic (as opposed to an aesthetic) rendering of a dance involves knowing about a choreographer's style, which, I argue, is linked to choreographic intention. My third issue is about performers' interpretation. For a discussion of this I draw on philosophers' essays which deal with the practice of musical interpretation, specifically performers' interpretation.[2]

Michael Krausz, in his introduction to a volume of essays on the subject, argues that considerations about musical (for which we can substitute dance) interpretation are both practical (in the sense of a performer) and philosophical and that both performers and philosophers need to take account of these issues; the situation is similar in dance.[3] Musical/dance interpretations depend on the performer's view of what a musical/dance work is:

---

1 The steps and positions of ballet referred to as the *danse d'école* are also described as the codified movement or academic dance. I use the latter term here.

2 My reason for advising dancers and rehearsal directors on interpretation is that many fail to understand or appreciate that performance of choreography takes priority over the execution of the dance lexicon. Many practitioners believe that the lexicon should be performed correctly at all costs and this frequently leads to a misrepresentation of the choreography. Dancers and directors need more dance education so that they understand the significance of choreography and that it is the choreography that is the art work and not the steps of the ballet lexicon. There is evidence to support my view of this misunderstanding in my article, 'Artistry or mere technique? The value of the ballet competition' (2008). Further evidence is available from studying the curriculum of any ballet conservatoire.

3 Although the score is differently regarded in dance, the concerns are to some extent similar.

For example, on whether it is fully embodied in a score, on how strictly all markings should be respected, on what pertinence historical research has to his performance, on how decisive is the role of a historical or reconstructed composer, and so on. (Krausz 1993, p.1.)

These are issues which concern both musicians/dancers and philosophers. But before dealing with these, I illuminate the problem. My discussion is concerned with a growing tendency to ignore choreographic style and thus homogenize performances of diverse choreographers. To support my arguments and defend them against objections by the profession, I start by giving some specific examples: firstly to explain how the confusion between academic dance and choreography has arisen and secondly to demonstrate how choreographed dances can be reduced to technical renderings. As the examples indicate, much of the profession either is unaware that there is a problem or does not consider it to be significant enough to explore the issue. So there is a lack of coherence between what performers do, or think they should be doing, and what philosophers, involved with dance, believe to be performance issues. In the following essay, I suggest some tentative solutions.

Confusing academic dance and choreography

Graham McFee makes the point that when ballet is criticized as having been too technical it is really an indication that there is a decline in the technique,[4] such that it becomes more a matter of the ability to execute 'circus tricks' rather than connect with the expressivity of the movement (1992, p.206). What is really at stake here is an ideological issue: should the dancer perform the dance's movement according to the current values of classroom technique (*danse d'école*) and thus emphasize the 'circus tricks' or should she adhere to the requirements of the choreography, which may involve cutting or adapting the classroom step? Expressivity is tied to choreographed movement rather than to that of the classroom and for a dancer to give an expressive performance, she needs to have an understanding of the choreography.[5] This is a problem, which is peculiar to ballet (though not confined to it), primarily because of the presence of the

---

4 By technique McFee seems to mean genre as in ballet or Graham technique or Cunningham technique. The ballet profession's notion of technique is tied to the steps and positions of the *danse d'école* and the profession considers a dancer to have a good technique only if she can perform these steps 'perfectly'. The notion of perfection is dependent on the values dictated by the contemporary era.

5 In an earlier article, I make the point that choreographed dances should be judged by artistic criteria while judgments about classroom movement are made by reference to aesthetic criteria. This means that expressivity is part of choreography and not necessarily embodied in the movement of the classroom (Morris 2008).

codified movement. The tendency in performances of choreographed dance is to isolate the aesthetic elements of the movement for their own sake so that the values intrinsic to academic dance take precedence over those of the choreographed dances. Ballet choreographers use the code as the basis for their choreography but each has a distinctive and highly personal approach and disregarding the alterations they make to it can lead to the loss of the dance's specificity; it reverts then to being (merely) classroom movement.[6] In other words, I argue that it is these alterations to the code, amongst other things, which constitute the identity of the work.[7] Ballet dancers need to have more knowledge of the choreography, to allow them to distinguish between it and codified movement. Barbara Newman, the dance writer, supports my concerns commenting that dancers' desire to attain perfection has led to a pervasive homogeneity. Not only does this make all the dances look the same, it also results in loss of artistry. And she argues that

> if no one [can] sustain a vision of the piece they [are] dancing, rather than of their own dancing in it, we [will] wind up with nothing to watch but technique and décor. (Newman 2004.)

The difficulty in perceiving the choreography has arisen in part because of the gulf that has opened between today's training and earlier choreography. For instance, during the latter part of the nineteenth century when Marius Petipa choreographed *The Sleeping Beauty* (1890) the two were closely linked. In the classroom, after *barre* work in the 'Class of Perfection' (the soloist class) the custom was to rehearse and perform the current solo variations as part of centre training (May 1998).[8] It was common too for ballet masters to invent long phrases of movement for training purposes and the choreographer sometimes also used these, slipping them into the dance. This meant that the phrases used for training became choreographed dance and consequently the context changed; they could now be manipulated for expressive purposes. As I will argue in due course, performances of these phrases can then be valued more for their style and meaning than their technical accuracy (Legat 1931). With the standardization of ballet in the Soviet Union in the late 1930s by Agrippina Vaganova, this practice altered significantly and each classroom step was taught as a separate entity and

---

6 I deal with the notions of the aesthetic and the artistic in due course.

7 My point is that they are a significant part of the style and so contribute to the dance's identity.

8 Almost all ballet classes begin with a series of exercises, designed to warm each part of the body, in which the dancer holds on to a waist-high length of wood known as a *barre*. Many pictures by Edouard Degas, show just this: see *La Salle de Ballet de l'Opéra, Rue le Pelletier* (1872), for example.

valued for the accuracy with which it was performed.[9] This approach to the technical elements of ballet is now widely taught. As a result, dancers are instructed to perfect the technical steps as separate units. Inevitably this slows down the dance phrase because each step has to be correctly (according to Vaganova's syllabus) completed and there is no recognition of the changes that occur in a step when its context is altered in a sequence of steps. This was very evident in the Soviet dancer, Rudolph Nureyev's performances. He frequently asked for the speed to be reduced in order for him to place his feet correctly for a *pirouette*.[10] As a result, choreography that relied on speed for its significance, is altered to suit the requirements of the contemporary classroom aesthetic. Misperceiving the choreographed step for that of the classroom means that the properties of the step as art are not discerned. Another example, from the Ballerina's first variation in Frederick Ashton's *Scènes de ballet* (1948), makes the point. When taught by Ashton, the dancer was instructed to bend over the raised knee (*retiré*) and worry less about turnout; consequently, the working leg was in a parallel position as opposed to a turned out one (Sibley 1996).[11] The expressive elements are in the speed of the movement and strongly bent torso: performing the classroom version would result in a slower pose and upright body.

McFee argues that treating a work as identical to one in another category means that the work is misperceived. I argue that this is also true of the movement that makes up the choreography: if it is taken to be the same as academic dance, it is misperceived (McFee 2011, p.48). What does this mean for the choreographed dance? If dancers only see academic dance, they are judging the technical aspects and not responding to the dance's significance. As McFee notes, this may not affect the beauty of the dance but a performance based only on the technical elements means that the dance's identity is compromised (McFee, 2011, p.12). That it was made by a choreographer allows it to be expressive, sad, witty, etc. which gives it meaning. The point can be developed further to show how misperceiving a dance in another genre can seriously distort our understanding. If, for example, we only know ballet, we see everything as ballet, and dances by Merce Cunningham or Paul Taylor become bad ballet, rather than being correctly perceived as modern dance which obeys different conventions and values.

---

9 I use the term 'step' to cover the ballet vocabulary in which a step generally means a combination of bodily movements, involving legs, arms, torso and head all occurring simultaneously.

10 See the recording of Nureyev in the duet from *Le Corsaire* (1963, *An Evening With the Royal Ballet*, British Home Entertainment, BEHO11).

11 *retiré* , a pose/movement in which one leg is raised to the side, turned out, with the knee bent, and the toe is pointed and placed on the knee of the supporting leg.

Two dance performances

Thus far, I have argued that ballet dancers and rehearsal directors frequently confuse the choreographed dance with academic dance, resulting in the loss of the expressive elements of the choreography and leading to the loss of the dance's identity. I want now to examine how omitting movements that are part of the style, but which limit the dancer's capacity to present a 'perfect' arabesque, can radically change former choreography. Previously, when investigating Ashton's dance movement style, I suggested that it comprises a web of interrelated elements (Morris 2012). These include the technical aesthetic of the era in which he worked; the contributions of the dancers; the contemporary stage dancing and the stylistic aspects of earlier dancers. All of these feed his style and he was not concerned with steps as such. Katherine Healy (1994), who worked with him on his revival of *Romeo and Juliet* in 1985, remembered that he was more insistent on details such as use of head, eye and arms and on the contrasting use of dynamics than on technical execution. To understand an Ashton dance, it is vital to notice the emphasis and timing of phrases and be able to perform the precise, yet intricate, footwork at a speed that is generally faster than that to which today's dancers are accustomed.

For Ashton expressive use of the body is also an important feature, much more important than technical accuracy (Nears 1988).[12] During a Masterclass in which he coaches Antoinette Sibley and Anthony Dowell in the final pas de deux from his ballet *The Dream* (1964), Ashton comments continuously on small details. The use of the shoulders is crucial and he insists that the impetus for the movement must come from the torso. He coaxes the dancers to make frequent alterations between languid moments and sudden forceful poses, encouraging them to slow down and then sparkle.

In *Masterclass* (1988), during the section where the two dancers have short solo phrases, Ashton admonishes Sibley for not using her shoulders more fully. He wants her to separate the arm movements so that one arm dives down before the other. But because he also wants her to pause after her *relevé* into *arabesque*, he suggests she play with the music. The section comprises a quick dive forward with a little jump from one foot to the other, ending in a crossed position with a pointed foot and a low bend forward of the upper body. The arms move from the shoulder circling down to focus on the foot, first the left, or open arm and then the right (crossed) follows just a couple of seconds later before she jack-knifes back into a momentarily held *arabesque*. The phrase has dynamic contrasts between the light, sparkling

---

12 This Masterclass was shown on television (BBC) in 1988 and is available for viewing at the British Film Institute. At the time of writing (2013), it is also available at http://www.youtube.com.

qualities of the beginning and the vigorous piercing qualities of the second part of the phrase. So it is not the bravura technique which is important but the qualitative elements which Ashton spends time conveying to Sibley.

Looking at a later version of the same section of the duet, performed more than ten years later by Alessandra Ferri and Ethan Stiefel of American Ballet Theater, crucial elements that Ashton encouraged Sibley to perform are ignored and the performance omits all of Ashton's directives as given within the earlier rehearsal footage.[13] It is not the same work. in the sense that reverting to classroom versions of the dance means that Ashton's choreography is no longer evident and thus in this performance the dance's expressivity is missing.

Ferri skips the dive forward and, instead of the circling arm projections, shrugs her shoulders. The first arm movement is absent, replaced by a shoulder shrug, and the second slides a little way down her leg, holding on to her skirt, and leaving out the deep forward bend. There is much less dynamic contrast between the two sections of the phrase and the dancer draws attention to herself through her high arabesque and strange, almost knowing, glance at the audience. The arabesque too is altered because the arms swing backwards into a position used more frequently in *Swan Lake* Act II. This is a case of the execution being so far removed from the choreography that it is difficult to recognize it as a performance of that choreographer's work. The movements have been altered, the directives ignored. Oddly, the dancers were coached by Anthony Dowell, the work's first Oberon, and Christopher Carr, a rehearsal director and notator, though it is possible that the directives were given and that the dancer ignored them in performance. She chose instead to adopt a classroom version of the movements: diving right down would have prevented her from achieving the high, swan-like *arabesque*, since, without significantly slowing down the music, she would have been constrained by tempo. As a result the identifying features were omitted and the specificity of the dance altered. Her performance manifests an emphasis on the aesthetic at the expense of the artistic.

Artistic or merely aesthetic?[14]

Both David Best and McFee distinguish between the notion of an aesthetic judgment or interest and an artistic one (Best 1978, pp.113-16, and 1985,

---

13 Diamond, Matthew (2004) *The Dream*, New York: Thirteen/WNET (Educational Broadcasting Company).

14 I have dealt with this contrast at length elsewhere (Morris 2008) and both Best and McFee deal extensively with it. I am broadly in agreement with them, though I develop their ideas and apply them to ballet.

pp.153-4; and McFee 1992, p.42).[15] They argue that our appreciation of art is different from the interest we take in natural phenomena, such as sunsets or seascapes, and, Best adds, the aesthetic sports, like gymnastics and ice-skating. This is because central to art is the expression of human concerns such as moral, social, political or emotional issues. Neither technical achievement nor an aesthetic sport, such as gymnastics, has as its aim the expression of life issues; both are concerned with achieving technical brilliance. Artistic judgments, on the other hand, are those we make about intentional objects made by humans, more specifically objects intentionally made as art. McFee's point is that our appreciation of an art work is different from that of an aesthetic object. More precisely, we should consider each under different categories and this means that the details of the work are altered when we see it as art. For instance, if we observe a dance but know little about it, we perceive it under aesthetic concepts and see only its beautiful or ugly features. In other words we do not have enough knowledge to understand it and are unable to recognize its significance, so we cannot see its stylistic or other meaningful features. McFee's distinction between the two kinds of judgments is important because, he believes, we need to apply different criteria when considering an art work. So when observing a dance we look for the formal aspects, the stylistic elements and the meaning but if (as ballet dancers) we look only at the performance qualities we may be enthralled by the brilliance of the dancing but miss the meaning. Performers should take a similar interest in the dance and need to distinguish between the dance as art, considering the style and meaning (of the dance movement), and the classroom movement from which it is drawn.

Choreographic intention and style

To determine how the dance should be danced, I consider choreographic intention (though not as any sort of 'inner state' of the choreographer) and its relationship to style. I have written in depth about this elsewhere (2012), so here I give a more condensed version of my arguments, which are drawn from McFee (1992 and 2011).[16] Central is the notion that a dance is more than its perceptible features. This means that both the context in which the dance was created and the choreographer's intention also need to be accounted for.[17] We can mis-read a dance if we know nothing

---

15 By 'judgment', McFee means appreciation of, or interest in, as opposed to an evaluation of something.

16 See Morris (2012), pp.10-16.

17 By intention, I do not mean that we need to have access to a choreographer's thoughts about a work but that, as McFee and others (for example, Rowell 2007, Cavell 1976, Dworkin 1998) have argued, art objects are intentional activities and thus embody the

of a choreographer's other works or her/his approach to style, so elements that seem to be outside the work do contribute to our understanding and performance knowledge. For instance, we could take Michael Fokine's *Les Sylphides* (1909) to be a classical ballet if we knew nothing of his other work or the prevailing artistic context of its creation and to perform it as having the values of classical dance would be to mis-represent it.[18] To understand it we need to know the dance tradition from which the choreographer came and both the historical era and geographical location in which s/he worked. At the heart of McFee's approach is the idea of choreographic intention, that the choreographer intended to make an art work. But to have access to this we need to examine other aspects, particularly the possibilities available to the choreographer at the time, from which the choreographer chose.

McFee focuses on individual style and the artist's use of material in a specific way. But for a dance work (or other art form) to be considered as art it needs to be decipherable. In other words, it has to be made in the context of artistic concepts; which effectively means that a choreographer has intentionally employed or rejected the canons and resources of the art form. So the conventions associated with the dance genre and the era in which it was made are central to the work. To discern a choreographer's style then the dancer (and observer) needs this knowledge together with information about the choreographer's own dance background, training and other influences as well as the training and dance style of the dancers with whom s/he worked. All of these aspects are part of choreographic style. So, in practice, how does this work?

In the case of my study of Ashton, whose work is in some measure derived from the balletic code, I was forced to confront a number of issues.[19] Ashton worked directly on his chosen dancers' bodies collaborating with them and encouraging them to contribute to his dances. He drew mainly from a group of dancers trained in a similar style. Thus both the values of the training style and the talents of the dancers fed his style as did the styles of the dancers and choreographers he admired. These included the dancers Anna Pavlova and Isadora Duncan and the choreographer Bronislava Nijinska. Aspects of their movement and approach to choreography can be discerned in his choreographic style. For example, in Nijinska's choreography (in the

---

choreographer's intention. We can discover intention by examining the work and by looking at the possibilities that were available to him/her at the time the work was made. This means that the context and the culture of the era are also part of the work and not extrinsic to it.

18 By classical dance, I mean performing it according to the values of late nineteenth century works like Marius Petipa's *The Sleeping Beauty* (1890)

19 See my recent book, Morris (2012) from which all of the information on this page is derived. David Vaughan's seminal work updated in 1999 is also relevant.

known, extant works, such as *Les Noces* (1923) and *Les Biches* (1924)), arms are pinned to the body, either placed on the shoulders or by the side of the body, this means that the impetus for the movement has to come from the torso. As already discussed above, this approach to movement is found in many Ashton dances. His passion for Pavlova was well known. She had, according to Ashton, beautiful feet, to which she drew attention in her dancing. In the first variation in his *Birthday Offering* (1956) the dancer (Elaine Fifield) was given movement which directs the audience's attention to the feet because Fifield too had Pavlova-like feet. This 'personal stamp' is what makes Ashton's dance movement particular to his choreography and not merely a replica of the academic code and this is true of most ballet choreographers whose stylistic preferences can be similarly identified. For the purpose of this essay, I am suggesting that identifying a dance involves not only considering both the written score and the verbal directions but also having some knowledge of the style: that is knowledge not only of a particular choreographer's approach to academic dance but also of the values of the contemporary training and his or her other artistic influences. This kind of information is needed by both performer and observers in order to interpret the dance.[20]

When the making of the dance is considered to be an intentional activity, we can access the intentions of choreographers by examining their other works. For instance we know that Fokine did not intend the choreography of *Les Sylphides* to be regarded as classical dance by examining his other works and his writings, so it can be said that Fokine's intentions encourage us to understand his works in a specific way. The style is embedded in the intention. This said, we need to be aware that we can only see a dance in performance, so we are to some extent dependent on the performance honoring the choreographer's intentions. Sometimes this means looking at early versions of the dance, performed when the choreographer or his rehearsal directors were still alive.

Music interpretation differs from that of dance

A small group of philosophers has written about performers' interpretation of music (see, for example, Krausz 1993), but there is almost no literature on the interpretation of ballet movement.[21] While the problems encountered

---

20 I have written at length on style in Morris (2012) drawing initially on the well-known articles by Armelagos and Sirridge (1978 and 1984) and Sirridge and Armelagos (1977) as a starting point but developing my approach beyond their arguments.

21 There are numerous references to interpretation in McFee's books both 1992 and in his most recent book 2011 but he is not dealing with interpretation in the sense that I am here. Julie Van Camp (1980) has also written about interpretation but she is referring to the difference between it and creativity. Her article touches on some of the problems

by musicians can be different, similar issues can also arise in the context of dance, and since there is little else available, I draw on the musical literature. Musicians have to interpret scores and, as Krausz points out, their interpretative decisions will depend on their relationship with the score.

This is not the case with ballet dancers who learn the dances from a rehearsal director or from a filmed recording of the work. The latter is already another dancer's rendering and so problematic. Dancers are generally taught to copy. They learn the classroom movement from watching a teacher and, when learning a dance, frequently do so from watching another dancer. This means that they are copying another interpretation rather than making one of their own. Though films are important too as a source of interpretation in that they can act as models of past performance traditions on which a new interpreter can build, they should only be viewed as a partial source. They are evidence of one performance only, and, as McFee argues, because dance is a performable art (it can be re-performed) a film is only one performance of the dance not the dance as such (2011, pp.8-9).[22]

Dances, like musical works, are also underdetermined, so each performance draws on different possibilities within the dance's context. In other words, dancers can choose to emphasize one aspect while disregarding another and still be giving an accurate account of the dance's choreographic style. So a film cannot be seen as something which must be copied by a future dancer.

Notation scores of most dances exist but are interpreted for performers by rehearsal directors, so dancers are confronting a prior interpretation rather than accessing the score directly. Scores are often initially the main source for reconstructing a dance once the choreographer has died, but in addition to a score, a rehearsal director may also be the dancer on whom the dance was first made. In this case, s/he can bring knowledge of the work's history of production. For example, the George Balanchine Foundation is an organization that promotes this kind of knowledge as important for reconstruction.[23]

Over the last fifteen years, the Foundation has been making recordings of older dancers, for the most part those on whom Balanchine created the roles, coaching today's dancers and instructing them in Balanchine style. These now provide a record of what was prescribed and proscribed

---

I am addressing here but she is not considering interpretation as the interpretation of choreography and choreographed dance movement.

22 McFee indicates that 'when watching a video recording counts as watching the dance, it is a performance, albeit an indirect or recorded one' (2011, p.9).

23 See, for example, the Foundation's website: http://balanchine.org The Balanchine Trust model has been adopted by several choreographers and organizations including the Frederick Ashton Trust, Jerome Robbins Trust, Glen Tetley Trust, the Gerald Arpino and Robert Joffrey Foundation and Anthony Tudor Trust.

by the choreographer and are available for dancers to use as a basis for interpretation but there are no such tools available for the work of most other choreographers.[24] Additionally, Balanchine introduced his own style of training and when this is retained, dancers can be in accord with the choreography. So having a style-based class might also provide a further tool to assist dancers in interpreting the choreography.

Scores

I turn now to the arguments of those philosophers who address performance interpretation and then examine how these are relevant to ballet. In the debates dealing with interpretation in music, two questions persist. The first considers the extent to which an interpretation is an interpretation of a given work and thus is more about the work's ontology and related questions of identity. The second is to do with the concept of interpretation. Ontology is not the focus of this paper and so I can deal only briefly with the issues surrounding relationships between the work, the score and its performance. This is a much larger debate and needs more detailed analysis than is possible here.

Most of the philosophers who deal with interpretation accept that scores are not the work, but instructions for its realization (Krausz 1993; Thom 1993; Hermerén 1993; Levinson 1993; and Margolis 1993). Those I consider also regard scores as underdetermining the work, which means there can be no single correct interpretation of the score, and that interpretation is central to the notion of performance. If all performances of a work were identical, not only would audiences lose interest, they would also be witnessing something closer to ritual.

The interpretation debate is also something that is discussed by musical performers who generally agree with the view that scores underdetermine works. In contrast to the philosophers, Daniel Barenboim (2008) makes the point that it is the score that is the work, that it has infinite possibilities and that it is the performance that is finite. He believes that because scores have endless possibilities, the performer can only choose to realize some of them, thus engaging with a score is a lifelong experience. But then there can be different interpretations of the same score, all of which comply with the score's instructions in at least some respects. Barenboim does not consider how to address the score's potential or what might be considered to be an acceptable interpretation, though he does indicate that some interpretations are unacceptable. Barenboim's view is not one that philosophers would accept. Scores cannot literally be the work for a number of reasons: if the score, whether in music or dance, is lost, it does not mean that the work

---

24 I am referring here to the practice of filming master classes with earlier dancers.

has also disappeared; scores do not have audible properties and works may have properties that are not evident in the score (be witty, imposing, stately, emotional etc.) and only become evident in performance. It is significant that no similar debate exists in dance and this might be because the score has a different status, though it is still acknowledged to be a major resource in at least some dance genres.[25]

Dance notation scores are more problematic than music scores because choreographers rarely write them; professional notators write them. They are thus an interpretation of the work by someone other than the creator, though they are generally written during the choreographic process, with the approval of the choreographer. This gives them authority and allows them to be identified as reliable instructions for performing the work, though they are not sufficient for the work's performance since more is needed. Notation scores are (usually) faithful, though underdetermining, representations of the dance movement, of the relationship between the movement and the music and sometimes also of the dynamic (effort) elements of the dance. However, lacking in a dance notation score are the subtle nuances that can be crucial to a choreographer's style, for instance, the ways in which the talents of the original dancer (for whom the dance was first made) are incorporated into the dance. Many choreographers choose a dancer because her specific skills suit the choreography. The choreography thus depends on the skills of that dancer; had she different abilities, the choreography would not be the same.

When working with the dancer Margot Fonteyn, Ashton drew the observer's eyes upwards, encouraging audiences to notice Fonteyn's expressive arms and upper body. She had soft, un-steely feet and he sought to detract attention from them. An example would be the variation in Act II of the ballet *Cinderella* (1948) where a sudden back bend during a phrase of intricate footwork attracts attention, drawing the focus upward (1964 DVD).[26] This has become a part of that dance's style and ignoring it affects the choreography. Balanchine too tended to use his dancers' skills, which then became part of the style of that dance. Suki Shorer, the renowned Balanchine teacher, explains:

> Suzanne Farrell had an unprecedented facility for dancing 'off-balance'. She could fall out of turns in a very interesting way. Patricia McBride covered space effortlessly, beautifully. Gloria Govrin had a huge, high, open jump, especially for a woman , and a slow, soft, catlike landing controlled with a very deep *plié*... (Shorer 1999, p.22.)

25 The existing philosophical literature on dance scores includes the work of Goodman (1976), Margolis (1984) and McFee (1992).

26 Vernon, John, dir. *Cinderella*, London, BBC Enterprises, 1964.

In the dances Balanchine made for these dancers, such traits are evident. While these aspects may be present in a score, scores do not draw attention to them, nor do they highlight that they are stylistic aspects. The main questions in the discussion of interpretation in music concern the *nature* of interpretation and whether a given performance is an interpretation or merely a realization of a sound structure. In dance the problem can be seen as similar, in that realizing classroom movement is not the same as interpreting a choreographed dance.

Philosophical approaches to interpretation[27]

Turning to the philosophers who deal with performers' interpretation, Krausz (1993), in common with Barenboim, argues strongly that scores allow for a multiplicity of admissible interpretations. But, he claims that we do not have to favour all of them; some interpretations are better, more acceptable than others. So it follows that the same work can have different interpretations, which can be good, bad, interesting or dull, though he accepts that these ascriptions apply not to the work but only to its performances. In other words, negative aspects of the performance do not affect the work; dull, bad or interesting performances are properties of the performance and not of the work itself. Which interpretations we favour depends on which set of standards we apply to the interpretation, since, Krausz maintains, the same set of standards cannot be applied universally. Yet scores indicate the essential features of the work that a performance must embody if it is to be a performance of that work. Or as Lawrence Kramer puts it, 'what a score prescribes is everything that [...] may not be left out of a performance' (2010, p.262).

Contrary to Barenboim, Krausz believes that no score can have all the instructions required for an interpretation; much is non-notatable. For instance, precise vibrato speeds, the position of the bow on a string or how much pressure should be applied, these, and other features he mentions, cannot be notated but knowledge of the contemporary performance practice could be useful in re-instancing them. Equally in dance, there are aspects that cannot be notated: precise dynamic, initiation of the movement and specific details of eye movement, for example. At least, these cannot easily be notated in Benesh, the most frequently used notation system in ballet companies.[28] Despite believing that scores can have multiple interpretations,

---

27 The discussion is limited here to philosophers who have written on interpretation in music as there is no similar discussion in dance literature on interpretation of choreography. The dance literature does not address the problem in the way in which those writing on music have done.

28 At least this is the case in the United Kingdom. The New York City Ballet favours Labanotation.

Krausz is not advocating interpretative anarchy. He argues that works can only be understood in the context of the practices in which they are 'found and fostered' (1993, p.75). These are historically located and vary according to when the music was written. What Krausz means is not totally clear. Is he suggesting that today's musicians need to include aspects of early performance practice or merely to be aware of their existence?

Paul Thom also argues that historical elements are part of the work. He notes that some of the instructions for performance are explicitly given, whereas others are implicit. By this he means that there are implied instructions to follow the performance practices of the cultures in which the work is located (1993, p.81). From these comments, I am assuming that knowledge of performance practice is a significant aspect of interpretation, even if it is not duplicated in a contemporary performance. Like Krausz, Thom does not propose an 'anything goes' approach, rather he insists that the performer is constrained by what is in the score or play text or notation and, equally, that an interpretation can be disvalued if it is incoherent or irrelevant to audience concerns (1993, p.98). In Thom's view, reading a work for performance means understanding it (Thom 1993, p.76). Formulating a reading of a work means identifying it and this depends on the potential performer understanding what is prescribed, proscribed and what is open to interpretation. According to Thom, works for performance carry sets of instructions for performance. But, of course, in dance these are generally not written, at least not by the choreographer.

Acceptable performances of (classical) musical works are those that comply with the score's instructions but, even in music, this is not at all straightforward. Later twentieth-century scores are more instructive than those written earlier. The latter relied on the performance practices of the time and so it was thought unnecessary to include overly detailed instructions for performance.

What is at stake here is the work's identity and both Krausz and Thom argue that if the interpretation cannot be justified by what is in the play text or score it is not an interpretation of that work but of a hypothetical work. And this is what happens in dance when a dancer mis-interprets a choreographic work and performs academic dance in place of the choreography: she is interpreting hypothetical dance, which replaces the movement as choreographed with academic steps.

Stephen Davies who has also written about performers' interpretations, broadly agrees with Krausz, with the added qualification that performers' intentions are a significant consideration (2003). If a performer intends to perform the work of Beethoven (in dance, Ashton or Fokine, etc.) then she must recognize that it is by Beethoven and not perform as though it was by Berlioz. In music, this may be less of an issue but in dance, the performer may intend to perform classroom steps, rather than the choreography. Jerrold Levinson goes further than Davies, distinguishing between an interpretation and a realization, stating that an interpretation

> must at least represent a set of choices to play a certain way, with some awareness of, if not active experimentation with, the alternatives available, and not merely a set of realizations of the sonic properties constitutive of the work. (in Krausz 1993, p.46.)

So the performer should bring knowledge and understanding to the work and this is broadly in line with Thom's arguments. Barenboim agrees, 'to be faithful to the score [...] means so much more than its literal reproduction in sound' (2008, p.53).

Like Krausz, Levinson does not countenance performers altering something to express their own flights of feeling. He does not consider this to be an interpretation. Thom (1993) clarifies the point, suggesting that all works for performance have opportunities for interpretation but that it is only performers who have the imaginative capacity for understanding a work and who can find ways of interpreting it in such a way as to make it artistically effective, who can be regarded as 'consummate performers'. It is the 'rank-and-file' orchestral player – or, by extension, *corps-de-ballet* dancer – who is reliant on others (conductors or rehearsal directors) to plan their execution of the work. They cannot be said to be creating an interpretation and present what can best be described as a realization of the bare movement structure (p.110).

So far there is agreement on the point that scores are underdetermined and that performers need to make knowledgeable choices as to their interpretation. But even Barenboim warns that not every interpretation is acceptable. For instance, he suggests that while exaggeration works well in Beethoven it would be totally unacceptable in Mozart. So, in common with Davies, he believes that an acceptable interpretation will also depend on knowing who wrote the music. But dancers are frequently not interested in that aspect. Unfortunately there are still many with no knowledge of the choreographer, much less the work's stylistic features and, consequently, we may no longer be seeing the work of a specific choreographer. As suggested earlier, Fokine's choreography is a case in point: because of misunderstanding, one of his important works has been lost from the Royal Ballet's repertoire and deemed not relevant to today's audiences. In a Royal Ballet performance of *Petrouchka* (1911) in 1995, Katherine Sorley Walker in her review claimed that

> It is the lack of an imaginative understanding of the part they are meant to play that makes the present crowd so lifeless and unconvincing. They seem to have little perception of the overall significance of the action.

They merely wear their costumes and mill around rather listlessly, following their prescribed lines of movement without any spontaneity or zest. (Sorley-Walker 1995, pp.772-3)

Petrouchka has not since been performed by the Royal Ballet. The rehearsal directors, it seems, were not to recognize the qualities that had been lost.

The philosopher Göran Hermerén tackles the issue of the recital which is unrecognizable as a performance of a specific work. He argues that when a musical interpretation is so different from the standard approaches it might no longer be identifiable as an example of that work (Hermerén 1993). This can be the result of omissions and additions to the notes, or, as in the above dance instance, as a result of misunderstanding the work's content. In common with the other philosophers in Krausz (1993), Hermerén believes that there must be some evidence that an interpretation is the result of considered, knowledgeable choices. And in the 1995 performance of *Petrushka*, there was no evidence that that process had occurred.

Of all the writers in Krausz's anthology, Hermerén gives the fullest account of what an interpretation might involve. Listing six key issues, he sets out the questions a performer might ask, only four of which are relevant to dance. These can be summarized as follows:

• the problem of interpretation: what does the interpreter want to know?

• the material used in interpretation: what sort of evidence is employed to support the interpretation?

• the method of interpretation: how should the performer prepare?

• the purpose of the interpretation: what does the performer wish to achieve: a presentation of the maker's intention; the most rewarding sound; an expression of her own feelings or a historical account and so on?

Hermerén admits that not all the categories are equally important and what is significant can depend on the choreographer/composer.

Applying Hermerén's suggestions for interpretation to dance

Hermerén's first point concerns the dancer's knowledge. What does the dancer need/want to know? What should interest him: past performances; finding out what the choreographer intended or, perhaps the dancers for whom the work was first made? While the dancer should not imitate past performers, as mentioned earlier, it can be the case that those performers' qualities are embedded in the work, as in Ashton's or Balanchine's dances but their movement style is not captured in notation. As the dance scholar

Victoria Watts points out notation is designed to encapsulate

the choreography, not one instance of performance...the score attempts to capture the essence of the work, the choreographic intent, independently from any individual iteration (2010, p.9).

So films of the earlier dancer can have a role in feeding dancer knowledge, though only in addition to the notation score. It is not for the interpreter to copy but to be aware of the dancer's skills and talent. For instance in a short extract from Ashton's *Daphnis and Chloe* (1951) where the dancer, Margot Fonteyn, directs attention to her head, eyes and upper body, it makes us less conscious of her feet and legs. Her dancing creates an impression of joy and abandonment and we are drawn into admiring the dance rather than noticing the technical challenges.[29] It is these kind of qualitative aspects which Fonteyn, the original dancer, brought to the role and today's dancers could be helped by observing this. It encourages them to focus more on the choreography and draw attention away from the technical features of the dance.

Hermerén's second and third points involve the material and the method used in an interpretation. For material, notation scores are of course important and tend to be the most accurate account of the dance. But, as indicated above, the interpretation of the score is subject to the rehearsal director's knowledge and skill. While there is little research on how rehearsal directors understand a score and because notation still has a marginal status within the dance field (Watts 2010), it tends to be used purely for information about steps and spatial placing rather than as the embodiment of the dance. Yet, as Watts indicates, it is just this aspect that the notation is aiming to capture. Today, many notation scores include other elements, such as supplementary notes and reviews or photographs. Whether the rehearsal director takes account of these extra elements is not documented.

Oral information from a past dancer can also be useful and this has been the established practice in ballet as is evident in the films made by the Balanchine Foundation. It can be controversial as dancers are not always reliable, though the earlier dancer may remember the choreographer's instructions and the feel of the movement. As with the musician, the performer's preparation depends on her attitude to the choreography. If she sees it as steps, she may work only on technique but if she considers it to be style, then she needs to have a greater understanding of the aspects that contribute to choreographic style.

For instance, training systems are not ahistorical and this needs recognition by the profession. These systems create bodies that have

---

29 There is currently a Youtube clip available of this but it is also available in the archives of the Royal Ballet and in the New York Public Library Dance Collection.

different skills and capabilities. In some systems, for instance, those of Enrico Cecchetti and Ninette de Valois, the focus is on rapid movement with quick footwork, in others, such as Vaganova and the Paris Opera, high extensions and an ability to cover space with huge and daring leaps are more valued. As well as forming specific bodily skills, the values and bodily abilities also change from era to era, so dancers have different criteria as to what can be considered as an acceptable performance. A further problem is that a dancer capable of the earlier approach will not be adept at managing the latter and vice versa. Consequently, dancers will seldom be able to manage a full range of styles, except in the very rare instance when an exceptional performer understands the training and the earlier dance style, despite being trained in a contemporary manner. For instance Mikhail Baryshnikov has assimilated both the postmodern stylistic aspects of Twyla Tharp's dance movement and the modernism of George Balanchine, despite having being trained in the Soviet Union.

Hermerén's last point is to do with the purpose of the interpretation. Is the dancer trying to give a particular rendering of the choreography, maybe even an historically truthful version, or merely replicate the steps accurately? This depends on the dancer's intention. While accuracy and truth to the choreography are crucial, performers also need to have some freedom. But how much can the dancer change the performance of movement without losing the choreography? Alterations to *the way* the movements should be performed can inhibit the dance movement's survival. Yet, paradoxically, changing the actual 'step' may not matter. What is significant is the process of movement, as opposed to the positional elements. In other words, dancers may need to discover the source of the movement, its initiation from the torso as opposed to the limbs, as is the case with, for example, Bronislava Nijinska's choreography. Today's aesthetic is concerned with accurate placing and achieving correct static positions and these values are much less applicable to the dances of Ashton or Macmillan, or even some earlier choreographers.

What then does it mean for a dancer to interpret the dance movement? They do not use a score, and apart from earlier recordings, what should they do and what is available to them? Understanding that choreography does not comprise codified steps is a beginning and accepting that their training may not have given them all that is required could also help.[30] The speed of the dancing can also be significant. Though dancing faster does not appeal to today's dancers, since it involves giving priority to motion and jeopardizing 'perfect' positions and high extensions, it can be the key to the dance's style. Flow and phrasing and relaxed turnout are critical aspects

---

30 The dancer and choreographer Bronislava Nijinska recognized that when she came to perform in the ballets of Fokine. See Nijinska (1981).

of some choreography, though many dancers would find this difficult to comprehend today. Audience expectations can also restrict what the dancer is able to present. They have been coaxed into believing that 180° turnout is the norm, so a dancer using semi-parallel movement could be considered sloppy. These are just some of the problems facing dance interpretation.

Conclusions

Attempting to find ways of addressing the problem of misperception in dance performance has taken me into arguments that might at first appear to be outside the issue. As a way of stopping dancers from executing academic dance when they should be performing choreography, I have suggested that they should adopt a concept of interpretation. This I have borrowed from philosophers of music who have written about that topic as it is not something that has really been addressed in dance. Adopting a concept of interpretation has led me to consider what kind of information a dancer needs in order to perform the dance knowledgeably. My contention is that if they misperceive the movement and take it to be academic dance, they are only giving an aesthetic rendering and not addressing the choreography's significance. When this happens, as it frequently does at present, the dancer does not present the dance as art and the stylistic aspects of the movement, which give the dance its significance, are missing. To prevent this, and provide information for the dancer, I have briefly explored the ways in which choreographic style is intentional and can be discerned by examining the codes and conventions of the art style from which the choreographer has drawn or rejected, the influences on the artist, and the contemporary context. From this it seems that in dance style is multifaceted. Consequently, dancers need to do more than replicate the movement.

The argument moved on to deal with the notion of performer's interpretation and whilst I recognized that the problems were different, I have explored what interpretation might be and examined how philosophers, writing about music, understand it. Classical music depends on having a score of some sort, while non-literate dancers have to look at context and develop practical, historical knowledge. This kind of knowledge is, as the musician and musicologist John Butt (2002) argues, potentially infinite and is highly relevant, particularly if it gives the performer new insights into the work. Where music and dance come together is on the question of performers' intention. The interpretation has to be knowledgeable and considered not simply a realization of sonic properties or of steps and positions. As Thom eloquently puts it 'to interpret is to go beyond what the work directs in ways that illumine its directives' (1993, p.95).

References

Armelagos, Adina and Mary Sirridge. 'The Identity Crisis in Dance', *Journal of Aesthetics and Art Criticism*, 37: 2, 1978, pp.129-139.

Armelagos, Adina and Mary Sirridge, in Sheets-Johnstone, Maxine (ed.), 'Personal Style and Performance Prerogatives', *Illuminating Dance: Philosophical Explorations* Toronto: Associated University Press, 1984, pp.85-99.

Barenboim, Daniel. *Everything is Connected*, London: Weidenfeld and Nicolson, 2008.

Best, David. *Philosophy and Human Movement*, London: George Allen and Unwin, 1978.

Best, David. *Feeling and Reason in the Arts*. London: George Allen and Unwin, 1985.

Butt, John. *Playing with History*, Cambridge: Cambridge University Press, 2002.

Cavell, Stanley. *Must we Mean What we Say?*, Cambridge: Cambridge University Press, 1976 [1969].

Davies, Stephen. *Themes in the Philosophy of Music*, Oxford: Oxford University Press, 2003.

Dworkin, Ronald. *Law's Empire*, Oxford: Hart Publishing, 1998.

Healy, Katherine. 'Recollections of Ashton's Juliet', *Dance Now*, 3:13, 1994, pp.14-23.

Hermerén, Göran. 'The Full Voic'd Quire: Types of Interpretations of Music' in Krausz, Michael (ed.) 1993, pp.9-32.

Kavanagh, Julie. *Secret Muses: The Life of Frederick Ashton*, London: Faber and Faber, 1996.

Kivy, Peter. *Introduction to a Philosophy of Music*, Oxford: Clarendon Press, 2002.

Kramer, Lawerence. *Interpreting Music*, Berkeley: University of California Press, 2010.

Krausz, Michael. 'Rightness and Reasons in Musical Interpretation', in Krausz, Michael (ed.), 1993, pp.75-88.

Krausz, Michael (ed.), *The Interpretation of Music: Philosophical Essays*, Oxford: Oxford University Press, 1993.

Legat, Nicholas. 'Twenty Years with Marius Petipa and Christian Johannsen', *The Dancing Times*, April, 1931, pp.11-14.

Levinson, Jerrold. 'Performative vs. Critical Interpretation in Music', in Krausz, Michael (ed.), 1993, pp.33-60.

McFee, Graham. *Understanding Dance*, London: Routledge, 1992.

McFee, Graham. *The Philosophical Aesthetics of Dance: Identity, Performance and Understanding*, Alton: Dance Books, 2011.

May, Pamela. 'Interview with author', July 1998.

Miller, Jonathan. *Subsequent Performances*, London: Faber and Faber, 1986.

Morris, Geraldine. *Frederick Ashton's Ballets: Style, Performance, Choreography*, Alton: Dance Books, 2012.

Newman, Barbara. *Striking a Balance: Dancers Talking About Dancing*, London: Elm Tree Books, 1982.

Newman, Barbara. 'Yuri Fateyev', in *Grace Under Pressure*, Alton: Dance Books, 2004, pp.301-313.

Nijinska, Bronislava. *Bronislava Nijinska: Early Memoirs*, Durham: Duke University Press, 1981.

Rowell, Bonnie. 'Choreographic Style: Choreographic Intention and Embodied Ideas', in Duerden, Rachel and Neil Fisher (eds.), *Dancing Off the Page: Integrating Performamce, Choreography, Analysis and Notation Documentaton* , Alton: Dance Books, 2007, pp.108-117.

Shorer, Suki. 'Balanchine Technique', *Ballet Review*, 27:3, Fall, 11-38

Sibley, Antoinette. 'The Ballerina's Solos from *Scènes de ballet*', in Jordan, Stephanie and Andrée Grau (eds.), *Following Sir Fred's Steps*, London: Dance Books, 1996, pp.138-146.

Sirridge, Mary and Adina Armelagos. 'The In's and Out's of Dance: Expression as an Aspect of Style', *Journal of Aesthetics and Art Criticism*, 26:19, 1977, pp.15-24.

Sorley Walker, Kathrine. 'A Quartet of Stravinsky Ballets', *The Dancing Times*, May, 1995, pp.772-3.

Thom, Paul. *For An Audience: A Philosophy of the Performing Arts*, Philadelphia: Temple University Press, 1993.

Thom, Paul. *A Theory of Interpretation: Making Sense*, Lanham, Boulder, New York, Oxford: Rowman & Littlefield Publishers, 2000.

Van Camp, Julie. 'Anti-Geneticism and Critical Practice in Dance', *Dance Research Journal*, 13:1, 1980, pp.29-35.

Vaughan, David. *Frederick Ashton and his Ballets*, London: Dance Books, 1999.

Watts, Victoria. 'Dancing the Score: Notation and Difference', *Dance Research*, 28:1, 2010, pp.7-18.

DVD

Diamond, Matthew, (dir.) *The Dream*, New York: Dance of America, Arthaus Musik, 2004.

Nears, Colin and Bob Lockyer, (dirs.) *Dance Masterclass: The Dream*, London BBC Productions, 1988.

Vernon, John, (dir.) *Cinderella*, London, BBC Enterprises, 1964.

Part III

Dance Expression and Representation

7. Expression, Music, and Dance

Noël Carroll

Introduction

In this essay, I would like to address the matter of the way in which music and dance conspire to project expressive properties. By 'expressive properties,' I have in mind such things as the kind of anthropomorphic attributions that we make when we say that 'the music is *angry*' or 'the music is *joyous*'. Expressive properties, in other words, are human qualities, like cheerfulness, or stateliness. Moreover, of these human qualities, those that are connected to affective or emotive states, such as sadness, are particularly important for our purposes, since they are often the primary focus of artworks, including danceworks-cum-music.

Of course, when we describe a dancer's movement as *sad*, we are not speaking anthropomorphically – unless the dancer is a robot – since the dancer is a human being. So in these cases, the phrase 'expressive properties' refers to human qualities – not to what is performed, but to the way in which it is performed, notably when the way in which it is performed manifests or exemplifies a discernibly pronounced human quality. Saying of the sailors' mien in *Fancy Free* that it is manly – or that it projects *manliness* – is to attribute an expressive property to their movement.

Both music and dance can be said to possess such pronounced human qualities. When the two art forms work in concert, they are capable of sensuously communicating these qualities with a very high degree of intensity. The aim of this paper is to advance a speculative account of how such expressivity is accomplished when music and dance co-operate in tandem, along with a suggestion about why the marriage of these two art forms can be so powerful. I will also conclude with some comments on the possibility of the music and the dance functioning more dialectically with respect to each other.

Perhaps needless to say, some readers might already be sceptical about the need for such an account. That dance-with-music can be expressive requires no explanation, it might be said, since the human body is expressive enough to explain the expressivity of the combination of music and dance. That's all we need to know here. That is, the expressiveness of the dancing body tells us why dancing with music is expressive. Thus, given this potential objection, part of the onus of this discussion will be to specify what music *adds* to the dance when the combination of these two art forms is so expressively effective.[1]

However, before embarking on an attempt to offer an account of the way in which music and dance in concert function to project consilient expressive properties, some disclaimers are in order. First, I am not suggesting that all dance is expressive in the way I will sketch in this essay. For example, some dance lacks musical accompaniment altogether and even attempts to bracket the natural expressivity of the human body. Here, I am thinking of certain of the reflexive task performances of the Judson era of postmodern dance, such as *Sticks* by Trisha Brown (1973).

Of course, not all dancing without music is bereft of expressivity; Doris Humphrey's (1928) *Water Study* manages not only to intimate flowing water, but flowing feelings, albeit evenly flowing feeling. Quite obviously, examples like this are not covered directly by my account, since they rely not at all upon the resources of music. Moreover, not even all dance that is co-ordinated with music is so yoked for the purpose of expression. Some combinations of music and dance are purely decorative, such as *Jardin Animé* from *Le Corsaire*, while other dance-cum-music may be primarily interpretive – what Margaret Moore and I describe as performative interpretations of the music (Carroll and Moore 2010). An example here might be found in George Balanchine's (1959) *Episodes* when the inversion in Webern's score is echoed by turning the ballerina upside down. That is, I am not concerned with every sort of music/dance relationship, but only those that have to do with the projection of expressive qualities.[2]

In virtue of all these qualifications, I hope that it is evident that I intend to theorize only about a certain type of dance, indeed, only a certain type of dance with music. What kind? Let me initiate the discussion by offering three examples.

---

1 Another sort of sceptic may claim that no explanation is necessary because it is obvious that the music is the source of the expression; the dance by itself is not expressive. This objection was put to me by a reader of this manuscript, but it seems hardly creditable to me. The human body, so to speak, 'in nature' is expressive. Why would it cease to be so when dancing? Were that the case, *it* would require an explanation. (Editors' note: see Julia Beauquel's essay in this volume for a critical discussion of the natural expressivity of the body in dance.)

2 In this respect, I am not attempting to cover the full range of dance/music relationships as one encounters in a work like Stephanie Jordan's important *Moving Music: Dialogues with Twentieth-Century Ballet* (Jordan 2000). For example, I am not trying to theorize about the structural relations of musical and choreographic structures, but instead am speculating about the relation of the perceived expressive contour of the music in relation to the perceived expressive contour of the dance. That is, I am more concerned with the projection of an expressive *gestalt* than I am with dissecting the steps or the score, although I believe that that too is an important area of research.

Three examples

The first example comes from Kurt Jooss's (1932) *The Green Table*.[3] The section that I want us to think about occurs right after the often satirical, but sometimes ominous, opening scene in which the ministers gather around the green table, haver, and then unleash war. What follows is a solo in which a skeletal-faced Death – done up like Mars – struts in a highly stylized fashion to the percussive pounding of a piano, playing in a minor key.

The music is dark, repetitive, and relentless. The dance movement is brutal. The figure of Death raises one leg and suspends it in midair before bringing it down with great force and weight, as if it were crushing anything beneath it as mercilessly as would the wheels of Juggernaut. The upper body movement consists, among other things, of fists jabbing into the air with fierce directionality. This movement, in association with the helmeted military garb from yesteryear, marks the figure not only as martial but powerfully aggressive and determined. The mechanical repetitions in the music are mirrored in the rigid, march-like cadence of the movement. The fraught, propulsive, repetitive music blends with the heavy, martial gestures to project an aura of pitiless, implacable violence – an unstoppable, vicious personification of Death, or, more specifically, Death in the time of war, indeed, Death as a war machine.[4]

For a contrasting example, consider Doris Humphrey's (1934) *Air for the G-String* to music by Bach.[5] Its sonorous melody, slowly emerging over a carefully constructed ostinato bass, communicates not only a sense of beauty, but one of a self-sufficient serenity, perhaps due to the repeated ascent and descent in the score – the cyclical repetition here suggesting equilibrium. The measured, restrained and stately processional music is re-articulated by the light, graceful movement of Humphrey's ensemble. Yet, as the group rises with opened arms reaching upwards – as if beseeching the gods – the serenity in the music becomes spiritualized.

That is, the movement seems hieratic. This is an effect that is undoubtedly accentuated by the flowing classical robes of the dancers and the Grecian columns in the background, both of which suggest that the dancers are priestesses assembled in a temple for worship. The swirling up and down, cyclically linked movement not only recalls the braiding in the music, but

---

3 Claims are based on the 1982 recording, distributed by WNET/Thirteen and available at the Dance Collection, New York Public Library for the Performing Arts.

4 A reader of this essay in manuscript has pointed out there is a mismatch between the rhythm of the dancer's heel stamps and the music which would appear to add to the disturbing character of the choreographic/music image.

5 See *Air for the G String and Etude Patetico. Doris Humphrey Technique: the Creative Potential* (Highstown, NJ: Dance Horizons Video, 1997).

gives the impression that the dancers have been gently transported to another level of embodied consciousness, infusing the audio-visual image as a whole with an almost sacred or numinous quality which, although it is not inconsistent with the music, is not salient in the music alone. That the serenity in the music becomes legible as spiritual serenity, it would appear, is a function of the union of the music with the dance.

My last example comes from the dance of the Snow Flakes which occurs just before the end of Act One of *The Hard Nut* by Mark Morris (1991).[6] Specifically, I want to call special attention to the vocal interludes. Here the music sounds euphoric (rather than dysphoric) – at least happy, maybe hopeful, perhaps joyous. As the dancers enter leaping, one arm reaching out from their body out toward the future, while, at times, the other hand sprinkles stage-snow, as if it were so much confetti, the optimistic mood of the music becomes concretized as celebratory. The twirling, vertical leaps amount to leaps of joy. In the final choral reprise, the dancers arms do not rise above their shoulders, nor do they bound off the floor; thus they are able to recalibrate the positive feeling in the music as calm.

With these three examples in hand, let us begin to try to account for what is going-on in this type of dance-cum-music. Since the expressivity of the music in these pieces presents us with the most challenging philosophical mystery, let us start with the music.

The music

That music is expressive is undeniable. Yet it is also philosophically perplexing. For, expression would appear to require a person – a sentient being – whose human qualities are being expressed. But pure music – music without words or a programme -- is not a person. So how is it possible for pure music to be expressive? That is, it makes sense to say that a person is sad or joyous. Those are states a person can undergo. Yet, it sounds strained to say that the music is sad or joyous. Or that, at least, is what the philosopher worries about. Indeed, there is a longstanding view in the philosophy of music that argues that absolute or pure orchestral music is not literally sad.

Ordinary folk, on the other hand, do not find it strained to speak this way – neither about music nor, for that matter, about other non-persons. They are happy to talk about the sadness of a weeping willow tree, along with the doleful visage of various breeds of dog, such as beagles and Saint Bernards. Perhaps by listening to ordinary folk, we can discover a way to answer the philosopher's query regarding the possibility of musical expressivity.

---

6 *The Hard Nut* (New York: WNET/Thirteen, 1992) available at the Dance Collection, New York Public Library for the Performing Arts.

When one looks at a tree and describes it as tortured, it is in virtue of the resemblance of the appearance of the tree to appearance of a person writhing or twisting in pain. Similarly, the weeping willow tree is said to be sad in virtue of appearing hunched over, recalling the bowed shoulders of mourners. Certain breeds of dogs are described as sad-faced, because they appear to wear a perpetual frown. In these cases, non-persons are thought to project human qualities – here, anthropomorphic ones – in virtue of the resemblance they bear to persons who appear to possess those qualities. It makes no difference that trees cannot be sad; they can nevertheless suggest sadness by appearing sad – by resembling the appearance of sad people in certain respects.

Indeed, it should be clear that being in a state like sadness is not necessary in order to appear sad, since actors (including for our purposes dancers) who are not sad can impart the impression of sadness, and other affective states, all the time without suffering those states. Indeed, were they wallowing, say, in sadness, they would probably forget their steps. Instead of being sad, they rather only project sadness. How do they do it?

They do it by imitating the typical appearance of people in the pertinent emotional states. In other words, they *look* sad, or joyous, or whatever. That is, actors/dancers, like the trees and puppies, can project expressive properties in virtue of resembling aspects of the regularly recurring appearances of persons in those states. And this suggests how it is possible for pure music to project expressive properties – namely, by imitation.

Initially, it may seem strange to say that music can imitate the appearance of persons in various affective states. Perhaps the strangeness here is due to our tendency to think of the imitation of the appearance of persons in visual terms. Music doesn't picture people. So, how it might be asked, can it imitate them?

Nevertheless, music does have certain features that it shares with persons. Foremost among these, I submit, is that music *moves* – specifically, it moves through time.[7] Indeed, there is evidence that music activates the pre-motor cortex of the brain. Moreover, it is in virtue of the impression of movement that music evokes that music may be deployed to imitate the movement of persons, especially the recurring movement-patterns of persons in various affective states. Ebullient people move expansively. Thus, music can suggest ebullience by moving likewise.

The notion that we hear movement in music is not incidental to music. Sound strikes us as music precisely because we hear it as moving in a certain direction with a discernible velocity and weight. These factors also pertain to movements associated with various affective states. A sad person typically moves ponderously with a slow and heavy gait. Sad music

---

7 For a defence of this notion, see Carroll and Moore 2010.

can approximately replicate cadences like that.

My own view is that it is primarily through the impression of movement that pure music – music without a text or a programme – is capable of projecting expressive properties. But there are other dimensions of imitation available to pure music as well. As Stephen Davies notes:

> [M]usic is expressive in recalling the gait, attitude, air, carriage, posture, and comportment of the human body. Just as someone who is stooped over, dragging, faltering, subdued, and slow in his or her movement cuts a sad figure, so music that is slow, with heavy or thick harmonic bass textures, with underlying patterns of tension, with dark timbres, and a recurrently downward impetus sounds sad. Just as someone who skips and leaps quickly and lightly, makes expansive gestures, and so on, has a happy bearing, so music with similar vivacity and exuberance is happy sounding. (Davies 2009, p.182)

Moreover, as has been frequently noted (see, for example, North 1959), music may imitate the sound of human voice without words in terms of various emotional states, thereby expressing such things as anger, sadness, joy, and so forth.

Of course, the expressive properties in the music of which we are speaking here are response-dependent properties – properties whose detection is dependent upon creatures with our sensory and affective constitution. Said properties might not be apprehended by an alien being with an alternative biology and a different perceptual apparatus. This does not mean that these properties are in any respect illusory. That dogs can hear pitches that humans cannot does not render them phantom pitches. The expressive properties grounded in the music – and especially in the appearance of musical movement – are intersubjectively accessible inasmuch as they are *real* response-dependent properties. Since these properties are rooted in imitating the expressive properties of persons, we can call this approach to expression in music, the imitation theory of musical expression.[8]

Since the imitation theory of musical expression maintains that we base our ascription of expressive predicates to the music on the basis of the certain correlations of musical patterning with the appearance of certain affective or characterological states in humans, it may be argued that that commits the imitation theorist to regarding the attribution of expressive properties to the music to be essentially metaphorical. On the one hand, it is not clear whether this would make any difference for the theory of the relation of music to dance that I will be propounding.

---

8 Other labels for this view are 'Appearance Emotionalism' and the 'Contour Theory.' Proponents of variations of this view include Peter Kivy (1989) and Stephen Davies (1994).

But, on the other hand, I am not convinced that the imitation theory of musical expression entails that the attribution of human qualities to music is necessarily metaphorical. We can agree that 'joyous' in the phrase 'joyous music' is not the primary use of that word. The primary use does undoubtedly apply to persons who are in joyous mental states. But even if 'joyous' here is a secondary usage, it is not evident that secondary uses of words are automatically metaphorical. 'Hand' in the phrase 'the minute hand of a clock' is a secondary usage, but it is also a literal usage. If it is metaphorical, it is a dead metaphor and dead metaphors are literal. Similarly, the attribution of human qualities – like sadness and stateliness – may be a secondary usage of those concepts with respect to music, but, nevertheless, may still be literal in a way that is strictly akin to notions like the minute hand of the clock. They are, through constant usage, literal descriptors of the qualities imparted by certain pieces of music.

On the view I am advancing, we detect the expressive properties in the music in virtue of the resemblance of the movement or some other feature in the music to comparable properties in persons. In some cases, the mode of detection might involve having certain feelings of movement aroused in us. In other instances, there may be no arousal of feeling; we simply perceive the music as moving quickly. We associate this movement, then, with certain broadly affective states.

Sceptics may object that this theory is both arbitrary and incomplete. It is incomplete because it does not tell us when parallels between musical structure and human qualities will function imitatively, and it is arbitrary because it does not tell us why the music functions imitatively when it does so. However, I do not think that these are questions that the philosophy of dance has to answer. Why creatures with our perceptual and affective constitution respond to certain correspondences rather than to others is a question for psychologists of music as is the question of the nature and operation of the mechanism that enables our detection of these correspondences. It is enough for the philosophers of dance to take note that these correlations obtain phenomenologically. The rest of the problem is for the psychologists to solve.

Furthermore, on the basis of phenomenological observation, we can say that music descending in a minor key is apt to call to mind a state somewhat indefinitely describable as down and dark. However, it is admittedly very difficult to locate with greater precision the affective properties projected by pure music, because, sans referential machinery, such music cannot specify toward what object the putative feeling being projected is directed. In this respect, the affective states suggested by pure music are better captured in the vocabulary of moods than they are in that of the emotions (Carroll 2010).

Moods are global states – like euphoria or dysphoria – that colour everything that comes under their aegis. When in a happy mood, we feel positively about whatever comes our way; the glass is always half full. Emotions, in contrast, are more highly selective; they focus upon our vital interests in the moment. If we perceive that we have been wronged, the emotion of anger battens upon all those elements of the situation that are pertinent to the injustice we think that we have been dealt. An emotion, in this regard, is like a spotlight; a mood, in contrast, is more like atmospheric lighting. The feeling qualities that pure music projects is moodlike insofar as it is global and somewhat vague and indefinite, because it does not refer to a particular object in such a fashion that it can be connected to a specific interest in the way that a fine-grained emotion like anger at the pickpocket with his hands on my wallet can be connected to injustice.

This feature of pure music has been evident to theoreticians for quite a long time. In the eighteenth century, James Beattie remarked that 'the expression of music without poetry is vague and ambiguous.' (1975, p.463). Peter Kivy has described this phenomenon as pure music's lack of emotive explicitness (Kivy 1980, p.98). According to Kivy, the expressive resources of pure, orchestral music were originally developed for the purpose of setting texts to music. Where music and text were conjoined, the text supplied the reference that allowed the feeling in the music to be labeled in terms of a definite emotional state. Where the text hails the Blessed Virgin Mary, the positive feeling in the music can be identified as adoration. But when pure orchestral music cuts its ties with texts, the music loses the kind of connection with an object required for emotive definition.

That is, emotions are directed at objects. Henry is mad at Henrietta. Emotive explicitness requires our knowing the particular object an emotion is directed at with reference to the vital interest that is at stake. Without that information, we may observe that Henry is excited, or even negatively so, but we can't get a closer fix on his emotive state. Similarly, by jettisoning the text, pure music severs its connection with particular objects and interests in such a way that we may say the music projects an aura of excitement without being able to say anything more refined about the nature of that excitement. Often we can say little more about the feeling the music expresses beyond identifying it as positively or negatively valenced – as being affectively up or down. Pure music in regard to expressivity is emotively inexplicit or, as I prefer to say, moodlike rather than emotionlike.

This emotive inexplicitness, moreover, is key to understanding the relation of music to dance when the two artforms come together for the purpose of expression as we shall see as we turn to the expressive resources of dance.

Dance

The emotive inexplicitness of pure, orchestral music is usually traced to its typical lack of referential machinery. There are, of course, exceptions to this generalization. Where orchestral music has a programme, like Pyotr Ilyich Tchaikovsky's *The 1812 Overture*, the positive feeling projected by the swelling music can be specified as an expression of a feeling of triumph. But without such reference, orchestral music of the sort that generally accompanies theatre dance is difficult to pin down emotively. However, this may not be immediately evident to many viewers/listeners. Audiences may take the music in our example from *The Green Table* to be brutal and determined. But this, I submit, is the result of what the dance has added to the overall composition. For with the dance comes reference, precisely what is needed in order to make the human qualities being expressed more and more explicit.

In many cases, the dance tells a story with characters. With these referents in mind, we come to hear the music as expressive of feelings that are appropriate to the scene before us. The languor and yearning in the music of Claude Debussy's *Prélude à l'Après-Midi d'un Faune*, choreographed by Vaslav Nijinsky (1912), becomes sexualized as erotic when coupled with the choreography portraying the faun in pursuit of the nymphs.

But even where there is no story, the dance movement can clarify the emotion in the composite audio-visual image. A *pas de deux* in a given piece of choreography may have no explicit story to tell. And yet the way in which the man and the woman partner generally projects very definite expressive properties.

Likewise, if, as in our previous example, we hear the music in *Air for a G String* as serene, it is the movement and gesture of Humphrey's dancers that specifies the feeling the piece imparts as a species of *spiritual* serenity. For, the bodies of the dancers supply the audience with referents, standardly bodies that are replete with expressive properties that are relatively explicit just because they are connected to human bodies. That is, the dancers supply the more specified feelings that are hinted at more vaguely in the music, supplying it with objects, and thereby rendering the expressive qualities of the image as a whole more perspicuous and defined.

Again the relation of the dance to the music in cases like these is reciprocal. The dance-theatre components – including not only movement and gesture, but, in many cases, costume, scenery, lighting, sometimes pantomime, and even a story – function as *indicators*. They indicate the reference of the concerted audio-visual image, thereby particularizing with greater clarity the feelings insinuated by the music.

In contrast, the music usually initially marks out a broad expanse of feeling tone – perhaps a positive or a negative mood. Then the dance elements focus that feeling within the range of possible emotions expressed by the music. The serenity in Bach's music is taken to express a spiritual equilibrium or a sense of inner peace when wedded to the movement, gesture, costume, and set in *Air for a G String*.

If the dance brings into focus the vague feeling lurking in the music in terms of a more fine-grained or particularized emotion, the music commonly serves to frame the dance by demarcating the kind of broad feeling under whose penumbra the dance belongs. In other words, the music functions rather like a mood calibrating our apprehension of the movement and gesture so that we are alerted to what to look for. The turbulence in the music by Alexander Scriabin helps guide our attention to the flailing fists of the female dancer in Humphrey's (1928) *Etude Patetico*.[9]

Viewing theatre dance, like viewing theatre in general, can be quite demanding as the eye struggles to find exactly where it should be looking. By carving out the broad affective terrain upon which the theatrical spectacle is situated, the expressive music in an audio-choreographic construction facilitates this task by informing viewers of the kind of emotive cues for which they should be on the lookout. Moreover, inasmuch as the music affectively saturates the action nonstop, this assures that the affective grip of the overall image never slackens, giving it an intensity that the action alone cannot continuously guarantee.

On the present account, the music affectively frames the dance-theatre components which when conjoined with the music focuses more precisely the pertinent emotive timbre within the range of affect circumscribed by the mood music. The music in *Air for a G String* is serene; the dance-theatre elements specify it as serene spirituality. The choral music in *The Hard Nut* is up; the accompanying dance defines it as celebratory, thereby transforming the winter snow storm into something anthropomorphically festive.

At first, it may be heuristically helpful to analogize the relation of the music to the dance to the relation of an adjective to a noun. For example, we might parse *Air for a G String* in terms of the music modifying the spirituality of the movement with the quality of sereneness. But, although suggestive, this analogy can also be misleading in at least two ways.

The first error would be to regard the dance-theatre components as only performing the function of fixing the reference of the audio-visual image. For, the dance movement, for example, does not merely designate the emotive object to which the mood music attaches. It also, most frequently, has expressive qualities of its own. Thus, it would be a vast oversimplification to suppose that the dance-theatre components supply nothing more than the reference of the audio-visual image. The brutal gestures of Death, not

---

9 See *Air for the G String and Etude Patetico. Doris Humphrey Technique: the Creative Potential* (Highstown, NJ: Dance Horizons Video, 1997).

to mention his make-up and costuming are highly expressive of his brutish implacability without the assistance of the music, although the music surely augments that quality immensely and never lets us forget it.

Similarly, it would be a mistake to imagine that music can never function referentially. For a non-dance example, consider Jimi Hendrix's rendition of 'The Star Spangled Banner' at the Woodstock Festival in 1969.[10] There, given the way in which Hendrix stressed his instrument, he recalled the sounds of bombing and strafing, thereby ironically contrasting the idealism of the American national anthem with the sounds of the alleged battle for freedom that the United States was waging in Southeast Asia.

Dance music, of course, may also function referentially. In Mark Morris's ballet-within-the-opera in John Adams's (1987) *Nixon in China*, the short strokes on the strings and the percussion represent aurally the beating of the heroine in the 'Whip her to death' scene.[11] Thus, just as the dance-theatre components can be expressive, so the music can be representational, thus undermining any simple analogy between the dance and nouns, on the one hand, and the music and adjectives, on the other hand.

Combining music with dance enhances expressive control over the movement by giving the movement an emotive frame of reference on a moment-to-moment basis. The music, so to speak, saturates the scene with a palpable, albeit broad, affective aura. It orients the viewer to the choreography, helping to disambiguate the dancer's gestures. And it keeps the audience attending to the movement continuously in light of the mood the music intones.

At this point, it might be objected that this account makes the music appear to be redundant. However, although it is true that the music is, in one sense, redundant, it is wrong to think that this is a basis for objecting to my account. The music *is* redundant in that it generally repeats information that may be available in the dance-theatre components sans music. But redundancy is not a flaw in art works. Generally, artworks have several channels of communication which very often deliver the same information. This assures that the artwork makes its point; informational economy is not a desideratum when it comes to art.

Furthermore, in the case of what we may call *framing music*, when it comes to dance, it would be more accurate to refer to it as *reinforcing* the expressive properties lodged in the dance-theatre array rather than repeating them monotonously. 'Redundancy' seems like the wrong notion here, not only because the music is in a different medium than the dance elements but also because the music is of a different order of generality than the movement

---

10 See the film *Woodstock* (dir. Michael Wadleigh, Warner Brothers, 1970).

11 *Nixon in China*, Brooklyn Academy of Music, Next Wave Festival, 1987, available at the Dance Collection, New York Pubic Library for the Performing Arts.

since it is, so to speak, disembodied.

By being embodied, the expressive properties, connected with the dancers' bodies, obtain a greater emotive precision which they lend to the music. The propulsive aggressivity of the music for Death in *The Green Table* accrues an aura of brutality when blended with Death's merciless march and manner. The dance-theatre elements, that is, enable us to hear the music as cruel, at the same time that the darkness in the music saturates the movement in a way that keeps the more ominous aspects of the movement constantly foregrounded. The music keeps the movement incessantly framed in terms of the apposite mood, while the movement makes that mood more emotively definite. Thus, the two elements support each other like stones in an archway.

An interim summation

So far, I have proposed that the relation of the music to dance in works that project expressive properties is reciprocal. Typically, in the type of expressive dance-cum-music we are discussing, the music frames the dance-theatre components by establishing broadly the range of affect that is pertinent to the movement. Generally, the mood of the music is indefinite – up or down, positive or negative, joyous or sad, and so on. The dance-theatre elements of the audio-visual array function in terms of focusing the expressive timbre of the piece more precisely – perhaps concretizing the dolours in the music as grief. Moreover, at the same time that the dance-theatre elements clarify the emotions expressed in the piece as a whole, the music constantly reminds the audience of the *kind* of affect they should be looking for, just as a mood-state governs our attention in everyday life.

It may strike some listeners as mysterious as to how audiences are able to extract expressive properties from dance with music. Yet I cannot resist speculating that it is an expansion of the ordinary capacities for mind-reading which evolution has bestowed upon us and which are so crucial to social beings like ourselves. Humans are particularly susceptible to emotional contagion. Figuratively speaking, we are capable of 'catching' the affects of our conspecifics. This is indispensable to the discharge of co-ordinated activity. When we converse with others we tend to adopt their posture, for example; this gives us a certain amount of bodily information about their inner attitudes. We use how we feel to get a fix on what they are feeling. This mirroring behaviour may be related to what are called mirror neurons. But the mirror-neuron hypothesis notwithstanding, it does seem indisputable that one of the ways that we attempt to glean knowledge about what is going on in others is by mimicking them.

Dance, it seems reasonable to conjecture, relies in part upon our tendency to imitate others in order to get a fix on their emotive states. We often find ourselves tapping our feet to the rhythm of the dancer's movement or swaying with her turns. Of course, we don't jump in our seats nor do we throw our arms upward. But our muscles do register the movement of the dancer's body, albeit discretely, in small inner pulls and spasms, tugs, tensions and releases that provide us with some limited simulacrum of what the choreographer intends to express through gesture and movement.

As creatures who would never have survived without society and the capacity to intuit – to a large extent – what others are feeling, our mind-reading abilities are keyed to very subtle cues. Mind-reading is so important to humans that our modes of detecting the feelings of our conspecifics are hair-triggered. That is why, I speculate, that we are capable of descrying human qualities in pure music. For insofar as it can imitate, however faintly, features of persons – such as movement and voice – that are associated with various affective states, we are predisposed to find it expressive. Admittedly, pure orchestral music can only convey very broad emotive states. But when united with dance, the emotive state characteristically becomes concrete in virtue of processes like emotional contagion, and, in virtue of the music, becomes pervasive.

A complication and a conclusion

Up until this point, I have only been considering cases where the music and the dance are co-ordinated in such a way that they appear to move phenomenologically, in a manner of speaking, in the same direction. The pounding propulsiveness of the music in *The Green Table* is consonant with the appearance of martial onslaught in the choreography. However, it is also possible for the expressive properties in the music and dance to head in different directions. The mood music may map a certain domain of affect, but the dance may stalk off along another pathway. In such cases, the dance may be adding a different emotive coloration to the overall image and/or may be ironically cancelling or at least modifying the affective address of the musical frame. Mark Morris's (1985) *One Charming Night* involves both undercutting and thereby modifying the expressive qualities of the music in a manner that renders the concluding overall images of the dance both sardonic and chilling.[12]

One Charming Night represents a young unsophisticated girl (she skips) being seduced by a vampire.[13] It opens with the girl alone on the stage, yearning for something of which she is dimly aware. We know that she is dimly aware, since she essays some of the gestures, like 'flying,' that will

---

12 *One Charming Night*, Brooklyn Academy of Music, 1997, available at the Dance collection, New York Public Library for the Performing Arts.

13 For more complete descriptions and analysis of *One Charming Night*, see Acocella (1993, pp.109, 155).

be the signature of her demon-lover to come. This yearning, moreover, can be heard in the music, although we may also sense that something may be amiss, since the girl's movement is sometimes spastic in contrast to salient regularity of the music – Purcell's *One Charming Night*.

Next the vampire arrives. He makes small hopping movements and patting gestures with his hands conjuring up vague animalistic associations; he does sophisticated *gargouillades* while she skips childishly around him; and he punctuates this with the 'flying' movements (sweeping across the stage with an arm raised behind him) that earlier signaled the girl's yearning. In short order, he succeeds in seducing her.

It is this point in the dance that is of especial interest for us. Once the vampire has won the girl, the gruesome process of vampirization occurs. The physical imagery is graphic, suggesting violent paedophilia as the lovers act out an exchange of blood. The musical accompaniment, however, is quite joyous as the vocalist intones 'alleluia' again and again. When the dance concludes, the girl, perched on the vampire's shoulders, 'flies' off, the music oxymoronically celebrating her brutalization (albeit a brutalization in which she is ambivalently complicit) and her damnation.

This dance is, of course, ironic at the level of the text. The accompanying songs, such as Walter Fuller's 'Lord, What is Man, Lost Man,' make reference to the Son of God. By associating the demonic figure of the vampire with Christ, Morris stages what in effect is a sort of Black Mass in which the girl is 'de-incarnated,' becoming a spirit of the night. But the sardonic effect is not merely achieved by literary means. It also benefits from the way in which the joy expressed by the music is incongruously yoked to the unnerving transformation of the girl into a monster. Musical rejoicing and perdition clash and then collude in an image that is at once chilling and cynical or, in short, satanic.

The fact that the expressive relation between music and dance is typically, reciprocally enabling also opens up the possibility of subverting this norm, although it must be acknowledged that this sort of deviation is fairly standard. It relies on the fact that audiences are sensitive to the expressive address of both the music and the dance not only when they move alone or move together, but also when they move apart. When that happens, the dance may ironically shift or displace the musical frame, or modify or 're-frame' it by adding a conflicting accent to the array, thereby resulting in a more complex expressive quality.[14] The dance puts pressure on the musical frame and the friction results in the emergence of a new expressive quality. In such cases, it is still the function of the dance-theatre elements to concretize

---

14 This possibility should not appear surprising. Insofar as emotions can initiate mood states, they are able to modify them, resulting in such things as composite expressive properties such as the bitter-sweetness of many melodramas.

the affect of the image as a whole by particularizing it, however, it may particularize it in a manner that recalibrates the mood-music by giving it a different accent in the way in which Morris's choreography makes Fuller's joyous and heartfelt refrain resonate with a certain fiendish glee, or, at least, a feeling of diabolical triumph.[15]

Nevertheless, whether the dance and the music are expressively consonant or dissonant, their projection of anthropomorphic qualities, it remains plausible to conjecture, most likely relies upon the rich mechanisms for affective mind-reading humans have developed to negotiate their greatest challenge – understanding each other. If dance tests the physical powers of the performers, it also puts the audience through its paces, testing our ability to detect and to recognize the temper and moods of others in motion.[16]

References

Acocella, Joan. *Mark Morris*, New York: Farrar Straus and Giroux, 1993.

Beattie, James. *Philosophical and Critical Works*, Hildeheim and New York: George Olms, 1975.

Carroll, Noël. 'Art and Mood,' in *Art in Three Dimensions*, Oxford: Oxford University Press, 2010.

Carroll, Noël and Margaret Moore. 'Feeling Movement: Music and Dance' in *Art in Three Dimensions*, Oxford: Oxford University Press, 2010, pp.489-510.

Davies, Stephen. 'Artistic Expression and the Hard Case of Music,' in Kieran, Matthew (ed.), *Contemporary Debates in Aesthetics and the Philosophy of Art*, Oxford: Blackwell Publishing, 2009, pp.179-191.

Davies, Stephen. *Musical Meaning and Expression*, Ithaca: Cornell University Press, 1994.

Jordan, Stephanie. *Moving Music: Dialogues with Twentieth-Century Ballet*, London: Dance Books, 2000.

Kivy, Peter. *Sound Sentiment*, Philadelphia, PA: Temple University Press, 1989.

Kivy, Peter. *The Corded Shell*, Princeton: Princeton University Press, 1980.

North, Roger. *Roger North on Music*, transcribed and edited by John Wilson, London: Novello, 1959.

---

15 Stephanie Jordan (2000, pp.73-102) points out that it would be a mistake to think of the relation of the music to dance as exclusively a matter of parallelism versus counterpoint, construed as contraries; rather it is better to think of the range of options as on a continuum between parallelism and counterpoint. Although my topic is different than Jordan's concerned with expressive properties as apprehended phenomenologically, rather than discrete musicological and choreographic structures, Jordan's warning is pertinent. As the above example shows, it is not that the choreography opposes the music; rather it moves or modifies its accent.

16 This paper benefited from the comments of the audience at the conference on philosophy and dance at Roehampton University in the Spring of 2011 and, also, especially, from feedback from Stephanie Jordan and Joan Acocella.

8. Physical and aesthetic properties in dance

Julia Beauquel

Introduction

Dance as art has been philosophically characterized as involving the natural expressiveness of human movements. But while some authors find the defence of expressiveness essential, others claim that it is not relevant to the understanding of dance and favour instead a focus on style, a supposedly more significant artistic feature.[1]

This paper is an attempt to provide an alternative account to both these positions, with the first (namely, that the dancers are supposed to convey emotions to us by their naturally expressive movements) seeming too naturalistic and the second (that dance only consists in the performance of complicated gestures of a certain style) overly stylistic.

The aim here is to consider the bodily movements neither from the perspective of spectators 'naively' attributing some *naturally expressive* properties to a dance, nor from the point of view of dancers whose main intention is to correctly perform a set of specific technical gestures. As we will see, dance cannot be properly analyzed by means of concepts implying a radical bifurcation of nature and culture, or of the audience's appreciation and the artists' intention.

Firstly, I will show that, as tempting as it seems to a philosopher of dance, insofar as the medium of the art form is the human body in movement, the notion of natural expressiveness is not unanimously accepted. Further thinkers have repudiated it for its misleading comparison with our common expressive behaviour. This essay will raise two objections to the empiricist implications of an aesthetic theory of dance appreciation focused upon the notion of natural expressiveness. First, such a theory seems indifferent to the cognitive aspects of aesthetic appreciation. It reduces our experience of dance to direct perception. Second, this perspective implies anti-realist, or at least relativist views according to which expressive properties are not real or objective, but subjective and relative to the individuals who perceive them.

Secondly, I will urge that the style approach, in overestimating the intentional and conventional features of dance, is not a relevant alternative to natural expressiveness. Again, two objections will be developed. On the

---

1 Joseph Margolis (1981) invokes the idea of natural expressiveness. A response to his paper is given by Mary Sirridge and Adina Armelagos (1983).

one hand, I will criticize the identification of style with technique and the neglect of both the meaning of dance and the expressiveness of the human body in favour of a strong interest in the dancer's intention to correctly execute the movements. On the other hand, I will claim that such a sharp distinction between the dancers' 'technical intentions' and the spectators' attributions of expressive properties to dance works is untenable.

This last objection will be deepened with the idea that a correct understanding of expression in dance cannot be based on a conception of intention as an internal mental state causing physical actions independent of a context. Such a view is not only unable to explain the dancer's expressive actions, but is also inadequate to the reality of many choreographers' creative processes. Expression is less the acting out of some inner mental life than the execution and composition of spontaneous and deliberate gestures that relate and respond to partially constraining contextual elements. As I will maintain, a growing tendency in the dance world is to create the dance work from a 'first performance' engaging one or several dancers. Many choreographers, such as Pina Bausch or Emanuel Gat, use the movement as a starting point: the definite theme, meaning, and structure of their works do not always precede, but progressively *emerge from the actions* performed in the studio. The analysis of choreographic expression should describe different kinds of movements involved in dancing and acknowledge their decisive role as well as the fact that they are not all as intentional or active as we think they are.

This essay moves away from the fruitless opposition between natural expressiveness and style. The focus will be on the physical dimension of human movement, suggesting that it obeys natural laws and thus cannot be considered purely artifactual, conventional, or even intentional. My examination of the art form does not deny the artistic significance of the various existing dance styles, both for the dancers who master them and the spectators who appreciate and identify them. There surely are important differences between a classical ballet like *Sleeping Beauty*, choreographed by Marius Petipa and first performed at the Mariinsky Theatre in St Petersburg, in 1890, and Pina Bausch's version of *The Rite of Spring* (1975) or *Points in Space* by Merce Cunningham (1986),[2] in terms of corporeal sensations as well as in terms of visual perception. Indeed, throughout history, the sense of space and the use of weight vary greatly from one dance style to another. This essay simply emphasizes that danced movements, preeminently with regard to their stylistic categorization, are the expression of our human nature, viz., movements that manifest the dispositions and capacities of a specific type of body. Allowing a different approach to expression in dance,

---

2 Clips of both the Bausch and the Cunningham works are, at the time of writing, available at http://www.youtube.com.

the notions of 'capacity' and 'disposition' are related to the philosophical problem of agency, and belong more generally to action theory.

Agency is the capacity of an agent to act in the world. Action theory, or philosophy of action, considers the nature and definition of action and agency, in particular, examining their relation to mental states: for instance, is an action necessarily *caused* by an intention? Are the expressive bodily movements of a dancer entirely active and intentional? A relevant understanding of dance, we will maintain, is an anticausalistic and externalist account that consists in recognizing that the movements are not strictly products of agency or effects of internal states and personal intentions. Rather, danced movements are contextual interactions that involve a measure of passivity and responsiveness, both on the physical and the aesthetic levels of description.

Finally, a discussion of aesthetic realism will complete my argument about the close relation of corporeal, contextual and aesthetic properties, maintaining that an adequate analysis of dance has to include all of them. The purpose of such an account is to defend an idea of continuity between natural and danced movements, in showing how physical and aesthetic or expressive properties of dance work together. This argument uses a logical and descriptive relation of 'supervenience' between these two types of properties, with a view to defending a realist conception of dance. Asserting that expressive properties such as 'passionate' or 'reserved' supervene on physical properties of movement means that the former depend on the latter, co-vary with them but are not conceptually reducible to them. Even though he did not use this term, such an idea has its origin in the work of Frank Sibley (2001).

Within this framework, what it means to have an appropriate aesthetic experience of a dance work is to be able to perceive and properly identify some physical properties as expressive thanks to a set of cognitive elements concerning its general context of production, including stylistic considerations. The audience does not perceive the expressive properties directly, but rather attributes them to the work on the basis of physical aspects that can cognitively be related to a context. For instance, when a spectator talks about an ethereal choreography or a tempestuous dance, it is in virtue of physical qualities enlightened by the knowledge of features allowing a differentiation between a classical and a modern style. Thus, a strictly empiricist account centered on the notion of natural expressiveness appears to be as misleading as a very strong contextualism excluding expressiveness in favour of style: generally, a correct understanding of this art implies both perceptual and cognitive faculties, both emotional and intellectual factors. Expressive and stylistic properties do not exclude one another. So the dichotomy of natural expressiveness and style is mistaken.

Natural expressiveness

Contrary to classical *expression* theories, the concept of *expressiveness* enables us to describe dance from an external perspective, without having to deal with the problem of the emotions and intentions, either real or hypothetical, of the dancer or choreographer. Speaking about the elegant, melancholic, soulful or joyful gestures of a dance consists in attributing to it some expressive properties that do not imply a reference to the artists' mental states. But the idea of a natural expressiveness has been criticized, mainly for its 'natural' connotation according to which the interaction between dancer and audience derives from our 'everyday expressive behavioural interaction' (Sirridge and Armelagos 1977, p.16). As Sirridge and Armelagos explain, the strong temptation to analyze dance in terms of natural expressiveness derives from the fact that 'the performer's body as a medium or instrument has a much more direct connection with the perceived artwork than in the other performing arts, for at least a part of what the dancer physically does is the most essential component of what the spectator perceives as the artwork with its characteristic expressive qualities' (1983, p.301). Such a view is compatible with an empiricist account of aesthetic experience in which sensation and direct perception play a primary role: our appreciation of dance is considered immediate, autonomous, non-conceptual. Created in order to generate a satisfying aesthetic experience, dance works are evaluated independently of their context of production; they are not 'over intellectualized'.

The limits of natural expressiveness

A first objection to an empiricist analysis of 'natural expressiveness' in dance concerns its inappropriate reduction of aesthetic appreciation to direct perception. As an art, dance does not stand on the same plane with ordinary expressive communication; such an explanation significantly impoverishes its artistic status by failing to account for the cognitive dimension of aesthetic experience. An adequate appreciation of dance's expressive properties requires at least minimal background information about the art form, its history, creative processes, techniques, styles, meaningful contents, and so on. Defended by Jerrold Levinson (for example, 2007) among others, this argument concerns not only the audience's appreciation, but also the dancer's practice. In ballerina Alicia Alonso's opinion, 'When you dance *Giselle*, whether you are a *corps de ballet* or a soloist or prima ballerina or *premier danseur*, you should know all about it. You should read and research the most you can about it, so you can portray the style and believe in what you are dancing' (in Newman 1998, p.59).

Secondly, this conception has relativist and subjectivist implications.

Being objects of immediate experience, expressive properties are not related to a relevant contextual and cognitive background: consequently, dance appreciation can consist in the attribution of *any* property to the works, depending on who experiences them. The aesthetic content, meaning and value of a choreographic work are subjective projections, relative to the perceiver. If the aesthetic judgment and properties are relative, then the works of art lack objective value and communicable meaning: such a view cannot warrant the claim that any interpretation of a dance is more correct than any other. On the contrary, the contextualism implies that our experience, whatever it is, is appropriate.

The style approach

Hence, 'there is no place in dance theory for [...] the notion of "natural expressiveness"' as Sirridge and Armelagos claim (1983, p.307). This natural expressivism does not reflect the reality of dance as art, which is best described in terms of style, roughly defined as 'the dynamic system of kinaesthetic motivation and movement ideals which guide the performer' in his performance (p.302). (For instance, in classical ballet, these ideals are line and fluidity.) According to the advocates of this approach, the fact that 'classical ballet has long been considered deeply expressive of a certain [...] range of emotions and feelings' has *nothing* to do with what a ballet dancer really does: she concentrates on the correct execution of the steps and on staying in line. Actually, 'a soloist is more interested in dancing *Giselle* brilliantly than in expressing sadness' (1977, p.15)[3].

Admittedly, a philosophical interest in dance as art must take into account the technical and stylistic aspects of the medium. These features play a part in dance appreciation. Identifying dance with the spontaneous and immediate performing of movements totally devoid of elaboration is a misconception. Should we conclude that dance styles and natural expressiveness are necessarily incompatible?

Two problems with the style approach

Despite its merits, the style approach encounters at least two major problems. One is that it tends to minimize *both* the importance of the *meaning* of dance *and* the *expressiveness* of the human body, identifying dance styles with pure technique and dancers with some kind of efficient machines. About performances of *Giselle*, dancer Alonso says: 'Today when you see a company, you notice [...] that one of the most difficult things for them is to

---

3 First performed in Paris in 1841, *Giselle* is a Romantic ballet originally choreographed by Jean Coralli and Jules Perrot, then re-choreographed by Marius Petipa for the Imperial Ballet.

believe in what they are doing when they do it' (in Newman 1998, p.59). Another dancer, Nora Kaye, discussing her attitude to some of the roles in the traditional repertoire, deplores this denial or underestimation of the role of affection and emotion in dance execution and aesthetic appreciation: 'you concentrate on your technique, your line [...] I wanted something with a little more emotion and not just steps' (in Newman 1998, p.58). If the performing of a dance merely consists in a correct execution, rather than in any kind of expressiveness, then the audience should pay attention to the way dancers succeed in achieving through the steps the movement ideals of a specific style. A spectator should be interested in watching how line and fluidity are exhibited, and remain indifferent as to the expressive, emotional and meaningful aspects of a particular dance.

However, a satisfying analysis of dance cannot totally neglect the empirical aspect of aesthetic appreciation or discredit the role of emotions in the identification of expressive properties and the understanding of dance meaning. Here is how Alonso describes the role of Giselle: 'In act I, when she comes out of the door, Giselle is life itself! [...] Slowly [...] you begin to understand that she is not just like all the other women, that there is something different on her, something more fragile. [...] It should make the audience hold their breath looking at her' (Newman 1998, p.59). As the film *Black Swan*[4] reminds us, dance is not just about technique, control and perfection, but also involves a capacity to communicate a meaning by exemplifying various expressive qualities – even though this process has nothing to do with the expression of some emotions felt literally (it is often a mistake to identify the emotion *expressed* with the emotion *felt* by this or that dancer). Surely, Nina's character is more interested in dancing brilliantly than in expressing the properties that must be manifest in her performance. But that is precisely why she is unable – at least, at the beginning – to perform the Black Swan part. And, I will maintain, any interpretation engages a disposition to be affected and to react to a context, which sometimes involves a passive use of the body and could well be seen as a form of *natural* expressiveness proper to each performer. This point will be addressed in what follows.

A second problem with the stylistic view is the internal/external distinction it draws. Maintaining that the attribution of a natural expressiveness to a dancer is not relevant insofar as she is centered on performing some correct steps unduly reduces dance to the description of its 'internal' part. Such a distinction between the activity of a dancer and the effects of her dance does not seem adequate to the art form. Notably, it seems to leave a mysterious chasm between the dancer's world and the spectator's. It neglects the expressive effects of the dancing body in virtue of an explanation focused on

---

4 Film directed by Darren Aronofsky, 2010.

the dancer's intentions (her activity, concentration and correction-seeking). Why would there be a radical dichotomy between what dance 'truly' is (some actions viewed from the perspective of a performing dancer) and what is only a deceptive appearance (these actions naively perceived as 'naturally expressive' by the spectators)? This philosophical study of dance seeks to include both what a dancer does (experienced dance) and what a spectator perceives (perceived dance).

Against two dichotomies: interiority/exteriority, style/expressiveness

Dance cannot be properly analyzed on the basis of a dichotomy of interiority and exteriority. A dancer performs gestures that are designed for an audience. These movements are intended to be shown: from dance learning to ballet rehearsals, they are constantly improved thanks to a person who teaches, observes and corrects them. The recognition that they are to be viewed is a presupposition of dancers' gestures being performed the way they are. A major part of dancers' practice consists in adjusting, thanks to an observing eye, their gestures to what will be the perceived effects of a work. The intentions conveyed in a dance are not independent of this eye; rather they are shaped by it. Thus, dance really ends up embodying an observer's directions and corrections, directions and corrections that are made with a view to the dance's being observed by an audience. The fact that observers help build the movement justifies the adoption of an externalist approach to expressive properties: these properties are extrinsic to the dancer; they are relational. In other words, they characterize the dance works but depend on the viewer's responses. The properties of *Giselle*, for instance, are those of gestures both as they are intentionally performed and as they are perceived.

Consequently, dancing *Giselle* brilliantly (the technique and style) and expressing sadness (the expressiveness and meaning) should not be considered two separate things. The first might be a way to do the second. One dance can fall under several correct descriptions, given by a dancer, a choreographer, a tutor, or a spectator: descriptions in terms of technical, intentional, stylistic, aesthetic and meaningful properties. Even if a dancer had no idea about the meaning of her execution, the action of correctly performing the gestures of *Giselle*'s choreography (the 'intentional' action, without observation), and the action of expressing sadness (the action observed and described as 'sad' by an observer who is able to perceive this property) are one and the same. Dance is not limited to dancers' intentionality or to their own description of what they do. The content that dancers manifest is largely impersonal. The important point is that there is someone, sometimes someone other than the artist, who is able to describe the action by highlighting its rationale. As Jerrold Levinson maintains: 'What an artist's work means [...], may very well be clearer to well-placed others than to him or her' (Levinson 2007, p.7).

Expression and the problematic relation between intention and action

A philosophical examination of dance shows that a conception of expression in which artists' intentions (those of dancers as well as those of choreographers) are considered internal mental states causing their actions independent of context, is untenable.

First, it does not reflect the reality of creative processes. Certainly, 'it is important to do justice to the connection between a work of art and its creator' as Graham McFee (1992, p.209) claims. But it is a mistake to believe that the movements of a dance only are the acting-out and the manifestation of mental states that a choreographer or dancer has the intention to express. The creative methods of Pina Bausch show that dance is not the result of prior, entirely determined intentions imposed on dancers by choreographers. Underlying both the importance of action and the collective aspect of creation, the famous choreographer confides: 'I cannot come and say: 'Here is what we will do'. [...] I like feeling that we are in the process without really knowing how we got there. There is no beginning. [...] I like us to move forward in the same direction rather than being followed.' (Bausch 2009). The work is progressively composed through the dancers' actions and the choreographer's selections. Dance works are very often created out of a series of individual or collective performances. Also invalidating the view of dance as a mere physical effect of some pre-existing intentional content, choreographer Emanuel Gat declares: 'I am not going to do a piece about the war in the Middle East but I will go inside a choreographic process that, if it has a strong inner logic, will reflect on so many other things' (Gat 2012).

Second, many issues that are raised by the notion of expression derive from our tendency to conceive it as a purely *intentional* and *active* process even though it is not. A danced movement can be intentionally passive (released, weighty), or unintentionally active, as when we run out of fear, by reflex. A dancer can convey expressive properties *without intending* to do so. In life in general, we routinely attribute expressive qualities to people who do not intend to have them. A joyful way of walking, the lassitude of a posture, a warm way of being, the sombre or radiant look of a face are not always the object of an expressive intention. The fact that these attitudes manifest the corresponding mental states does not imply that the people concerned actually *intend* to express and transmit them to an observer or an interlocutor.

Similarly, not every expressive property conveyed by dancers is the fruit of an intention. McFee explains: 'the artist's intentions are not, or not necessarily, things he actually or explicitly thought or intended: that is to say, the implicit intentions, thoughts, ideas (unconscious ones) must be respected' (1992, p.209). As Merce Cunningham himself said, anything the human body does is expressive, even when it is not infused with intention and emotion. As an example, a piece like Yvonne Rainer's *Trio A*,[5] which aims at being devoid of emotion, hierarchy, repetition, and any form of emphasis conveys a 'touching, upright girls-college seriousness', according to critic Joan Acocella (1990, p.13). Thus, even if we accept the thesis that dancers only care about their execution's correctness (rather than their interpretation's rightness), this does not justify the exclusion of their expressiveness.

An expressive property can be the symptom of a specific corporeal constitution or the manifestation of a distinctive temperament. A willowy body with long muscles will not produce the exact same effects as a smaller and very toned body; and it is likely that, with similar intentions, a dancer with an impulsive and nervous temperament dances very differently from a calm, or even lethargic personality. As we will see, 'our intentional actions are *not always as active as we think* they are' (De Sousa 1987, p.11). Of course, a dancer initiates, performs and ends her movements whenever she decides to. But falls, turns, jumps, or runs and other movements involve a physical dimension of weight and inertia that is not entirely under her control. Later, I will highlight the inextricable combination of activity and passivity that constitutes dance.

Conative and cognitive orientations

For now, the idea that expression is not a strictly active, subjective or projective phenomenon can be deepened by the distinction drawn between the conative and the cognitive 'direction of fit'.

This distinction can be illustrated by a question raised by Plato about the nature of piety: do we desire X because X is desirable, or do we consider X desirable simply because we desire it? Roughly, the first alternative is objectivist (the desire depends on a property of the object). This is the cognitive orientation, characterized by a 'mind-to-world' direction of fit. The second alternative is subjectivist (the desire depends on the subject). This conative orientation is the opposite: it consists in a 'world-to-mind' direction of fit. We will or desire what does not yet exist, and our desire is satisfied if the world provides what we want.

---

5 First performed on January 10, 1966 at the Judson Memorial Church in Greenwich Village by David Gordon, Steve Paxton and Rainer herself.

Here, I maintain that expression in dance combines and manifests both directions of fit. Through movement, dancers both express subjective characteristics and respond to objective elements, such as musical properties. As spectators, we generally expect more than seeing dancers conscientiously rehearsing a habitual sequence of steps. We enjoy being able to identify how they respond to each other and how they relate to a context. We are particularly touched when a dancer lets herself go or surprises herself. These remarks apply equally to technique, creation, and interpretation.

Therefore, rather than analysing expression in dance as a causal relation between an internal intention (for instance, to correctly perform some gestures) and a physical action ('wrongly' perceived by the audience as expressive), a conception of the art form should take into account the dancers' interaction with the context of a work that constraints and influences their movements. As an organization of some more or less active and intentional relations to the specific context of a work, dance includes a measure of passivity and receptivity that should not be neglected. A relevant approach to expression may be inspired by ideas such as those defended by Elizabeth Anscombe in her book *Intention* (2002), where she argues that we should replace the causal explanation of the relation of intention to action with an observation of the conditions under which our actions' descriptions are intentional. Here, the description we suggest employs the notions of capacities and dispositions, as well as the categories of activity and passivity.

Reconciling different perspectives

To sum up, a stylistic or conventionalist account of dance is no more acceptable than an empiricist or naturalist view. As we have seen, the emphasis on natural expressiveness reduces dance experience to relative appreciations or judgements of taste, whereas the focus upon style and dancers' practice and intentionality tends to ignore the expressiveness of the dancing body. Considering dance as the natural performing of expressive movements offered to immediate subjective and sensible experience or exaggerating the importance of stylistic aspects by putting aside the impact of corporeal expressiveness upon our perception and emotions seem equally inappropriate.

Furthermore, style and expressivity should not be set against each other on the basis of what is intentionally and consciously controlled by a dancer and what is not, or what is active and what is passive in her dance. The distinction between what is intentional and what is not, if it is too hastily conceived as a distinction between what is conscious, voluntary, active or controlled on the one hand and what is unconscious, involuntary, passive or uncontrolled on the other hand is an obstacle on the path to dance understanding.

We could content ourselves with the idea that there is no point in matching the natural expressiveness approach against the style approach. After all, these views complement each other, dealing with the description of one phenomenon from different perspectives: the spectator's point of view, in terms of movement's expressiveness, and the dancer's point of view focused on rightly performing some sophisticated movements. But such a distinction between experienced and perceived dance can also leave us unsatisfied: there seems an obligation to explain how the expressive properties and the stylistic aspects relate to each other, keeping in mind that dance is neither a purely natural expression, nor a pure set of stylistic conventions.

A more appropriate and fruitful approach to dance analysis is to consider the nature of the movements themselves, setting aside the aesthetic intentions of both those who perform them and those who attribute expressive properties to them. I suggest an explanation that is not purely aesthetic; it is borrowed from action theory. It consists in examining dance in terms of active and passive movements. This conception which first accommodates physical movements, then aesthetic qualities should allow us to clarify the way in which dancers' natural expressiveness and choreographic styles can be reconciled. This raises the question what dance does and how it does it.

Dance and action theory

In a paper about 'agency' and 'patiency' (i.e., the quality of being passive, or the condition of being acted upon by another) in nature, Mikael M. Karlsson (2002) briefly presents Fred Dretske's (1988) theory of action as a rare attempt to distinguish between active and passive movements without appealing to the notion of intention. Here, my question is whether such a theory, dealing with natural movements *in general*, can clarify the somewhat mysterious notion of natural expressiveness and provide us with a way to analyze dance as a set of physical movements without having to deal with the choreographer's or dancer's intention and the audience's appreciation.

Dretske's distinction between what a subject does and what happens to it is not based upon a contrast between what is intentional and what is not, but upon a distinction between internal and external causes of movement. On the one hand, agency concerns everything a subject does, even involuntarily. It is the agent's behaviour. The location of the movement's cause is internal (for instance: trembling, coughing, crying, blushing, inhaling, exhaling). On the other hand, a subject is acted upon, or has something happen to it when something external moves it, in other words when the location of the movement's cause is external to the subject (for instance, being bitten by a dog).

Of course, philosophical inquiry into dance should not reduce this art form to an activity devoid of intention. The aim is simply to focus, at least initially, on a movement's basic properties. For it is far from obvious that every movement in a dance is intentional. And after all, dancers are natural beings; their properly human capacities and technical, artistic abilities, as developed as they are, never totally eliminate the effects of nature on their bodies and movements. Rather, these danced movements can be conceived, in a sense, as the expression of a nature that is realized to some degree.

Unfortunately, Dretske's distinction between agency and patiency on the basis of a distinction between internal and external causes of change leads to counterexamples: according to Dretske's theory, Karlsson asserts, some 'paradigm cases of *having something happen to one* rather than of *doing something* (namely, we *suffer* hair loss and are *victims* of heart attacks and epileptic fits)' just because they are *internally caused*, count as things that a person *does*, not things that she undergoes (Karlsson 2002, pp.62-3).

Applying this to dance, a dancer who performed the wrong steps or lost her balance not because of an external event but because she is in bad shape or has a cramp (i.e. an *internal* cause) would be considered the *agent* of her movement. Is it right to classify this movement – that would commonly be considered accidental – in the same category as the correctly performed actions? In this conception, some unpredicted and uncontrollable movements, because they have an internal cause, count as a dancer's actions. But as cases like the awkward movement caused by a cramp show, a dancer is not the agent of every internally caused movement any more than the bald man is the agent of his hair loss. This conception exaggerates the role of the agent's activity, failing to account for the intrinsic passive phenomenon (such as hair loss, epileptic fits, unpredicted movements caused by a pain).

These problematic examples show the contestable character, notably concerning dance, of an account that distinguishes between *agency* and *patiency* on the basis of a distinction between some *internal* and *external* causes of movement.

Active and passive powers

Nonetheless, thanks to the notion of passive powers, it is possible to improve this conception in order to make it relevant for an analysis of dance. Karlsson defines a passive power as 'a power of something to be affected by something else in a certain way' (2002, p.54). The examples he uses to illustrate this are those of a splinter of iron attracted by a magnet, a football kicked by a footballer and a field mouse carried off by an owl. Whereas the magnet, the player and the owl are agents, the movements of the splinter, the football and the field mouse are passive. Karlsson writes: 'they do not act, but are acted upon; being attracted, kicked and carried off are evidently not things that they *do*, but things that *happen* to them' (Karlsson 2002, p.63). The major difference with Dretske's theory is that this power of being affected is *intrinsic* (or *internal*) to these things or beings. The attraction of the splinter by the magnet depends on a passive power of the iron, a property of this material: its susceptibility to being attracted by the magnet (a property that neither copper nor aluminum possesses). Yet we cannot, as Dretske would, speak about a *behaviour* of the splinter, the mouse and the ball. Karlsson asserts: '*agency* should not be attributed on the basis of the exercise of a *passive* power'. It would be paradoxical. And he continues: 'a subject *acts* or *does something*, as opposed to *being acted upon* or *having something happen to it*, insofar as its motion is brought about by the exercise of an *active* power: a power to do rather than to be affected, an *ability* rather than a *susceptibility*' (2002, p.64).

To a large extent, dance consists in the *experience* and *manifestation* of our active and passive intrinsic powers. Let us consider the dancer's body as having both active properties like those of the magnet, owl and footballer and passive properties like those of the iron splinter, the mouse and the ball: her movements that derive from active powers are similar to the action of the magnet, the kick of the footballer and the movement of the owl catching its prey, whereas her movements derived from passive powers are similar to those of the iron splinter attracted by the magnet, the mouse carried off by its predator, and the ball.

What fascinates us in dance seems to partake of its power to exemplify, at a high level of complexity, such a mix of activity and passivity. Every movement that yields to the force of gravity exhibits passivity: as an example, the fact of coming down on the floor after a leap does not seem attributable to an activity of the dancer's body; her dangling arm movements obeying her chest rotations do not seem more active. Most of the bodily movements that are mainly due to weight or inertia are attributable to a form of passivity rather than an activity. Thus, when a dancer lets herself fall, even if she decided to do so and if she demonstrates an ability to fall, the fall itself is a 'letting-go' rather than a 'doing': the dancer lets the natural movement of her weight go. No intention, will or decision to let her self go can make this abandon entirely active. The most a dancer can 'do' in such a released movement is to train her self to partially control the fall. In other words, no human being is the *agent* of her body's attraction by gravity. Thus, in every movement due to the body's weight or inertia (the off-balance, falls, bounces, spins) the dancer experiences a passivity that she learns to partially control but that she cannot quite seize. This is what Aristotle calls *nature: the motion whose source is intrinsic to the thing but that is not derived from the thing itself.* Through this type of movement, the dancer *exemplifies* and *manifests* this nature that does not belong to her and yet characterizes her. A dancer's passive movements just depend on a disposition of her body.

If this is correct, the concepts of activity and passivity are relevant for the purpose of understanding natural as well as danced movements, provided that one does not distinguish them on the basis of Dretske's internal/external contrast. They show that it is not absurd, as some think it is, to speak of a form of *natural* expressiveness of danced movements, which consists in using weight and energy in an active way, but also in a passive manner. To understand this, it is neither necessary to examine the dancers' emotions, nor to wonder about what comes under the intention to correctly perform the movements of a given dance style or what is part of a dancer's natural expressiveness instead. Dance literally exemplifies our bodily capacities and susceptibilities.

Aesthetic implications

So far, I have examined dance in terms of some of its physical properties; I can now consider the aesthetic level. The use of active and passive powers may help to explain some major differences between dance techniques and styles. Depending on the importance that they attach to these powers, these techniques and styles produce some movements that *feel* very different to the dancers and *look* very different to the spectators. Put simply, classical dance technique largely privileges the learning and mastery of active powers; the active, risen-up and controlled movements continuously escape from weight, in a tireless fight against gravity. These extremely active body movements are particularly appropriate to the expression or 'exemplification' of light themes, literally as well as figuratively. Catherine Z. Elgin thus writes: 'Classical ballet [...] literally exemplifies properties such as grace, delicacy, and beauty; and metaphorically exemplifies properties such as love and longing, weightlessness and ethereality' (2010, p.86). As Nelson Goodman explained, the exemplification of a property P means that P is both instantiated and referred to (Goodman 1976; see also Elgin 1996, pp.170-183). In other words, a dance exemplifies lightness and joy when it possesses *and* draws attention to these properties.

When dancers came to think of the expressive power of classical dance as limited, they progressively introduced opposing tendencies of movement in attributing a greater importance to the exemplification of passive powers by using weight in a released manner[6]. An example provided by Elgin is

---

6 Sirridge and Armelagos (1977, p.21) claim: 'we might, then, suppose that dancers have rejected traditional ballet because they have disliked or been unable to tolerate the limitations on expressive potential which they saw reflected in the usual choice of subject matter'.

Martha Graham's works, insofar as they 'literally exemplify that the body of the dancer has a certain weight – that it is subject to literal as well as metaphorical gravity [...] [They] metaphorically exemplify psychological properties such as grief, regret, horror and hope' (Elgin 2010, p.86). Thus, modern, postmodern and contemporary techniques and styles appeared with all the new properties they express, literally as well as metaphorically related to gravity. So dance can be the object of various aesthetic descriptions: we speak highly of the graceful, elegant and ethereal classical style or admire the intensity of an impetuous contemporary style.

This very sketchy portrayal simply aims to show how physical properties can generate various sorts of aesthetic properties (expressive then stylistic). The nature of dance aesthetic properties partly depends on a measured use of active and passive powers of physical movement.

The important point is that this use is not strictly physical, but also aesthetic. In addition to the active/passive use of weight and inertia, either in resisting gravity or on the contrary giving in to it, dancers can let themselves be affected and guided by the music, or can act against it in various ways. Many choreographers and dancers' creations still derive from and depend upon musical works: their improvised movements as well as their compositions are closely related to the musical properties that inspire them. This is particularly obvious in Anne Teresa de Keersmaeker's works since 1980 and, for instance, in Mark Morris's *Mozart Dances* (2006).[7] Thus soft and joyful or sad and plaintive music has the power to infuse the danced movements with its nuanced rhythmical and melodic properties. Its power is even stronger, since music does not only affect the movement qualities, but determines the movements themselves, as Noël Carroll and Margaret Moore claim (Carroll and Moore 2010). In some dances indeed, the turns, arm movements, leaps and many other gestures are the embodiment or reflection of some musical movements. In these cases, it seems appropriate to describe dance as deriving from passive powers: dance exemplifies a power to be affected by music. But dance, of course, can also act in contrast to a melody, or simply be totally independent of it, as it is shown by many pieces by Cunningham and John Cage.

Impenetrable and porous dances

I suggest a distinction between some 'impenetrable' and some 'porous' dances, depending on whether the active or passive movements prevail. This distinction is not a mere conceptual exercise but aims to point out some very

---

7 A clip of *Rosas Danst Rosas* (1983), filmed by Thierry de Mey, the composer, and an interview with Mark Morris, plus rehearsal footage of *Mozart Dances* are (at the time of writing) available on http://youtube.com

different tendencies that can be discerned in dance works and revealed by the dancer's testimonies.

The impenetrable tendency is to dance in an extremely active way. The movement is first. The dancer claims that she does not have time to interpret, 'it goes too fast'. The mere performance of the gestures demands all the focus. The purpose is *the correctness* of the performance: 'impenetrable dancers' concentrate on the rigour and precision of the executed steps, in sum on the technical virtuosity of the performance.

As for the 'porous' tendency, it consists in performing the movement in an open way, as a manifestation of what affects us. The movement is second: it is a response to something else. The purpose here is *the rightness* of the performance: the right response to this 'something'. The 'porous dancers' focus on the quality of the choreography and the will to serve something else: a melody, some emotional properties, in short a meaning conveyed by the movements.

'Supervenience' and aesthetic realism

My explanation of dance in terms of active and passive powers that are literally and metaphorically employed intends to support the thesis that dance appreciation and understanding imply both *the perception of physical properties* of corporeal movement and *the identification of stylistic properties*. This way of combining the physicality of dance with its aesthetic features is compatible with a realist account using the logical relation of supervenience to describe the dependence of aesthetic properties upon physical properties.[8] This description of the way in which we are in relation to the choreographic works allows us to maintain that these two types of properties are neither radically distinct nor identical: aesthetic properties supervene upon the basic or physical properties, co-vary with them, but are not conceptually reducible to them. A vigorous, harmonious or smooth dance is what it is in virtue of other properties that are not aesthetic, upon which it depends, with which it covaries, but to which it is not reduced.

Dance cannot be properly reduced to physical movements and gestures. It is made of corporeal and intentional actions possessing properties that characterize it as an art form and can be adequately perceived. Aesthetic properties of dance supervene not only on physical properties but also on contextual properties such as those of choreographic vocabularies, styles, techniques, creation processes, artistic evolutions, and so on. Our attribution of aesthetic properties does not derive from purely subjective impressions: speaking about dance, we refer to real features. These characteristics are physical, spatial, formal, structural and contextual

---

8 For such a conception, see particularly Pouivet (2006) and (2010).

(cognitive, intentional, historical, cultural).

Aesthetic realism has two major advantages. First, acknowledging the normativity of aesthetic experience, it does not reduce dance to physical bodies in motion. The content and meaning of dance works depend upon physical as well as stylistic properties. Second, it shows that aesthetic properties are not determined by subjective projections, experiences or reactions. They are real (the dance works possess them) and relational (related to human intentions and to a context). That we can say why we attribute certain properties to a dance does not imply that we can attribute to it *any* property depending upon our own subjective experience. We cannot adequately attribute just any kind of property to any choreographic work. Dance is not condemned to relativism of appreciation but is a reality that can be the object of an actual knowledge. We can learn to appreciate it correctly. An appropriate aesthetic experience including both the cognitive and the perceptive or emotional aspects of dance is possible.

Conclusion

Certainly, aesthetic realism is not nowadays the most prevailing conception in the art world, especially concerning dance. The corporeal dimension of the art form, its stylistic diversity and variety of content, combined with the fact that many choreographic works are not narrative may explain why subjectivism is dominant in the dance world. Dance is an art form that is apparently impenetrable, or seems on the contrary immediately accessible, in a 'non-cognitive mode'.

But there is no reason to think that we cannot learn to understand dance, to develop a capacity to perceive its real properties and refer to them adequately in making right and reliable judgements. Dance as art includes movements and gestures that we can learn to identify; and it comprises works that are excellent, good, mediocre, poor, clear or confused, memorable or insignificant.

This does not mean that we must renounce our perceptual and emotional faculties in favour of conventional information or knowledge of things like stylistic elements. The opposition of style and expressiveness is mistaken: there is no incompatibility, but rather a continuity relating these notions. It is not necessary to make a choice between a view of dance as a set of bodily movements perceived by spectators as naturally expressive on the one hand and, on the other hand, an analysis of this choreographic art as a set of stylistic gestures performed by dancers principally preoccupied with the perfection of their technique.

Of course, classical dance, which is extremely codified, lends itself to a stylistic approach, whereas contemporary dance may seem or be described by its practitioners as more natural. But an explanation of dance in terms of active and passive powers highlights that generally, in every dance style, the movements exemplify the actions and passivity of the natural beings that we are. They exemplify the capacities and dispositions of a certain type of body; the body that constitutes us as human beings. This is what dancers do, and what spectators see. On different levels (basic or physical, and aesthetic), we act and undergo what surrounds us; we are able to react and respond in various nuanced ways, in a more or less appropriate manner. In any case, the wide diversity of danced movements is the expression *par excellence* of our complex nature.[9]

References

Acocella, Joan. 'Imagining Dance', *Dance Ink*, 1:2, 1990.

Anscombe, G. E. M. *L'intention*, trans. Mathieu Maurice and Cyrille Michon, Paris: Gallimard, 2002.

Aristote. *La Métaphysique*, trans. Jules Tricot, Paris: Vrin. Tome I, 1991, and Tome II, 2000.

Bausch, Pina. In *Hommage à Pina Bausch*, revue *Danser*, 2009.

Beauquel, Julia. 'Le mouvement et l'émotion', in Beauquel, Julia and Roger Pouivet (eds.), 2010, pp.65-77.

Beauquel, Julia. *Le Danseur et le réel, une philosopie de la danse*, Rennes: Presses Universitaires de Rennes II, collection Aesthetica, forthcoming 2014.

Beauquel, Julia and Roger Pouivet (eds.). *Philosophie de la danse*, Rennes: Presses Universitaires de Rennes II, collection Aesthetica, 2010.

Carroll, Noël and Margaret Moore. 'La communication kinesthésique, par la danse, avec la musique', in Beauquel, Julia and Roger Pouivet (eds.), 2010, pp.99-114.

Carter, Alexandra (ed.). *The Routledge Dance Studies Reader*, London: Routledge, 1998.

Cunningham, Merce and Jacqueline Lesschaeve. 'Torse: There Are No Fixed Points in Space', in Carter, Alexandra (ed.), 1998, pp.29-34.

Cunningham, Merce. 'L'art impermanent (1955)', in Ginot, Isabelle and Marcelle Michel (eds.), *La danse au XXᵉ siècle*, Paris, Larousse, 2002.

De Sousa ,Ronald. *The Rationality of Emotion*, Cambridge, MA: MIT Press, 1987.

Dretske, Fred. *Explaining Behavior: Reasons in a World of Causes*, Cambridge, MA: MIT Press, 1988.

Elgin, Catherine Z. *Considered Judgment*, Princeton, Princeton University

9 For extended views on this matter, see Beauquel (forthcoming, 2014).

Press, 1996.

Elgin, Catherine Z. 'L'exemplification et la danse', in Beauquel, Julia and Roger Pouivet (eds.), 2010, pp.81-98.

Farjeon, Annabel. 'Choreographers: Dancing For De Valois and Ashton', in Carter, Alexandra (ed.), 1998, pp.23-28.

Gat Emanuel. 'Playing Games: The Choreographic Process', Sadler's Wells, London's Dance House website, 2012, http://www.sadlerswells.com/page/screen/1162333620001#.

Goodman, Nelson. *Languages of Art*, 2nd edition, Indianapolis: Hackett Publishing Company, 1976.

Hilton, Rebecca and Bryan Smith. 'A Dancing Consciousness', in Carter, Alexandra (ed.), 1998, pp.72-80.

Jeyasingh, Shobana. 'Imaginary Homelands: Creating A New Dance Language', in Carter, Alexandra (ed.), 1998, pp.46-52.

Karlsson, Mikael M. 'Agency and Patiency: Back to Nature?' in *Philosophical Explorations*, 5:1, 2002, pp.59-81.

Karlsson, Mikael M. 'Les lapins pourraient-ils danser?' in Beauquel, Julia and Roger Pouivet (eds.), 2010, pp.45-64.

Levinson, Jerrold. 'Aesthetic Contextualism', *Postgraduate Journal of Aesthetics*, 4:3, 2007.

Margolis, Joseph. 'The Autographic Nature of the Dance', *The Journal of Aesthetics and Art Criticism*, 39:4, 1981, pp.419-427.

McFee, Graham. *Understanding Dance*, London, Routledge, 1992.

Newman, Barbara. 'Dancers Talking About Performance', in Carter, Alexandra (ed.), 1998, pp.57-65.

Pouivet, Roger. 'Survenances', *Critique*, 575, 1995, pp.227-249.

Pouivet, Roger. 'On the Cognitive Functioning of Aesthetic Emotions', *Leonardo*, 33:1, 2000, pp.49-53.

Pouivet, Roger. *Le réalisme esthétique*, Paris: Presses Universitaires de France, 2006.

Pouivet, Roger. *L'ontologie de l'œuvre d'art : Essais d'art et de philosophie*, 2nd edition, Paris: Vrin, 2010.

Schmidt-Garre, Jan (ed.). *You Don't Do Anything, You Just Let It Evolve*, Documentary on Sergiu Celibidache, Paris Media Production, co-prod. ZDF, 2005.

Servos, Norbert. 'Pina Bausch: Dance and Emancipation', in Carter, Alexandra (ed.), 1998, pp.36-45.

Sheppard, Anne. *Aesthetics, An Introduction to the Philosophy of Art*, Oxford: Oxford University Press, 1987.

Sibley, Frank. 'Aesthetic and Non-aesthetic (1965)', in *Approach to Aesthetics*, Oxford: Clarendon Press, 2001, pp.33-51.

Sirridge, Mary and Adina Armelagos. 'The In's and Out's of Dance:

Expression as an Aspect of Style', *The Journal of Aesthetics and Art Criticism*, 36:1, 1977, pp. 15-24".

Sirridge, Mary and Adina Armelagos. 'The Role of "Natural Expressiveness" in Explaining Dance', *The Journal of Aesthetics and Art Criticism*, 41:3, 1983, pp.301-307.

9. Visible symbols: dance and its modes of representation

Henrietta Bannerman

Introduction

In this essay I interrogate what it is that we mean when we talk of dance as representation, arguing that we need to move beyond any notion of dance simply imitating or simulating human reality. Often in the sphere of aesthetics, representation is most readily aligned with *mimesis* (Hursthouse 1992), or the way in which the art object communicates textually, visually or aurally by copying or resembling a pre-existing reality. However, many, particularly post-nineteenth-century forms of art are not imitative especially since within the period of modernism artists in several disciplines departed from the custom of mimesis. For them, representation became as Mitchell says, 'an extremely elastic notion, which extends all the way from a stone representing a man to a novel representing the day in the life of several Dubliners' (1990, p.13).

I am interested in demonstrating how it is possible to link questions about the nature of representation with the methodology of dance analysis and in so doing I turn to the work of Charles Sanders Peirce (1931-1958). In particular, I will examine how Peirce's notion of the triadic sign can bring out connections between object and meaning other than imitation as traditionally conceived. In the last part of the essay, I analyze two scenes from Hofesh Shechter's *Political Mother* (2010-2011), I show how applying Peirce's sign theory can help explain how this work communicates its meaning to the viewer with the affective intensity for which Shechter's choreography is renowned.

Interrogating representation, mimesis and the symbolic

It is important to question the representational in dance in an era when it is sometimes said that what we see in a theatre is not representative of anything but rather is real life as it is lived by the flesh and blood people on stage. Norbert Servos, for example, writes that Pina Bausch's "theatre of experience' [...] does not *pretend*. It *is*' (Servos 1984, italics in original). As a major figure in the genre of *Tanztheater* and precursor of British physical theatre, Bausch led the way in providing audiences of the late 20th century with productions rooted in reality. However, I contend that a theatrical production, no matter how life-like, is not everyday reality but is better understood as a form of representation, indeed under the rubric of Aristotelian mimesis. It is important, however, to establish that the mimesis of ancient Greece was not understood in quite the same way as it is today. The Greek scholar Gilbert Murray remarks: 'if we wonder why Aristotle, and Plato before him, should lay such stress on the theory that art is imitation, it is a help to realize that common language called it 'making', and it was clearly not 'making' in the ordinary sense', (1920, p.8).

Murray reminds us that the poet who was the "maker of a Fall of Troy 'did not make the real Fall of Troy. He made an imitation Fall of Troy' (*ibid.*). In more modern times and within the context of linguistic theory, we have come to understand that all texts, no matter how realistic they may appear, are constructed according to the author's view of the world, an observation that applies surely to Bausch's productions, meanwhile, which are celebrated for their ability to 'refer the onlooker directly back to reality' (Servos 1984, p.21), thus constituting what we might term an augmented mimesis.

This augmented mimesis is like that characterized by Susan Kozel who draws upon Luce Irigaray's feminist oriented 'new symbolic', to argue that mimesis in Bausch is:

> based on a principle of repetition or analogy which is not one of identical reproduction or simple imitation. There is always a moment of excess[1], or a remainder in the mimetic process, something that makes the mimicry

---

1 Kozel's notion of excess, I claim, chimes with the theories of Monroe C. Beardsley (1982), in particular his characterization of dance as constituting 'an overflow or superfluity of expressiveness,' qualities that extend beyond the practical necessities of ordinary behaviour or in various types of choreographed rituals (1982, p.35). This view is contested by Noël Carroll and Sally Banes (1982) who point out that such excess or extremes of expressivity in movement, are not commensurate with dances typical of the Judson era such as Yvonne Rainer's *Room Service* (1963), a dance designed as they put it 'to make ordinary movement *qua* ordinary movement perceptible,' (1982, p.37) and thereby uninflected by any degree of physical or emotional intensification. In particular they describe a section from the dance as it was performed in 1964 as comprising 'two dancers carrying a mattress up an aisle in the theatre, out one exit, and back in through another' (1982, p.37). I propose that *Room Service* (and dances that are similarly task-based), often performed within a theatrical or performance setting, present an overabundance of normative signs. If these signs are decoded through Peirce's second triad, the viewer is directed towards an experience which is transformative in that its meaningfulness exceeds that of watching everyday behaviour. This is not in fact to argue against Carroll and Banes who recognize the prosaic activities comprising *Room Service* as a dance and as symbolic (1982, p.38) but rather to recast Beardsley's theory and propose that an excess of the mundane is regarded as 'an overflow or superfluity of expressiveness,' as I hope to demonstrate in the analysis of Jerome Bel's *Shirtology* (1997) made later in this essay (see Davies, D. 2004 pp.17, 56, 59 and 2011 pp.10-14 for further comment on Beardsley's and Carroll's and Banes' views on the expressive and anti-expressive aspects of dance).

different from that which inspired it, and which transforms the associated social and aesthetic space. (Kozel 1997, p.100)

In calling for a new female-centred social and political order and the requirement for a new symbolic to underpin it, Irigaray opens the way for the body to be combined with language, thereby creating scope for what Kozel calls a 'physical symbolic' (p.107). Bausch exposes as Kozel puts it, 'not just the power relations between men and women but the entire web of conventions and representations which shape us' (*ibid.*). Kozel's physical symbolic, then, is a key term for this essay as is the way that it gives precedence to the body's movements and thus reinforces the power of dance as non verbal communication.

We might further propose that in comparison to the artificial medium of verbal language, all live dance performances are real. A word (sign) is not the thing it represents, whereas a movement is the movement one sees whether or not it is intended to represent something other than itself. In this respect I recall the words of the sculptor Anthony Gormley who in a television arts programme spoke of his admiration for the non narrative work of Merce Cunningham and of dancers as the 'bravest and most direct artists because they use life itself and being as their medium of expression' (BBC2 2011). It does not follow, however, that the reality of the stage and of everyday life is synonymous, as each constitutes its own sphere of engagement. This surely is what the writer Albert A. Johnstone means when he maintains that dance which aims to develop characterization or narrative does so on the basis that the movements performed are real, but that the ideas, emotions and beliefs attributed to the dancer performing those movements are illusory (1984, p.171).

Nonetheless, notions of the illusory do not rest comfortably with Bausch's *Tanztheater* where the emotions or states of being portrayed by the dancers emanate from their personal, real, lived experience (Fernandes 2001, pp.25-31). This reiteration of the real leads writers and commentators like Ciane Fernandes to argue that Bausch does not present illusion as such but frames human experience in a theatrical context as a transcendence of the real or as a re-presentation of reality (Fernandes 2001). It is then a lived aspect of theatrical verisimilitude, or as Kozel puts it a physical symbolic that re-energizes the concept of mimesis as a transformational mode of representation.

For the purposes of this essay, we need to further examine how the term representation in dance studies has been theorized in ways other than the mimetic and with this enquiry in mind I include references to Noël Carroll's and Sally Banes' categories of representation (1999) which form part of the small body of theoretical writing about interpreting dance. I am also drawn to Susan Foster's writing about the symbolic and to her four modes of representation since I want to compare them with Peirce's theories. Foster defines these modes and illustrates each using the example of how a river might be represented. Thus, for Foster *resemblance* embodies 'a certain quality or attribute of the river, perhaps its winding path,' in other words, 'I am river;' while choreography considered under the category *imitation* produces 'a schematized version of the river's appearance', or 'I am like the river. *Replication* is a more complex idea according to which the river is represented as 'a dynamic system [...] the movement replicates the relationship [...] for example, between the flowing water and the bounded channel or between the current and a small island,' – 'I am riverness.' About *reflection* Foster says, 'by reflecting its own movement the dance can suggest the river as one of many possible associations evoked by the activity of moving.' She explains that this category is the most dance-specific of the four she describes because reflective representation is ambiguous in the way that it 'makes exclusive reference to the performance of movement and only tangentially alludes to other events in the world.' Through *reflection*, the dance signifies movement, of the river or whatever else the viewer sees (1986, pp.65-67).

I hold that Foster's forms of representation situated within the practice of dance analysis could be subsumed under Peirce's sign classification in that resemblance and imitation represent in the iconic mode and replication and reflection follow principles of indexical signification. I shall give further attention to Peirce's categories of sign function later in my discussion but at this juncture I want to investigate Foster's concept of the symbolic which I claim chimes with the symbolic dimension of representation discussed in relation to Bausch, Kozel and Irigaray. In full acknowledgement that Foster writes about dance as it occurred in a very different social context from the traumatic period of Bausch's post Second World War Germany, I maintain the view that Kozel's definition of the symbolic order as a 'conglomeration of representations which [constitute] all of our experiences' pertains to the following passage about Renaissance dance:

> A man and woman joining hands in a dance could represent the golden mean, a resolution of the tensions inherent in the contrast between men and women. The man's hardiness, strength, and courage, as represented in the vehemence of his movement, combine with the mild, timorous nature of the woman, as reflected in the delicacy and prettiness of her movements. Dancing together, they produced magnanimity, constancy, continence, and a host of other virtues. (Foster following Elyot 1986, pp.116-117)

Foster's words depict an image that resembles a harmonious union based on compliance with a 16th century world view. Yet there is a hint of Kozel's physical symbolic in the way that social mores and gender politics of the historical period are embodied within this act of dance thereby symbolizing or displaying in concrete form the various qualities associated with the otherwise abstract concept of virtue (Foster citing Sir Thomas Elyot, 1986, p.116). There are further claims as to the symbolic resonances of this dance when Peirce's theories are brought into consideration because I would argue that this excerpt from a Renaissance dance represents through the modes of resemblance (icon), existential connection (index) and convention (symbol or sign proper).

In later sections of this essay, I shall account for the ways in which Peirce's system extends comprehension of the symbol's flexibility and significance as a means of representation in dance. But before developing these ideas in more detail, I consider other more general aspects of the symbol and of the symbolic because I contend that these terms are rarely questioned or analysed. I aim, therefore, to review instances of the symbol as a form of metaphor or metonym.

The symbol and symbolic representation

The term symbol is widely applied in different contexts and an exhaustive review of its diverse character would exceed the time and space available in this article. On a common sense basis we can think of an object as a symbol when through conventional use it acquires a meaning that allows it to represent another object, idea or situation. Thus all manner of entities are symbols including flags representing countries; scales denoting justice; crosses, religion; a dove, peace; words constituting language; numbers representing various quantities. We also speak of musical and dance notation as symbol systems because they function on a code-based principle that is similar to verbal language. In other words both forms of notation operate in connection with convention in the way that the user acquires the knowledge and competence to recognize the symbol or sign and the connection between it and its referent.

Nevertheless, throughout the history of aesthetics the symbol has been treated as a flexible mode of representation and was often used to convey allusive and even enigmatic concepts. As Terry Eagleton says, when discussing the force of symbolic reference in 18th century aesthetic theory, 'the symbol fused together motion and stillness, turbulent content and organic form, mind and world' (1983, p.22). The symbolist art movement of the late 19th century is associated with enigmatic and allusive imagery that tantalizingly evokes rather than literally describes or illustrates its themes and subjects. I propose that in the context of 21st century art, the symbol continues to substantiate the elusive or intangible in concrete visible, auditory or lexical form. One might wonder, however, if the symbol differs from the metaphor and its close relation the metonym since in the arts the metaphor and the metonym are used in the general process of representation.

The literary metaphor is as slippery a concept as the symbol but it is most often described as a figure of speech or trope in which one thing is understood in terms of another. When we consider the poet Heinrich Heine's familiar remark, 'experience is a good school, but the fees are high,' (Heine in Woods 1967, p.493) we note that the primary subject *experience* is expressed in terms of the secondary subject *school*. We realize that there is no literal connection between the idea of experience and a place of learning but we appreciate the metaphor's appeal to an equivalent notion of the educative nature of both school and experience. The metaphor, therefore, in the words of McLaughlin is 'a compressed analogy' (1990, p.83). On the other hand, the metonym represents either a quality of an object standing in place of the object itself, for example *the deep* replacing *the sea*, or as the part representing the whole, as in the phrase, *the stage* as a shorthand for the wider theatrical profession.[2]

On this basis, I propose that as far as dance is concerned, the physical symbol combines the metaphor and the metonym. We can think, for example, of a motif from Martha Graham's movement vocabulary called 'the dart.'[3] This two-dimensional movement in low arabesque with one arm raised and angled sharply at the elbow, appears in the Greek-inspired tragedies such as *Cave of the heart* (1946), *Night Journey* (1947) and *Clytemnestra* (1958) and consequently might be described as a metaphor for emotional suffering as well as a metonym for the tragic circumstances of Graham's heroines. The dart becomes a visual symbol because it is a movement which is meaningful on several levels and in addition is typical of Graham's style. Similarly when Laura Cappelle refers to the 'light, artless pointe work' of the fiancée in Roland Petit's ballet *L'Arlésienne* (1974) as a 'symbol of earnest simplicity', the term symbol represents how the use of flexed feet within the dancer's pointe work is both metaphoric and metonymic. This is because the movement is analogous with the peasant society which forms the background to the ballet and indicative of the young woman's anxiety about her troubled fiancé (Cappelle 2011).[4]

---

2 See Lepecki 2006, p.55 for an analysis of Bel's solo *Shirtologie* [sic] (1997) in relation to metonymy.

3 This movement is a stride forwards with the heel of the foot leading as the second leg extends to the back of the body in a low *arabesque*. The opposite arm to extended leg is raised in an angular shape and the cupped hand is held in line with the forehead. For further information see Bannerman 1999, pp.15, 33; Bannerman 2006, pp.4, 16.

4 Laura Cappelle wrote the words quoted in the programme for English National Ballet's

For Foster the relation between the symbol and its referent is one of 'shared essence' (1986, p.233). In other words dance in the symbolic mode does not necessarily imitate the reality it represents but, as we saw from the example of Renaissance dance, embodies the mores, belief systems and order of the society in which it takes place. Foster's idea of shared essence is similar to metonymic attributes or qualities and so it is useful for the purposes of this essay to recognize that one way of defining the visual symbol is to regard it as occupying the territory of both the metaphor and the metonym. Whilst I contend that arguing for the representational properties of the metaphor and metonym is one of the methods of theorizing symbolic representation I concentrate for the remainder of this essay on semiotic theory especially in relation to Peirce's sign and how his system of symbolization is applied to dance in forming a physical symbolic as posited by Kozel.

The sign

In the process of formulating his often convoluted theories on the process of human communication or semiotics, Peirce identified a triadic group of signs (Peirce 1932, 2.247) comprising the icon, index and symbol.[5] This typology of signs has been influential amongst Peirce's followers (Hawkes 1977, p.128). I shall demonstrate how the typology is relevant to the analysis of dance meaning, but also how these categories are not necessarily autonomous but interdependent because they can be different aspects of the same sign (Hawkes 1977, p.129).[6]

---

farewell tribute to the French choreographer Roland Petit who had recently died. They performed Petit's *Carmen* (1949), *Le Jeune Homme et la Mort* (1946) and *L'Arlésienne* (1974) at the London Coliseum from July 21-24 2011.

5 Peirce was an intellectual polymath who fulfilled a unique role in the history of American philosophy (Hartshorne and Weiss in Peirce, 1931, p.iii). Described by Jonathan Culler as a 'wayward philosophical genius,' Peirce was 'denied tenure by the Johns Hopkins University at Baltimore' (1981 p.25) but despite this setback to his career, he became the founding father of the American system of semiotics.

6 In order to contextualize Peirce's work on the sign, it is useful to refer to his continental counterpart, Ferdinand de Saussure, who in a similar but unrelated manner to Peirce offered a theory of signs and sign function. Saussure treated language as a system of signs (words). He described the sign in terms of a double-sided coin in that it comprises on the one side what he called *signification* (concept) and on the other, *signal* (sound pattern) (Saussure 1983, pp.66–7). We must note that within the usage of semiotic theory, the *sign* has come to be commonly understood as constituting a *signified* which semioticians agree does not refer to a real 'thing' (Barthes' quotation marks, 1967, p.42), but rather is 'a mental representation of a "thing" (*ibid.*)'. Thus in addressing the mental or psychological aspect of sign theory, we enter the domain of human consciousness and subjectivity because the exchange of signifiers is socially and culturally mediated. Peirce's model is similar to the one formulated by Saussure although it is my view that Peirce's method is more useful because it is based on a signifying process that is extremely

For Peirce a sign begins as a *representamen*: something which stands to somebody for something in some respect or capacity. It addresses somebody, that is, creates in the mind of that person an equivalent sign, or perhaps a more developed sign. That sign which it creates I call the *interpretant* of the first sign. The sign stands for something, its *object* not in all respects, but in reference to a sort of idea, which I have sometimes called *ground* of the representamen. (Peirce 1932, 2.228).

In line with the above quotation and earlier comments Peirce's representamen or sign comprises three essential elements. The *representamen* is 'something which stands to somebody for something in some respect or capacity.' The representamen or sign 'addresses somebody, that is, creates in the mind of that person an equivalent sign, or perhaps a more developed sign.' The sign stands for its '*object*' or the entity to which the sign refers (Peirce 1931, 2.228). It is important to note that for Peirce this cognitive or psychological aspect of his sign theory referred to as the '*interpretant* of the first sign' is a combination of 'sign, thing signified, cognition produced in the mind' (Peirce 1931, 1.372) and may be thought of as the *sense* made of the sign. Importantly for Peirce, the interpretant or signified (mental image, idea) in turn becomes a sign thus unleashing an unlimited process of semiosis or activity of sign production (Eco 1979; Peirce 1932, 2.273–274, 300).

We can understand the act of signifying through the process of semiosis if we bring to mind the symbolic use of colour in various cultures. For example in the West according to background, education and culture we treat the colour red as a symbol of danger. The chain of signification begins perhaps with the idea that red represents fire or blood and in turn red as a sign or symbol unleashes further signification relating to harmful situations and conditions. We might also have learned that red infuriates animals such as bulls and more commonly that when a light glows red, we are prohibited from entering a room or proceeding along a road when driving.

Bright red costuming in dance signifies in line with the context of a work, as for example in Ashton's *Marguerite and Armand* (1964). When first encountering Marguerite as a fashionable courtesan flirting with her admirers, we note her blood-red ball gown, a colour closely associated not only with the danger of her sexuality but also with the consumptive illness from which she suffers. Thus the viewer decodes or makes sense of this visual information through the process of semiosis, where the colour red functions within a chain of sign production (Eco 1979, p.68).

Semiosis then reveals the way in which the sign is a slippery entity and cannot be pinned down to any one self-contained referent. There is a sense in which Peirce's concept of unlimited sign production foresees the

dynamic in the way that Peirce provided taxonomies of the sign.

poststructuralism of theorists such as Jacques Derrida. Poststructuralists rejected the secure correspondence of signifier and signified as theorized by Saussure (1983) prompting Derrida to write of what he called the play or freeplay of signifiers. He held that signifiers are not fixed to their signifieds but point beyond themselves to other signifiers in an 'indefinite referral of signifier to signifieds' (Derrida 1978, p.25). Thus Derrida's notions resonate with Peirce's interpretant which as we have seen is indefinite or open-ended in the way that one sign leads to another with no ultimate sign referring only to itself.

Peirce's triadic sign

We must acknowledge that some of Peirce's 'best thought was devoted to logical problems' including 'the logic of classes and relations' and to 'the theory of signs' (Hartshorne and Weiss 1931, p.iii). Within the first volume of his *Collected Papers* (1931) Peirce writes that 'logic is simply the science of what must be and ought to be true representation so far as true representation can be known without any fathering of special facts beyond our daily life. It is in short the philosophy of representation' (1.539). Slightly later in this section of the *Collected Papers*, Peirce introduces 'three kinds of representation' (1.558), the icon, index and symbol (1.564), 'conceptions' which he considered to be of the most 'fundamental' importance to the 'science of logic' (1.559) and first published in 1867 (Peirce 1.564). Since in his writings Peirce constantly returned to this 'division' (1.564), it is the icon, index and symbol to which I now turn my attention.

The icon

For Peirce '[...] a sign may be *iconic*, that is, may represent its object mainly by its similarity, no matter what its mode of being (Peirce 1932, 2.276). In his earlier writings, he often referred to iconic signs as *likenesses* (1931, 1.558), so it follows that the iconic mode describes the signifier as resembling or imitating the signified (recognizably looking, sounding, feeling, tasting or smelling like it) – being similar in possessing some of its qualities as, for example, in a portrait, a cartoon, onomatopoeia, metaphors, representational sounds within programme music, sound effects in radio drama, soundtrack, imitative gestures). It is important, however, to point out that for Peirce the iconic sign represents its object 'mainly by its similarity' (Peirce 1932, 2.276). This is a complicated idea since for Peirce the iconic similarity between a representamen and its object (or a signifier and its signified) is one of 'an analogy between the relations of the parts of each [...] many diagrams resemble their objects not at all in looks; it is only in respect to the relations of their parts that their likeness consists' (1932, 2.282).

Within current semiotic practice, however, iconic signification is more commonly connected to the notion that a sign *resembles* its object, in the way that a drawing or a cartoon *looks like* its object. In the cases of linguistics or music, the icon *sounds* like the object it represents. For Carroll and Banes, this form of representation is *unconditional* as exemplified by the ballet *Romeo and Juliet* where there is unambiguous mimesis or iconic signification in the way that the men fight one another. Again, the peasant dances in *Giselle* feature costumes, props, music and choreographic formations that help the audience to recognize that they 'stand for harvest celebrations' (1999, p.24). In addition to the iconic mode, we can also argue that the harvest dances act as symbols because we have come to think of this style of sophisticated and technically proficient dancing as classical ballet and in this sense they represent dances about dancing.

The index

Peirce explains that, '[a]nything which focuses the attention is an index. Anything which startles us is an index, in so far as it marks the junction between two portions of experience'. (Peirce 1932, 2.285). In the indexical mode of signification, the signifier is not arbitrary but is directly connected in some way (physically or causally) to the signified (regardless of intention) – this link is observed or inferred as for example in natural signs (smoke, animal tracks,) medical symptoms (pains, rashes); measuring instruments (weathercock, barometer); signals (as in a knock on a door or a telephone ringing); pointers (a pointing index finger, a directional signpost); personal trademarks (handwriting, catch-phrases) (Peirce 1932, 2.286).

In dance, torso-centred movement such as the Graham contraction produces indexical signification because in western culture, the contraction points to or is symptomatic of feeling. The framework or context of individual dances and in accordance with other signs brought into play, the contraction indicates a particular state or shade of emotion. Thus, unlike the symbol/ sign proper both the icon and the index are motivated in the way that they have a natural or physical connection between sign and object.

The symbol

Amongst Peirce's more succinct definitions of the symbol is his explanation that it is 'a sign which refers to the object that it denotes by virtue of a law' (Peirce 1932, 2.249), thus in the symbolic mode, the sign denotes in line with rule or convention or as Saussure specified the meaning of the sign or symbol is fundamentally arbitrary and therefore 'fixed by rule' (1983, p.68). The symbol is most readily associated with the linguistic sign because the relationship between signifier and signified (representamen and object) must be agreed upon and learned; this situation applies also in the case of a numbers system, Morse code, traffic lights, national flags and so forth.

Peirce's symbol corresponds to Carroll's and Banes' mode of 'lexical representation' (1999, p.21) according to which in dance the viewer understands specific gestures or actions on the basis that they have learnt the conventions or codes that underpin these gestures. Carroll and Banes observe, for example, that the ability to decode classical ballet mime or the way 'an averted glance and a forfending backhand raised to the face' represents 'contempt,' requires the viewer to be well versed in specific areas of 'ballet practices,' (Carroll and Banes 1999 pp.21-22). It is pertinent to add that the symbolic mode of representation in dance applies also to a more general body language where, as with the words of natural language, specific gestures such as a handshake are tied by social convention to their meanings.

One must not be misled, however, into considering these Peircian categories of sign as independent of one another. As Terence Hawkes points out, it is important to be aware that the 'triad involves, not mutually exclusive *kinds* of sign, but three modes of a relationship between sign and object or signifier and signified' (1977, p.129).These modes of the triadic sign 'co-exist in the form of a hierarchy in which one of them will inevitably have dominance over the other two' (*ibid.*).

Thus, for Peirce neither photographs nor portraits serve as pure icons. A portrait, he held, does not replicate exactly the subject it represents and the quality of resemblance is achieved through stylized methods of reproduction and so bears traces of the symbol. Similarly a photograph is indexical because it was produced under circumstances that physically forced it to 'correspond point by point to nature' (Peirce 1932, 2.276). We might follow Roman Jakobson and refer to a portrait as a symbolic icon (Jakobson 1971, p.335; Hawkes 1977, p.129) and a photograph as an indexical icon.

It is worth mentioning that other modes of representation as theorized by Carroll and Banes, notably their category of *conditional generic representation* is similar to Peirce's triad since under the conditions of this category, the spectator 'needs a clue that something [specific] is being represented' (1999, p.22). This is tantamount to the concept of indexical signification. Carroll's and Banes' example of an instance of conditional generic representation is Simone Forti's *Planet* (1976) because, as they reason, 'the title alerts us that representation is afoot. Thus we are predisposed to see the dancers moving from crawling on all fours to walking to running as a representation of the process of evolution' (1999 p.27).

Whilst interesting as an illustration of a particular category of representation, Peirce's semiotic theory is more useful to the dance analyst. As described by Carroll and Banes, *Planet* combines symbolic, indexical and iconic signification, and thus Peirce's triad provides tools that account most readily for how it is that we interpret the images and actions of dance.

Peirce's theories of representation allow us to dissect the symbolic, a concept described but not analysed in detail by Foster, Johnstone and Kozel, nor addressed fully by Carroll and Banes. It can be argued that the visual symbol when treated as Peirce's triadic sign, embraces at least three levels of representation in the way that it becomes the bearer of meaning that transcends the imitative or informational. Under these conditions the visual symbol, or in Kozel's terms the physical symbol, if treated as Peirce's hybrid sign, is analogical or metaphoric because it is descriptive through resemblance (iconic), evocative and allusive in accordance with the indexical or metonymic mode, and most often conventional in line with the sign/symbol proper.

I would argue that even a relatively sign-neutral *avant-garde* production such as Jérôme Bel's *Shirtology* (1997), is suitable for analysis in accordance with Peirce's system as I aim to demonstrate in the following analysis.

The man in Bel's solo (Bel 2012) does not conform to what society is taught about dancers and consequently subverts the notion of symbol. As he stands facing the audience eyes cast downward, this dancer is an icon of an ordinary man but whose slightly dishevelled appearance and submissive posture creates indexical signification of self-deprecation and vulnerability. His repeated actions of discarding, one after another, the array of t-shirts that he wears, provides indexical-symbolic signification because we understand that this is not everyday behaviour and in fact we associate stripping away clothing in public with striptease. However, the lack of any hint of sexuality in the dancer's clothing, posture or demeanor does not support this interpretation so we must exert our powers of semiosis or mental sign production and seek other visual and aural clues.

The t-shirts bear numbers and words and once or twice, pictures. These symbols and icons acquire indexical signification in the way in which Bel presents them to view for up to 30 seconds at a time. We ponder the significance of the symbols for the dancer since on one occasion he reads the message printed on the front of the shirt and on another depicting musical notation, he sings snatches of the tune represented in musical form. Several times the dancer complies with the slogans that the t-shirts advertise as when revealing the word 'Replay', he reprises a song that he intoned moments before. The steady but uninflected pace of his phrasing and lack of emotional expression are indexical in the way that the dramatic neutrality points to dances such as Yvonne Rainer's *Room Service* (1963), symbols of dance art radicalism and pedestrianism (see note 1).

In connecting the various signs with each other, we can find several layers of meaning in Bel's solo. Aside from its reference to the Judson Dance Theater legacy, the solo demonstrates that we are symbol making beings. It also questions identity – the t-shirts may be autobiographical by representing stages this man has passed through in his life. On the other hand, pictures of sports heroes shown on the back of one t-shirt and of a young woman in an athletic dance pose on the front of another – a pose which the dancer tentatively reproduces in his own movement – suggest the ideals that dominate society and which we struggle to live up to. The combination of symbolic, iconic and indexical signification presented by Bel's minimalist dance renders the solo meaningful in terms of its comments on dance itself, and on the extent to which we are motivated, but controlled by the symbols we create.

I propose then, that when thought of as a visual or physical symbol, Peirce's triadic sign is effective in accounting for how it is that all manner of theatrical productions act upon or affect the viewer. I have chosen the opening scenes of the Israeli choreographer, Hofesh Shechter's *Political Mother* (2010) as a further illustration of Peirce's sign theory applied to dance in order to demonstrate how the exercise of this system reveals these dance episodes as deeply affective and meaningful experiences for the viewer.

Hofesh Shechter's *Political Mother*

The lights lower in the auditorium leaving the audience enshrouded in a smoky darkness made ominous by the low-pitched tones of funereal music. Red plush curtains part to reveal a solitary male dancer crouched low on stage picked out from the shadowy background in the down-light of a single spot. In these opening moments of the dance, the audience witnesses the death throes of this lone figure dressed in a costume resembling a samurai warrior's armour.[7] The blows of the warrior's sword and cries of pain are vivid iconic signs in terms of action and sound but the representational effect of these images is strengthened because they are symbolic and indexical icons.

As we sit in the darkened auditorium before the curtain rises our sensory awareness has been aroused through the cultural association of mist and mystery further enhanced by the low sombre music, indexical signification which warns of the shadowy world that awaits us as the curtains disclose the darkened stage. The soldier's death is heavily symbolic because it is culturally embedded within the experience of those who recognize the ancient practice of ritual suicide or *seppuku* traditionally committed by the Japanese samurai. In addition to its status as symbolic icon, the suicide is an

---

7 This description is based on the 2010 production of *Political Mother*. In its latest manifestation (July 2011) this scene is similar but it is preceded by a longer musical passage played live and a battery of percussion. Nevertheless, the soldier's death is repeated and his cries are still audible amidst the densely textured sound accompaniment.

emotionally stirring index in the way that it points to or leads us to empathize with the soldier's physical pain and with his psychological suffering.

Before the stage lights go down on the soldier's final death throes, the viewer is jolted out of the dream-like state induced by his suicide and transported into another precarious situation as amplified techno music pierces the misty darkness. As though catapulted from some parallel universe, two men in jeans and t-shirts appear downstage in a sudden blaze of light, knees bent low, chests hollowed, arms outstretched as if imploring us to enter their world of desperation. Another blackout and the two become a group magnifying the gesture of entreaty.

The music's rhythmic beat sends the dancers into heavily accented runs, feet dragging behind, their arms held aloft as though forced to surrender to an unseen accuser. Darkness again, broken this time by rays of light pointing downwards from the flies onto the buttoned jackets of five soldiers, their heads lost in the otherwise pervading gloom of the stage space. Each man relentlessly pounds the drum in front of him, beating it into a torrent of sound that sends shock waves around us holding the viewer hostage to impending doom (Brighton Dome, May 20, 2010). Throughout these opening scenes, our senses are bombarded by a welter of images and sounds which form as Kozel puts it, a 'conglomeration of representations' which we interpret through the mental act of semiosis. Shechter provides a combination of iconic, indexical and symbolic signification within these theatrically potent scenes thus plunging the viewer into the midst of what we recognize as the representation of a pressurized society or community beset by the strictures of an unseen but dominant force.

If we stop to consider the words of the title *Political Mother* in relation to these opening scenes we need think only of the overall reference to hegemonic regimes. In the passage featuring the soldier's ritual suicide we have a strong iconic representation of the abstract quality of loyalty. Contrasting with this first set of images is the gesture of entreaty, an indexical icon of supplication which alerts the viewer to the plight of these people. Any quarter or solace that might be offered is immediately obliterated by the ear-splitting barrage of the soldiers' percussion.

As the violent preface to a gritty production saturated in all three of Peirce's categories of sign and loaded with messages about the trauma of power, political aggression and its human toll, the soldier's suicide and the dancers' gestures of supplication appear to symbolize the death of a society's ideals in the face of a harsh and intolerant regime. Yet it has to be acknowledged that *Political Mother* has a sense of optimism in the way that the choreography also includes Israeli folk dance motifs which act as indexical signs indicating the resilience of the human spirit unwilling to succumb to the will of forces intent on crushing it.

Conclusion

I have argued that in visual culture especially, the symbol is a complex mixture of representational devices and that it is tantamount to Peirce's triadic sign. As a symbolic icon, Peirce's sign provides a window onto the world of the art work and its re-presentation of real events and situations, but as an indexical symbol it also opens a door onto an invisible, interior world of ideas and emotions. If we analyse the warrior's death from *Political Mother* in accordance with Peirce, we become aware of meaning beyond a 'simple' representation of honourable death. As spectators we can connect the existential ramifications of this act with loyalty and with the sense of idealistic dedication or devotion which it represents.

Representation in dance depends to some extent on mimesis but we need to be aware that visual works are cognitively as well as visually stimulating, that they demand our intellectual and physical responses. I propose that Peirce's theories help to explain the underlying processes of representation or as I have argued symbolization through which dance productions, like *Political Mother* transport the viewer from the everyday environment into a world of the choreographer's making. This world of choreographic imagination becomes real as it unfolds before us through the flesh and blood dancers, the reality of their movements, and the choreographer's creation of symbols that provide the viewer with access to both visible and invisible layers of meaning.

References

Bannerman, Henrietta. 'An Overview of the Development of Martha Graham's Movement System (1926-1991)', *Dance Research*, 17:2, 1999, pp.9-46.

Bannerman, Henrietta. 'A Dance of Transition: Martha Graham's Herodiade (1944)', *Dance Research*, 24:1, 2006, pp.1-20.

Barthes, Roland. *Elements of Semiology*, trans. Lavers, Annette and Colin Smith, London: Jonathan Cape, 1967.

Barthes, Roland. *Mythologies*, London: Vintage, 1993.

Beardsley, Monroe C. 'What is Going on in Dance?' *Dance Research Journal*, 15:1, 1982, pp.31-36.

Bel, Jérôme. *Jérôme Bel Shirtology.– Performance room:* London: BMW Tate live (March 29), 2012.

Cappelle, Laura. 'Laura Cappelle Explores Roland Petit's Style', in *Roland Petit's Carmen with Le Jeune Homme et la Mort and L'Arlesiénne'*, Programme for English National Ballet Season at the London Coliseum, July 21-24, 2011.

Carroll, Noël and Sally Banes. 'Working and Dancing: A Response to Monroe

Beardsley's "What is Going on in a Dance?",' *Dance Research Journal*, 15:1,1982, pp.37-41.

Carroll, Noël and Sally Banes. 'Dance, Imitation and Representation', in McFee, Graham (ed.), *Dance, Education and Philosophy*, Oxford: Meyer & Meyer Sport, 1999, pp.13-32.

Culler, Jonathan. *The Pursuit of Signs*, London: Routledge, 1981.

Derrida, Jacques. *Writing and Difference*, London: Routledge, 1978.

Davies, David. *Art as Performance*, Oxford: Blackwell, 2004.

Davies, David. *Philosophy of the Performing Arts*, Oxford: Blackwell, 2011.

Eagleton, Terry. *Literary Theory: An Introduction*, Oxford: Blackwell, 1983.

Eco, Umberto. *A Theory of Semiotics*, Bloomington: Indiana University Press, 1979.

Fernandes, Ciane. *Pina Bausch and the Wuppertal Dance Theatre: The Aesthetics of Repetition and Transformation*, New York: Peter Lang, 2001.

Foster, Susan Leigh. *Reading Dancing: Bodies and Subjects in Contemporary American Dance*, Berkeley: University of California Press, 1986.

Gormley, Anthony. *The Culture Show*, BBC 2, June 2, 2011.

Hawkes, Terence. *Structuralism and Semiotics*, London: Routledge, 1977.

Hursthouse, Rosalind. 'Truth and Representation', in Hanfling, Oswald (ed.), *Philosophical Aesthetics: An Introduction*, Milton Keynes: The Open University and Blackwell, 1992, pp.239-296.

Jakobson, Roman. *Selected Writings. Vol. 2. Word and Language*, The Hague: Mouton, 1971.

Johnstone, Albert A. 'Languages and Non-languages of Dance', in Sheets-Johnstone, Maxine (ed.), *Illuminating Dance*, London and Toronto: Bucknell University, 1984, pp.167-187.

Kozel, Susan. 'The Story is Told as a History of the Body: Strategies of Mimesis in the Work of Irigaray and Bausch', in Desmond, Jane (ed.), *Meaning in Motion*, Durham and London: Duke University Press, 1997, pp.101-109.

Lepecki, André. *Exhausting Dance: Performance and the Politics of Movement*, London: Routledge, 2006.

Matthews, Eric. *Twentieth-century French Philosophy*, Oxford: Oxford University Press, 1996

McFee, Graham. *Understanding Dance*, London: Routledge, 1992.

McLaughlin, Thomas. 'Figurative Language', in Lentricchia, Frank and Thomas McLaughlin (eds.), *Critical Terms for Literary Study*, Chicago: The University of Chicago Press, 1990, pp.11-22.

Mitchell, William. 'Representation', in Lentricchia, Frank and Thomas McLaughlin (eds.), *Critical Terms for Literary Study*, Chicago: The University of Chicago Press, 1990, pp.80-90.

Murray, Gilbert. 'Preface', in *Aristotle on the Art of Poetry*, trans. Ingram Bywater, Oxford: Oxford University Press, 1920, pp.3-20.

Peirce, Charles Sanders. *Collected Papers of Charles Sanders Peirce*, Hartshorne, Charles and Paul Weiss (eds.), Cambridge: Harvard University Press, 1931-1958.

Saussure, Ferdinand. *Course in General Linguistics*, trans. Roy Harris, London: Duckworth, 1983.

Servos, Norbert. *Pina Bausch - Wuppertal Dance Theater, or, The Art of Training a Goldfish: Excursions into Dance*, Köln: Ballett-Büchnen-Verlag, 1984.

Shechter, Hofesh. *Political Mother*, Brighton: Concert Hall, Brighton Dome, May 21, 2010.

Shechter, Hofesh. *Political Mother: The Choreographer's Cut*, London: Sadler's Wells Theatre, July 15, 2011.

Woods, Ralph Louis. *The Modern Handbook of Humor*, New York: McGraw-Hill, 1967.

10. The intrinsic significance of dance: a phenomenological approach[1]

Jonathan Owen Clark

Introduction

This essay aims to answer a simple question: why dance *matters* to us. I will argue that of all the philosophical approaches to aesthetics, it is phenomenology that is best equipped to answer this question satisfactorily.[2] Other approaches, which derive from poststructuralism, critical theory, semiotics or historicist hermeneutics, for example, tend to assimilate meaning in dance to the specific socio-cultural and historical contexts in which dance works were produced, and hence to methodologies aligned with the linguistic or literary turns in intellectual history and the human sciences. These approaches neglect the foundational nature of dance *as movement*, the distinctive way in which it reveals and epitomizes our *animate* nature. Whilst other theories attempt to explain what a dance means or could mean, a phenomenological approach shows how it comes to be meaning-bearing at all, why it is that it seems to us that dance has something to say to us, without our being able to necessarily put this into words.

Above all, the phenomenological approach taken here aims to explicate the *intrinsic, intuitive* and *aesthetic* significance of dance by showing how it, in common with other artforms, 'aesthetically exemplifies factors which are basic to our cognitive and metaphysical inherence in the world' (Crowther 2009, p.31). I will aim to explain why dance engages our attention at all, prior to any semiological (or other) abstractions of its content. This will involve explicating how some of the basic factors at work in our movement, perception and spatial positioning are exemplified and transformed through dance, seen as both a visual *and* kinaesthetic medium.

The essay is structured as follows. I will first give an account of Paul Crowther's 'analytic phenomenology' of art, which provides the methodology to be utilized in what follows. I will describe how this methodology outlines

---

1 This essay is dedicated to the memory of the dancer and dance educator Gill Clarke.

2 Phenomenological approaches to dance are of course not new. For representative examples in the literature, see: Sheets-Johnstone (1966); Mickunas (1974); Levin (1983); Fraleigh (1987); Bernard (1993); Parviainen (1998); Kozel (1998); McNamara (1999); Rouhiainen (2003). However, none of these approaches present the material in the same way as is done in the present essay. For a recent collection of reflections on the current state of phenomenology in dance, see a special issue of *Dance Research Journal* (43:2, 2011) entitled 'Dance and Phenomenology' (Mark Franko, ed.).

the varying phenomenological depth factors[3] at work in different forms of art and aesthetic experience, giving relevant examples.

In the second part I give an expository account of Edmund Husserl's seminal ideas on the visual and kinaesthetic components of perception, and more specifically, the *correlation* between the two. This section will also show how an appeal to Husserl's conception of kinaesthesia is inadequate to the study of dance, and that an extension of his ideas is needed. This extension is provided primarily in the work of Maxine Sheets-Johnstone, which I also sketch. In this section I will also look at some objections to the scope and role of kinaesthesia that have appeared in the dance literature.

With the philosophical preliminaries out of the way, I will then present six speculative 'theses' that aim to answer why dance *matters* to us, that reduce to factors relating to (in order): path-dependency and spatial trajectory; the 'three-foldedness' of dance; imaginative and projective aspects of kinaesthesis; the virtualization of expression; intermedial interpenetration; intercorporeality and intersubjectivity.

Paul Crowther's analytic phenomenology of art

In a range of recent monographs, Paul Crowther (2001, 2002, 2009, 2012) has put forward a theory of 'analytic', or more recently, 'post-analytic' phenomenology that aims to provide a non-exegetical account of the thinking of the founding phenomenologists,[4] allied to rigorous lines of argumentation that are derived from analytic aesthetics (but without recourse to the overemphasis placed in the latter tradition on the *logical* structure[5] of artworks).

Such a theory is necessary, Crowther claims, because of the ubiquity, some might say hegemony, of recent reductionist philosophical approaches to visual (and other) art that are derived from poststructuralism and historicist hermeneutics. Crowther writes:

Cashed out in more specific terms, this [reductionist] reading of visual 'production' emphasizes such things as the immediate material, social, and institutional circumstances in which the image was produced,

---

3 This is Crowther's term, which draws on a convergence of ideas in Merleau-Ponty, Hegel and Kant, and which 'centres on the *ontological reciprocity* of the subject and object of experience' (Crowther 2009, p. 3). In this essay I will be concerned primarily with how dance aesthetically highlights aspects of this reciprocity.

4 Such as Edmund Husserl, Martin Heidegger, Henri Bergson and Maurice Merleau-Ponty.

5 Crowther claims that this overemphasis can be traced to the work of Arthur Danto and Nelson Goodman. Other approaches within analytic aesthetics that specifically refer to the artform of dance can be found in the work of Joseph Margolis, Noël Carroll, Graham McFee and Francis Sparshott.

the stylistic and cultural sources it draws upon, its conscious and 'unconscious' modes of displaying them, what audiences it addresses and creates, and its modes of reception and transmission amongst various 'constituencies'. The overriding tendency, here, is to reduce all questions of meaning to issues of socio-historical contexts of production and reception (Crowther 2009, pp.11-12, [my addition]).

Social reductionism[6] of this kind is often combined, Crowther claims, with a related *semiotic* reductionism,[7] which attempts to explain the visual dimension of painting and sculpture on the basis of models derived from literary analysis; for example, in terms of the denotation/connotation relation. The upshot of all these theories, is that despite the fact that they have contributed greatly to the study of art,[8] they struggle to come to terms with something more fundamental, namely what it is about art that *enables* it to be semiotically significant or act as a site of cultural production at all. Crowther's central claim is that this *intrinsic significance* of the image, the foundation for its meaningfulness, can only be explained via *phenomenological depth* factors associated with the *ontological reciprocity* of the subject and object of experience that are involved in the perception of artworks.[9]

Let us firstly define these terms carefully. The term ontological reciprocity is meant to indicate that the animated human subject is immersed in a physical world which is mind-independent, but which itself determines the conditions for the subject's continued survival. At the same time, the nature of this physical world in perception (what we might call the *phenomenal* world) is shaped by the subject's innate cognitive and movement abilities, so that 'The ontological structure of the subject and its objects of experience are thus reciprocally related in key respects. At the experiential level, each is, in effect, part of the full definition of the other' (Crowther 2009, p.3). A phenomenological approach elucidates the complex nature of this

---

6 Crowther invokes the names, in visual art theory, of Griselda Pollock, John Barrell, Carol Duncan and Albert Boime, but the tendency is far from being imprisoned there. In music for example, we can think of the 'New Musicology' movement, comprising scholars such as Susan McClary and Leo Treitler: see, for example, the wide-ranging collection of essays in Cook and Everist (1999). In dance, one thinks of the collection in Desmond (1997). Another approach to contemporary dance that utilizes ideas from critical theory and poststructuralism can be found in Lepecki (2006).

7 In visual art, the work of Rosalind Krauss, W.J.T Mitchell and Norman Bryson. In music, one thinks of the work of Enrico Tiasti, Kofi Agawu, and, above all, Jean-Jaques Nattiez. In dance, explicitly semiotic approaches include Foster (1988).

8 It is imperative to note that Crowther is not opposed to such theories, just to the reductionism inherent in their ubiquitous application. Phenomenology and semiotics should be *complementary* theories.

9 Crowther shows how these factors are routinely ignored in both hermeneutical and analytic aesthetics, at the same time as they actually ground both.

reciprocity, which involves *relations* between the subject and world and how these relations change on the basis of the subject's modes of perception, knowledge and movement. I also stress the *pre-reflective* and *pre-conscious* nature of many aspects of this reciprocity, which means that some of these relations are sensed without us necessarily being aware of them, as a result of their embedding in all kinds of habitual and 'learned' cognitive skills, including our own ability to *move*, that are *practical* in nature, *not* linguaform or conceptual, and *not* based on inferential aspects of perception itself.

These pre-conscious factors of phenomenological depth include, according to Crowther: *the tacit enabling conditions of immediate perception* (hidden orderings of the perceptual field, based on our current positioning, which organize how we are aware of some but not all of the items present to consciousness at once, combined with the move from perception to apperception); *the constitutive role of imagination* (how our perception of an object depends, for example, on the simulation of other perceptions of the same object that are not currently present in experience); *understanding of the basic structure and scope of self-consciousness and agency* (our awareness of ourselves and others as free volitional agents, and the understanding of our own bodies in terms of repertoires of 'I cans' and 'I cannots').

Note how such an approach to visual art and aesthetic experience via an appeal to a ground of phenomenological depth factors resists the ubiquity of social or semiotic reductionism: it appeals instead to the intrinsic, or *transhistorical* significance[10] of the image (or artwork) which is bound up with the conditions of embodied human subjectivity, a significance which 'aesthetically exemplifies factors that are basic to our cognitive and metaphysical inherence in the world' (Crowther 2009, p.31).

Crowther stresses that each form of art is grounded in phenomenologically different ways. Think for example, of how the themes in visual art history of space-occupancy and implied motion, the generalized ontology of spatial relations achieved through perspective, the depiction of objects via marks on a surface, the 'projection' of a virtual 'elsewhere' from a material base, the disruption of spatial context through framing etc. are all basic to acts of picturing *as such*.

These aspects of the embodiment of phenomenological depth in and through a visual medium may change, be recombined or even disrupted in different historically contingent ways pertaining to specific aesthetic *styles*, but they have a significance that is not reducible to history alone. Such intrinsic significance is however not at all 'ahistorical' but is historically revealed and identified through those features that make a work of art a mode of reference *at all*, and thus depends on 'those transhistorical ontological structures that are basic to individual kinds of cultural phenomena and

---

10 See Crowther (2002).

[which] form conditions which enable their more historically specific transmissions' (2009, p.22 [my addition]).

Such significance, which depends on phenomenological depth factors, is moreover *shown* rather than *spoken*. In art, one of Crowther's central claims is that 'features basic to the reciprocity of subject and object of experience are *made to exist in a heightened and enduring form*' (2009, p.5). I would suggest that the word 'heightened' is apposite here, but I would also extend this to 'transformed' as well: art can both heighten and, in some cases, question or negate our habitual interactions with objects and the environment.

Perspective painting, for example, both expresses the systematicity of ordinary visual perception and depicts a virtual space into which we can imaginatively project ourselves. The painting also manifests agency: we sense the 'presence' of the artist and his/her understanding of the scene depicted. The task of the last section will be to explain some of the intrinsic significance that is specific to dance as an art form, and to show how dance similarly can heighten, transform and make enduring facets of experience.

As a final aside, note that these phenomenological assumptions also question, or even directly contradict, those of the orthodox 'classical cognitivist'[11] approaches in the philosophy of mind which stress instead of the subject-world correlation: computation *over* previously constructed mental representations (such as 'sense-data' or symbols); *neutrality* of the observer; *modularity* of cognitive architecture in the 'processing' of mental representations; reducibility of the conditions of experience solely to neural, and not bodily substrates.

As such, much of what I have to say about dance and movement will be consistent, subject to some important caveats, with the *enacted* or *embodied* approach to cognition,[12] but also with a wide range of other sources in philosophy.[13] Central is the idea that perception is a constructive process that is not neutral with respect to our animation and movement, but arises from innate *coupling* of the human organism with its own environment (and not merely with its social milieu) (see Ankersmit 2005, p.248).

Husserl and Sheets-Johnstone on kinaesthesia

In this section, I consider accounts of vision, tactility and kinaesthesia that seem fundamental to any philosophical account of dance. If, as Crowther stresses, the task of a phenomenological account of art is to locate particular

---

11 For example, see Fodor (1979).

12 This already vast field perhaps owes its modern inauguration to the work of Francesco Varela, Evan Thompson and Eleanor Rosch (1991). For an update on this work, see Thompson (2005). See also Noë (2004) and Clark (2008).

13 Such as Husserl, Bergson, Dewey, Deleuze and Merleau-Ponty.

aspects of perception, imagination and agency that are heightened, transformed and made enduring via a particular artform (and in which he locates the particular and singular 'intrinsic significance' of that artform), it would seem sensible to choose these three aspects of perception.

This is because when dance is made or watched, we don't just *see* what is being danced; we also *feel* its dynamics, the intentional arcs of its movement, its innate tactility and its tactile-kinaesthetic *qualia*. Perhaps a useful way of describing the latter phenomenon, which in the dance literature has become known as 'kinaesthetic empathy',[14] is through Theodor Adorno's idea of 'mimetic re-enactment' (1984). 'In the process of mimetic (re)enactment, we reach behind the already formed figures of meaning back to the dynamics, force, and energy of their formation' (Menke 1998, p.51). Note that this sense of mimesis is not simply the projection of our own affective and other responses onto the dancers themselves, nor is it an attempt to mirror or duplicate the dancers' own internal experience (which is, in the final reckoning, inaccessible to us anyway). It is more like Husserl's concept of 'pairing' [*Paarung*]: according to Husserl, in perceiving and coming to understand the other, I draw on my own bodily experience, but through my encounter with the other, this same experience is also modified.[15] The intersubjective encounter is neither a simple projection, nor is it merely a question of a kind of subjective introjection. In the case at hand, what I bring to my perception of dancers' movements are prior kinaesthetic and tactile experiences and visual expectations; through pairing or (re)enactment, these aspects of my prior experience are changed or transformed in new ways. The case for the existence in dance performance and spectatorship of pairing, mimesis or 'kinaesthetic empathy', and indeed the importance of kinaesthesia to dance studies *tout court* is the subject of some considerable debate, and I will deal with some serious objections to these ideas in the next section. But for now, let us take the case as given, or a least plausible. The result is that the perception of movement needs to be assessed in

---

14 For an extensive account of this phenomenon within a dance context, see Foster (2008, 2010). Approaches to the concept in the dance literature are somewhat divergent. Much of the dispute is essentially related to the *type of mediation* between dancer and spectator being claimed for. Many dance theorists (e.g. Hagendoorn 2004) have appealed to the discovery of 'mirror neurons' (Rizzolatti and Sinigaglia 2008) as an empirical basis for a natural, spontaneous and causative type of mediation (mirror neurons respond when a particular goal-directed action is performed, *and* when it is witnessed). Foster (2010) appeals instead to a mediation that is historically contingent, and in doing so emphasizes sociocultural *construction* rather than the empirical causation. In a similar vein, Paterson (2012) warns against the speculative re-application of a decontextualised empirical theory to the phenomenology of dance performance.

15 For more on 'pairing', see Zahavi (2003, p.112f).

terms of both its visual and kinaesthetic-tactile manifestations.[16] In order to accomplish this task, we need to take a closer look at both vision and kinaesthesia, to which I now turn.

Edmund Husserl's 'Ding und Raum'

Husserl's aim in this book is to provide a systematic and rigorous account of how perception gives rise to both spatial items (objects) and the sense of spatiality itself, utilizing the familiar method of phenomenological reduction, or 'bracketing'.[17] I would like to bring out three core elements in Husserl's thinking.

The first element is that it is a necessary fact about visual perception that only one 'profile' or 'adumbration'[18] of an object appears at any one time. Objects have occluded sides, and in order for the perceiver to overcome this radical incompleteness of perception, we have to consider not just temporally isolated profiles of an object, but temporally extended perceptual series that allow for the increasing specification and determination of this same object: 'A sort of connection of perceptions belongs to the essence of every perception: that is, to its essence belongs a certain (temporal) extension' (Husserl 1997a, §19). It is only via these temporally extended series that we can arrive at fuller knowledge of the object, which is achieved, Husserl claims, via a *synthesis* of all these separate profiles, taken together in their unity.

Secondly, what makes this synthesis possible? Husserl claims that of vital importance here, is that the transition from one profile to the next has to occur *continuously*. Note that this is not to say that discontinuities in the presentative contents of the perceptual series do not exist or are not important, just that they take place against a backdrop of continuity: 'It is only when, in the unity of experience, the continuous transition from one perception to the next is warranted that we can talk of the evidence that identity is given. The unity of the object only certifies itself as such in the unity of a synthesis that continuously ties together the multiple perception' (§44).

However, the unity of a *particular* given series is not yet enough. Husserl also shows that the imaginative projection of *possible* series in relation to the object is also necessary, in which case: 'It [the object] is what it is only as the identical in the systematic unity of these appearances or possibilities of appearances' (§30, [my addition]).

---

16 This is not to elide other aspects of dance spectatorship, such as audition. See numbers four and five of the six 'theses' presented later, which overlap substantially with this sensory modality.

17 Put simply, a filtering out of unnecessary prior understandings of the natural world: for a concise account, see Zahavi 2003, pp.43-79.

18 Husserl's term.

The third element is the most important for our purposes. For the constitution of spatiality via the synthesis of temporal series of real or possible appearances is not yet sufficient either: we also must consider the role played by *kinaesthesis*. Visual contents by themselves cannot account for our experience of three-dimensionality, because without an awareness of the direction of *our own movement* in relation to the object, we would not be able to discern the difference between the object's movement independent of us, and the appearance of an object at rest from a changing perspective. And this felt awareness of our own movement is what is meant by the term kinaesthesia.

In addition, Husserl claims that certain *types* of motion, like receding from and approaching the object, are necessary for the constitution of spatiality, and that the *correlations* of these movements, or 'kinaesthetic series' with the series of visual appearances that accompany them are what is necessary to make possible 'a new dimension, that makes a thing out of a picture, space out of the oculomotor field' (§67).

Husserl also stresses elsewhere the importance of the kinaesthetic self-awareness of movement to the possible (virtual) series of perceptions that aim at imaginative capture of the absent profiles of an object. These series operate as 'if-then' loops that correlate virtual visual appearances with virtual kinaesthetic sensations: 'All possible profiles of an object, as a spatial object, form a system that is coordinated to one kinesthetic system, and to this kinesthetic system as a whole, in such a way that "if" some kinesthesis or other runs its course, certain profiles corresponding to it must necessarily also run their course' (Husserl 1997b, p.390).

To summarize, every perception has an inherent duality. There exists a series of background kinaesthetic experiences *and* a functional correlation with a set of visual, or other[19] appearances. It is this functional correlation that gives rise to our sense of space and objects in space, in such a way that 'perceptual intentionality presupposes a moving and therefore incarnated subject... the crucial point made by Husserl is not that we can perceive movement, but that *our very perception presupposes movement*' (Zahavi 2003, p.100). Why is all of this relevant to the perception of dance? Husserl shows how a sense of kinaesthesia is vital to all perception, and not just to the perception of artforms traditionally associated with kinaesthetic experience, like dance. But dance, I will argue below, takes this basic aspect of our everyday perception, and then heightens or transforms it in determinate ways.

Sheets-Johnstone and kinaesthesia

Despite Husserl's insights into the necessary role of kinaesthesia in perception, his account, at least from a dance perspective, seems incomplete.

---

19 Such as tactile series.

This is because Husserl never granted kinaesthesia the status of a *bona fide* sensory modality in its own right, relegating it instead to a question of the simple awareness of movement and positioning relative to external objects, or to a question merely of spatial displacement and pointillistic sensation. This clearly restricts his account of kinaesthesia: specifically, it elides the dynamic and continuous nature of the experience of self-movement.

Sheets-Johnstone has rectified this discrepancy in Husserl with her own systematic account of kinaesthesia and kinaesthetic consciousness (Sheets-Johnstone 2011, pp.113-150). I will give only a short summary here and again will emphasize four important aspects of Sheets-Johnstone's thinking, namely the qualitative structure of movement; the 'two-foldedness' of kinaesthesia as felt *and* as perceived; the 'dynamic congruency' between emotion and movement, and the intermodality of vitality affects, with reference to the work of child psychologist Daniel Stern.[20]

The dynamics of movement, Sheets-Johnstone claims, are grounded in its structure which has four basic qualities: *tensional, linear, amplitudinal,* and *projectional,* which are separable only reflectively. Experientially they all combine in a global sense to form the distinct qualitatively felt dynamic phenomenon of any particular self-movement, or 'kinesthetic melody', a term Sheets-Johnstone, following Husserl, often uses:[21]

> the felt tensional quality has to do with our sense of effort; the linear quality with both the felt contour of our moving body, and the linear paths we sense ourselves describing in the process of moving; the amplitudinal quality with both the felt expansiveness or contractiveness of our moving body and the spatial expansiveness or constrictedness of our movement; the felt projectional quality with the way we release force or energy. (Sheets-Johnstone 2011, p.123)

Linear and amplitudinal qualities clearly relate to *spatial* aspects of movement, tensional and projectional qualities to *temporal* aspects. We can now see why Husserl's conception of kinaesthesia is insufficient for a phenomenologically accurate account of dance; it tends to reduce this complex dimensionality of movement to just one of its aspects, the sense of linear displacement in space in a particular direction or path. Husserl elides the particular qualitative aspects of the dynamic acts that are essential to his 'if-then' loops correlating perception and movement.[22] And as adults we can also easily pass over our kinaesthetic experience and its complex

---

20 See Stern (1985)

21 Husserl (1966) used the example of the perception of a musical melody in his original exposition of the nature of subjective time consciousness.

22 But Husserl nevertheless retains at least a *minimal* aspect of kinaesthesia, namely the *felt* difference between certain movement patterns, such as approaching and receding.

qualitative dynamics. But as Sheets-Johnstone notes of our self-movement: 'any time we care to pay attention to it, there it is' (Sheets-Johnstone 2012, p.6). And in terms of dance:

> The qualitative dynamics of movement are obviously central and foundational to the aesthetic creation and realization of a dance. As a formed and performed art, dance is grounded in the qualitative intricacies, complexities, and possibilities of human movement. Kinesthesia is in turn a sensory modality basic to the art of choreography and the art of dancing. An important fact attaches to this truth. Kinesthetic experience is not a matter of sensations, but a matter precisely of dynamics. (p.11)[23]

The second important aspect I want to highlight is that kinaesthesia has both 'inner' and 'outer' components. Through kinaesthesia, we experience directly our ability both to feel and to perceive our own movement.[24] To perceive our own movement as a three-dimensional phenomenon, as a *spatial happening*, is rooted in kinaesthetic experience, as when we are working to perfect certain movements in sport. And during a dance performance, we readily and easily perceive the qualitative dynamics of the movement, the dynamics that the dancers are kinaesthetically experiencing *and* constituting by this same movement.

The third aspect is the linkage Sheets-Johnstone makes between emotion and movement: joy 'moves' us in ways different from anger and 'moves us to move' in ways different from fear, and so on. Emotions, Sheets-Johnstone claims, are linked to tactile-kinaesthetic bodies via a 'dynamic congruency' between their qualitative aspects: an ongoing kinetic form has a distinctive spatial-temporal envelope that matches the form of an ongoing affective feeling.[25] Note that 'dynamic congruency' does not entail formal identity, and it is precisely because such a difference exists that we can separate out the emotion from the movement, as when we feign or imitate an emotion. And we recognize the kinetics of emotion and can detect such differences on the basis of our own affective/tactile-kinaesthetic experience of our own emotions.

Sheets-Johnstone, drawing on the work of child psychologist Daniel Stern (1985), links this 'affect attunement', or the matching of the dynamics of another person's feelings to *intermodal* 'vitality affects' that emphasize the purely *dynamic* aspects of varied phenomena: a sound or a pain can *burst*

---

23 The account given here of the centrality of kinaesthesia is not universally accepted within the dance literature, and I will outline one main objection to this view later.

24 Husserl refers to this as *Innen-* and *Aussenleiblichkeit*. See Zahavi (2003, p.101f) for more details.

25 See Sheets-Johnstone (2011, pp.453-472): the argument here is reminiscent of that of Susanne Langer (1996).

forth with a certain distinctive activation tone and contour; a touch, gesture or aroma can be *fleeting* or *attenuating*, and so on. These vitality affects resist our attempts at taxonomy and classification in language, but are linked profoundly to the tactile-kinaesthetic body: 'every time one moves a vitality affect is present' (Sheets-Johnstone 2011, p.222).

But at this point we should perhaps deal with some objections to the account given so far in this section of kinaesthesia and its relation to dance performance. These objections can be considered to be twofold. The first relates to an important problem in philosophy generally, namely the difficulty in translating what are essentially first-person experiences, arrived at via phenomenological reduction, into claims about *intersubjective* experience. Put differently, how can we move from statements about the first-person experience of self-movement to statements about the experience of the movements of others? To answer this question, let us return to the 'inner' and 'outer' aspects of bodily experience, and the phenomena of mimesis or pairing that we described earlier. My body is given to me *both* visually and tactually in terms of a body-as-object, *and* as a volitional interiority, a body-as-lived. And it is precisely this dual experience, Husserl claims, that makes intersubjective empathy possible: one reason why I am able to recognize and non-inferentially experience other embodied subjects is that the experience of my *own* body has this 'remarkable play between *ipesity* and *alterity* characterizing double-sensation' (Zahavi 2003, p.104). When I touch one hand with the other, I experience both the hand *touching* and the hand *being touched*: 'When my left hand touches my right, I am experiencing myself in a manner that anticipates both the way in which an Other would experience me and the way in which I would experience an Other' (*ibid.*). And Husserl only refers to tactility here as one specific example that can be generalized. We can also speak of visual resemblances, and of movement pairings; the latter constituting a move from empathy to kinaesthetic empathy proper. Other bodies *act* similarly to our own, they move in similar ways, and one important aspect of intersubjective pairing is the correspondence between intentional behaviour and expressive movements, a correspondence that seems to be detectable, as we have seen, cross-modally.

But there is a second objection that we must answer that questions the importance given in our account to the connection between kinaesthesia and dance. This objection is raised by Graham McFee, who argues that *even if* such a sense exists,[26] this still raises the question of whether the consideration of kinaesthesis 'could make much of a contribution to our knowledge or understanding of meaning of dances' (McFee 1992, p.269). McFee claims this is because the acquisition of knowledge or the attribution

---

26 McFee argues kinaesthetic sensation cannot really be considered as a sensory modality in the same way as the usual five senses (McFee 1992, p.264f.).

of meaning in art is tied to our recognition of formal features in the artwork (including recognition of their status *as* formal features) that can only be effectively dealt with by *projectional* sensory modalities such as sight and hearing. These are modalities where idiomatically there is a *gap* between the subject and object of perception. Without going into the details of why this is the case here, we can nevertheless take issue with the claim that kinaesthesia is of little importance to dance studies because a consideration of it makes no contribution to *meaning-attribution*. This is just a variety of the hermeneutic reductionism critiqued earlier. It ignores the argument that artworks, in the words of Hans Ulrich Gumbrecht, typically engender 'meaning-effects' *and* 'presence-effects', as well as oscillations between the two. The over-emphasis on the former has led to an institutional bias in the humanities in which 'the absolute dominance of meaning-related questions has long led to the abandonment of other types of phenomena or questions' (Gumbrecht 2004, p.16). These 'other types of phenomena' or presence-effects include things like kinaesthetic *qualia*, images, vitality affects, and experiences of heightened somatic intensity that have 'no message' (p.98). For if what 'meaning' is deemed to be entails solely the conceptual, propositional or semiotic, then these phenomena are not related to meaning-attribution, as McFee claims. But there is a historical body of work in philosophy that stresses how this conception of meaning itself is too narrow when it comes to an adequate description of perceptual and aesthetic experience. These approaches to the problem at hand stress an alternative and enlarged account of 'meaning' itself, seeing it as something that arises 'through embodied organism-environment interactions in which significant patterns are marked within the flow of experience' (Johnson 2007, p.273). Under this rubric, we can insist that kinaesthetic experiences *are* meaningful, just in a different way. They can become marked in our experiential flux as certain patterns (or Sheets-Johnstone's 'kinesthetic melodies'), and become part of a nexus of meaning that consists of 'connections to past, present and future experiences, actual or possible' (*ibid.*). A particular difference in kinaesthetic quality may be felt during a dance performance that becomes marked against a background of other such experiences. This quality, via this marking, can be reactualized in future dance performances, remembered, or projected purely imaginatively. The interconnections between all these occurrences of a kinaesthetic quality and other experiences *are* its meaning. This is a redefinition of meaning that is prefigured in the work of pragmatist philosophers like John Dewey and William James, and taken up by the current 'embodied' or 'enacted' approaches to cognition.[27] And the vital point is that many of these thinkers stress the *connectedness* and *continuity* between, on the one hand, formal, conceptual and structural aspects of

---

27 See, for example, Lakoff and Johnson (1981, 1999).

experience, and preconceptual, nonformal, and felt dimensions on the other.

But to summarize, the importance (or not) of kinaesthesia to dance studies seems to depend less on direct experiential considerations than on whether kinaesthetic experiences can be successfully integrated into theories that have wider philosophical mandates, particularly aesthetic theories that consider the problem of meaning-attribution (in the conventional analytic sense) to be central to their functioning. But with some of these objections to kinaesthesia aside, we can now move to a consideration of our central question, the elucidation of the intrinsic significance of dance.

Why dance matters – six theses on intrinsic significance

Let us recall then Crowther's account of the intrinsic significance of different artforms. He claims that this significance depends on factors relating to perception, imagination and agency 'which are fundamental to our knowledge of self and world' (Crowther 2009, p.11). That is they are, generally speaking, pre-reflexive, subjectively experienced factors pertaining to phenomenological depth. What art does *aesthetically*, that is through the creation of certain *styles*, is to heighten, transform and make enduring these factors, and each artform has to be investigated individually for its own singularities in this regard. For each, at a basic level, can involve different sensory modalities, which combine aspects of perception, imagination and agency in different *autonomous* ways.

We have seen that in the case of dance, we need to pay particular (but not exclusive) attention to the sensory modalities of vision, tactility and kinaesthesia, and we have learned from Husserl and Sheets-Johnstone that these modalities are (a) fundamentally functionally correlated in all perception, and that (b) kinaesthesis in particular needs to be considered as a sensory modality extending beyond merely pointillistic sensation and involving a specific qualitative dynamic of change, not just the registering of spatial displacement. In what follows, I will present six theses that aim to precisely explicate how dance as an autonomous artform heightens, transforms and makes enduring certain aspects of visual and tactile-kinaesthetic correlation.

Thesis one: trajectory and path-dependency

This thesis is the easiest to state succinctly. In our normal 'naïve' interactions with the world, we are often not entirely conscious of our kinaesthetic modality. This is because our movements, for the most part, are *goal-directed*. Our bodies traverse areas of space with a specific intentional functionality: we reach for an object; we remove something in our path; we speed up and slow down because we are late or early etc. What we seldom pay attention to is that each of these goal-directed movements exhibit both spatial and kinaesthetic *path-dependency*; that is, if we so choose, we can reach for an object or remove something from our path via separate spatial trajectories, or speed up and slow down in *this* particular way, or in a qualitatively different way. Each of these separate trajectories exhibits its own qualitatively different kinetic-affective dynamic; one that, if we wish, we can become fully conscious of: 'anytime we choose to pay attention to it, there it is' (quoted earlier).

In dance, and to the contrary, these aspects of path-dependency, rather than remaining submerged, come to the fore. Dance reveals through its material our innate ability to move path-dependently. In dance, this path-dependency becomes coupled with aesthetic style; the *way* certain dancers traverse space, even in simple ways such as walking, becomes the focus of our attention.

The minimal geometries traced by performers in the early works of Rosemary Butcher provide an example of this;[28] the choreography makes us aware of both spatial path-dependency, through a deliberate restriction to simple repeated trajectories such as squares and circles. And we also become aware, *via* this restriction, of kinaesthetic path-dependency; the reduction of spatial trajectory makes us aware of other, less visible details in the movement, namely the small kinaesthetic differences exhibited by the dancers who share the same choreographic material.

Thesis two: the 'three-foldedness' of dance

I would not hesitate to say that I believe this thesis to be fundamental to why dance matters to us. We saw earlier, how our experience of our own body is essentially two-folded; we can both *feel* our own movement *and* perceive our own movement. This latter perception of our own movement suffers however from two distinct limitations.

The first is that although we can perceive our own movement visually, there are natural biomechanical impairments to our ability to do this, due to our own self-positioning relative to our own bodies; I cannot see directly how the back of my head is moving, for example. Note that I am not claiming here that this self-perception of movement need be necessarily a visual matter, just that it *can* be.

The second limitation relates to the *felt* dimension of kinaesthesia, which is at least partly an awareness of the repertoire of 'I cans' and the 'I cannots' of our own body; what it is that we are able to accomplish (or not) kinetically. What I want to suggest is that in dance, and in place of the usual

---

28 Representative examples might include *Catch 5-Catch 6* (1978) and *Shell Force Fields and Spaces* (1981). Photographs of both can be viewed at: www.rosemarybutcher.com [accessed Jan. 2013].

two-foldedness of the kinaesthetic feeling and perception of our own body, we become aware of a certain *three-foldedness*. The introduction of another body (or bodies) into our perceptual field *triangulates* the relationship we have with our own bodies, and in doing so, introduces two crucial new (and related) phenomenological factors. The first is that perception of dance involves both an *extension* and *heightening* of the kinaesthetic relationship we have to ourselves: we can perceive the body of another visually with much greater determination than we can visually perceive our own; the occluded parts of our own bodies are now, in some sense, visible. In addition, by perceiving the body of another, we become aware, and no more so than in the case of dance, of the potential extension of the repertoire of kinetic 'I cans'. And this intrigues us.

But the crucial point is this. The triangulation just mentioned does not result in the estrangement of our kinaesthetic link with self. Through the processes of mimetic (re)enactment and pairing described in the last section, or the 'making oneself similar to' of kinaesthetic empathy, the triangulation *both extends and consolidates* this link with self. It preserves something of the inner link at the same time as extending it outwards. We understand and appreciate the movements of others through our own self-understanding of our own movement; it is only on this basis that we are aware of the triangulation *as* an extension at all.

Moreover, dance – considered in an extended sense that includes physical theatre etc. – does this *autonomously*. There is no other artform in which the 'inner' and 'outer' aspects of kinaesthesia, which are partly constitutive of all perception, are *both* extended and consolidated in this way through a triangulation to another body.

Thesis three: kinaesthesia and imagination

Let us take Husserl's favourite example of phenomenological bracketing in *Ding und Raum*, that of the perception of a cube. We do not, as we have seen, have access to this cube all at once due to our necessary profiling towards it. Our perception of it however is linked not just to the *actual* (and correlated) series of visual appearance and kinaesthesia that we carry out in relation to it, but to virtual *possible* series too, which are structured in terms of 'if-then' loops. The synthesis of both actual and virtual series is necessary for our perception of the cube as an identical object.

Now, let us consider the case of these *possible* series more carefully. When we are apprehending the occluded sides virtually ('*if* I perform this movement, then what *would* I see of the occluded sides'?), we can say that there is a strong path-dependent nature to this. The possible series of visual appearances is correlated to a *particular* continuous and indivisible kinaesthetic arc that has to be intentionally protended (to use Husserl's term).[29] In imagination, we project path-dependent intentional arcs of movement.

In dance perception, we do the same. The movements of the dancers that we see are internally mimetically (re)enacted. In doing so we create protentions as to how the path-dependent movement is to be continued. And this creates *expectations* as to whether the movement that is subsequently perceived 'matches' our own *felt* protention. Again, dance both heightens and consolidates our own imaginative kinaesthetic faculty.

A piece by William Forsythe exemplifies this. In a section of the ballet *Artifact* (1984), a group of dancers is performing to J.S.Bach's 'Chaconne'.[30] The movement is interrupted periodically by periods of darkness on stage, or by the theatre curtain falling prematurely. During these periods, we become aware precisely of our own kinaesthetic *and* visual protentions. Despite the complete lack of visibility, we still imaginatively project movement trajectories happening in the darkness *as if* they were still visible, and this involves both a kinaesthetic protention or felt continuation in our own bodies, and a projected visual image, each entrained to the other. The piece seems designed to excite and then accentuate these visual and kinaesthetic images.

Thesis four: virtualization of expression

The fourth thesis describes something that dance shares with other temporal artforms, such as music[31] and theatre. The key is that the difference between the perception of dance *as art* and ordinary pedestrian movement is that it is *aesthetically framed*: by this I mean that a dance spectator tends to pre-reflexively assume that the movement is both a) potentially repeatable within another aesthetic context, and b) exhibits at least some type of minimal formal organization. This opens up an irreducible ontological gap between the experience and perception of something *as art* and typical non-aesthetic experience. The consequence of this gap is that the kinetic-affective dynamics of dance assume an 'as such' quality, which results in an experience of *agentive ambiguity* as to the source of the affect. When we affectively perceive dance, it is not simply a question of the agentive attribution of the exhibited affects or emotions to the particular performer in front of us; the gap opened up by the potential repeatability and formal organization of the material means that the affect or emotion seems instead to be a *virtualized expression* of the affect or emotion 'as such'.

---

29 See Husserl (1966).

30 Seen live by the author at Sadler's Wells, April 2012.

31 For more on this with regard to music, see Crowther's (2007; Ch.7) reading of Langer and Schopenhauer.

Thesis Five: intermedial interpenetration

Let us consider again the 'vitality affects' that Daniel Stern (1985) has mapped in relation to intermodal aspects of psychology: the way for example a gesture or sound can both be described as 'attenuating' or 'bursting forth'. Consider also Sheets-Johnstone's assertion that all self-movement, together with its mimetic (re)enactment, always already constitutes a type of vitality affect. In dance, I propose, something is created where, via the introduction of music and lighting etc., these vitality affects become dispersed and become interpenetrated in and between different media. A dance performance creates a type of aesthetic 'atmosphere' in which there exists an intermedial interpenetration of vitality affects.[32] For example, such interpenetration can arise from the effect of entrainment or metric synchronization between visual and sonic aspects of the performance material, as is the case in much classical dance. In other cases, such as in the work of Cage and Cunningham, this entraining relationship of music to dance is deliberately suspended, in which case new aspects of intermediality become subjectively constructed: the metric incommensurability of the visual and sonic does not force the absence of intermedial relation, but the construction of new relations.[33]

Thesis Six: intersubjectivity and intercorporeality

Stern (1985) also posits that it is characteristic of human subjective development that we begin to relate to others in and through movement, through a kinaesthetically and kinetically inflected intercorporeality. Affective modes of receptivity and responsivity to others, affective accordances and disacccordances with others and so on, are anchored and articulated in felt dimensions of bodily movement. Most of the time we are not aware of such interactions. But dance makes them publicly accessible and enduring. And it does so whether we are 'actually' physically moving with the dancers or not; we simulate the same interactions internally via movement pairing or mimesis.

We can also refer here to the 'perceived' dimension of kinaesthesis: What we perceive primarily is the geometric *three-dimensionality* of our own movement: that is, the spatial volume of one's movement becomes apparent. This is also how we are aware of the possible collision of our movement paths with nearby objects in our surroundings or with other persons, and: 'The fact that one is or can be perceptually aware of one's own movement as a kinetic worldly reality is obviously significant with respect to interpersonal

---

32 The term 'aesthetic atmosphere' comes from the work of Gernot Böhme, who draws attention to the ease in which we transfer attributes such as 'sharp', 'cold', or 'heavy' in such a way that the transfer is not metaphorical, but dependent on primary intersensory qualities or atmospheric 'characters'. See Böhme (2001, p.96).

33 For more on this, see Deleuze (2005, p.216f.).

relations; one can become aware of the literal or figurative impact of one's own movement dynamics on others' (Sheets-Johnstone 2011, p.517). In dance, these (otherwise avoided) collisions and relations are productive and generative of new movement: think for example of contact improvisation. In this way, dance epitomizes and extends interpersonal affective relations and questions of intersubjectivity and intercorporeality.

References

Adorno, Theodor. *Aesthetic Theory*, trans. Christian Lenhardt. Boston: Routledge & Kegan Paul, 1984.

Ankersmit, Frank. *Sublime Historical Experience*, Stanford: Stanford University Press, 2005.

Bernard, Michel. 'Sens et fiction ou les effets étranges de trois chiasmes sensoriels,' in *Nouvelles de danse* 17, 1993, pp.56–64.

Böhme, Gernot. *Aisthetik. Vorlesungen über Ästhetik als allgemeine Wahrnehmungslehre*, Munich: Wilhelm Fink, 2001.

Bowie, Andrew. *Music, Philosophy and Modernity*, Cambridge: Cambridge University Press, 2007.

Clark, Andy. *Supersizing the Mind*, Oxford: Oxford University Press, 2008.

Cook, Nicholas and Mark Everist (eds.). *Rethinking Music*, Oxford: Oxford University Press, 1999.

Crowther, Paul. *Art and Embodiment: From Aesthetics to Self-Consciousness*, New York: Oxford University Press, 2001.

Crowther, Paul. *The Transhistorical Image: Philosophising Art and Its History*, Cambridge: Cambridge University Press, 2002.

Crowther, Paul. *Defining Art, Creating the Canon*, New York: Oxford University Press USA, 2007.

Crowther, Paul. *Phenomenology of the Visual Arts (Even the Frame)*, Stanford: Stanford University Press, 2009.

Crowther, Paul. *Phenomenologies of Art and Vision: A Post-Analytic Turn*, London: Bloomsbury, 2013.

Deleuze, Gilles. *Foucault*, London: Continuum, 1988.

Deleuze, Gilles. *Cinema 2: The Time Image*, London: Continuum, 2005.

Desmond, Jane, (ed.) *Meaning in Motion: New Cultural Studies of Dance*, Durham: Duke University Press, 1997.

Fodor, Jerry. *Representations: Essays on the Foundations of Cognitive Science*, Cambridge: MIT Press, 1979.

Foster, Susan Leigh. *Reading Dancing: Bodies and Subjects in Contemporary American Dance*, Berkeley: University of California Press, 1988.

Foster, Susan Leigh. 'Movement's Contagion: the Kinesthetic Impact of

Performance,' in Davis, Tracy C. (ed.), *The Cambridge Companion to Performance Studies*, Cambridge: Cambridge University Press, 2008.

Foster, Susan Leigh. *Choreographing Empathy: Kinesthesia in Performance*. London: Routledge, 2010.

Fraleigh, Sondra. *Dance and the Lived Body*, Pittsburgh: University of Pittsburgh Press, 1987.

Gumbrecht, Hans Ulrich. *The Production of Presence: What Meaning Cannot Convey*, Stanford: Stanford University Press, 2004

Hagendoorn, Ivar. 'Some Speculative Hypotheses about the Nature and Perception of Dance and Choreography,' *Journal of Consciousness Studies*, 3:4, 2004, pp.79-110.

Husserl, Edmund. *The Phenomenology of Internal Time Consciousness*, trans. James S. Churchill, Bloomington: Indiana University Press, 1966.

Husserl, Edmund. *Thing and Space: Lectures of 1907*, trans. Richard Rojcewicz, Dordrecht: Kluwer Academic Publishers, 1997a.

Husserl, Edmund. *Psychological and Transcendental Phenomenology and the Confrontation with Heidegger (1927-1931)*, Sheehan, Thomas and Richard E. Palmer (eds. and trans.), Dordrecht: Kluwer Academic Publishers, 1997b.

Johnson, Mark. *The Meaning of the Body: Aesthetics of Human Understanding*, Chicago: Chicago University Press, 2007.

Kozel, Susan. *Closer: Performance, Technologies, Phenomenology*, Cambridge: MIT Press, 2007.

Langer, Susanne. *Philosophy in a New Key*, 3rd edition, Cambridge: Harvard University Press, 1996.

Lakoff, George, and Mark Johnson. *Metaphors We Live By*, Chicago: University of Chicago Press, 1981.

Lakoff, George, and Mark Johnson. *Philosophy in the Flesh: The Embodied Mind and Its Challenge to Western Thought*, New York: Basic Books, 1999.

Lepecki, André. *Exhausting Dance: Performance and the Politics of Movements*, New York: Routledge, 2006.

Levin, David Michael. 'Philosophers and the Dance,' in Copeland, Roger and Marshall Cohen (eds.), *What is Dance? Readings in Theory and Criticism*, New York: Oxford University Press, 1983, pp.85–94.

McFee, Graham. *Understanding Dance*, London: Routledge, 1992.

McNamara, Joann. 'Dance in the Hermeneutic Circle,' in Fraleigh, Sondra and Penelope Hanstein, (eds.), *Researching Dance*, Pittsburgh: University of Pittsburgh Press, 1999, pp.162–187.

Menke, Christoph. *The Sovereignty of Art: Aesthetic Negativity in Adorno and Derrida*, Cambridge: MIT Press, 1998.

Mickunas, Algis. 'The Primacy of Movement,' *Main Currents in Modern Thought* 31, 1974, pp.8–12.

Noë, Alva. *Action in Perception*, Cambridge: MIT Press, 2004.

Parviainen, Jaana. *Bodies Moving and Moved: A Phenomenological Analysis of the Dancing Subject and the Cognitive and Ethical Values of Dance Art*, Tampere: Tampere University Press, 1998.

Paterson, Mark. 'Movement for Movement's Sake? On the Relationship Between Kinaesthesia and Aesthetics,' *Essays in Philosophy*, 13:2, 2012, pp.471-497.

Rouhiainen, Leena. *Living Transformative Lives: Finnish Freedance Dance Artists Brought into Dialogue with Merleau-Ponty's Phenomenology*, Helsinki: Theatre Academy, 2003.

Rizzolatti, Giacomo and Corrado Sinigaglia. *Mirrors in the Brain: How Our Minds Share Actions, Emotions, and Experience*, trans. Frances Anderson, Oxford: Oxford University Press, 2008.

Sheets-Johnstone, Maxine. *The Phenomenology of Dance*, Madison: University of Wisconsin Press, 1966.

Sheets-Johnstone, Maxine. 'Movement and Mirror Neurons: A Challenging and Choice Conversation,' *Phenomenology and the Cognitive Sciences*, 11:3, 2012, pp.385-401.

Sheets-Johnstone, Maxine. *The Primacy of Movement*, expanded 2nd edition, Amsterdam: John Benjamins, 2011.

Smyth, Mary M. 'Kinaesthetic Communication in Dance,' *Dance Research Journal*, 16:2, 1984, pp.19-22.

Stern, Daniel. *The Interpersonal World of the Infant: A View from Psychoanalysis and Developmental Psychology*, New York: Basic Books, 1985.

Thompson, Evan. *Mind and Life: Biology, Phenomenology, and the Sciences of Mind*, Cambridge: Belknap Press/Harvard University Press, 2007.

Varela, Francesco and Evan Thompson and Eleanor Rosch. *The Embodied Mind: Cognitive Science and Human Experience*, Cambridge: MIT Press, 1991.

Wittgenstein, Ludwig. *Zettel*, Oxford: Blackwell, 1981.

Wolin, Richard. 'Utopia, Mimesis, and Reconciliation: A Redemptive Critique of Adorno's Aesthetic Theory,' in *Representations* 32, 1990, pp.33-49.

Zahavi, Dan. *Husserl's Phenomenology*, Stanford: Stanford University Press, 2003.

Part IV

Dance and Philosophy / Dance as Philosophy

11. Dance and/as art: considering Nietzsche and Badiou

Catherine Botha

Introduction

French philosopher Alain Badiou asserts that 'Dance is not an art, because it is the sign of the possibility of art as inscribed in the body.' (Badiou, 2005, p.69). In the context of Badiou's inaesthetics, an approach to art which he claims exclusively considers 'the strictly intraphilosophical effects produced by the existence of some works of art' (Badiou, 2005, p.12), it seems that 'ultimately only two arts are required [...]: the poem as affirmation, as inscription of a disappearance, and theatre as the site wherein this affirmation turns into mobilization' (Rancière 2004, p.235). In Badiou's inaesthetic approach, dance is denied artistic status, acting instead only as the metaphor of thought.

Provoked by Badiou's claim, this paper examines the relationship between art and dance by means of a consideration of selected aspects of the works of Friedrich Nietzsche and Alain Badiou. I first present a reading of Badiou's writing on dance and his claims regarding its status as non-art. Subsequently, I provide an interpretation of Nietzsche that attempts to show that he does not only use the symbol of dance as a metaphor (as Badiou does), but also acknowledges the centrality of dance for the development of the body-self. Even though I show that both positions are deficient in certain respects, I suggest, in the final section of the paper, that some of the claims of both theorists can fruitfully contribute to a different way of approaching the question of whether and how dance can be considered an art.

Badiou and dance as non-art

Badiou's *Handbook of Inaesthetics* (2005) commences with a call for a revival of the lost relationship between art, philosophy, and the education of the youth. As he describes it, this relationship has historically been constituted by one of three schemas: the didactic, the classical, and the romantic. In the didactic schema, of which Plato is seen as representative, art is thought of as being incapable of truth, or, at least, all truth is considered to be external to art (Badiou 2005, p.2). In the romantic schema, of which Heidegger could be seen as representative, art *alone* is considered as being capable of truth (pp.3, 6). Between these two positions, Badiou identifies the classical schema as represented by Aristotle. In this schema, the proper purpose of art is not truth, but rather catharsis, and so the fact that art is incapable of truth is viewed as unproblematic (p.4). As Badiou explains, from the point of view of the classical schema, '[a]rt has a therapeutic function and not at all a cognitive or revelatory one' (ibid.).

Badiou's complaint is that, in his view, none of the above-mentioned schemata, nor the three main tendencies of thought that he identifies as emerging in the twentieth century (Marxism, psychoanalysis and German hermeneutics), have been able to produce a new schema for linking together art, philosophy, and education (Badiou 2005, p.5). As a consequence, Badiou aims to rethink aesthetics from within his own theory of truth events. For Badiou, it is only by turning back to truth that aesthetics can regain its proper relation to philosophy and education since 'the only education is an education by truths' (p.14).

What then does Badiou mean by truth? Badiou characterizes truth as fidelity or faithfulness to an event (Badiou 2002, p.42), which allows for the infinite transformation of a system of knowledge (pp.67-70). What he essentially means by this is that for a truth to arise, something must happen within an established field of knowledge (p.122). Badiou describes this happening as a truth – a rupture that introduces the new. As he remarks: 'A truth punches a 'hole' in knowledges...' (p.70). In this way, the Badiouian event can be described as a happening that reveals the ongoing discrepancy between the domain of knowledge and the domain of being itself.

Badiou further stipulates that truth events do not carry a guarantee as to their identity as events, and so he explains that, as such, events must be named by a subject – the one who bears the process of truth (Badiou 2002, p.43). When the subject names the event as an event, it simultaneously establishes itself as a subject due to its faithfulness to the procedure needed to verify the truth of that event. As Badiou points out, the subject does not exist before the event, but rather only arrives with the naming of the event (ibid.). This then is Badiou's 'immortal' subject: irreducible to the 'psychological subject, the Cartesian reflexive subject, the Kantian transcendental subject' (ibid.), or the finite, biological subject – the 'living organism pure and simple.' (p.11).

On the basis of Badiou's description of truth and the subject, it seems then that truth-procedures cannot be grasped on the level of animal or bodily existence. How then does the body figure in Badiou's thinking, if at all? It certainly does, and we see it in his claim that it is dance that 'produces the idea that the body is the bearer of ideas.' (Badiou 2005, p.72). In his exploration of Nietzsche's various aphorisms concerning the dancing body, Badiou begins, in the chapter on dance in his *Handbook of Inaesthetics*, with an interpretation of the Nietzschean view that the body in dance is a body at play – 'it is a body that forgets its fetters, its weight' (Badiou 2005, p.57). Badiou relates how Nietzsche contrasts this playful, light dancing body with the body of the military parade – the homogenized, heavy and stultified body (p.59). While the body of the parade conforms to external laws and habits, Badiou, through Nietzsche, reads the body in the moment of dance as being subject only to *internal* restraint:

> Dance is in no way the liberated bodily impulse, the wild energy of the body. On the contrary, it is the bodily manifestation of the disobedience to an impulse in the form of the power of restraint. [...] *Dance offers a metaphor for a light and subtle thought* precisely because it shows the restraint immanent to movement and thereby opposes itself to the spontaneous vulgarity of the body. (p.60, emphasis mine)

Badiou concludes from this reading that, for Nietzsche, the 'affirmative power of restraint' seen in the dancer is what demonstrates that 'the will is capable of learning' (p.61), and it is from this insight that Badiou then develops his own position: that dance provides the metaphor for the fact that 'every genuine thought' depends upon an event, before this thought has received a name (*ibid.*). In this way, Badiou is able to emphasize the relation between dance, truth, and education by developing a particular reading of the Nietzschean position, where the restraint that characterizes dance metaphorically transforms the animal body into the body of humanity as infinite – the body of a humanity that is *capable* of art (p.70).

But does the fore-going discussion allow one to conclude that Badiou adequately addresses the question of whether dance is an art? As Giorgio Agamben points out, 'Badiou [...] still conceives of the subject on the basis of a contingent encounter with truth, leaving aside the living being as 'the animal of the human species,' as a mere support for this encounter'(Agamben 1999, p.229). Here Agamben is claiming that, by describing the body as a body that has overcome its animality to become immortal in the moment of dance, Badiou includes the animal body into thought 'only as its exclusion' (*ibid.*).

Why should this be a problem in the context of the question of whether or how dance can be considered art? Even though Badiou's examination of the relation between aesthetics, philosophy, and education through the figure of dance is certainly instructive, the reductive thinking that relegates the body (of the dance) to a secondary position – a mere means to the naming of an event – seems to me to be unhelpful in deciding why it is that we would still intuitively want to characterize dance (or at least some forms of dance) as art. As I show in the second section of this paper, this reduction does not, I believe, happen if we read Nietzsche's work on dance in a way different to Badiou. By allowing for dance to function both as a metaphor for thinking (which Badiou adopts, and that I agree is a reading that is faithful to Nietzsche's statements on dance), as well as an integral part of the bodiliness that is human being, reading Nietzsche in a different way allows us to side-step this problem.

A second and related concern that could be raised is whether Badiou adequately addresses the question of the definition of dance. If we wish to decide whether dance is an art, it seems reasonable to ask for some form of definition of dance (and art), even if we do, in the end, reject the idea that dance or art can be defined.

In his discussion of Nietzsche's characterization of dance as a 'compulsory metaphor for thought,' Badiou mentions dance as 'an image of a thought subtracted from every spirit of heaviness' (Badiou 2005, p.57). The complex metaphorical network that Badiou identifies in Nietzsche's writings on dance includes connections with images of the bird, flight, air and fountains; as well as with the concepts of innocence and forgetting (pp.57-58). But most crucially, Badiou isolates one specific formulation as a very 'elegant definition of dance': 'A wheel that turns itself' (p.57). In this context, he explains that dance is 'like a circle in space, but a circle that is its own principle, a circle that is not drawn from the outside but rather draws itself' (ibid.). From this it seems that a very particular and narrow understanding of dance is being used – only lightness and the release from constraint are included, while weightiness and the heavily choreographed are excluded[1].

In my view, it is only because Badiou defines dance in this way, i.e. that he draws upon the very narrow understanding of dance that he reads Nietzsche as espousing, that he can claim that dance is *not* an art. Or, to put it differently, by excluding what he calls the 'regime of the body in which the body is exerted for the sake of its subjection to choreography' (Badiou 2005, p.59), Badiou can then claim that the dance that Nietzsche refers to cannot be an art.

The question then emerges as to whether there is not another way of reading Nietzsche on dance that will perhaps allow for a different conclusion.

---

1 This kind of characterization would then exclude hip hop as dance since to dance hip hop, the body must be held tight and focused, with strong weight - a strong contrast with the desire for weightlessness in ballet. See Thomas DeFrantz (2004) for a discussion of the aesthetic of hip hop dance.

Nietzsche: dance, art and philosophy

Nietzsche's thinking on the relationship between dance, art and philosophy is a theme that has received much attention from varying points of departure (Daniel Conway (1992), Jacques Derrida (1978), Sarah Kofman (1993), and Kimerer LaMothe (2011) are but a few examples of commentators who consider this theme in varying degrees of detail). The gist of these readings of Nietzsche's writings on dance is that Nietzsche sees dance as metaphor – a view which, as has already been mentioned, Badiou adopts. But does Nietzsche not go beyond merely claiming that dance is a mere metaphor for philosophical thinking – that light and joyful thinking that is able to escape the spirit of gravity that Nietzsche decries in the nihilism that he diagnoses in 19th century culture? To attempt to answer this question, I begin this section with a brief explanation of Nietzsche's evolving views on the nature of art and its value, then provide an exposition of the dominant readings of Nietzsche's view on dance as metaphor, and finally consider attempts to read Nietzsche's statements on dance in a way which allows for a different interpretation to the dominant views.

Many commentators, including Alexander Nehamas (1985), E.E. Sleinis (1994), Aaron Ridley (2007), and Julian Young (2009, pp.438-441), agree that Nietzsche's thinking on art in general is not static, but rather evolves throughout his writings. In his early work, of which the *Birth of Tragedy* is the most significant example, Nietzsche asks about how a culture can survive the absurdity and flux that is life, and turns to the ancient Greeks to investigate their approach. He holds that the Greeks survived through the balance of two competing, but complementary impulses – the Apollonian and the Dionysian (BT § 1).[2] Nietzsche describes Apollonian art (exemplified in the work of Homer, and emphasizing form and balance) as a 'glorification' of the phenomenon of human existence that allowed the Greeks to veil the horrors of life (BT § 3). Yet for Nietzsche, the beautiful illusion of the Apollonian must be balanced by its opposite – the Dionysian. Dionysus, the god of the non-representational art of music, is linked with 'formless flux, mystical intuition and excess'; a world where 'individual identities are dissolved' (Ansell-Pearson 2006, p.34).

Nietzsche posits that the tragedy of Ancient Greece was the highest form of art due to the balance of Apollonian and Dionysian elements exhibited.

---

2 The following abbreviations are used to refer to Nietzsche's works in this paper: BGE: Beyond Good and Evil; BT: The Birth of Tragedy; CW: The Case of Wagner; GM: On the Genealogy of Morality; GS: The Gay Science; HH: Human, All Too Human; TI: Twilight of the Idols; WP: Will to Power; Z: Thus Spoke Zarathustra. All references are translated from the *Kritische Studienausgabe* (KSA), excepting for references to *The Will to Power*. Full details are available in the reference list.

In tragedy, we subject ourselves to the terrible in life voluntarily, in order to experience the sublime (BT § 7). As such, the tragic is able to remind us of 'another state of being and a higher pleasure' (BT § 21). Art, in the balance between the Apollonian and the Dionysian, is then a way to cope with the flux and absurdity that is life for the early Nietzsche.

In *Human, All too Human*, however, Nietzsche qualifies the idea that he seemed to promulgate in *The Birth of Tragedy:* that there exists a metaphysical world relative to which nature is mere appearance. Although he does at this stage still grant that there *could* be a metaphysical world, he claims that all we can say about it is that it has a 'differentness' that we cannot access (HAH § 9). In section 10, he explains that art (as well as religion and morality) cannot provide us with access to another dimension of reality because we always find ourselves within representation (HAH p.10). So during this period, art is not considered a viable alternative to the sciences as a source of knowledge. Art is, however, not seen as completely useless, since from art it will, says Nietzsche, be easier to 'go over' to a 'truly liberating philosophical science' (HAH § 27), but the usefulness of art lies only in its being preparatory for science: 'The scientific man is the further evolution of the artistic' (HAH § 222).

This view is, however, reversed in the *Gay Science*, where Nietzsche tells us that it is *only* as an aesthetic phenomenon that existence is still bearable for us (GS p.107). Without the anaesthetization provided by art, we would succumb to nausea and suicide (*ibid.*), and so Nietzsche encourages us to learn from artists to use 'artistic distance' (*ibid.*; see also GS p.299). Here then we have a return to the idea that redemption from the flux of life can come only through the illusion that art teaches us – the theme that was first explored in the *Birth of Tragedy*.

As is pointed out by Hussain (2007, p.137), what is special about art for Nietzsche is its use of honest illusions: 'art alone is now honest'. This view is most clearly expressed in the *Genealogy of Morality*, where Nietzsche is looking for an alternative to the ascetic ideal, that heaviness that he claims is characteristic of the Judeo-Christian tradition. He finds this alternative in art since in art 'the lie is sanctified and the will to deception has a good conscience' (GM III, p.25). Why? Because Nietzsche believes that (good) art sees its illusions for what they are, without the illusions themselves being undermined (Hussain 2007, p.172). Of course, Nietzsche admits that art can be a dishonest illusion and so criticizes the likes of Wagner, Liszt and Victor Hugo (see for example CW § 8), but his point remains that redemption from the nihilism he diagnoses in his culture is possible through art.

From the above it is clear that Nietzsche generally sees art as having the potential to enhance life. But, has Nietzsche provided a way to determine whether a specific practice or artefact counts as art? In admitting that art can be a dishonest illusion in some instances, and by specifying the importance of the balance between the Dionysian and Apollonian in Greek tragedy, he certainly has provided a means to determine the difference between good art and bad art; but at this point it remains unclear as to how his discussions of art and artwork provide a means to make a determination as to whether a specific practice or artefact counts as art. As Sleinis (1994, p.127, emphasis mine) notes, Nietzsche's theory is 'a theory about the *function* of art, and it embodies a criterion of what constitutes good art.' However, since Nietzsche does characterize dance as an art (in GS 381 for example), it seems appropriate now to ask why and how he does so, in order to further explore whether his position can be extended in some way to provide us with a way to decide whether dance can be considered an art.

Dance is a theme that appears in a myriad of forms in Nietzsche's texts. Nietzsche characterizes dance in various ways, including as an experience of rapturous intoxication (BT §1), as a language of gestures (BT § 3), an epidemic (BT § 8); an ideal (GS 381), and as an art (GS 381). What is critical for the purposes of the current paper is that Nietzsche uses dance images mostly when he describes what he calls the 'revaluation' of all values [*Umwertung*] that he proposes as solution to the nihilism he diagnoses in 19th century European society, and it is this that encourages the dominant view of Nietzsche's writings on dance – that he sees dance only as a metaphor for philosophical thinking.

With the recognition of the death of God that Nietzsche announces in the *Gay Science* § 125, the foundation for values disintegrates. Devoid of this grounding, new, life-affirming values are needed to overcome the ensuing threat of nihilism. How is this to take place? As Nietzsche metaphorically describes it in *Thus Spoke Zarathustra*, the lion (which could be taken as representative of the human spirit) must conquer the great dragon (representing traditional morality), in order to create a space in which new values can be created (Z 26). The lion's 'I will' is opposed to the 'Thou shalt' of the camel – the plodding beast of burden that does not see any need to create new values. But the lion can only destroy and not create new values in Nietzsche's view (*ibid.*). As such, it must give way to a third metamorphosis – the child. The child represents 'innocence and forgetting, a new beginning, a game, a self-propelled wheel, a first movement, a sacred 'yes" (*ibid.*), and so is able to engage in the creation of new values.[3] It is this image of innocence represented by the child that Badiou highlights in his reading of Nietzsche's statements on dance, and in his definition of dance.

The characterization of the creation of new values in *Thus spoke Zarathustra* is comparable to where, in *Beyond Good and Evil*, Nietzsche

---

3 My intention here is merely to describe Nietzsche's vision of the revaluation of all values and not engage in a critical discussion thereof.

distinguishes genuine philosophers from what he calls 'philosophical labourers.' Philosophical labourers fail to engage in the revaluation of values; rather, they simply 'press into formulas' existing values (BGE 211) in Nietzsche's view. Genuine philosophers, in contrast, are engaged in the revaluation project and thus are the ideal type that Nietzsche wishes to cultivate. Genuine philosophers distinguish themselves by legislating and creating new values: 'they say, "*thus* it *shall* be!" ' (*ibid.*).

What is of relevance to the current paper is that Nietzsche oftentimes characterizes this revaluation that the genuine philosophers may bring to pass as dancing. As LaMothe describes it: 'Dance repeatedly appears to signal both the means and the fruit, the practice and the performance, of creating life-affirming values and learning to *love* life' (LaMothe 2011, p.2). How? Just as a dancer has to work many hours off stage to perfect his[4] bodily movements, his rhythm and balance, so Nietzsche is arguing that in order for a revaluation of values to take place, the free spirit must *learn* to think, a process that entails much effort and dedication. As he says:

> Learning to *think*... logic as a theory, as a practice, as a *craft* is beginning to die out ... there is no longer the remotest recollection that thinking requires a technique, a teaching curriculum, a will to mastery - that thinking wants to be learned like dancing, as a kind of dancing. Who among Germans still knows from experience the delicate shudder which light feet in spiritual matters send into every muscle? (TI § 7 'What the Germans Lack')

In the same way that dancing must be learned, Nietzsche's free spirits must learn to *overcome* life-denying values, and develop the strength needed to affirm life.

From the very succinct reading I have provided so far, it seems that the dominant readings are right – that Nietzsche merely sees dance as a metaphor, a way of describing the manner in which the spirit of gravity can be overcome by his free spirits. Yet, Nietzsche's writings can also be read as implying that he sees dancing as an important tool for maintaining the health of bodies in the culture to be founded by philosophers of the future.

Dance as more than metaphor?

Kimerer LaMothe (2011), Bruce Ellis Benson (2008) and Horst Hutter (2006) represent some recent examples of theorists who interpret Nietzsche's references to dance as more than a mere metaphor for the kind of thinking

---

4 In an attempt to achieve gender neutrality, for the sake of consistency, as well as to eliminate the stylistic awkwardness resultant from the use of paired pronouns (Dumond 1990), I choose to use the masculine pronoun throughout this paper. I do not, however, alter any quotations by other authors, but rather leave them in their original format.

Nietzsche is advocating as a means to overcome nihilism. LaMothe, for example, claims that for Nietzsche, Isadora Duncan, and Martha Graham:

> [D]ancing is a theopraxis – an activity in which people image, elevate, and sanctify their highest ideals, and thereby enact the process of becoming of self-overcoming that Nietzsche claims 'life' is. (LaMothe 2011, p.109)

Many of the theorists who advocate a reading similar to this – one that reads Nietzsche's pronouncements on dance as more than merely metaphorical – rely especially on a particular reading of the previous quote from *Twilight of the Idols*. When we consider this passage again, it seems that Nietzsche is not only saying that we should learn thinking 'like' dancing. As I have shown in the previous section, he certainly does say that, but, as LaMothe (2011), Benson (2008) and Hutter (2006) relate, he continues here and elsewhere to make another claim. He seems to be encouraging readers to learn thinking *as a kind of* dancing, i.e., as a species of dancing. This would seem to imply that a person who wants to know how to think must know *how* to dance.

This reading sits well with Nietzsche's understanding of the human being. A human being is seen by Nietzsche as a body, a multiplicity of changing desires, instincts and sensations (HAH § 39, 106). This is in contradistinction to the metaphysicians' misunderstanding of the human being as 'an *aeterna veritas*, as a thing that remains constant in the midst of all turbulence, as a sure standard of things' (HAH § 2). For Nietzsche, our thoughts and convictions are then simply 'judgments of our muscles' (WP § 314, see also BGE § 36), with human life being made up of our nervous stimuli, our physical sensations, our instincts, feelings needs and emotions. There is no 'essential self', no independent rational mind or soul that can be freed from bodily desires and forces. We are simply a plurality of moods and instincts held together by a will (GS § 354, see also WP § 492). As a result, Nietzsche can say through Zarathustra:

> A man's stride betrays whether he has found his own way: behold me walking! But whoever approaches his goal dances...And though there are swamps and thick melancholy on earth, whoever has light feet runs even over mud and dances as on swept ice (Z §17 'On the Higher Man')

It seems then that Nietzsche can then be interpreted as claiming that thinking is a bodily discipline requiring a physical technique. If this is right, then dance and other body-centred practices can be viewed as important practices suggested by Nietzsche as a part of the yes-saying and constructive labours as related in *Zarathustra* (Hutter 2006), and not only as metaphors for thinking.[5]

---

5 This interpretation of Nietzsche could be seen as complimentary to the somaesthetic theory developed by Richard Shusterman. Shusterman (1999, 2007) does indeed

I have very briefly shown that even though a reading of Nietzsche's writings on dance as metaphor is accurate, his views on the bodily nature of human beings, and a specific reading of some of his claims, does allow for a broader interpretation that invites us to see dance as an integral part of human bodily existence. Dance becomes one of the tools that encourage human beings to practice the art of living – to turn their lives into works of art. However, does this way of reading Nietzsche's statements on dance provide us with an adequate answer to whether dance is an art? In my view, even though reading Nietzsche differently to the dominant interpretations provides a more nuanced answer to the question of the artistic status of dance than does Badiou, reading Nietzsche in this way still does not provide us with a clear enough answer as to why one would want to say that dance is an art. Dance is certainly given a transformative power in its ability to synthesize the Dionysian and the Apollonian, but I remain skeptical of whether there can be, even on a reading that sees Nietzsche as claiming that dance is more than a metaphor for thought, a convincing explanation of why dance is an art. The reason is, as previously stated, that Nietzsche's writing on art seems only to provide us with a way to distinguish between good and bad art, between the life-affirming and the life-denying practices in which we could engage, but he does not seem to provide a way to determine whether a particular practice or artefact counts as art.

Another approach

As has been previously mentioned, in my view, Badiou's claim that dance is *not* an art depends upon a very specific understanding of dance, and a very narrow reading of Nietzsche's pronouncements on dance. It is only because Badiou reads Nietzsche as claiming that dance is only a metaphor for thinking that he can then embark upon his project of rethinking aesthetics from within his own theory of truth events. As has been shown, it is possible to understand Nietzsche's claims about dance differently, and so call Badiou's conclusion into question. Using Badiou's revival of the question of whether dance is an art as a starting point, the task remains to consider why one would indeed want to call (at least some forms of) dance art.

Intuitively, most would probably agree that the dancing beagles we can watch on *YouTube* or the lone human dancing for joy in his apartment, would not count as instances of dance as art. What would be our reasons? We could argue that these instances of dance do not take place in a theatrical setting and so do not count as art. This kind of view, which emerges from the turn to the extrinsic or relational properties of art is, as is well-known, developed in the work of Arthur Danto (1981), George Dickie (1984) and

---

acknowledge and draw upon Nietzsche's thinking in the development of his theory.

Jerrold Levinson (1990). Danto's claim that what makes something art is its embeddedness in an artworld; Dickie's development of Danto's theory into the institutional theory of art;[6] and Levinson's historical definition of art (where he claims that what makes something a work of art is its relation to previous works of art) are all inspired by a rejection of the position best represented by Morris Weitz's 1956 paper 'The Role of Theory in Aesthetics.' (Yanal 1994, p.x). In his paper, Weitz rejects the attempt to define art, since he posits that all we can say about the practices or artefacts we call art is that they, *a la* Wittgenstein, exhibit family resemblances. Art is, for Weitz, an 'open concept' and trying to find intrinsic properties common to all 'artworks' is misguided.

The institutional/historical response to Weitz's position has been, rightly in my view, accused of a vicious circularity.[7] In addition, if we take contemporary examples of dance into account, the institutional/historical position cannot always explain why we would want to call these works art. Take for example, *mapantsula* dancers performing on the streets of Johannesburg in the 1980s.[8] Today some might want to call their dancing art, but the dance events did not take place in a theatrical setting, and their dancing was not (yet) embedded in an artworld (in fact, it was a rejection of the institutional). Although one could claim that the works were related in some way to previous works of art in Levinson's historical sense, in the case of mapantsula, the relation was such that Weitz's claim about family resemblances would be more accurate than Levinson's position in this particular case, in my view.[9]

In response, I propose that what makes an artefact or practice distinguishable as art is that its maker should possess an artistic[10] intent, and that this

---

6 It must be acknowledged that Dickie does not claim works have to be presented in a gallery or theatre to count as art.

7 See Wollheim (1980) and McFee (1985). It must also be noted that Dickie (2003) acknowledges the circularity of the institutional theory, but denies that this circularity is vicious. It is not within the scope of this paper to engage in a full discussion of this issue, but I do contend that Dickie cannot completely avoid the problems raised by his critics.

8 *Pantsula*, a 'flat-footed tap-and-glide' style of African dancing, became a popular dance form in the 1980s in South African townships. The dance was a reflection of township culture at the time. Today, the *pantsula* and its accompanying music - *kwaito* - has moved out of the townships onto theatre stages. See Tomaselli (1991) for a more detailed discussion of this dance form.

9 The reason why I make this claim is that, with theorists like Davies (2003), I question whether it is *necessary* that the nature of art be determined by its historical unfolding. Weitz' family resemblance view seems to me preferable in this instance since it avoids this problem. This is not, however, to deny that there are no problems with the family resemblance view. See Nicholas Moutafakis (1975) for a discussion.

10 I purposefully use the term 'artistic' rather than 'aesthetic' since, as has been pointed

should be combined with an artistic expectation by some form of audience. This would mean that dancing beagles do not count as art, for example, since even though there might be an artistic expectation by an audience in some form, we can assume that the beagle has no artistic intent.

The importance of the role of the artist and his intentions is something that is strongly highlighted by Nietzsche, especially in the *Genealogy of Morality*. In his discussion of Kant, he points out that 'Kant, like all philosophers, just considered art and beauty from the position of "spectator", instead of viewing the aesthetic problem through the experiences of the artist (the creator), and thus inadvertently introduced the '"spectator" himself into the concept "beautiful"' (GM III: § 6). But Nietzsche has been accused of swinging too far over to the other side. As Heidegger notes in 'The Will to Power as Art', Nietzsche views art (only) through the eyes of creators and not spectators (Heidegger 1991, p.71). Is this correct? It is to some extent, but Nietzsche certainly does give more attention to the role of the audience than Heidegger allows. The most striking example is his rejection of the idea that the audience is (or should be) somehow disinterested in contemplating a work of art. Again, his ire is directed towards Kant: 'Kant said "Something is beautiful if it gives pleasure without interest." Without interest!' (GM III: § 6). As was alluded to in the previous section, for Nietzsche, art must be capable of profound effect: 'Art is the great stimulus to life: how could it be thought purposeless, aimless, *l'art pour l'art?*' (TI IX: § 24).

Using Nietzsche's attention to both creator and contemplator of art as a starting point, I propose that deciding whether a particular practice counts as art can be determined to the extent that both the artistic intention of the creator of the work, and the artistic expectation of the audience be present to some extent. On this definition then, dancing beagles do not count as art since the intention of the beagle is not to create something beautiful or striking even though some of us might think that the hopping about of a dog is aesthetically pleasing in some way. The lone dancer in the apartment would not be thinking that he is creating art, but merely be expressing his emotion through bodily movement, and of course, there would be no audience with any expectations about the movements performed.[11] But the

---

out by McFee (1992, pp.42-44), our appreciation for aesthetic objects, such as sunsets or mountains is distinct from our appreciation of works of art.

11 It could be argued that our lone dancer catches a glimpse of his movements in a mirror, and decides that his movements count as artistic. This would seem to imply that, on my proposal, the lone dancer's dance would not count as art since there is no expectant audience. However, as I argue elsewhere (Botha 2012), for dance performance to take place at all the dancer must 'be able to see and feel himself dancing (in both a metaphorical and literal sense) – to be his own perceiver, and the perceiver of his fellow dancers if there are any – whilst also being the actor – the executor of the movement and stillness of the dance'. As such, the lone dancer's efforts could still count as art under

choreographer who crafts a dance work can be said to have a specific intent – an artistic one, and the audience who observes that work could be said to have specific artistic expectations about that work.

So, on my view, we cannot uncritically say that dance is art, but only that certain forms of dance count as art, and the criterion I propose to use to decide whether a sequence of human bodily movements counts as art is the confluence between the intent of the creator of that sequence, and the expectations of the audience towards that artwork. My approach has certain advantages. Considering certain practices using this definition could, for example, make it easier to decide whether, say, stripping or gymnastics count as art, and it also provides us with a definition that is broad enough to allow for bad dance (art) to be acknowledged as such.

My proposed view does, however, raise a number of questions, of which I briefly mention and discuss only a selection here, all clustered around what I consider the most pressing problem – the provision of a clear explanation of what is meant by the terms artistic intent and artistic expectation. The first pole of my proposed way of determining whether certain dance forms count as art does show strong affinities to that of Monroe C. Beardsley (1982) and Berys Gaut (2000). Gaut proposes a list of properties which are jointly sufficient for being a work of art.[12] The tenth property in the proposed list is 'being the product of an intention to make a work of art' (Gaut, 2000) - the second pole of my proposal.[13] Similarly, Monroe C. Beardsley's definition of art is that artwork is: 'either an arrangement of conditions intended to be capable of affording an experience with marked aesthetic character or (incidentally) an arrangement belonging to a class or type of arrangements that is typically *intended* to have this capacity' (Beardsley 1982, p.299, emphasis mine). In my view, however, both Gaut and Beardsley do not

---

my proposal, since the dancer himself acts as both intentional executor and expectant perceiver of the artwork.

12 Gaut's list of properties are: that an artwork should (1) have positive aesthetic properties; (2) be expressive of emotion; (3) be intellectually challenging; (4) be formally complex as well as coherent; (5) be able to convey complex meanings; (6) show an individual point of view; (7) be original; (8) be the product of a high degree of skill; (9) belong to an established artistic form; and (10) be the product of an intention to make a work of art (Gaut 2000). For Gaut, none of the properties listed is a *necessary* condition for an artifact or performance to be called a work of art. Rather, the properties listed are only jointly sufficient for such a classification.

13 My proposal further has affinities with Gaut's view in its being an anti-essentialist position – I agree with Gaut that there is no *fixed* essence of art to be discovered. Anti-essentialism in aesthetics is often viewed as espousing a kind of relativism, but this is a misunderstanding of the anti-essentialist position. Being anti-essentialist means that my view can accommodate the idea that new forms of art, in this case, dance, are constantly possible, but does not, however, accommodate the claim that there are no necessary conditions of being a dance.

sufficiently develop their conceptions of intent, something that I believe is essential for my own proposal. I can only discuss selected aspects of this problem here, the first of which is the question of whether the maker can fail in his intent to make art, and how this affects the question of whether artistic intent and expectation are sufficient for art-making.[14] On my view, the creator of a dance can certainly fail in his intent to create a dance, but this would not have any effect on whether the dance work counts as art or not. Rather, that particular dance work may be regarded by its maker (as both intending creator and expectant perceiver), as well as its audience, as an example of bad art.

The second problem raised by my proposal is to consider how that intent is affected when the intent of the creator of a dance is explicitly to use dance to provide social or political commentary, or for some other purpose. It is important to point out that there can be a myriad of interwoven intentions involved in the creation of an artwork. Saying that dance works such as *Hoppla!* or *Bleeding Fairies* are works created specifically to question society's obsession with thin, ethereal female bodies, does not preclude the possibility that the intent of the choreographers is also artistic, for example. My point is that an artistic intention need not be the only intent with which a work is created, but for a dance to count as art, its creator needs to have some artistic intention with his creation.

The third related problem is how we can know what the intentions and expectations of dance creator and audience are, when intentions and expectations could be claimed to be seen as private desires that might not always be accessible. Both the second and third problems I have raised are closely related to the first. Although leaving these questions unanswered at this point leaves my proposal incomplete and imprecise, with further development, I believe that using such a definition of art can be a fruitful and meaningful way of deciding whether certain dance forms can be considered art.

Conclusion

The aim of this paper was to investigate the question of why and how we could characterize dance as art. I have shown that reading Nietzsche in a way different from the dominant interpretations allows for a more nuanced understanding of the role of dance in society than my reading of Badiou's claims regarding dance's status as non-art. I concluded that if we acknowledge Nietzsche's contention that dance is a metaphor for thinking, *and* supplement this with a reading that acknowledges the centrality of dance for the cultivation of the body-self, Badiou's classification of dance as

---

14 Thank you to an anonymous reviewer for pointing out this important question.

metaphor can in some respects be seen as incomplete.

Using Badiou's denial that dance is an art as impetus, I then proceeded to draw upon elements of Nietzsche's thinking in an attempt to develop another approach to the question of whether and how we can claim that certain dance counts as art. I proposed that for certain human bodily movements to count as art, the confluence between the intent of the creator of that sequence, and the expectations of the audience to that artwork are integral.

References

Agamben, Giorgio. *Potentialities: Collected Essays in Philosophy*, Stanford: Stanford University Press, 1999.

Badiou, Alain. 'Art and Philosophy' in trans. Jorge Jauregui, *lacanian ink* 17, Fall 2000, pp.48-67.

Badiou, Alain. *Ethics: An Essay on the Understanding of Evil*, London: Verso, 2002.

Badiou, Alain. *Infinite Thought: Truth and the Return to Philosophy*, London: Continuum, 2003.

Badiou, Alain. *Handbook of Inaesthetics*, trans. Alberto Toscano, Stanford: Stanford University Press, 2005.

Beardsley, Monroe C. *The Aesthetic Point of View*, Ithaca, New York: Cornell University Press, 1982.

Benson, Bruce Ellis. *Pious Nietzsche: Decadence and Dionysian faith*, Indiana Series in the Philosophy of Religion, Indiana: Indiana University Press, 2008.

Botha, Catherine F. 'En-visioning the Dance: the Audience as Mirror', unpublished conference paper, *Dance Through the Looking Glass*, An International Conference on the Philosophy of Dance and Moving Bodies, University of Ghent, 1-2 June 2012.

Conway, Daniel W. 'Nietzsche's Art of This-Worldly Comfort: Self-Reference and Strategic Self-Parody,' *History of Philosophy Quarterly*, 9:3 July 1992, pp.343–357.

Danto, Arthur. *The Transfiguration of the Commonplace*, Cambridge: Harvard University Press, 1981.

Davies, David. *Art as Performance*, Oxford: Blackwell, 2003.

DeFrantz, Thomas. 'The Black Beat Made Visible: Hip Hop Dance and Body Power' in Lepecki, Andre (ed.), *On the Presence of the Body: Essays on Dance and Performance Theory*, Connecticut: Wesleyan University Press, 2004.

Derrida, Jacques. *Writing and Difference*, trans. Alan Basset, London: Routledge, 1978.

Dickie, George. *The Art Circle*, New York: Haven, 1984.

Dickie, George. 'The New Institutional Theory of Art' in Lamarque, Peter and Stein Haugom Olsen (eds.), *Aesthetics and the Philosophy of Art – The Analytic Tradition*, Oxford: Blackwell, 2003, pp.47-54.

Dumond, Val. *The Elements of Nonsexist Usage: A Guide to Inclusive Spoken and Written English*, New York: Prentice Hall, 1990.

Gaut, Berys, 'The Cluster Account of Art,' in Carroll, Noel, (ed.), *Theories of Art Today*, Madison: University of Wisconsin Press, 2000, pp.25-45.

Goodman, Nelson, *Languages of Art: An Approach to a Theory of Symbols*, Indianapolis: The Bobbs-Merrill Company, 1968.

Hallward, Peter. *Think Again: Alain Badiou and the Future of Philosophy*, London: Continuum, 2005.

Heidegger, Martin. *Nietzsche Volume 1: The Will to Power as Art*, trans. David Farrell Krell, San Francisco: Harper Collins, 1991.

Hussain, Nadeem J. Z. 'Honest Illusion: Valuing for Nietzsche's Free Spirits' in Leiter, Brian, and Neil Sinhababu *Nietzsche and Morality*, Oxford: Clarendon Press, 2007, pp.157-191.

Hutter, Horst. *Shaping the Future: Nietzsche's new regime of the soul and its ascetic practices*, Lexington Books, 2006.

Kemal, Salim, Ivan Gaskell and Daniel W. Conway. *Nietzsche, Philosophy and the Arts*, Cambridge Studies in Philosophy and the Arts. Cambridge: Cambridge University Press, 2002.

Kofman, Sarah. *Nietzsche and Metaphor*, Large, Duncan (ed. and trans.), London: Athlone Press, 1993.

LaMothe, Kimerer L. *Nietzsche's Dancers: Isadora Duncan, Martha Graham, and the Revaluation of Christian Values*, New York: Palgrave MacMillan, 2011.

Levinson, Jerrold. *Music, Art, and Metaphysics*, Ithaca: Cornell University Press, 1990.

Moutafakis, Nicholas J. 'Of Family Resemblances and Aesthetic Discourse,' *Philosophical Forum*, 7:1, 1975, pp. 71-89.

Nehamas, Alexander. *Nietzsche: Life as Literature*, Harvard: Harvard University Press, 1985.

Nietzsche, Friedrich. *Beyond Good and Evil: Prelude to a Philosophy of the Future*, trans. Walter Kaufmann, New York: Vintage, 1966.

Nietzsche, Friedrich. *The Will to Power*, trans. Kaufmann, Walter and Richard J. Hollingdale, New York: Vintage, 1968.

Nietzsche, Friedrich. *The Gay Science*, trans. Walter Kaufmann, New York: Vintage, 1974.

Nietzsche, Friedrich. *Human, All Too Human: A Book for Free Spirits*, trans. Richard J. Hollingdale, Cambridge: Cambridge University Press, 1996.

Nietzsche, Friedrich. *Sämtliche Werke: Kritische Studienausgabe in 15 Bänden*. Colli, Giorgio and Mazzino Montinari (eds.), Berlin: De Gruyter, 1999.

Nietzsche, Friedrich. *The Birth of Tragedy and Other Writings*, Geuss, Raymond and Ronald Speirs (eds.), Cambridge: Cambridge University Press, 1996.

Nietzsche, Friedrich. *The Anti-Christ, Ecce Homo, Twilight of the Idols and Other Writings*, Ridley, Aaron and Judith Norman (eds.), Cambridge: Cambridge University Press, 2005.

Nietzsche, Friedrich. *Thus Spoke Zarathustra: A Book for All and None*, del Caro, Adrian and Robert Pippin (eds.), Cambridge: Cambridge University Press, 1996.

Nietzsche, Friedrich. *On the Genealogy of Morality*, Ansell-Pearson, Keith (ed.), trans. Carol Diethe, Cambridge: Cambridge University Press, 2007.

Rancière, Jacques. 'Aesthetics, Inaesthetics, Anti-Aesthetics', in Hallward, Peter (ed.), *Think Again: Alain Badiou and the Future of Philosophy*. London: Continuum, 2004.

Shusterman, Richard 'Somaesthetics: A Disciplinary Proposal' *The Journal of Aesthetics and Art Criticism*, 57:3. Summer, 1999, pp.299-313.

Shusterman, Richard 'Somaesthetics and the Revival of Aesthetics' *Filozofski Vestnik*, 28:2, 2007, pp.135–149.

Tomaselli, Keyan. 'Popular Communication in South Africa: 'Mapantsula' and its Context of Struggle', *South African Theatre Journal*, 5:1, 1991, pp.46-60.

Weitz, Morris. 'The Role of Theory in Aesthetics,' *Journal of Aesthetics and Art Criticism*, 1956, 15, pp.27-35.

Wollheim, Richard. 'The Institutional Theory of Art,' Supplementary Essay 1, in Richard Wollheim *Art and Other Objects*, Cambridge: Cambridge University Press, 1980, pp.157-166.

Yanal, Robert J. *Institutions of Art: Reconsiderations of George Dickie's Philosophy*, Pennsylvania: Penn State Press, 1994.

Young, Julian. 'Nietzsche, Friedrich (Wilhelm)' in Davies, Stephen, Kathleen Marie Higgins and Robert Hopkins (eds.), *A Companion to Aesthetics* Blackwell Companions to Philosophy, 2nd edition, John Wiley and Sons, 2009.

12. Dance and the historical imagination

Larraine Nicholas

Introduction

Thinking historically about dance as a performing art takes place in the present tense reflecting on a disappeared past. It entails complex considerations. Not only are there broader contexts of political, social and artistic environment with all their specifics of time and location to take into account, but also dancing bodies and watching bodies that were real people with all their physiological and psychological specificities. Then there is also the thing being danced (dance work, class), an event with its own motives and aesthetic features. Dance history raises this specific problem that evidence of its essential activities (the making and performing of movement as cultural product) is missing in its original form and often we lack moving image primary source material. So the historian of dance is often required imaginatively to explore a terrain that has few solid landmarks. Unravelling the claims to knowledge embedded in historical communications, whether in printed, oral or danced form is not the issue here. Rather, I want to take a step backwards to examine some aspects of historical thought. As historians we have recourse to various strategies. We investigate all the sources with rigour; we attempt to mediate between conflicting pictures of what happened, conscious of the theoretical frameworks that focus different interpretations. Is this enough? Should we know more about what processes underpin historical thought? Here I aim to explore only one of these: that faculty of mind called imagination.

The case study

I am in an archive and start through a collection of letters between dancers whose working relationship appears to be breaking down. The letters allude to conversations and arguments, sometimes obliquely. They discuss institutional arrangements in present circumstances; personal competence to carry out tasks; this or that person's domineering character. My protagonists visit each other to discuss matters although they seem now to have been dispersed far apart in localities other than London; references to these conversations condense and perhaps misrepresent what was said. As I read, mental images course through my head. I see their faces and try to judge their states of mind. Do they sit down at the table with some tea, I wonder, or do the hot words come too soon for that? I try to hear their voices and see their body language. My research objective is to explain the basis of the disagreement.

This is a three-sided letter exchange. Leslie Burrowes (formerly a student of Mary Wigman) and Louise Soelberg (formerly with Ballets Jooss) have been colleagues in The Dance Centre, in London, a joint organization for the promotion of modern dance. The third, Diana Jordan, was trained as a physical education teacher, working now in dance in educational settings; she has been a student of Burrowes and performed with the Dance Centre Group. Now it is England, 1940, so they have pressures that are not just about their artistic visions but also about the Blitz and danger of invasion.[1] Burrowes has moved away from London and feels suspicious of what Soelberg wants – an alliance with the Ling Physical Education Association towards furtherance of modern dance in education, specifically working jointly with *émigré* dance artists Rudolf Laban and Lisa Ullmann as colleagues. Apart from the variables of political and social circumstances, I know I will need to consider aesthetic and cultural differences since these personalities have individual perspectives on their German modern dance training.[2]

What is happening as I read these letters? Certainly I am subject to a whole series of mental images which come about quite spontaneously, without effort on my part. First there are the aspects of my characters that I know already. When I read Burrowes' letters I see in my mind's eye her face, her hair and her slim, toned body so it appears that mental imagery is arising from my memory of photographic source material.[3] I know Soelberg and Jordan less well, but their faces easily come to me by the same route. But memory is not the only source of these images. Although I do not know where these conversations take place and where my subjects write their letters, in my efforts to think about their values and motivations, images of locations occur spontaneously, fuzzy though they are. It seems that my imagination really takes flight into fiction sometimes.

Up to a point, then, mental images occur as a natural and unbidden aspect of my research process. Some of these images are based upon memory, integrating previously known source material into the current ones. Others have no basis in a reality I know of, remaining pure possibilities and often floating freely without any effort on my part.

Visualization ('seeing in the mind's eye') is not the only aspect of mental imagery, although sometimes the easiest to pinpoint. In the case of this

---

1 For details of this case study see Nicholas (2010a).

2 Laban represents the inaugural generation of German modern dance, with Ullmann as his student, originally in Germany now in Britain. Laban's students, Wigman and Jooss, had developed their own unique styles. As students of Wigman and Jooss, Soelberg, Burrowes and Jordan were removed two generations from the Laban source.

3 See Nicholas (2010b). The Leslie Burrowes Collection at The National Resource Centre for Dance (University of Surrey) includes books, albums, photographs, programmes, letters and other documents relating to Burrowes' career.

research, I struggle to 'hear' voices, and can only manage an approximation based on my knowledge of the backgrounds of the dancers I research. Whether and why I should try this is another matter. Is it really germane to the issues at hand? Perhaps not, but I do feel the need to immerse myself in my subjects. I do not have any moving picture evidence but there are photographs which I return to in memory and search for any hint of what is not in print, trying to make images of their moving bodies. To question aesthetic differences I can push that thought stream further by considering how it might feel to dance like this; to attempt quasi-kinaesthetic imagery of the feeling in executing one of Burrowes' famous leaps or backbends, or quasi-tactile mental images of the sensation, touching the fabric of a costume.

I have referred to spontaneous quasi-sensory images, some from memory, but others unrelated to any factual evidence, and also to more effortful and controlled imaginings as I reach for understanding. I define these as images of imagination, forming in the absence of immediate perception. There are features that distinguish these mental objects from ordinary sensory perceptions: their tendency to be variable in quality, discontinuous in time and space (a filmic quality), incomplete in a way that cannot be improved by changing physical adjustments, and not open to external verification (Casey 2000, pp.146-173).

In many ways the very label of 'image' is unhelpful, seeming to privilege the visual and static, but mental imagery as it is conceived in philosophical and scientific disciplines can exist in any sensory modality – if there is a 'mind's eye', there is also a 'mind's ear', etc. To take a neurobiologist's definition, images are 'mental patterns with a structure built with the tokens of each of the sensory modalities – visual, auditory, olfactory, gustatory, and somatosensory' (Damasio 2000, p.318). Such a definition appears to make no distinction between immediate perception and imaginary sensations but is useful as scientific confirmation of the presence of multi-sensory imagery. I acknowledge the heated controversy in the field of mental imagery research which questions whether these really are instances of object-like representation in the mind or a kind of description in a language ('mentalese') known only to the mind. I skirt these debates in order to focus on the experience of imagery and imagination from the perspective of a historical researcher. [4]

In my thought experiments, I have noticed some processes that occur during historical enquiry, lurking beneath the surface of what we normally claim to do in the methodology of dance history. Of course academic rigour and empirical data must guide us but surely something else is at work? While neuroscience works to verify and locate the presence of mental imagery,

---

4 For a survey of these debates see Thomas (2011).

it remains a problem for philosophy to consider how these phenomena relate to meaning, thought and knowledge. What is the connection between mental imagery and the extremely fluid term 'imagination'? Does spontaneous mental imagery have any part to play in what must in the end be a scholarly investigation? What is the status of my intentional imaging, when I seemingly test the ground for probability?

The notion of an 'historical imagination' can be found in the work of philosopher-historian R.G. Collingwood. Such a concept is often mentioned but has resisted a deep interrogation in the meta-disciplines of history let alone in dance history. The terminology as used in history suffers from the same problematic that affects any philosophical discussion of imagination. The creative and uninhibited connotations of the term clash with the rational and cognitive. Hayden White's influential *Metahistory: the historical imagination in nineteenth century Europe* (1973) focuses on analysis of the meaning-making of literary tropes in historical writing and is thus different from the methodological concept of historical imagination I am pursuing in this essay. In an encyclopaedic volume, Alun Munslow (2000, pp.124-129) defines historical imagination as 'the application of the general capacity of the human mind for comparison, connection, analogy and difference to the study of the past and its sources', which sounds like the beginning of a methodological argument, yet he follows White in emphasising the imaginal nature of the metaphorical form of explanation in history writing. The continuously updated textbook, *The Pursuit of History* by John Tosh (2009) gives equal weight to the need to get an imaginative insight into the sources for what they can reveal about the past and for finding a fluent, accessible literary form. What this actually means in terms of an historical imagination working at the moment of historical research is not spelled out.

Imagination

What is imagination? In 1990, Francis Sparshott summarized twelve different meanings of imagination and did so in a form that tried to suggest the fluid, unregulated way in which imagination often takes hold of our thoughts, as is suggested in my own thought experiments. The sheer range of meanings shows what a problematic terminology this is, ranging across a spectrum from normal comprehension of perceptions to acts of creativity or innovation; from projections of desire or innocent day-dreams to culpable misrepresentations of events or mistaken suppositions. Sparshott refers to usages of the word 'imagination' as a 'radical heterogeneity' but claims that there are some linkages across them. The broadest of these is that imagination stands for the ability to conceive of alternative worlds, 'interestingly different from our own but also interestingly accessible from it' (1990, p.7). In these terms, imagination is seen as reaching out into an unknown that can be the once existing past as well as worlds of pure fantasy.

There are a number of distinctions within the Sparshott list. Mistakes, delusions, false suppositions and optical illusions are not part of my investigation since they refer to a mistake in interpretation of current reality that can be corrected. Another major division is that between the usages that refer to creativity, specifically in the arts, and those that link mental imagery and hence 'imagination' to everyday cognition. The latter has a long tradition going back at least to the seventeenth century, in which the nature of ideas was often considered by philosophers such as Descartes, Hobbes, Hume and Kant, in terms of images residing in the mind as the result of perceptions of the world, hence 'imagination' acquired these connotations.[5] Nearer our own time, Mary Warnock (1980) wove together threads from this tradition, particularly those of Hume and Kant, with different notions of imagination from the nineteenth and twentieth century, including those of Romantic poets and phenomenology. She made connections between the cognitive and creative functions of imagination; between perception, thought, absent things and creative expression:

> there is a power in the human mind which is at work in our everyday perception of the world, and is also at work in our thoughts about what is absent; which enables us to see the world, whether present or absent as significant, and also to present this vision to others, for them to share or reject. (Warnock 1980, p.196)

Between them, Sparshott and Warnock condense centuries of thought on imagination and highlight the complexities of the cluster of meanings while drawing out an important idea to be pursued in the highly specialized field of historical imagination: images and imagination have an important part to play in the way we interpret the world, even the absent one of the past.

Collingwood and *The Historical Imagination*

The historical imagination's best known delineation is in a lecture (it was his inaugural as Waynflete Professor of Metaphysical Philosophy at Oxford University) by the philosopher-historian R.G. (Robin) Collingwood (1935) published posthumously in *The Idea of History* (1946, ed. Knox).[6] Between

---

5 See section 2.3, 'Images as Ideas in Modern Philosophy' in Thomas (2011).

6 There have been a number of posthumous publications of Collingwood's writings. *The Idea of History* (ed. Knox 1946) was a compilation of published and unpublished essays, lectures (including the Waynflete Lecture), and fragments towards Collingwood's uncompleted major work, *The Principles of History*. The second, revised edition (ed. Van der Dussen, 1993) appends Lectures 1926 – 1928, including 'Outlines of a Philosophy of History'. Depositions of manuscripts at the Bodleian Library have brought more to light including notes on the Waynflete Lecture that expand on some of its ideas and more

that and his death Collingwood (1889–1943) published *The Principles of Art* (1938), in which theories of imagination in relation to art were developed. It will be seen that there are connections to be made between his concepts of aesthetic and historical forms of imagination.

The Waynflete Lecture's premise is that historical thought, in its most important details, is quite different to the kind of thought that is about an object of direct perception, since historians must think about people and events that are not available to the senses in the present (Collingwood 1993, p.233). In this sense, historical thought is 'imaginary'. Collingwood critiques what he calls the 'common-sense' theory of history, which assumes that historical thought is about an already existing truth out there to be discovered through the evidence of the so-called 'authorities' (i.e. the remaining traces, that are close enough to the past event to represent some supposed special knowledge). If that theory were valid it would be constantly under attack from the practising historian's need to select and interpret information.[7] Far from this 'common-sense' theory, the historian is autonomous, 'his [*sic*] own authority' (1993, p.236). In order to write a coherent account there must be selection, interpolation (historical construction by joining up isolated evidence), and above all criticism of the sources (pp.236-7). It is the exclusive province of the historian (of appropriate qualifications) to validate the 'authorities', to accept them as evidence, *or not*, based upon the criterion of historical truth 'by reference to which the authorities themselves are judged' (p.240). This critical criterion of truth has a specific meaning to Collingwood's analysis of historical knowledge as discussed later.

Enlarging on interpolation, Collingwood takes as examples fragments of information that need to be bridged by what is implied from isolated pieces of evidence (naturally evidence the historian is happy to consider valid). This is the first time imagination is invoked in this published lecture. '[W]hat in this way is inferred is essentially something imagined.' He insists that this is not the same as the 'ornamental' imagination that makes for an engaging and interesting historical text, but indicates the kind of imagination that structures historical thought.

> The historian's picture of his subject, whether that subject be a sequence of events or a past state of things, thus appears as a web of imaginative construction stretched between certain fixed points provided by the state-ments of his authorities; and if these points are frequent enough and the

---

sections of *The Principles of History*. Rough Notes to the Waynflete Lecture were published in 1999 together with the surviving sections of *The Principles of History* as *The Principles of History and other writings on the philosophy of history* (edited by W.H. Dray and J. Van der Dussen).

7 This comes as no surprise to the twenty-first century historian, but it is highly probable that this 'common sense' views still persists in the general population.

threads spun from each to the next are constructed with due care, always by the *a priori* imagination and never by merely arbitrary fancy, the whole picture is constantly verified by appeal to these data, and runs little risk of losing touch with the reality which it represents. (Collingwood 1993, p.242)

This is not as complacent a belief as it might appear. He is not suggesting that primary sources are transparent evidence of what really happened: this has already been denied (pp.235, 245). Instead the historian is critically interrogating the sources (p.237) so that these seemingly fixed points of data in the web are constantly having their worth and meaning reassessed. In Collingwood's description, this web seems to have both the steely strength attributed to spiders' webs, and their potential to be broken up and remade in another coherent form. In this first aspect of his theory of historical imagination, the historian's task is critical and constructive, founded upon knowledge and judgment, therefore not fanciful but expanding rationally on what might be known from the traces.

The above quotation might also prove confusing. How can this bridging of evidential gaps be *a priori* since it appears to be dealing with empirical data? It might appear that this aspect of historical imagination is simply inference from sources, dependent on empirical experience and perception, therefore not *a priori*. However, Collingwood argues, perception deals with the here and now while history deals with the past, 'something which never can be a this, because it is never a here and now' (1993, p.233). The traces, available to ordinary perception, do not become historical until worked upon by the imagination of the historian. Fixed points of data can only be arrived at through constructive and critical thinking and there is never the final conclusion on a particular historical problem that will last for all time. (p.243).

Now he returns to what he calls 'the criterion of historical truth'.

That criterion is the idea of history itself: the idea of an imaginary picture of the past. That idea is, in Cartesian language, innate; in Kantian language, *a priori*. It is not a chance product of psychological causes; it is an idea which every man possesses as part of the furniture of his mind, and discovers himself to possess in so far as he becomes conscious of what it is to have a mind.(Collingwood 1993, p.248)

This claim has been called 'astonishing' and 'obscure' (Dray 1995, p.200) and certainly seems to be both rhapsodic and vague. The key terms ('idea', 'imaginary picture' and 'mind') all declare Collingwood's commitment to history being defined as a specific kind of thought. Elsewhere he writes about 'The Ideality of History', meaning that history is 'an object of thought without actually existing.' The 'truth' of this thought cannot be arrived at by recourse to perception or by recourse to a universal truth (Collingwood 1993, p.440). It is another thing with its own rules. He knows very well that any truth claims by the historian are subject to change and rethinking by other historians. What endures is the truth of the methodology, the true guidance of the critical-constructive historical imagination. What is more, he hints at another sense of history's *a priori* nature: that it is founded on a sense of temporality that is a necessary condition of humanity.

Collingwood also identifies two other 'functions' of *a priori* imagination, 'pure or free' imagination exemplified in the creative work of an artist, and 'perceptual imagination' referring to the ability to imagine what we cannot actually perceive, but what we know of as objects of *possible* perception (insides of closed boxes etc.) (1993, p.242). This is also implicated in the act of decoding text, where the reader sees through the symbols to an underlying meaning (Hughes-Warrington 2003, pp.144-5). But the historian's *a priori* imagination is different to these because there is no possible object of perception.

In relation to the original problems posed by my thought experiments, Collingwood's analysis of historical imagination seems to be only one step on the rung of explanation. While he confirms a belief in historical thought as a kind of imagination that is removed from direct perception, but rational, constructive and critical, there is no phenomenological account of the process that might explain the quasi-sensory imaging of my experience.

Marnie Hughes-Warrington suggests that Collingwood viewed imagination as instantiated in a 'scale of forms', each one in the scale, from bottom to top, characterized by a greater application of cognition (2003, pp.135-154). His notion of the scale of forms, something adapted from Aristotle's *De Anima*, is set out in his *Essay on Philosophical Method* (1933) in which he aimed to show how philosophical distinctions could be made between overlapping concepts. In this dialectical methodology 'each term in the scale renders explicit what for the previous term was only implicit.' (editors' notes, Collingwood 2005, p.xxv). In the *Essay*, he uses this method to differentiate between different forms of philosophy. 'If the concept of philosophy is a philosophical concept, different groups of philosophical topics will not only overlap, they will be philosophical in different ways and also to varying degrees' (Collingwood 2005, p.189), advancing towards a fuller realization of the central concept. Hughes-Warrington argues that the central concept in Collingwood's scale of the forms of imagination is the advancing degree of intellectual control that characterizes the change of form. Although not stated explicitly by him, the Rough Notes for the lecture suggest that he was thinking of historical imagination in terms of a scale of forms (Hughes-Warrington 2003, p.149). Thus, for Hughes-Warrington, at the bottom of the scale is 'imaging', to which I must return later. Next comes the 'pure' or 'free' imagination as used by artists in its most advanced form. In a romantic vein, Collingwood views artistic creativity as potentially difficult to control (p.136). Then comes the perceptual imagination, referring to the ability to imagine what we cannot actually perceive, but what we know of as objects of possible perception (insides, backs etc.) and allowing us to believe in the continual existence of objects, even though we are not constantly observing them (the ship that we observe at different points in its journey, Collingwood 1993, p.241). At the top of the scale of forms is the historical imagination, characterized by the most complete intellectual control. He refers to it as a 'self-dependent, self-determining, and self-justifying form of thought' (p.249)

This scale within imagination does not imply a movement up from poorer to best, but that the lower ones in the scale are contained within the higher, moving towards a more profound application of judgment (Hughes-Warrington 2003, p.149). All of these separate sub-concepts within imagination can be part of the historical imagination: the fuzzy and transitory images; the free imagination that may suggest new formats and language to communicate historical research and offer possibilities that might conform to my evidence; the perceptual imagination that obliges me to understand the continuity of my object of research between the points at which it can be viewed in my data; and the fulfillment of the historical imagination in the critical-constructive historical imagination guided by the *a priori* 'idea of history'.

Alongside his theory of historical imagination, Collingwood is known for the controversial concept of re-enactment. That there is no present object of the historical past is made explicit in the theory of historical imagination that I have just outlined. Yet, anterior to this is the notion that there must be something of the past available in some way to the work of the critical-constructive historian. The theory of re-enactment takes this further by stating that history is the re-enactment of past thought. Collingwood argues the possibility of this on the basis that the nature of thought is something autonomous from individual instantiations in the minds of different people (1993, pp.282-302). Thus, to entertain a reconstruction, or in Collingwood's terms, 're-enactment' of past thought, is to rehearse the *same* thought. 'Yet if I not only read his argument but understand it, follow it in my own mind by re-arguing it with and for myself, the process of argument which I go through is not a process resembling Plato's, it is actually Plato's so far as I understand him rightly' (p.301).

Re-enactment is one aspect of the critical-constructive historical imagination and should be seen in relation to his notion of the ideality of history, rather than recommending an empathic relationship with the historical subject. In his use of the verbal phrase 'so far as I understand him rightly' in the above quotation, he makes it clear that it is the process of properly informed thinking that is valued. There is always the possibility that the historian does not understand and always a gulf between past and present that defies connection.

To further unpick the scale as suggested by Hughes-Warrington really demands more interrogation of what is actually implied by 'imaging' as the first step towards the fully autonomous historical imagination. There does seem to be a tension within the scale between the sensuous nature of imaging and the higher order of intellectual activity as in the historical imagination which Collingwood does not tease out. He comes nearer to discussing imaging in *The Principles of Art* where he equates imaging with raw sensory-emotional input (Collingwood 1958, pp.190-2). He is concerned to show the connection between imaging (sensation or mental imagery) in its raw form, and intellect: 'it is not sensa as such that provide the data for intellect, it is sensa transformed into ideas of imagination by the work of consciousness' (p.215). This is achieved through giving attention (an aspect of consciousness) to sensations, in order to select and achieve control over them. Thus they become imagination, a kind of thought, but not a very discriminating one. 'The conceptions of past, future, the possible, the hypothetical, are as meaningless for imagination as they are for feeling itself. They are conceptions which appear only with a further development of thought' (p.224). This development he calls the intellect, which is able to consider deeply the relationships between things (p.216). This is clearly where the rational, critical and constructive historical imagination is situated.

Collingwood's historical imagination has a 'family resemblance' to the other forms of imagination identified by Sparshott and Warnock. The historical imagination is a kind of thought dealing with a wholly absent thing (the past) and is thus in Collingwood's own word, 'imaginary'. It happens as the result of the accumulation of transformations by the imagination, converting raw sense data or mental imagery into thought, thus an intermediary between perception and cognition and the work of the intellect. It takes information from imaging, 'free' and perceptual imaginations but does not depend totally on them.

Some answers and some questions

In my originally described thought experiments I identified a major historical question related to the research I was undertaking, that is, to explain the basis of the disagreement between the dancers whose letters I was reading. I then also asked some questions about the mental imagery I experienced and whether there was a legitimate methodology in my imaginative experience. I asked if there was anything historically significant in the spontaneous images in my head; whether it was important to push these further to make more difficult imaginings, or whether it was sheer indulgence, a distraction from making rational judgments based on source material. Collingwood's position on historical imagination has answered some of these questions. I am satisfied that what he describes as historical imagination is an intellectual activity by which the historian constructs an historical account through criticism of sources, intelligent interpolation and selection. This is what he describes as constructive history. I am less sure though, about how my spontaneous and more contrived mental imagery activity fits into his account. His own clearest examples of mental imagery are concerned with perceptual imagination, such as imaging the grass hidden by the mullion of the window or the inside of a matchbox (Collingwood 1958, pp.172, 192); or, they illustrate imaginative interpolation between fixed points of data, as with Caesar's journey from Rome to Gaul (Collingwood 1993, p.240). However, in neither case is there much to account for the way that imaging is really integrated into the constructive historical imagination.

His explanation of the theory of historical re-enactment clearly derives from his practice as philosopher and historian of Roman Britain in which the motivations behind his protagonists' actions were an important thread to follow through the method of re-enactment of their thought. I see that re-enacting the thoughts of the letter-writers in my own historical research is a valid method and one that comes to me spontaneously. Is it also a theory that can be broadened to take in the virtual or actual reconstruction of dance? Reconstruction is a word Collingwood sometimes uses as an alternative to re-enactment. It is true that Collingwood's dependence on the language of mind and thought suggests that he discounts the notion of a thinking body, but I believe that in this he is only typical of his time in the language he uses. Elsewhere he agrees that, 'The language of total bodily gesture is ...the motor side of our total imaginative experience' (1958, p.247). In relation to my research questions, I can see that the virtual reconstruction of movement through quasi-sensory imaging is a valid device to attempt understanding of the aesthetic processes of my historical subjects, given that, in Collingwood's words this can only be 'so far as I understand [them] rightly.' Interestingly, an analogy Collingwood uses for re-enactment/reconstruction of past thought is in relation to the history of music. In order to understand the music of the past, it must be performed in the present and he does not rule out that the performance may be in imagination (1993, p.441). Since he takes music to be equivalent to thought, we can assume that dance is also.

There remains the problem of the place of mental imagery in the concept of historical imagination. Does the mental imagery of pictures, feelings, smells, sounds, and muscle sensations have any role in producing the rigorous historical account that must come from my research?

Collingwood downgrades imaging and it seems to be minimally present in his conceptualization of the constructive historical imagination. So I seek another account that offers more support for my experience of imagining during historical research.

Integrating imaging into imagination

Phenomenologist Edward Casey posits three potential streams of imagination, side by side, crossing over or nesting inside each other: imaging, *imagining that* and *imagining how*. Imaging is the quasi-sensory mind's eye, ear etc. that is familiar already. Note that Casey conceives of this as relatively simple in the object of its imagining and always in the sensory mode. *Imagining that* brings to mind a state of affairs that could possibly exist or could conceivably have been the case. It implies a state of knowing things to be related in a particular way that is not necessarily accompanied by mental imagery, but may be so. This is interesting, recalling the philosophical debate over whether imagination is more 'language-like' than 'image like'. *Imagining how* has similarities to *imagining that* but turns the thoughts inwards: How would it feel if this was the case? It enables a first person quasi-observational sensation or a first person quasi-participant sensation from inside the situation (Casey 2000, pp.41-48).

Working with these concepts in terms of my research case study raises some interesting issues. I could be *imagining that* the three letter writers of my research intend to have a meeting. It would be unlikely that I could represent this idea in a quasi-sensory image, not only because I cannot mentally represent their thoughts and I cannot visualize them because the decision, if taken, would happen in different locations and perhaps not simultaneously. This is likely to be an example of non-sensory *imagining that*, but at the same time I could be imaging Leslie writing a letter or orally confirming her decision. The two modes of imagination entwine and support each other. In another example I could be *imagining that* Leslie, Louise and Diana are having a rehearsal. This is a state of affairs that could present itself to me as a multi-sensory *imagining that*, visualized and audialized, within which particular instances of imaging might momentarily occupy my imaginary field, the image of Louise's face, for example. Casey's phenomenology allows for imaging and other forms of imaginative knowing to exist in the same imaginary event. This is a satisfactory adjustment to Collingwood's hierarchical scale of forms and more faithfully represents my own experience.

But I find there is a problem in relating this process to instances of imagining in the critical-constructive historical imagination as Collingwood describes its constraint by the evidence. My solution is to adjust Casey's term so that *imagining that* must always be relative to the historical traces.

For example, on the basis of the evidence of letter *x* and press cutting *y*, I can *historically imagine that* a state of affairs existed. I am not permitted to *historically imagine that* all three intend to have a meeting unless there is evidence to suggest it. I *am* permitted to do so for a state of affairs for which I have historical evidence, for example that all three are having a rehearsal.

The qualitative aspect of *imagining how* in historical terms is quite different to *imagining that*. It allows for a personal imaginative insertion of imaginer into the historical state of affairs in order to imagine, for example, *how* a situation feels to a participant or *how* a series of actions is performed. Casey notes that this kind of imagination is distinctive from *imagining that*, in the way that it allows a series of events to unfold. With the aid of ephemera I can *historically imagine how* a dance performance unfolds over time. The succession of individual pieces, the specific performers, the titles and the musical accompaniments can all tell me something about the event. Again this kind of imagining can be sensory or non-sensory. Notice how all three forms of imagination blend together. I may set up the state of affairs by *historically imagining that* the Dance Centre Group is giving a performance of this program on a specific date. As I imagine the programme, images of costumes, photographs and suggested movements come spontaneously, *imagining how* the event might appear to its spectators. This kind of imagining with its multi-sensory dimensions '*how* it is to do, feel, think, move, etc. in a certain manner' seems very useful in dance history (Casey 2000, p.45).

For Casey the most sincere form of imagination deals in 'pure possibility', that is undertaken as imagining for its own sake with no aim or goal. On the other hand my historical imagination should be constrained by the demands of historical evidence, conforming more to 'hypothetical possibility', where possibilities are being tested for fitting a set of circumstances.[8] I say 'should' but as previously shown, imagining does stray into playing with pure possibility, imaging things I cannot know, attempting to encounter my subjects more closely even though fictionally. *Imagining how* sometimes seems like this. Is this pure fancy or could it serve some historical function?

Can I really experience how it would feel to be one of the dancers whose careers were blocked by the political situation of 1940 or how it would feel to be the possessor of that particular body of dance knowledge? The issue of presumed empathy has been high on the agenda of false historical thought for deconstructionist historians for decades (Jenkins 1991, pp.39-47). Access to other minds is impossible. Yet imagining other minds remains an absolute essential of human conduct. Based upon her historical analysis of imagination, Mary Warnock describes 'a strong philosophical tradition which gives to imagination the task of allowing access not only to the

---

8 For Casey on pure and hypothetical possibility see 2000, pp.113-119. However he does seem to admit that these two varieties often merge into each other.

natural, external world as a whole, but also to the thoughts and feelings of other people' (1994, p.21). Those characteristics of imagination already noticed, the connection with a world of absent things including the past and other minds, gives to imagination the faculty of sympathy which requires us to attempt an understanding of another's feelings rather than replicate them as in empathy. Sympathy is a much more achievable goal.

In my final point I return to one of my original questions. Is it an indulgence to imagine during historical research? Attempts to be guided by the constraints of historical imagination are often subverted by spontaneous imaging and *imagining how*. There seems to be a real need to broaden out the picture of the past, to make a human contact that sometimes escapes the rational historical construction. Imagination seems to have an inner direction towards a fuller picture of these people, to hear their voices and see and feel their dances. Does this have any purpose even though pure imagination sometimes escapes into places that historical imagination cannot follow? I say that it does. Imagination has an affective quality of pleasure that can become addictive. Immersion in the lives of historical subjects through imagination provides a vivid sense of their existences that hopefully can be transferred to enthusiasm in historical communication. We owe it to our historical subjects not to remain aloof from them. In a way this pleasure seems to be justified payment for the work we do to bring the past to current knowledge.

Conclusion

Casey's phenomenological account of imagination supplements Collingwood's analytical system. Collingwood's theory of historical imagination describes the autonomous historian working with sources through selection, interpolation and criticism, offering plausible access to the world of ideas from the past. Yet in his belief in the power of the intellect, he downgrades the more pleasurable and vivid aspects of imagery. Casey reverses some of this. Imagining for him is a combination of quasi-sensory and non-sensory ideas that twine together in the flow of thought. It can easily be seen how this informs my own imaging during research. Casey favours the free flow of pure possibility, while Collingwood makes the case for cognitive controllability. So if we can combine both theorists, imagination has this double aspect of controllability and free flow that I experience.

Mental imagery can arrive in any of the sensory modalities including the kinaesthetic kind which can be so powerful in dance history. Thinking about dances from the past can be a way of attempting to access the thought of the past as a re-enactment that must surely involve mental imagery. History is a construction that takes place in the imagination of the historian, constrained by evidence but nevertheless imaginary. This being so, it matters very much that we continue to ask the question: What are we doing when we think historically about dance?

References

Casey, Edward. 'Imagination: Imagining and the Image,' *Philosophy and Phenomenological Research*, 31:4, 1971, pp.475-490.

Casey, Edward. *Imagining: A Phenomenological Study*. 2nd edition, Bloomington and Indianapolis: Indiana University Press, 2000.

Collingwood, R.G. *The Principles of Art*, Oxford: Oxford University Press, 1958.

Collingwood, R.G. *The Idea of History, revised edition, with Lectures 1926-1928*, Dussen, Jan van der, (ed.), Oxford: Oxford University Press, 1993.

Collingwood, R. G. *An Essay on Philosophical Method, new edition*, Connelly, James and Giuseppina D'Oro, (eds.), Oxford: Clarendon Press, 2005.

Damasio, Antonio. *The Feeling of What Happens: body, emotion and the making of consciousness*, London: Heinemann, 2000.

Dray, William. *History as Re-Enactment: R.G. Collingwood's Idea of History*, Oxford: Oxford University Press, 1995.

Furlong, E.J. *Imagination*, London: George Allen & Unwin, 1961.

Hughes-Warrington, Marnie. *How Good an Historian Shall I Be: R.G. Collingwood, Historical Imagination and Education*, Exeter: Imprint Academic, 2003.

Jenkins, Keith. *Re-Thinking History*, London: Routledge, 1991.

Kind, Amy. 'Putting the Image Back in Imagination,' *Philosophy and Phenomenological Research*, 62:1, 2001, pp.85-109.

Munslow, Alun. 'Historical Imagination', in *The Routledge Companion to Historical Studies*, London: Routledge, 2000, pp.124-129.

Nicholas, Larraine. 'The Dance Centre: Finding a Place for Laban', *Movement, Dance and Drama* 29:1, 2010a, pp.23-24; and 29:2, 2010a, p.9.

Nicholas, Larraine. 'Leslie Burrowes: A Young Dancer in Dresden and London, 1930-34', *Dance Research*, 28:2, 2010b, pp.153-178.

Sparshott, Francis. 'Imagination: The Very Idea', *The Journal of Aesthetics and Art Criticism*, 48:1, 1990, pp.1-8.

Thomas, Nigel J.T. 'Mental Imagery', *The Stanford Encyclopedia of Philosophy* (Winter 2011 Edition), Zalta, Edward N. (ed.), URL = <http://plato.stanford.edu/archives/win2011/entries/mental-imagery/>. Accessed August 2012.

Tosh, John. *The Pursuit of History*, 5th edition, Harlow: Longman, 2009.

Warnock, Mary. *Imagination*, London: Faber and Faber, 1980.

Warnock, Mary. *Imagination and Time*, Oxford: Blackwell, 1994.

White, Hayden. *Metahistory: the historical imagination in nineteenth century Europe*, Baltimore: Johns Hopkins University Press, 1973.

13. The thinking body: dance, philosophy and modernism

Kristin Boyce

Introduction

There are two different ways to understand the phrase 'philosophy of X,' understandings which depend upon two different ways of construing the genitive 'of'. The 'of' can be construed as an objective genitive or it can be construed as a subjective genitive.[1] Consider, for example, the phrase, 'philosophy of Kristin,' if the 'of' is construed as an objective genitive, the phrase refers to the philosophy which takes Kristin as its object. If, on the other hand, the 'of' is construed as a subjective genitive, the phrase refers to the philosophy that belongs to Kristin: Kristin's philosophy. It is worth noting that these two senses of 'the philosophy of Kristin' are not incompatible. Kristin's philosophy might be a philosophy which takes Kristin as its object. In this case the 'of' in the phrase 'the philosophy of Kristin' is doing double duty: it is functioning as both a subjective and as an objective genitive.

There are two corresponding ways to understand the phrase 'philosophy of dance.' If the 'of' is construed as an objective genitive, the phrase refers to the philosophical reflection that takes dance as its object. This is how the phrase is usually understood. But if the 'of' is construed as a subjective genitive, the phrase refers to the philosophical reflection that belongs to dance itself: dance's philosophy. When the 'of' is construed in this second way, dance is understood not simply as *material* for philosophical reflection (material which might occasion new or revised theories about the relation between mind and body, for instance) but rather as in some sense the *subject* of such reflection.

The overarching aim of this essay is to investigate the possibility of 'philosophy of dance' understood in this second sense. Its scope is, for the most part, limited to dance's philosophy of dance – that is, to philosophy of dance in which the 'of' functions as both a subjective and an objective genitive[2] – and it will be concerned only with dance considered as a fine art (not with forms of ritual or social dance).

When I speak of a form of philosophical reflection that belongs to dance that is *art*, what I will mean is that there is a necessary relation between

---

1 Paul Griffiths makes this point with respect to the phrase 'philosophy of religion,' (Griffiths 1977, pp.615-620).

2 For indications of how dance's philosophy might be extended to topics other than dance, see Elgin 2010 and Noë 2007.

the philosophical reflection, which is in some sense 'present in' the dance, and the artistic value or power of the dance. So what I will be exploring is the possibility that for some dance such a necessary relation obtains. A subsidiary aim of the essay will be to clarify the *strongest* possible sense in which such a relation could obtain – the strongest possible sense, that is, in which a form of philosophical reflection could belong to dance.

The strategy of the essay is to focus on one resource for those who have sought to illuminate the cognitive ambitions and value of certain forms of dance: conceptions of modernism that were developed in the first instance by Clement Greenberg in order to explain changes in the visual arts.[3] Scholars such as Sally Banes, Noël Carroll, Roger Copeland and David Michael Levin have all sought to adapt these conceptual resources to dance. In the first half of the essay, I make explicit an approach to philosophy of dance that I take to be shared by and implicit in these writings. I call this the *standard approach to philosophy of dance*. I argue that this approach fails to fully clarify a sense in which philosophical reflection might genuinely belong to dance and that it fails in part because of the particular way these writings both elaborate and criticize Greenberg's framework. In the second half of the essay, I develop an *alternative approach to philosophy of dance* by taking my bearing from a very different way of elaborating and criticizing that framework – that which is found in the writing on modernism that Stanley Cavell and Michael Fried developed together. I argue that the alternative approach clarifies not just *a* sense in which philosophical reflection might belong to dance but also the *strongest possible sense* in which this might be the case.

In seeking to clarify the salient differences between the standard and alternative approaches, a helpful organizing metaphor will be that of 'direction of fit'. This metaphor is often used to illuminate the difference between two mental states, belief and desire. Belief has a world-to-mind direction of fit: the mind fits itself to the world by tracking the way things are in the world. Desire, by contrast, has a mind-to-world direction of fit: it aims to fit the world to itself, to make it the case that the way the world is conforms to the desire.[4]

---

3 It is no reach to suggest that these conceptual resources should have application to dance. From its earliest dialectical unfolding, western theatrical dance has been shaped by developments in the visual arts. For choreographers as foundational to the development of the art form of classical ballet as Jean-Georges Noverre, for example, painting served as the model of what ballet must become if it were to develop into a serious art (cf. Carroll 2003). The relation between dance and the visual arts is no less intimate by the 1960s. Martha Graham, Merce Cunningham and the Judson Church choreographers collaborated with many of the visual artists with whom Greenberg and his successors were centrally concerned.

4 This metaphor was introduced as a (perhaps inadequate) way of glossing the point of a thought experiment that is introduced at the beginning of Elizabeth Anscombe's

The metaphor of 'direction of fit' helps to illuminate the standard and alternative approaches to philosophy of dance in the following way. The picture that guides the standard approach is one of a philosophy-to-dance direction of fit that is of dance as in some way fitting itself to philosophy. There are multiple variations of this approach but in its baldest form, the 'necessary' relation between dance and philosophy is spelled out in terms of a sense in which dance is understood to depend upon (or follow as a consequence of) an explicit and accompanying activity of theorizing about dance. This suggests one alternative to the standard approach: reverse it so that the guiding picture is one of a dance-to-philosophy direction of fit. On that picture, philosophical conclusions derive from (or follow as consequences of) the artistic value or power of certain dances – from the style of the movement in Graham's *Appalachian Spring*[5], perhaps, or Crystal Pite's *The Second Person*[6]. This picture is compelling, but I think it is nevertheless inadequate. The alternative that I propose rejects the metaphor of direction of fit altogether. It seeks to clarify the possibility that for some forms of dance, there is a reciprocal relation of mutual dependence between artistic and philosophical achievement.

Modernism and the standard approach

Until recently, it might have been hard to imagine how dance could fruitfully be conceived as involving *any* form of reflection, let alone a form of philosophical reflection. Copeland, for example, argues that for much of its history, dance has suffered the effects of a deeply entrenched Cartesian dualism: because its medium is the human *body*, dance has been conceived (and often conceived itself) as 'mired' in the body, feeling and subjectivity – more suited to serve as a therapeutic antidote to the 'abstractions and deceptions' of reason than as a medium of thought (Copeland 2004, pp.13, 89, 122).

For scholars who have sought to bring out the cognitive ambitions or value of certain forms of dance, Greenberg's writings on modernism in the visual arts have been an important resource. Greenberg motivates the cognitive turn that he takes to be constitutive of modernism in the visual arts in terms of the Enlightenment. In the wake of newly developed scientific methods, the arts (along with religion and philosophy) were denied the kind of seriousness they had traditionally been taken to have – seriousness as sources of *knowledge*. They were therefore faced with the task of demonstrating that

---

Intention. For a summary of this thought experiment and a critique of common readings of it, see Vogler 2001.

5 First performance: 30 October 1944, Library of Congress, Washington D.C.

6 First performance: 15 February, 2007, Lucent Danstheater, The Hague.

they were necessary, to show that they afforded a kind of experience that was 'valuable in its own right and not to be obtained from any other kind of activity,' (Greenberg 1993, p.86). As Greenberg understood it, this involved each art turning inward, using its own procedures to 1) produce the kind of experience or effect that it alone could produce, and 2) *show* that it alone could produce it by demonstrating that the conditions for the possibility of that experience were the possibilities unique to its medium.

Establishing the limits of a given art (or of art more generally) involved eliminating from art any effect that was proper or more natural to another – that is, 'any effect that might conceivably be borrowed from or by the medium of any other art,'(p.86). Consider, for example, Greenberg's explanation for modernist painting's turn to *abstraction*. He argues 'some of the greatest feats of Western painting' have been due to its efforts to eliminate effects borrowed from sculpture – the art form to which Western painting owes perhaps the greatest debt – and to realize the possibilities that are unique to its particular conditions of possibility, namely, the flatness of the painted surface. Modernist painting becomes increasingly abstract 'not because it has abandoned the representation of the recognizable objects in principle' but because doing so is necessary in order to free painting from its dependence on sculpture:

> All recognizable entities . . . exist in three-dimensional space, and the bar-est suggestion of a recognizable entity suffices to call up associations of that kind of space . . . and by doing so alienate pictorial space from the literal two-dimensionality which is the guarantee of painting's independence as an art. (p.88)

As Greenberg puts it, modernist painting shifts from the 'tactile' (from paintings which give the impression that one could walk through them) – to the purely 'optical' (to paintings that can 'be travelled through only with the eye)' (p.90). Understood in this way, modernism does not, as it is often thought to, represent a radical break with tradition. It represents instead an effort to clarify and inherit what is best and most vital in the tradition of a painting, 'continuing in the direction' of traditional painting while rendering more explicit the conditions for the possibility of its value.

Three theorists who draw on different aspects of Greenberg's work in order to illuminate the cognitive ambitions and achievement of certain choreographers – namely, Merce Cunningham and the Judson Church Choreographers – are Sally Banes, Noël Carroll and Roger Copeland.[7] For Banes and Carroll, what is most important is Greenberg's conception of modernist art as engaged in investigating its own conditions of possibility.

---

7 Because Levin draws not just on Greenberg but also on Fried, I postpone consideration of his work on until Part Two.

Carroll makes this especially explicit in his article, 'The Philosophy of Art History, Dance and the 1960s.' As he understands it, such investigation is one project among many that a given art might undertake. Drawing on Arthur Danto's developmental history of painting, Carroll describes the history of dance as a succession of such projects. In the early stages of its development, he argues, dance, like painting and drama, devoted itself to a 'mimetic project': that of approximating, with ever-increasing verisimilitude, significant dramatic action. For various reasons, the mimetic project came to a close and the 'authority of the view that representation is the essence of art eroded' (Carroll 2003a, p.84) This created a problem: the arts, including dance, needed a new 'project' or 'vocation'. Artists and philosophers, aiding and abetting each other at the levels of theory and practice, identified several different options: formalism, expressionism and modernism. Dance that devoted itself to the formalist programme sought to create works that afforded a species of 'aesthetic experience'. Dance that devoted itself to the expressionist project developed forms of movement that were 'dictated by the logic of inner feeling,' And dance that devoted itself to the modernist project undertook the theoretical or philosophical task of 'defining its own essential nature' or 'interrogating its own conditions of possibility,' It is in terms of this latter project that Carroll seeks to do justice to the achievements of the Judson Church choreographers in particular (pp.87, 90).

Although Carroll takes his conception of the basic cognitive project that is constitutive of modernism from Greenberg, he argues (following Danto) that the historical development of both the visual arts and dance showed Greenberg to be wrong about what the essential conditions for a given art *are*, as well as how far the project of investigating those conditions could be taken by the arts themselves. Greenberg assumed that the essential conditions for the possibility of a visual art like painting were 'perceptible properties' – e.g., 'flatness' – and that 'interrogating its own nature' involved an art in 'deploying . . . its perceptible properties reflexively,' (p.89). But the Judson choreographers showed that there *were* no such properties – that in the case of dance, there were no perceptible properties that distinguished dance *from* ordinary movement. In so doing, they brought the modernist project as close as dance *could* bring it to completion.[8] They also returned dance to the *real* world. As Banes and Carroll characterize it, adoption of the 'modernist project' had represented a sterilizing and elitist inward turn: it 'advocates that art be about itself – that art is a practice that is separate

---

8 Since there were no perceptible properties that distinguished dance for ordinary movement, the problem of determining the real conditions for the possibility of dance – i.e., contextualization within the art world – could not be completed within the arts themselves, but only in the medium of philosophy (Carroll 2003, p.89).

from other social enterprises.' The Judson Church choreographers, part of the 'integrationist avant-garde,' by contrast, 'agitated for the blurring of the boundary between art and life,' (Banes and Carroll 2006, p.52). In other words, they returned dance from its self-preoccupation to an engagement with the world and human concerns.

Copeland, too, builds upon (and distances himself from) Greenberg in order to illuminate the distinctively intellectual aspirations and achievement of the Judson Church choreographers as well as their predecessor, Merce Cunningham. In *Merce Cunningham: The Modernizing of Modern Dance,* Copeland argues that modern dance prior to Cunningham, especially that of Martha Graham, embraced a form of Cartesianism about the mind and body. Because dance is so intimately related to the body, Graham and her predecessors in effect saw it as the art form most advantageously positioned to resist the 'cerebral excesses of technocratic civilization and its Cartesian habits of thought' (Copeland 2004, p.207). Dance, as they conceived it, freed a spectator from such excesses by immersing her in powerful and immediate emotional and bodily experiences. To this end, they developed forms of movement that reduced the distance between audience and dance, emotionally and personally involving the viewer by eliciting powerful tactile responses.

Ironically, Copeland argues, the effect of such intrusive stimulation of the viewer's emotions and bodily sensations was not to free her but instead to reinforce a kind of passivity and vulnerability with respect to the many other forms of stimulation and manipulation to which our feelings and desires are routinely subjected in contemporary life.[9] Cunningham, by contrast, put dance on the *other side* of the Cartesian divide by creating dance that left the feelings and bodily experiences of the viewer 'out of the equation' and instead created a 'purely conceptual experience,' (pp. 92, 206). Cunningham's choreographic ambition, as Copeland understands it, is captured in the following question: 'Can the artist ... function principally as a Cartesian mind pried loose from a body?' (p.206). Instead of drawing a spectator nearer, Cunningham strove to facilitate the capacity for critical, analytic distance in the face of the forms of stimulation that assault the senses.[10]

In making this argument, Copeland both acknowledges Greenberg's importance and distances himself from what he takes to be Greenberg's 'overly narrow' conception of modernism. For example, he adapts to dance Greenberg's discussion of a shift from 'tactility to opticality':

9 cf. especially Copeland 2004, pp.87-94.

10 Copeland draws attention to the following remarks of John Cage's: 'I wanted art to change my way of seeing, not my way of feeling. . . . I don't want to spend my life being pushed around by a bunch of artists' (Copeland 2004, p.92).

Clement Greenberg, probably the most important art critic of the period, discusses the essentially 'optical' (as opposed to tactile) nature of painting in the early 1960's . . . What Greenberg says of painting applies, mutatis mutandis, to early post-modern [as well as modernist] dance. (Copeland 1986, p.9)

But he attributes quite a different purpose and significance to this shift than Greenberg does. As we saw, for Greenberg the shift is important because it is part of how painting acknowledges one of the possibilities unique to its own medium – flatness. For Copeland, the shift is important because it is part of how dance shifts from the wrong to the right side of the Cartesian divide: by shifting to an emphasis on sight, the sense which, Copeland argues, is most closely associated with the intellect and 'analytical detachment.'[11]

We can begin to see how the interpretations developed by Banes and Carroll as well as Copeland imply a standard approach to philosophy of dance – that is, one which is characterized by a philosophy-to-dance-direction-of-fit – by exploring a significant way that both interpretations depart from Greenberg's model, albeit without thematizing that deviation. Like Greenberg, these theorists motivate the philosophical or cognitive turn with which they are concerned in terms of a crisis of confidence and the necessity for justification. But they conceive the form of self-justification at stake differently than Greenberg does. The difference might be summarized this way. While Greenberg argues that the arts take a cognitive turn in order to show the value that they have, the standard approach suggests that it is in virtue of taking such a turn that dance comes to *have* value.

Consider Copeland first. By his lights, the crisis of confidence has to do with the medium of dance: because its medium is the human body, dance is the art form which appears to stand at the furthest remove from those human capacities that are presumed to be most important and most distinctively human: our conceptual capacities. Copeland repeatedly highlights the intellectual ambitions (as well as insecurities) of Cunningham and his collaborators. For example, he reads Cunningham's choreographic ambitions through a comparison with Duchamp:

Duchamp . . . seemed to suffer from an intellectual inferiority complex – or at least a fear that the visual arts were perceived as less 'mentally demanding' than the verbal arts. In a remarkable burst of candor, he once admitted, 'the painter was considered stupid, but the poet and writer were intelligent. I wanted to be intelligent'. (Copeland 2004, p.226)

---

11 Levin, too, adapts this aspect of Greenberg's argument to dance, arguing that Balanchine's black and white ballets also effect a shift from tactility to opticality. In his case, though, it is not at all clear what motivates this shift, other than perhaps an attraction and desire to 'adopt' the 'new aesthetic' that he saw in painting (Levin 1983, pp.126-7).

The ambition, in light of this worry, is to create art (for Cunningham, to create choreography) that had the kind of value it was presumed to lack and which, in their estimation, most dance *did* in fact lack.

Especially in 'Art History, Dance and the 1960s,' Carroll highlights a similar crisis of confidence. Since the inception of its ambition to be accepted as a fine art, he argues, dance has sought to gain respect by conforming itself to standards of other, more firmly established 'fine arts,' especially painting. This can be seen as early as the ballet d'action of Jean-Georges Noverre, writing and choreographing in France in the 1760s. Noverre, Carroll argues, 'was a man with a mission. As a choreographer, he was committed to getting dance taken seriously ... he wasn't interested in describing dance as it was. He was concerned with saying what dance should become – what dance should become in order to be considered art,' and this committed him to making dance which could be understood to meet the specifications of the 'presiding theory of art' at the time: the imitation theory (Carroll 2003a, 90-1). Fast forward to the 1960s and dance is essentially in the same position: still insecure as an art form, still looking to painting for a model of what it means to be 'serious'. Only now the prevailing theory of 'serious' art (or at least one such theory) is that there are no perceptible differences between art and ordinary life – in the case of dance, no difference between 'dance movement' and 'ordinary movement' – and that therefore *anything* can be art (p.95).

The philosophy-to-dance direction of fit that this implies is underscored by the way in which Banes and Carroll describe the choreography of Yvonne Rainer. Like the minimalists in the visual arts and music whom the Judson school claimed as predecessors, Rainer accorded priority not only to the activity of making dances but to an additional and accompanying activity of theorizing *about* dance. For example, in conjunction with her break-through work, *Trio A*, Rainer also publishes a manifesto which attempts to offer an articulation of the theoretical commitments exemplified in this, 'A Quasi Survey of Some 'Minimalist' Tendencies in the Quantitatively Minimal Dance Activity Midst the Plethora, or An Analysis of Trio A'. As Rainer's friend and colleague Simone Forti puts it 'You don't start by experiencing the movement and evolving the movement, but you start from an idea that already has the movement pretty well prescribed,'(quoted in Burt 2009, p.9). And as Carroll and Banes put it, the movement 'implies' or 'insinuates' a theory of dance that is 'easily stateable in propositions' and the 'works in questions can be seen as [the] consequences' of those theories. (Carroll and Banes 1982, pp.39-40; Carroll 2003a, p.94).

This suggests one way of understanding how philosophy might be conceived as *necessary* to this dance and therefore how such dance could be conceived as providing a paradigm of 'dance's philosophy.' Philosophy, one might think, is necessary to such dance because it *justifies* it. Dance is conceived as the conclusion of an aesthetic inference in something like the way action is understood as the conclusion of a practical inference. But can such philosophical theorizing *provide* this kind of artistic justification? Here is how Cavell puts the point with respect to minimalist musicians:

> I am not suggesting that such activity [i.e., the theorizing engaged in by the minimalist musician or by the 'minimalist' choreographer like Rainer] is in fact unimportant, nor that it can in no way be justified, but only that such philosophizing . . . does not justify it and must not be used to protect it against aesthetic [artistic] assessment. (Cavell 2003, p.196)

If the 'philosophizing' that is present in the dance is *not* 'justifying' it, then these accounts have failed to give us the resources to identify a sense in which philosophical reflection is necessarily related to the artistic achievement of some forms of dance. In other words, they have failed to provide a compelling point of departure for something deserving the title 'philosophy of dance,' when 'philosophy of dance' is understood in the second sense.

There are places in Banes and Carroll's writings in particular where it becomes apparent that it is not in fact clear how, on their account, the philosophical and artistic achievements of Rainer's choreography *are* related to each other. For example, there are a number of places where they characterize the artistic value of Rainer's work in terms of how dance reshapes attention to and appreciation for the 'everyday'[12]. But Carroll, especially, often characterizes this value as distinct from and in addition to the theoretical or philosophical achievement of the work. For example, in 'Yvonne Rainer and the Recuperation of Everyday life,' he describes Rainer's commitment to the theoretical project of minimalism as telling 'only part of the story' that explains her commitment to exploring everyday movement; it is her second project, that of 'restoring an appreciation for what was wondrous and simple in everyday movement,' that tells the rest of the story (Carroll 2003b, pp.72-3). And in 'The Philosophy of Art History, Dance, and the 1960s,' the independence of these two 'projects' is made even more explicit: 'Everyday work movements are presented in a dance-world context in order to recall to mind the intelligence exhibited by the body in discharging mundane tasks. *Theoretically, however, the work also suggests* that movements that do not look like dance can be dance,' (Carroll 2003a, p.94; italics mine). It simply isn't clear how, on this account, we should understand the relation between what the dance accomplishes theoretically (demonstrating that there is no perceptible property that distinguishes dance movement from everyday movement) and what it achieves artistically (transforming the quality of our attention to the everyday).

---

12 Most recently in Banes and Carroll 2006, p.62.

An alternative approach to philosophy of dance

In this section, I sketch an alternative approach to philosophy of dance. In seeking to differentiate this approach from the standard one, it might seem most natural to simply reverse the picture that guides the standard approach. In that case, the guiding picture for the alternative approach would be one of a dance-to-philosophy direction of fit. To a certain extent, this is what I do. On the alternative approach, an explicit and accompanying activity of philosophical explication enters, if it enters at all, only to explicate something that is already *in* the movement. In this sense, an explicit and accompanying activity of philosophical explication can be understood as 'fitting itself to dance'. In a deeper sense, however, the alternative approach rejects the metaphor of direction of fit altogether. For on this approach, what the explicit and accompanying activity of theorizing explicates is a form of reflection whose medium is, and is *necessarily*, the movement itself. With respect to such dance, I will argue, there is a *reciprocal relation of mutual dependence* between the philosophical and artistic achievement of the work. For such dance, two conditions hold simultaneously:

• It is in virtue of what the work achieves *as art* that it achieves something philosophically important.

• It is in virtue of what it achieves *philosophically* that the work succeeds as art.

In developing this alternative approach, I draw on the writings on modernism in the visual arts and music that Cavell and Fried develop together. Like Carroll and Copeland, Cavell and Fried both build on and criticize aspects of Greenberg's writings, but it is their particular way of doing so that opens the possibility for an approach that succeeds in getting into view a form of philosophical reflection that genuinely belongs to dance as art.[13]

As we saw in the first section, Carroll and Copeland re-conceive the 'necessity' which motivates the cognitive turn that is constitutive of modernist dance. As they understand it, the necessity at issue is *external*: in order to become valuable, dance must conform itself to an external standard; it must acquire the value that attaches to the cognitive project it takes on. In a certain sense, the necessity that figures in Greenberg's account is also external: the necessity of showing, in the face of suspicion to the contrary, that dance provides a unique and valuable form of experience. For Cavell and Fried, by contrast, the necessity at issue is *internal*: dance as an art form reaches a point in its historical development such that in order to remain *art*,

---

13 Neither Cavell nor Fried writes extensively about dance, but Cavell acknowledges a role for dance in philosophical reflection in Cavell 2005, p. 3.

it is necessary for it to engage in critical reflection upon its own conditions of possibility.

Dance reaches this point when 'the relation between the present practice of [dance] and the history of [dance...] has become problematic': when it is no longer clear whether or how it will be possible to continue to produce dance that, as Fried puts it, is capable of compelling conviction that [it] can 'stand comparison' with dance of the past whose quality seems 'beyond question', (Cavell xxxiii; Fried 1998, p.98). Cavell puts this point in terms of the capacity to continue to produce work that can matter to us or 'absorb us in the way that art does,' that is, in a way that carries with it the conviction that others should care about it, too, and it matters to one that they do (Cavell 2003, p.197). At such a point, the conventions that had hitherto been relied upon in order to produce dance that could matter to us in this way can *no longer* be so relied on (pp.xxxii, xxxvi).[14] It therefore becomes necessary to discover what, under present conditions, 'we will accept as [dance] and why we so accept [it],' (Cavell 2003, p.219). This is not an investigation that could be carried out in a medium other than dance itself: the only way to discover what can absorb us the way great dance of the past absorbs us is to produce work that, when 'tested against oneself', succeeds in doing so.

Conceived in this way, the cognitive project that is constitutive of modernist dance is not one which can be 'brought to a close' in the way that Carroll suggests – by clearing up, once and for all, what the essential conditions for anything to count as dance *are*. As Cavell and Fried conceive it, that project is not one of 'discovering the irreducible essence or timeless conditions for the possibility of a particular art form'. After all, the problem is precisely that conventions, which might have been thought essential to something's being dance, can no longer be relied upon to produce new work capable of mattering to us in the way that art does. The task is rather, as Cavell puts it, to discover what, under present conditions, will make it possible to produce such work and why.

With respect to such dance, there is a *reciprocal relation of mutual dependence* between the philosophical and artistic achievement of the dance. Its artistic

---

14 In her exploration of a 'specific form of knowledge of dance', Gabriele Brandstetter suggests that clarifying such a form of knowledge in effect requires a kind of Kuhnian paradigm shift in the arts. She asks: 'Can a pattern comparable to the paradigm shifts described in the history and theory of science be transferred to dance? More precisely: to dance as an art form of body motion in space and time?' (Gabriele Brandstetter 2007, p.42). As Cavell and Fried conceive it, arts 'enter the condition of philosophy' in virtue of undergoing this kind of artistic version of a Kuhnian paradigm shift. Cavell acknowledges his connection to Kuhn in Cavell 1982, pp.xix, 121 and 164 as well as Cavell 2010. See also Fried 1998, p.99. Brandstetter's question is further evidence that Cavell and Fried offer valuable resources for those interested in dance as forms of knowledge and/or philosophy.

achievement depends upon its entering 'the condition of philosophy,' where this means that what dance *is* – what the present conditions for the possibility of dance are – has become an inescapable subject for dance itself (Cavell 1979, p.14; Cavell 2003, p.xxxxvi). But at the same time, such dance succeeds *as philosophy* only in virtue of its artistic power: it is only by producing work that can absorb and matter to us that such dance succeeds in showing what its present conditions of possibility *are*.[15]

When philosophy of dance is conceived along the lines of the alternative approach, the choreography of Rainer and Cunningham might still be understood to afford paradigmatic instances of dance's philosophy, but *not* because their choreography avoids engaging the feelings and imagination (Copeland) or because it abandons an 'expressive project' to adopt a 'philosophical' one instead (Carroll). From the vantage of the alternative approach, to say of Rainer's or Cunningham's work that there is a form of philosophical reflection that *belongs* to it as art is to say that in order to succeed *as art*, their work *must* undertake to discover what forms of bodily movement can, under their respective conditions, matter in the way certain forms of dance were once able to do.

One might see an earlier stage of this project in the response of choreographers like Balanchine and Martha Graham to a moment in which the conventions of classical ballet begin to lose their authority, a moment in which: (a) ballet movement starts to feel artificial and confining, a denial of the 'natural' movement of the body, (b) costumes start to register as covering or concealing the body, or (c) narratives full of fairies and birds and royalty start to seem silly and distracting. Graham and Balanchine 'enter the condition of philosophy' (albeit in very different ways) by finding ways to produce works that, when tested against their audience, compel conviction that [they] 'can stand comparison with [dance of the past] whose quality seems beyond question' (Fried 1998, p.99). While the ways of working that Graham discovers require eschewing the ballet vocabulary altogether,

---

15 In 'Balanchine's Formalism', Levin brings not only Greenberg but also Fried to bear in his interpretation of Balanchine's black and white ballets. But he does not track the aspects of Fried's and Cavell's work that I am arguing are most valuable for the present purpose. Levin does not track their objections to the essentialism that figure at least in Greenberg's more programmatic essays, nor their corresponding sensitivity to the necessity that figures in the self-reflexive turn that is constitutive of modernist art. By Levin's lights, ballet takes such a turn because Balanchine chooses to adopt the new modernist aesthetic that had already gained predominance in visual arts and replaced the aesthetic of 'mimetic connotation and transcendent symbolism'(Levin 1983, p.126). As he sees it, Balanchine made some really beautiful ballets and the interested observer can identify in them many important 'affinities' with the aesthetic that 'defines the paintings and sculptures', among them a shift to 'opticality' and a commitment to 'reveal, to make present . . . [ballet's] defining condition as art' (p.127). In this way, Levin's way of drawing on Greenberg and Fried lends itself to a standard approach to philosophy of dance.

those discovered by Balanchine involve working with and transforming that vocabulary. Cunningham and Rainer, then, might be understood to work at a moment when the new possibilities that Graham and Balanchine 'discovered' have started to lose *their* authority, when they have started to appear distractingly overblown and theatrical.[16] In other words, while the standard approach holds that Cunningham and Rainer are located at one extreme of a continuum from most to least philosophical, and Graham at the other, the alternative approach suggests a more fundamental affinity. On this approach, Cunningham, Rainer and Graham appear to be working equally, when they work successfully, in the condition of philosophy.

One important implication of this alternative way of conceiving both modernism and 'philosophy of dance' is that it refuses the dichotomy between dance that is concerned with itself and dance that is, as Banes and Carroll put it, concerned with 'the world, the flesh and/or the devil as they exists off camera' (Banes and Carroll 2006, p.52). Part of what the alternative approach clarifies is what is humanly at stake in dance's philosophy of dance. Dance that enters the condition of philosophy exposes the fragility and partiality of our capacity to understand and be responsive to our own needs. Who are we such that certain forms of bodily movement can matter to us in ways that carry the conviction that others should care and that something is at stake for us in whether they do or not? Why has the life gone out of certain ways of working that were once able to produce work that could matter to us in this way? Will we be able to discover new ways of working that can produce such work? If not, what exactly will have been lost? What do radical changes in what can absorb us (or even whether we can be absorbed at all) reveal about how we have changed or how our world has changed?

A second implication of the alternative approach is that getting dance's philosophy clearly into view provides a vantage from which to reconsider what philosophical reflection *is*. As we saw, the standard approach attempts to secure the respectability of certain forms of dance by arguing that they have the kind of seriousness that philosophy is generally understood to have. For the alternative approach, by contrast, getting clear about the kind of seriousness certain forms of dance (or sculpture or painting) have makes it possible to get clearer about the kind of seriousness that *philosophical reflection* has. Philosophy is often understood to have the seriousness it has *in virtue of forgoing* dependence on anything as tenuous as the subjective response of a reader or viewer. But on the alternative approach, it is not

---

16 Mark Franko suggests that Graham's work did not lack the reflexivity that is constitutive of modernist dance, but only a 'critical witness to articulate its modernism in words'. In fact, he suggests, Graham's mentor, Louis Horst in effect 'outlines a Greenbergian reflexivity before the fact' in his theory of the archaic. See Franko 1995, pp.39,47.

possible to recognize the philosophical work done by some forms of dance *as philosophical* unless one can recognize the dance's capacity to matter to its viewers – to elicit from its viewers a certain kind of response – as constitutive of at least some forms of philosophical reflection.

Part of what is so powerful about Cavell's work is that he takes this particular form of philosophical reflection to have important implications for our understanding of the character of philosophical work more generally, particularly the work of the ordinary language philosopher. The ordinary language philosopher's claims about 'what we would say when' are, as Cavell puts it, 'at least as close to what Kant calls aesthetical judgments as they are to ordinary empirical hypotheses' (Cavell 2003, p.94). What he means by this is that the claims of the ordinary language philosopher call for and depend on being tested against oneself – by being tested against what one is inclined, as a native speaker of English, to say in a certain set of circumstances.

Conclusion

In this essay, I have explored the possibility of a 'philosophy of dance' in which the 'of' is construed subjectively: that is, the possibility of a form of philosophical reflection that *belongs* to dance as art. Because dance has often struggled to be taken seriously as an art, it can be easy for an interest in dance's philosophy to register as an effort to secure respectability for dance by associating it with a form of human activity that is assumed to be paradigmatically 'rational' and 'serious'. In the first half of the essay, I argued that implicit in some influential writing about the cognitive value of dance, is a standard approach to the philosophy of dance that makes just this kind of move. On the standard approach, dance is understood to involve philosophical reflection insofar as it fits itself to ends that are traditionally associated not with art but with philosophy and the value of such dance is understood to derive from the philosophy that is present in it. Such an approach, I argued, does not succeed in clarifying a sense in which philosophical reflection might genuinely belong to dance as an art form.

In the second half of the essay, I sketched an alternative approach to philosophy of dance, one that I argued clarifies not only *a* sense in which philosophical reflection might belong to dance, but *the strongest possible sense* in which this might be the case. On the alternative approach, philosophical reflection belongs to some forms of dance in virtue of a reciprocal relation of mutual dependence that obtains between the artistic power of the dance and the philosophical reflection that is present in it. From the perspective of this approach, dance's philosophy is not of interest because it appears to secure respectability for dance. It is of interest because investigating a proximity between philosophical and artistic power, which has been poorly understood, promises to deepen our understanding of both philosophical and artistic endeavour. It is easy to avoid that promise by simply projecting onto dance unsatisfying (though familiar) assumptions about philosophy. But Cavell and Fried's work, I have argued, stands as a reminder that it is possible not to take this form of the easy way out.

In exploring dance's philosophy, I have limited the scope to dance's philosophy *of dance*. This might seem to have arbitrarily excluded the forms of dance's philosophy that are most interesting. Consider, for instance, Alva Noë's discussion of what Karen Nelson's *Tuning Scores* might teach us:

> A first answer is that *Tuning Scores* cast light on dance itself. They inform us of dance possibilities. This may be so. But it is not the answer I am looking for. It does not satisfy. For one thing, it is not surprising to learn that the *Tuning Score* method will teach us about *dance*. The question is whether dance, explored by using *Tuning Scores*, can teach us about something *else* (i.e., the mind). (Nöe 2007, p.125)

Similarly, in seeking to clarify the 'cognitive value' of what she calls 'dance about dance', Catherine Elgin articulates what she takes to be a common frustration (although she also takes there to be a good response to that frustration):

> There is something irritatingly self-indulgent about artists' talk of exploring the limits of their medium. One wants to reply, 'Yes, yes I can see why artists working in a medium and art students studying a medium need to care about the limits of the medium. But why should the rest of us care? What sort of understanding does such an exploration yield for us? (Elgin unpublished, p.12)

For Elgin, the interest of such exploration lies in what it can illuminate about topics in philosophy of mind and action: the relation between mind and body and the nature of intelligent spontaneous action.

I, too, am interested in how dance might illuminate topics that extend beyond the reach of aesthetics proper. But there is, I think, a connection between the perspective from which dance seems in need of some form of external grounding or justification and the perspective from which dance's philosophy starts to look interesting *only* once we can see that its scope extends beyond dance itself. Whatever dance's philosophy might contribute to reflection upon topics in philosophy of mind and philosophy of action will come by way of working through difficult questions about what dance itself is and why it matters to us in the way it does.[17]

---

17 This article was completed with support from an American Council of Learned Societies New Faculty Fellowship. Portions of the material were presented at Roehampton University's 2011 *Thinking Through Dance* conference, the 2011 meeting of the *American*

References

Banes, Sally and Noël Carroll. 'Cunningham, Balanchine and Postmodern Dance,' *Dance Chronicle*, 29, 2006, pp.49-68.

Brandstetter, Gabrielle. 'Dance as Culture of Knowledge' in Gehm, Sabine, Pirkko Husemann and Katharina von Wilcke (eds.), *Knowledge in Motion: Perspectives of Artistic and Scientific Research in Dance*, Piscataway: Transcription Publishers, 2007, pp.37-48.

Burt, Ramsay. 'The Specter of Interdisciplinarity', *Dance Research Journal*, 41:1, 2009, pp. 1-17.

Carroll, Noël. 'The Philosophy of Art History, Dance, and the 1960s' in Banes, Sally (ed.), *Reinventing Dance in the 1960s: Everything Was Possible*, Madison: University of Wisconsin Press, 2003a, pp.81-97.

Carroll, Noël. 'Yvonne Rainer and the Recuperation of Everyday Life' in Sachs, Sid (ed.), *Radical Juxtapositions: 1961-2002*, Philadelphia: The University of the Arts, 2003b, pp.64-85.

Carroll, Noël and Sally Banes. 'Working and Dancing: A Response to Monroe Beardsley's "What is Going on in a Dance?",' *Dance Research Journal*, 15:1, 1982, pp.37-41.

Cavell, Stanley. *The World Viewed*, New York: The Viking Press, 1971.

Cavell, Stanley. *The Claim of Reason: Wittgenstein, Skepticism, Morality and Tragedy*. Oxford: Oxford University Press, 1982.

Cavell, Stanley. *Must We Mean What We Say?* New York: Cambridge University Press, 2003.

Cavell, Stanley. 'Fred Astaire Asserts the Right to Praise,' *Philosophy the Day After Tomorrow*, Cambridge: The Belknap Press of Harvard University Press, 2005.

Cavell, Stanley. *Little Did I Know: Excerpts from Memory*, Stanford: Stanford University Press, 2010.

Copeland, Roger. 'The Objective Temperament: Post-Modern Dance and The Rediscovery of Ballet,' *Dance Theatre Journal*, 1986, 4:2, pp.6-11.

Copeland, Roger. *Merce Cunningham : The Modernizing of Modern Dance*, New York: Routledge, 2004.

Elgin, Catherine Z (unpublished). 'Emotion, Expression and Exemplification.' Access to this article was obtained through communication with the author. It has been published in French: 'Exemplification et la Dance' in *Philosophie de la Dance*, Rennes: Presses Universitaire de Rennes, 2010, pp.81-98.

*Association for Aesthetics,*as well as the University of Chicago's *Wittgenstein Workshop*, and *Practical Philosophy Workshop*. I benefited especially from questions raised by Jenny Bunker, Noël Carroll, Renee Conroy and Graham McFee. I am grateful to Aili Bresnehan, James Conant, James Hamilton and Daniel Morgan for helpful comments on earlier drafts.

Fried, Michael. *Art and Objecthood: Essays and Reviews*, Chicago: The University of Chicago Press, 1998.

Franko, Mark. *Dancing Modernism/Performing Politics*, Bloomington: Indiana University Press, 1995.

Greenberg, Clement. *The Collected Essays and Criticism: Modernism with a Vengeance, 1957-1969*. Chicago: The University of Chicago Press, 1993.

Levin, David Michael. 'Balanchine's Formalism' in Copeland, Roger and Marshall Cohen (eds.), *What is Dance?*, New York: Oxford University Press: pp.123-42. Originally published in *Dance Perspectives*, 55:3, 1973.

Nöe, Alva. 'Making Worlds Available,' in Gehm, Sabine, Pirkko Husemann and Katharina von Wilcke (eds.), *Knowledge in Motion: Perspectives of Artistic and Scientific Research in Dance*, Piscataway: Transcription Publishers, 2007, pp.121-8.

Vogler, Candace. 'Anscombe on Practical Inference' in Millgram, Elijah (ed.), *Varieties of Practical Reasoning*, Boston: MIT Press, 2001.

14. Choreography as philosophy, or exercising thought in performance

Efrosini Protopapa

Introduction

In seeking to understand how choreography may work as philosophy, one could turn towards certain contemporary dance works, particularly by European choreographers, that seem to be seeking, or often claiming, a relationship to philosophy. Similarly, insofar as philosophy can be understood as a practice of thinking, we could approach the exercising of thought in/ as (choreographed) performance, by looking at the ways in which such works seem to pursue or present philosophical thought. The task here is one of identifying precisely what type of relationship between choreography and philosophy that is in these performances, or how we are to perceive or understand this link as spectators of such works. Even further perhaps, a question could be posed about whether philosophy actually appears somehow in choreography. And if so, how?

In order to address such issues, the main part of this essay will examine the ways in which certain philosophical ideas seem to be inspiring contemporary choreographers particularly in Europe, further focusing on the specific case of Jérôme Bel and a lecture performance he gave in 2008 on his work *The Last Performance* (1998). The French choreographer will be looked at here not only because of his prominent place in the European dance scene I refer to, but also precisely because of the explicit reference he has often made to philosophy both within his pieces and in interviews and other literature surrounding his works. In order to take the discussion further, the final part of this essay will then introduce propositions by Gilles Deleuze and Félix Guattari, as well as Hélène Cixous, on philosophy itself, which enable us to think through the appearance of the philosophical in contemporary choreographic works, in a way that is perhaps different to how we would approach such works according to the claims made by the choreographers themselves.

Before that, however, and in order to contextualize this discussion, it is necessary to briefly outline developments in contemporary European choreography in the past two decades, which have given rise to the controversial term 'conceptual dance', particularly in reference to works that allude to the philosophical or theoretical. I would argue that such developments also potentially link to the ways in which debates on practice-led research have recently grown, particularly in the UK, the US and Australia, where we often find a relationship being pursued between philosophical writing and choreographic practice. Indeed, I propose both these two contexts – the contemporary European dance scene and the academic debates on practice-led research – as platforms where we can trace the philosophical as it appears in/as contemporary choreography. Alongside my discussion of Bel then, I will also briefly refer to writings by Susan Melrose, who was one of the first academics in the UK to articulate the complex relationship between practice and theory or between performance-making and writing in practice-led research.

Choreography producing new concepts of dance

In attempting to depict the kind of contemporary developments in choreography that are of relevance here, it is quite revealing to look at the 'Call for Papers' that André Lepecki and Ric Allsopp sent out as editors of the *Performance Research* journal issue entitled 'On Choreography' in 2007.[1] Lepecki and Allsopp suggest that since the 1990s 'choreography' started to shift, both as a term and as a practice, so that it cannot be defined anymore as concerning the composition of bodily movement in time and space; rather, it has now become a practice that questions precisely the relationships 'between movement, composition and the production of dance' (Allsopp and Lepecki 2007, [email / electronic announcement]). In this way, they argue, choreography has now expanded 'to include a wide range of conceptual tools, materials and strategies' (*ibid.*). They continue by observing that such a conceptualization of choreography has produced performance work that is often self-reflexive, in the way it questions 'the orthodoxies of contemporary art work and practice' (*ibid.*). Choreography, as they characterize it, appears to be questioning its own mechanisms, conditions of work, processes and products. This seems aligned with Bojana Cvejić's argument (2006, [online]) that defining choreography as the composition of movement in time and space gives a very vague idea about the processes and operations involved in choreographic practice, and in this way also limits our understanding (or perhaps also the potential) of choreography.

More recently, choreography has been presented as an expanded practice in a conference devised by Mårten Spångberg, in collaboration with Cvejić and Xavier Le Roy,[2] on the occasion of the exhibition *Retrospective* by the choreographer Le Roy, who has very much shaped the developments in

---

1 *Performance Research*, 'On Choreography', 13:2, was published in March 2009. The 'Call for Papers' I refer to here was sent via email on 6 July 2007.

2 MACBA, Fundació Antoni Tàpies, Mercat de les Flors, Barcelona, 29-31 March, 2012. For more information: http://choreographyasexpandedpractice.wordpress.com/2012/02/25/choreography-as-expanded-practice-barcelona-29-31-march-2012-2/ [accessed 5 November 2012]

European choreography mentioned here (alongside Bel). In their opening statement, the organizers describe how 'in the last few years, the term 'choreography' has been used in an ever-expanding sense', so that it 'is not *a priori* performative, nor is it bound to expression and reiteration of subjectivity'. Rather, as they argue, it may include choreographic strategies that remain unrelated to dance, but also expanded practices often developed by choreographers, such as the devising of situations, social choreography and any 'rethinking of publication, exhibition, display, mediatization, production and post-production' (Spångberg, Cvejić and Le Roy 2012, [online]). We therefore find in such statements the idea that choreography has shifted away from the notion of dance composition or the art of making dances, and has become an expanded practice that potentially engages with strategies and modes of doing from various fields, including visual art, art history, performance studies, cultural studies and philosophy.

Alongside these developments, and if we are to zoom into the specific relationship of choreography to dance and movement, André Lepecki's book *Exhausting Dance: Performance and the politics of movement* (2006), has been key in providing 'a discussion of some recent choreographic strategies where dance's relation to movement is being exhausted', otherwise framed as 'a choreographic questioning of dance's identity as a *being-in-flow*' (Lepecki 2006, p.1, his emphasis). Lepecki claims that the 'dismantling' of a certain notion of dance as displaying continuous movement in-flow, or else 'the deflation of movement' in recent dance performance, have problematized pre-established ways of viewing dance and of writing on dance. Most significantly, these tendencies comprise a broader 'critical act of deep ontological impact', as they seem to question the very basis of dance – what Lepecki names: 'the bind between dance and movement' (*ibid.*). Again, certain contemporary experimental choreography could be conceived here as a practice which comes to redefine the ontological ground of dance, 'its essence, nature, purpose, means of production and modes of manifestation' (*ibid.*). Notably, the choreographers that Lepecki discusses in his book, as well as those meant by other writers who are concerned with new conceptions of choreography today, include, alongside Bel and Le Roy, Vera Mantero, Boris Charmatz, Jonathan Burrows and Matteo Fargion, Raimund Hoghe, La Ribot, and the younger makers Thomas Lehmen, Ivana Müller and Nicole Beutler, whose works indeed I have often heard being classified under the somewhat puzzling term 'conceptual dance'.

It is useful then to return to Bojana Cvejić, who sees the term 'conceptual dance' as a consequence of critical theory's 'incursion' into choreography, given that many of the above-mentioned choreographers openly invoke philosophical writings as inspirational sources for their expanded choreographic practice. This particularly includes, as we will see later, the writings of philosophers such as Roland Barthes, Jacques Derrida, Michel Foucault, Gilles Deleuze and Felix Guattari. Within this context, and as a result of its dialogue with critical theory, it is proposed that choreography now introduces concepts of its own about what dance performance is and how it is made. The proposition is put forward that, as soon as choreography starts operating as an expanded field of practices it not only becomes freed up by the obligation to produce a composition of dance or movement, but it also gains the capacity to produce concepts of dance itself. As Cvejić claims, by sourcing concepts from 'other domains of knowledge, theoretical discourses and cultural practices', which do not specially, autonomously or intrinsically belong to dance, choreographers are now conceptualizing dance – not *in* or *on* dance, but conceptualizing *dance* – through choreographic practice, through the very making, producing and presenting of dance performance. She therefore suggests that, whereas 'until the 1990s one could [get away] with speaking about dance performances by asking what kind of object of dance a performance produces; by defining, first, style with a formalist concern with the body as the instrument for a certain technique and, second, subject matter by way of metaphoric representation', today, because of some dance's inspiration from philosophical thinking, we are able to ask 'not what kind of object a dance performance is, but what kind of concept of dance it proposes' (Cvejić, 2006, [online]).

Whether or not we name certain dance 'conceptual' seems partly irrelevant here. In fact, as much as a key feature of the types of works I am discussing is that they produce 'concepts of dance', which seems to allude to the philosophical, it is also clear that the term 'concept' itself remains quite vague and problematic in this context.[3] A further question could be raised then about which dances and whose practices we mean when considering choreography that introduces new concepts of dance – but also, what kind of concepts are we speaking about here, and how are they introduced through choreographic works? Le Roy himself has admitted: 'I don't know of one choreographer who works in dance without a concept. [...] There is also a problem with the generalities – people are being grouped in this category or that but within these groups what I see is only people with very different ways of working and very different subjects' (in Burrows, Le Roy and Ruckert 2004, p.10).

---

3 See Le Roy, Cvejić and Siegmund (2006) for a detailed discussion of the similarities and differences between conceptual (visual) art and conceptual dance. A useful observation is made here that conceptual dance practices share a kind of self-reflexivity with conceptual art, but in a much less discursive/linguistic or epistemological and a much more perceptual/anti-essentialist way. Further differences are then noted about how each of these 'movements' relate to abstraction and modernist questions, but also to institutions and the arts market.

It is different though to claim that all choreographers work with a concept and that all choreography produces a concept of dance. While it could be argued that any choreographed piece that presents itself as dance potentially proposes a concept of dance by its very nature (of being dance), there is a sense in which the choreographers mentioned above consciously and systematically seek to question what dance is and how it is made. This suggests experimentation with the ways in which they set up their processes, or create new premises within which to work choreographically.[4] Furthermore, this kind of self-reflexivity, which Cvejić suggests 'is directed towards the *dispositif* of theatre, the conditions, roles and procedures whereby a spectator is presented [with] something as dance' (2006, p.50), is precisely what the openness to other fields of knowledge potentially facilitates. It therefore leads to the discovery and employment of new modes of working *as* choreography, which may potentially also lead to new understandings of what dance is and how it is made.

In other words, choreographers such as Bel and Le Roy do not make works which comment on and/or (re)present ideas or concepts through (choreographed) dancing, as this would affirm pre-existing concepts of dance (as composed movement). In this case, one would leave the performance with a sense of what the work looked like and what it was *about* (which is the mode of operation dance has most traditionally adopted as a theatrical art form). Rather, the choreographers discussed here are seen to be producing new concepts *of* dance by practicing choreography as an expanded practice, so that one leaves their shows with a proposition about what dance performance could be, or about how dance performance could function in ways other than those traditionally assumed through choreographed (composed) dancing.

On theorizing in practice-led research

If these propositions also remind us of discussions on practice-led research, it is because they too seek to describe the possible relationships that are being pursued between theory (philosophy, often) and practice in dance research. Here, too, I would distinguish between choreographic practice that explores concepts or ideas *through choreography*, and that which aims to put forward new understandings *of choreography*. Similar to this line of thought

---

4 What I have called the set-up of the process or the premise for creation, Mårten Spångberg has in fact described as a concept, in a workshop he led with Xavier Le Roy (Vienna, 2010). Moreover, in attempting to depict the differences between the ways in which a concept (or protocol, as he said) works in choreography, he distinguished between: 1. the concept on display (eg. Jérôme Bel's *The Last Performance*), 2. the concept as embedded in the work (Xavier Le Roy's *Product of Circumstances*), 3. the concept as a motor machine (eg. Xavier Le Roy's *Rite of Spring*).

is the way in which Melrose has systematically posed a series of questions about the relationship between writing on performance and what she calls 'mixed-mode' and 'multi-participant' performance practices, or between the practices of theorizing in writing and those of theorizing in/as performance-making practice (2006, p.125). More specifically, Melrose regards theorists/ writers as expert-spectators, in the sense of academics who write from the point of view of the spectator (rather than that of the artist as doer). Such writers, I would imagine, approach the work aiming to understand it through a theoretical perspective, or by applying a philosophical framework to facilitate an understanding, or even interpretation, of the work. Melrose, however, is primarily concerned with the ways in which theorizing might also be happening by artists themselves as expert-practitioners, especially within collaborative contexts (2005). In this case, I suggest, the work of the writer as expert-spectator changes; rather than them doing the theorizing, they are presented with a kind of theorizing that happens by the artist through practice. This does not necessarily have the same aims as a written theorization, and for this reason, it does not come to replace a writer/expert-spectator's written response. Rather, as I shall show through the work of Bel, its whole function, purpose and nature is different; it belongs, as Melrose would say, to a different professional context and a whole different 'economy'.

It is important then to add that Melrose often stresses the notion of the singular expert signature(s) behind artistic practice, and is particularly interested in understanding the modes and operations of the economy that guides art-making processes as 'professional singularities' (2005: [online]). The notion of an economy is useful here, particularly if we are to understand it as the field of conditions in which the work develops and appears, affecting the way the expert-artist works, how they make decisions during the creative process, but also how they produce and share their work within a broader artistic, economical, social and political context.[5] In fact, Melrose considers this economy in which the expert performance-maker operates as significantly different to that of (academic) writing on or about performance, and often speaks of 'a lack of fit between *two complex economies of practice* [her emphasis]' (2003, [online]); a lack of fit, that is, between the economy of performance-*writing* and that of performance-*making*. While the

---

5 A similar notion of an eco-system came up, in a talk by Franck Leibovici and Matthew Gale as part of 'Performance Year Zero: A Living History', a symposium at the Tate Tanks on issues of documenting and preserving performance art, 5-6 October 2012. For more information: http://www.tate.org.uk/whats-on/tate-modern-tanks/conference/performance-year-zero [accessed 5 November 2012]. Leibovici spoke against the autonomy of an artwork and suggested it belongs to a whole eco-system which someone needs to be part of or reconstruct in order to fully understand it within its social, economic and political context.

former is a post-event writing *about*, the latter is conceived as the 'emergent event' itself. Hence, the act of theorizing performance (as event) in writing is concerned with 'work already made' and involves a 'looking backwards'. On the contrary, professional artistic practice, which is concerned with the making of work, and all the theorizing that might be happening as part of that practice, evolve within an 'intermix of *continuity* with *futurity*' (Melrose 2006, p.126, her emphasis). This is because the artist looks forward with curiosity, as Melrose claims, not necessarily with a view to producing something new, but certainly with a desire to facilitate 'the emergence of something not yet seen but recognized, something both continuous with, and judged to be *better* than, the already-seen' (*ibid.*, her emphasis).

Following Melrose then, could we suggest that one way in which professional artistic practice operates in order to pursue the emergence of something 'not yet seen' with continuity and futurity, is by turning to philosophy? If so, then what I aim to show in what follows is that this in turn does not have to do with a borrowing of philosophical concepts or ideas, or with philosophical writing. Instead, I am interested in work that operates itself as philosophy; in other words, work that borrows something of philosophy's nature as a specific kind of practice, of thinking and of elaborating such thinking for another. In this way, I would argue, not only does dance exercise the philosophical, but it is allowed to start discovering and generating original modes of thought from within its own complex economy of practice.

Staging theory, philosophizing in/as performance

In order to explore the above propositions further and tackle the dialogue that current choreography seems to be pursuing with critical theory and philosophy, I will first examine the case of the talk that was offered *instead of* Bel's 1998 piece *The Last Performance*, as part of the season called 'Jérôme Bel Showtime', at Sadler's Wells in London in February 2008. Instead of the actual work, Bel presented a lecture demonstration on *The Last Performance* – and, indeed, this is how the evening was advertised – consisting of a talk intersected with sections from another piece of his, *Shirtology* (1997), which was performed live in-between his speaking. What is of particular interest here is the explanation Bel gave to the audience about why this piece had become a lecture and was not touring as a performance anymore. On the one hand, he said, this is because *The Last Performance* was an unsuccessful performance piece, in the sense that it did not work with the public: people got bored throughout it, did not understand it, and often left the theatre in the middle of the show. On the other hand, it was because, as Bel admitted, he still thought the philosophical ideas that had inspired the work were crucial to his thinking and work overall, and so he hoped that these ideas could potentially be interesting for an audience, if only he could communicate them in a different format; hence he chose the set-up of what he called a lecture demonstration.

For the most part, Bel's talk revolved around issues related to the role/ death/function of the author and the role/birth/function of the audience, as proposed by Roland Barthes ('The Death of the Author', 1977[1968]) and Michel Foucault ('What is an Author?', 1984[1969]). He also at some point discussed the nature or ontology of performance as an art of (re) presentation which resists reproduction, following Peggy Phelan ('The ontology of performance: representation without reproduction', 1993).[6] He then claimed that some ideas, such as the above, are better told in words rather than through (choreographed) performance. I suggest, however, that this is not the only issue at stake here; rather, as Jérôme Bel talks, there are a couple of other things that perhaps we do not become aware of in the first instance; and it is in these more detailed observations that we might start to understand how the philosophical appears in his work.

Firstly, and although I have only seen *The Last Performance* recorded on video, it does not seem to me that this work was ever *about the theoretical ideas* that Bel discussed in his talk. If I were to describe the piece to someone, I would probably say that it is a piece based on a sequence such as this: performers appear on stage one by one, only to introduce themselves, as Jérôme Bel, Susanne Linke, André Agassi, Hamlet or Calvin Klein, for example, and then perform something ranging from a one-minute stillness timed by the performer, or the iteration of the phrase 'to be or not to be', to a short game of tennis, or a short dance, depending on who they have previously introduced themselves as. So, for example, if the performer appears on stage wearing a tennis player's outfit, and tells us 'I am André Agassi', then they play a bit of tennis against the back wall of the stage; if they appear wearing a white silk night gown and introduce themselves as Susanne Linke, then they perform a dance by Susanne Linke; and so on and so forth. Costumes, declarations (starting with the phrase 'I am' and followed by a proper name such as the above), and subsequent acted-out sequences of utterances and movements, all gradually get combined in different ways, so that the audience is given more and more combinations and possible variations of combinations on the existing elements (or variables). It is all a game of establishing and then gradually destabilizing what André Lepecki terms as 'layered connections

---

6 In fact, it could be argued that conceptual visual artists have been discussing similar ideas, or even referring to the same philosophers, when discussing their practice. For example, Sherrie Levine cited these very same philosophers in denying the existence of originality in her work *After Walker Evans* (1979). The scope of this chapter does not permit me to expand on the analogies between conceptual visual art and what has been termed 'conceptual dance', but see also footnote 3 for further reading on this matter.

between self and body, identity and body-image, being and its social surface'
(Lepecki 2000, [online]). Given such a framework, it could be claimed that
the interplay between names, identities, cultural signs, appearances and
actions, provides rich material for discussion, especially alongside Barthes'
and Foucault's essays on authorship. Similarly, the display of citation, in
the form of re-enacted material, whether dance material (Linke) or other
(Agassi), as well as its re-appearance in performance, each time in a
slightly altered way, certainly foreground issues of copying, difference and
repetition – other favourites of Jérôme Bel – and potentially persuade us of
the impossibility of reproducing 'the live (performance)', which would bring
us back to Phelan as discussed by Bel in his talk.

On the one hand, however, it does not seem to me that *The Last Performance*
is a re-presentation of those philosophical concepts on stage; nor is it a
translation of theoretical ideas into performance. In other words, this is
not a case of a choreographer reading Barthes and then creating a work
as a response to the ideas he found in the text. And, on the other hand, I
would also tentatively suggest that an ordinary (non-philosopher) audience
member might have seen other things in *The Last Performance*, than those
issues brought up by Bel in his talk. For example, the simplicity of the piece's
structure and the humour with which it teases the audience as more and
more Linkes and Agassis appear on stage, and even the pure skill involved
in playing tennis alone against the back wall of a theatre, or in re-enacting
a solo by Susanna Linke with such care and exactitude as it is performed
in *The Last Performance*, are only two of the things that struck me when
seeing the work on DVD, which Bel, for example, did not choose to touch
upon in his lecture. Of course, as Bel has told us, the lecture performance
works as a format through which to speak about theoretical ideas that have
struck him and have influenced his thinking and making process for *The Last
Performance*, not about the structure of the work or the skill and virtuosity
involved in its creation. However, this lecture demonstration does not
stand *in place of* the performance, as he tries to convince us in his opening
statements; in the end, what it achieves is certainly not to tell us what the
original piece used to tell us only in another (more successful) medium, but,
rather, to tell something of its own.

Moreover, and in order to better understand what the lecture
demonstration might actually be saying or doing, I return to Melrose's
writings and, in particular, to her proposition that it is often through the
perspective and powerful position of the expert-spectator that academics
usually theorize performance work. One could claim, in this sense, that Bel
assumes exactly such a position in his talk, despite being the choreographer
(expert-practitioner) of the original work. Which is to say, by looking back at
his own work, the readings, ideas and thinking processes that informed the

creation of *The Last Performance*, he is rehearsing a 'looking back', instead of operating within continuity and futurity. I would suggest however, that, indeed, this is what he *seems* to be doing. Certainly, this is what he is staging: a post-event looking-back, from the point of view of the theorist who is engaging with philosophy, or the expert-spectator, who attempts to fill in the gaps that were left open or vague, or became confusing, for audiences of the original piece. And yet, what we are being presented with here I would describe more in terms of 'a concealed expert-spectator'. Not only does Bel sell this evening as a lecture performance, rather than an ordinary show; not only does he provide us with convincing arguments as to the reasons he has chosen to do so, which involve a catchy story about an unsuccessful, boring show; what is more, we sit in the auditorium and listen to him speaking about philosophy in an informative, yet at the same time entertaining way, as if we are invited to discover the magic of certain concepts with him, so that we somehow 'buy into' his proposition that what he is doing is *just* revealing to us the philosophical inspiration of a 'missing' show – at least, I do.

Upon closer examination though, what we see is that the most powerful operation going on here is this: Jérôme Bel taking the stage to perform that specific persona that Bauer has described, the one wearing the pink buttoned-down shirt with the orange undershirt, trendy shoes and comfortable loose trousers; the one looking troubled, thinking and doing playful gestures, smiling and laughing as if surprised by his own words as he speaks (Bauer 2008, p.46). And so, while to begin with it seems that this lecture is just the way in which Bel has chosen to articulate the philosophy 'behind' the creation of an older work, in fact he is using this as a different sort of opportunity to perform; he is choreographing a new work. He is still appearing on and creating for the stage, and therefore he is still operating in the modality of performance-making. The philosophical content of the talk and the decision not to present the work might trick us into perceiving this event as a thinking on performance. However, as soon as the persona of Jérôme Bel appears so carefully choreographed, onstage, we are already dealing with nothing other than, indeed, an actualized instance of performance. In fact, we are looking at a choreographic (and choreographed) work. Going back to the notion of choreography as an expanded practice, I see Bel here exercising precisely this broader understanding of choreography. The lecture demonstration is a choreographed dance piece not because it shows composed movement in time and space, but because in presenting it Bel is exercising his singular expert choreographic practice. At the same time, and in line with Melrose's observations on the economy of different practices, his lecture demonstration clearly belongs to an economy of dance-making, because he stages it as part of a showcase festival of his choreographic work, in a theatre venue for dance, and has also carefully and professionally selected, as an expert artist would do, his costume, way of speaking, relationship to the audience, and all the other details that make this lecture demonstration a dance piece in the place of the original show.

In fact, it might also appear as if Bel's decision to present a lecture demonstration on the philosophical ideas that informed the original work (instead of the original work) raises questions about the relationship between philosophy or theory and performance practice, and the (in) capability of one to translate into the other; or, questions regarding the specificity, the aims and the limits of certain thinking or ideas and the way in which they work (or do not work) in different modes of practice. In truth, such issues are certainly raised by Bel, but not from his decision to talk about Barthes, instead of performing 'him' (as if this is what he was doing); but, rather, because in the end we see that he cannot escape performance even when he supposedly 'speaks theory'. A pure reference to philosophical material, in other words, does not guarantee a shift into a different mode of operation. Bel's performance seems so carefully thought-through, his stage-persona so purposefully *constructed*, that the whole event of his lecture performance clearly (and consciously) operates within rules of its own and within a complexity that is specific to it. One could name this a kind of knowledge complexity, or an economy of choreographic practice that relies on professional, expert knowledge. As soon as Bel takes to the stage, he is re-affirming his position as an expert-practitioner, rather than a theorist engaging with philosophical texts, or an expert-spectator (regardless of the seemingly philosophical-analytical perspective he adopts – or pretends to adopt – as part of his 'looking-back').

One could go even further and propose that what Bel might be doing from within this position of the expert-practitioner could be perceived as a theorizing *in performance*. Again, though, the theorizing here does not refer to the philosophical content of his lecture (i.e. the discussion of Barthes, Foucault and Phelan, for example), but to his particular expert-performance itself (which might have something to tell us, for example, about the unavoidable sense of purposeful constructed-ness we perceive in the event of something or someone appearing onstage). And yet, on her side, Melrose is very clear in claiming that expert-practitioners indeed 'might *theorise* in modes and registers of complex practice which operate wholly or in significant part outside of writing', so that in this case 'the term 'theoretical' might be non-identical with the specific registers of writing through which it is widely articulated' (Melrose 2005, [online] her emphasis). And so, although Melrose herself admits that it is not always easy to identify and describe what we might mean by 'the *already-theoretical status of certain expert or signature performance practices*' (*ibid.*, her emphasis), it is at least clear that this status is to be sought for or traced inside the performance work, rather than in any accounting of it from the outside, whether that is a piece of writing, or, indeed, a lecture or talk which operates in a 'looking-back' mode, analogous to that of the expert-spectator's writing on performance.[7]

The particular case of Jérôme Bel therefore takes us back to writings by Cvejić and Melrose referred to earlier, and allows us to tentatively make the following proposition: that certain choreographic works' relationship to philosophy need not necessarily be traced in the way such works present (or have been inspired by) philosophical texts or ideas, but more specifically by the way in which they operate as philosophy themselves. And even though philosophy too, it could be claimed, is sometimes analytical, in the sense that it seeks to clarify and understand concepts that organize language and action, it is meant here as a practice of thinking which brings forth new concepts, unknown yet, but recognizable. It is this type of philosophy, as I will argue in what follows, that I find emerges as a mode of doing in the work of Bel and other artists who have been described as conceptual.

Philosophy: creating concepts as (choreographic) acts of thought

If this last proposition of works operating as philosophy has something to do with choreographers self-reflexively inventing concepts of performance through the very practice of performance-making, then this idea indeed corresponds perfectly to Deleuze and Guattari's description of philosophy as 'the art of forming, inventing, and fabricating concepts' (Deleuze and Guattari 1994, p.2). In their 1994 book *What is philosophy?*, the authors set out to revisit what philosophy is, in order to define more clearly 'its occasion and circumstances, its landscapes and personae, its conditions and unknowns' (*ibid.*), as they say. Here, they argue that philosophy is the discipline of creating concepts, and in fact they put an emphasis on creation, given that they do not perceive the concept as something pre-existing, or ready-made, but exactly as an unknown. The concept does not feature as a simulation that the philosopher discovers or seeks; rather, it appears through and as an act of thought. It is created *as one thinks*. It is presented as

---

7 It should also be clarified that the point being made here is not one in favour of what has been named 'performative writing'. My sense is that such writing, even if, or precisely as, it takes place on the page, operates in a mode similar to that of Bel when he takes the stage to speak through theory; it attempts to perform on the page. Here, however, we are concerned firstly with the idea that the practitioner can perhaps theorize only *in practice*, and secondly, as I will show later on, with the proposition that, if the practitioner were to write in some sort of relationship to her own practice, then this relationship would be of a different nature to that often pursued by theorists as expert-spectators (even when they exercise performative writing).

a 'becoming'; although singular and specific, it has a history and it relates to other concepts. What it needs, however, is a conceptual persona to create it through thinking and the philosopher to speak that thought. The conceptual persona is the one who thinks through the concept, while the philosopher is the one who presents it and makes it convincing. More specifically, Deleuze and Guattari describe the conceptual persona as the very potential of the concept, the one without whose signature the concept would be nothing (1994, p.5).

Although the relationship Deleuze and Guattari set up between the notions of the concept, philosophy, thought and the conceptual persona are too complicated to sufficiently unpack in the context of this chapter, it is useful to think through these initial propositions they make in relation to a potential suspicion that arises as we try to believe in the philosophical nature of Jérôme Bel's work based on his quoting of Barthes or Foucault. Bel's work can indeed be thought of as philosophical, but this has to do with the concept of performance (and of dance) that he works through and presents (convincingly) with each one of his works. As I have proposed, it is in this way that choreography becomes a practice of philosophy, when and as it produces new concepts of dance. Bel becomes, in this sense, a conceptual persona, 'a presence that is intrinsic to thought', as Deleuze and Guattari would argue, or 'a condition for the exercise of thought' (as a mode of creating concepts) (1994, p.3). In other words, he becomes a conceptual persona because he is the condition for the new concept of dance to appear, and hence he is intrinsic to that concept of dance. It therefore becomes even clearer that Bel is not a translator of post-structuralist thought into performance terms; nor does he operate as a double of Barthes or Phelan in another medium. Bel's creation is singular and bears his own signature; we could even suggest that this is precisely what he does not seem able to escape from.

But what distinguishes the notion of a conceptual persona to that of the philosopher? And how could this inform the way we look at what Bel 'does' in this lecture performance? Deleuze and Guattari write that '[the] conceptual persona is not the philosopher's representative, but, rather, the reverse: the philosopher is only the envelope of his principal conceptual persona and of all the other personae who are the intercessors [...], the real subjects of his philosophy' (1994, p.64). Elsewhere, they argue that 'conceptual personae are only thinkers', aiming to produce movement by thinking something, rather than to perform a speech act, to do something by saying it (1994, pp.64,69). On the one hand, then, Bel constructs – he invents and fabricates – the concept of the choreographer who performs himself as a thinker negotiating ideas of Barthes and Foucault. And since this produces a new concept – a movement of thought in us as we expand our understanding of what a dance piece is and how choreography functions – he becomes a conceptual persona. On the other hand, he performs his thinking, and himself as a thinker, so that he also becomes a philosopher speaking the philosophical speech act, as Deleuze and Guattari suggest. I would argue, however, that it is in the first of these operations wherein his philosophical practice lies, not in the (philosophical) ideas themselves that he references, nor in the type of persona that is performed, which could also potentially be seen as a caricature of the philosopher, an appearance of philosophy rather than philosophy itself.[8]

The philosopher's aim: reminders, recollection, ownership

Finally, I turn to Hélène Cixous and her differentiation between the practice of the philosopher and that of the writer (of literature or poetry, for example) (Cixous 2010, [video lecture][9]), in order to take the proposal above further and to make some final remarks, which also relate to Bel's *theatrical dramaturgy*. I will refer here to a conversation between Cixous and Adrian Heathfield, video recorded by Hugo Glendinning in October 2010.

Towards the end of their conversation, Heathfield prompts Cixous to speak about the apparent schism that she has identified between writing literature and writing philosophy; he is specifically interested in the question of loss, and the conditions of passage or duration in writing, and asks her about the impression she feels her writing makes or leaves, 'not something that cannot be recalled, but that must be recalled, again and again', as he describes it. Cixous then speaks about writing as an instrument or a tool that focuses on sparks of thinking that are not yet thought. In fact, she considers writing itself as that which is not yet thought. As she says, at some point writing does become thought, it formulates into something, and from that point on you can repeat it... it is grasped. She then adds:

> Philosophers work in this way. REAL philosophers. I'm not a philosopher. Though I write philosophically, my voice and traditions are literary. I am more a writer than a philosopher because the philosopher wants and has

---

8 See also Maaike Bleeker's account of Ivana Müller's *How Heavy Are My Thoughts?* (2009), where a similar differentiation is made between the act of thinking and the speech act based on Deleuze and Guattari's description of the philosopher and the conceptual persona. Bleeker draws on Deleuze and Guattari in order to examine the operation of Müller's transformation into I.M. as part of this particular work and raise questions about theatricality as a constitutive of modern thinking.

9 Hélène Cixous, in conversation with Adrian Heathfield (2010). *Writing not yet thought*. A video recording by Hugo Glendinning, presented as part of 'Performing Idea: Performative Writing', an international symposium in the context of *Performance Matters*. Organised by the Live Art Development Agency; Goldsmiths, University of London; and Roehampton University. Toynbee Studios, London, 8 October 2010.

to be recollected. [...] And he posts – I say 'he' because until now it is mostly men – he posts reminders. But the aim, the ambition, the desire is [...] to insert reminders that are decisive [...] there are everywhere assertions, as if he were climbing up the Himalayas, and you have grasps, I mean he doesn't lose grip in between the different steps. (Cixous 2010,[video lecture])

And therefore, Cixous continues to argue that this type of 'grasping' or 'inserting reminders' is not the purpose of a writer, who is more focused on exploring dimensions of the other, on othering her own self. The writer others herself, according to Cixous, so that she can never 'self'. So she concludes: 'Everything I've written is not me. I'm not even sure that somebody else who I could name hasn't written it. I don't think a philosopher would accept that disowning. I disown' (*ibid.*). A philosopher would not, is probably what she implies.

I now go back to Jérôme Bel one last time. What is interesting here is that, rather than othering, it seems that with him it is as if we are witnessing an over-selfing process. Not only does he not disown the work as he takes to the stage to discuss *The Last Performance*, but he claims authorship with his performing, so that in fact he skilfully performs his ownership of the work too through the lecture performance that looks back at the (his own) original. As for the grasps Cixous mentions, those reminders that aim to help one keep a sense of the whole, recollect and go further and further in their experience of the work, these bring to mind another claim Bel has made about his work: that he makes it in such a way that spectators of his pieces should be able to describe them bit by bit to someone who was not there, from start to finish, moment to moment.

One could say a lot here about the expectations Bel has around language and description of course; but this is most probably another topic. What is more important is that, in order to enable this possibility, Bel pursues a type of dramaturgy that operates, I would suggest, precisely in the way that Cixous describes the way the philosopher writes. Bel's works are very often a series of images that follow one another in a way that seems absolutely necessary, logically structured, often exhaustive and in this way take the spectator further and further through sign-posting. Therefore, one is able, with the help of those reminders, those grasps, to reconstruct through memory one's whole journey as a spectator; because this particular choreographer, as many more whose work has been described as conceptual, wants to (and perhaps has to) be recollected in a very specific way, in order for their proposed concept of dance to appear through thought.

A tension however emerges if we go back to Deleuze and Guattari: their notion of the conceptual persona implies not the philosopher as a person who owns what they say, but rather a condition through which thought appears, which seems more comparable to Cixous's writer rather than the philosopher who 'owns'. On the surface then, these two positions seem to sit quite uncomfortably next to each other, while we are left wondering about the philosophical nature of Bel's work. Indeed, this is a very productive tension. It takes us right back into the theatre, where Bel appears to be doing something as an expert performance-maker. Here, we find a performance of owning, a performance of philosophical thinking, while at the same time the exercising of thought is happening in and with us. In listening to Bel and trying to understand all the complex ideas on authorship and representation about which he speaks, still sat in our seats as spectators in a theatre, we are in fact already engaging in and constructing choreography as an expanded practice. The creation of the new concept of dance, of choreography and of spectatorship happening with this lecture performance is precisely what makes it philosophy, and this is not a process owned by Bel. This type of ownership or authorship is a (theatrical) tool through which philosophy happens in the theatre. But the philosophy itself is disowned. On these grounds, we could undoubtedly say that Jérôme Bel is an expert in what he does: as a performance maker, he does not abandon the theatre to become a philosopher on the page, but he uses choreography to do philosophy on stage; in so doing, he performs thinking so as to create a movement of thought in us and with us, in the theatre.

Concluding thoughts

In conclusion, and zooming out of the case of Jérôme Bel, it seems necessary that we re-examine some of the works that have been characterized as conceptual dance precisely in order to make the term conceptual appear under new light and become more specific, given the distinct ways in which different types of conceptual dance pieces create concepts, think or work philosophically. Works such as those of Bel are not conceptual because they are intellectual, difficult and dry; conceptual, not necessarily because they seem to be repeating a similar gesture in the history of dance that conceptual art made in the history of the visual arts by self-reflexively proposing 'this is dance' or 'this is choreography'. Rather, conceptual, because these works present us with new concepts of performance, because their choreographers follow a practice that is philosophical in the way it operates, and whose site remains the body and/or the stage. Moreover, it is important to understand the types of philosophy that happen in expert performance-making, which might indeed be different to what I have described in the example of Bel's lecture demonstration. Following Melrose, we might further want to ask, what are the philosophical operations of a discipline-specific expert intuition, that of the choreographer?

Furthermore, I would like to suggest that by examining further the ways in which philosophical enquiry operates within or as choreography, we might be able to pin down the specifics of the relationship between philosophizing and choreographing, which could certainly be diverse and multiple across different types of works. In this way, we could re-think new ways in which choreography thinks and demands us to think, as expert writers and spectators, but also, potentially, re-imagine philosophical thought, the creation of concepts, *as* choreography.

References

Allsopp, Ric and André Lepecki. '*Performance Research*: Call for Papers' [email / electronic announcement], 6 July 2007.

Barthes, Roland. *Image Music Text*, London: Fontana Press, 1977.

Barthes, Roland. 'The death of the author', *Image Music Text*, London: Fontana Press, 1977 [1968], pp.142-154.

Bauer, Una. 'Jérôme Bel: An Interview', *Performance Research*, 13:1, 2008, pp.42-48.

Bel, Jérôme and Jonathan Burrows. 'Artist Talk: Jérôme Bel', Lilian Baylis Studio, Sadler's Wells Theatre, London, 16 February 2008 [my notes].

Bleeker, Maaike. 'Thinking Through Theatre', in Cull, Laura (ed.), *Deleuze and Performance*, Edinburgh: Edinburgh University Press, 2009, pp.147-160.

Burrows, Jonathan, Xavier Le Roy and Felix Ruckert. 'Meeting of Minds', *Dance Theatre Journal*, 20:3, 2004, pp.9-13.

Cixous, Hélène, in conversation with Adrian Heathfield, *Writing not yet thought*, a video recording by Hugo Glendinning, Paris, September 2010. Presented as part of 'Performing Idea: Performative Writing', an international symposium in the context of *Performance Matters*, Toynbee Studios, London, 8 October 2010 [my notes and transcription of conversation on DVD]. Organised by the Live Art Development Agency; Goldsmiths, University of London; and Roehampton University. DVD published by Performance Matters.

Cull, Laura (ed.). *Deleuze and Performance*, Edinburgh: Edinburgh University Press, 2009.

Cvejić, Bojana. 'Learning by making and making by learning how to learn (Contemporary Choreography in Europe: When did theory give way to self-organization?)', 2006, [online]. http://summit.kein.org/node/235 [Accessed: 25 June 2007].

Deleuze, Gilles and Felix Guattari. *What is Philosophy?*, trans. Hugh Tomlinson and Graham Burchill, London: Verso, 1994.

Foucault, Michel. 'What is an Author?', in Rabinow, Paul (ed.), *The Foucault Reader*, London: Penguin Books, 1984 [1969], pp.101-120.

Hochmuth, Martina, Krassimira Kruschkova and Georg Schöllhammer (eds). *It takes place when it doesn't: On dance and performance since 1989*, Frankfurt: Revolver, in collaboration with Tanzquartier Wien, springerin and Theorem / Culture 2000 programme of the European Union, 2006.

Kelleher, Joe and Nicholas Ridout (eds.). *Contemporary Theatres in Europe: A Critical Companion*, London: Routledge, 2006.

Lepecki, André. 'Crystallisation. Unmaking American dance by tradition', 1999, [online]. http://www.sarma.be/text.asp?id=868 [Accessed: 18 May 2005].

Lepecki, André. 'Wake up call. Citation and the unmaking of amnesia in The Last Performance', 2000, [online]. http://www.sarma.be/text.asp?id=869 [Accessed: 18 May 2005].

Lepecki, André. 'Exhausting Dance: Themes for a Politics of Movement', in Heathfield, Adrian (ed.), *Live: Art and Performance*, London: Tate Publishing, 2004, pp.120-127.

Lepecki, André. *Exhausting Dance: Performance and the politics of movement*, New York: Routledge, 2006.

Le Roy, Xavier, Bojana Cvejić and Gerald Siegmund. 'To end with judgement by way of clarification', in Hochmuth, Martina, Krassimira Kruschkova and Georg Schöllhammer (eds.), *It takes place when it doesn't: On dance and performance since 1989*, Frankfurt: Revolver, in collaboration with Tanzquartier Wien, springerin and Theorem / Culture 2000 programme of the European Union, 2006, pp.48-56.

Melrose, Susan. 'The Eventful Articulation of Singularities - or, "Chasing Angels"', 2003, [online]. http://www.sfmelrose.u-net.com/chasingangels/ [Accessed: 23 March 2006].

Melrose, Susan. 'Out of Words', 2005, [online]. http://www.sfmelrose.dsl.pipex.com/outofwords/ [Accessed: 23 March 2006].

Melrose, Susan. 'Constitutive ambiguities: Writing professional or expert performance practices, and the Théâtre du Soleil, Paris', in Kelleher, Joe and Nicholas Ridout (eds.), *Contemporary Theatres in Europe: A Critical Companion*, London: Routledge, 2006, pp.120-135.

Melrose, Susan. 'Still Harping On (About Expert Practitioner Centred Modes of Knowledge and Models of Intelligibility)', 2007, [online]. http://www.sfmelrose.org.uk/MELROSEAHDSperfarts.pdf [Accessed: 5 November 2012]

Phelan, Peggy. 'The Ontology of Performance: Representation Without Reproduction', in *Unmarked. The Politics of Performance*, London: Routledge, 1993, pp.146-166.

INDEX